The Handbook of Fede Leadership and Admin

M000077197

The editors have assembled a first-rate group of contributors to assess the enduring questions about federal executive branch leadership and bureaucratic service in America. The authors' mix of academic and practical experience provides the reader a nice balance of perspectives. They recognize that effective federal bureaucratic leadership is more important than ever.

Paul Teske, University of Colorado Denver, USA

Public management is context dependent, rather than generic. That may sound obvious, but in the late 1920s through the 1930s, a dominant strand of thought considered public administration to be a "single process," wherever practiced. Today by contrast, federal administration is distinguished from private enterprise, nonprofit management, and state and local governmental practices by the combined effects of its scope and scale; the constitutional separation of powers, federalism, and protection of individual rights; and administrative law requirements for stakeholder participation, representation, transparency, privacy, due process, and other democratic-constitutional values. *The Handbook of Federal Government Leadership and Administration* is a state-of-the-art guide to the unique features of federal administration, informed by the latest theoretical developments, research, and practical applications and the leadership and management of federal agencies.

Written by "pracademics" with federal practitioners specifically in mind, the handbook is designed to bridge the gap between academic and applied public administration by identifying what resonates with practitioners as they search for usable theories and research findings to improve performance. Combining rigor and relevance in the study and practice of federal administration, it includes chapters on theory, history, reform initiatives, leadership, necessary skill sets, budgeting, power and influence, political embeddedness, change management, separated and shared executive, legislative, and judicial powers, effective communication, ethics, and emerging concepts and challenges. It will be essential reading for federal practitioners, scholars, and "pracademics" alike.

David H. Rosenbloom is a Distinguished Professor of Public Administration in the School of Public Affairs at American University, USA.

Patrick S. Malone is a professor and the Director of Key Executive Leadership Programs in the School of Public Affairs at American University, USA.

Bill Valdez is a retired Senior Executive, having served 20 years at the U.S. Department of Energy, and is the President of the Senior Executives Association and an Adjunct Faculty at American University.

American Society for Public Administration
Series in Public Administration and Public Policy
David H. Rosenbloom, PhD, Editor-in-Chief

Mission: Throughout its history, ASPA has sought to be true to its founding principles of promoting scholarship and professionalism within the public service. The ASPA Book Series on Public Administration and Public Policy publishes books that increase national and international interest for public administration and discuss practical and cutting-edge topics in engaging ways of interest to practitioners, policy makers, and those concerned with bringing scholarship to the practice of public administration.

Recent Publications

Community Action Leaders
Rooting out Poverty at the Local Level
Beverly S. Bunch and Dalitso S. Sulamoyo
with J. Travis Bland, Aaron M. Itulya, Lorena Johnson, and Junfeng Wang

Participatory Budgeting in the United States
A Guide for Local Governments
Victoria Gordon, Jeffery L. Osgood, Jr., and Daniel Boden

Government Contracting
Promises and Perils, Second Edition
William Sims Curry

Managing Public Sector Projects
A Strategic Framework for Success in an Era of Downsized Government, Second Edition
David S. Kassel

The Handbook of Federal Government Leadership and Administration
Transforming, Performing, and Innovating in a Complex World
Edited by David H. Rosenbloom, Patrick S. Malone, and Bill Valdez

The Handbook of Federal Government Leadership and Administration

Transforming, Performing, and Innovating in a Complex World

Edited by David H. Rosenbloom, Patrick S. Malone, and Bill Valdez

Routledge
Taylor & Francis Group
NEW YORK AND LONDON

First published 2017
by Routledge
711 Third Avenue, New York, NY 10017

and by Routledge
2 Park Square, Milton Park, Abingdon, Oxon OX14 4RN

Routledge is an imprint of the Taylor & Francis Group, an informa business

Library of Congress Cataloging-in-Publication Data
Names: Rosenbloom, David H., editor. | Malone, Patrick S., editor. | Valdez, Bill, editor.
Title: The handbook of federal government leadership and administration: transforming, performing, and innovating in a complex world / edited by David H. Rosenbloom, Patrick S. Malone, and Bill Valdez.
Description: New York, NY: Routledge, 2016. | Series: ASPA series in public administration & public policy | Includes bibliographical references and index.
Identifiers: LCCN 2016020666 | ISBN 9781498756402 (hardback: alk. paper) | ISBN 9781315439242 (ebook)
Subjects: LCSH: Administrative agencies—United States—Management. | Public administration—United States. | Government productivity—United States.
Classification: LCC JK421 .H287 2016 | DDC 352.23/60973—dc23
LC record available at https://lccn.loc.gov/2016020666

ISBN: 978-1-498-75640-2 (hbk)
ISBN: 978-1-315-43924-2 (ebk)

Typeset in Times New Roman
by codeMantra

Contents

Figures

Tables

Preface

David H. Rosenbloom

The *Handbook of Federal Government Leadership and Administration: Transforming, Performing, and Innovating in a Complex World* uniquely contributes to contemporary knowledge about U.S. federal administration. First, it provides a state-of-the-art guide, informed by the latest theoretical developments, research, and practical applications, to the leadership and management of federal agencies. Second, it is largely written for federal practitioners by "pracademics" (public administration practitioners, with academic appointments who teach graduate courses at universities). Third, it can help bridge the gap between academic and applied public administration by identifying what resonates with practitioners as they search for usable theories and research findings to improve performance. In short, the book is a self-conscious collaborative effort by pracademics, practitioners, and academics, mostly associated with American University's Key Executive Leadership Programs, to achieve the elusive goal of combining rigor and relevance in the study and practice of federal administration. Each of these distinctive features of the book merits further elaboration.

The underlying premise for the book's focus on federal leadership and administration is that public management is context dependent, rather than generic. Nowadays this may seem obvious, but that was not always the case. In the late 1920s through the 1930s, a dominant strand of thought considered public administration to be a "single process," wherever practiced. Today by contrast, we recognize that federal administration is distinguished from private enterprise, nonprofit management, and state and local governmental practices by the combined effects of its scope and scale; the constitutional separation of powers, federalism, and protection of individual rights; and administrative law requirements for stakeholder participation, representation, transparency, privacy, due process, and other democratic-constitutional values. The distinctive characteristics of federal administration are analyzed throughout the book's chapters on theory, history, reform initiatives, leadership, necessary skill sets, budgeting, power and influence, political embeddedness, change management, separated and shared executive, legislative, and judicial powers, effective communication, ethics, and emerging concepts and challenges.

The book's editors relied heavily on pracademic authors in an effort to combine theory, research, and practice. Failure to connect these three aspects of applied knowledge has been a longstanding problem in the field of public administration. Although handbooks have been a staple of the literature on U.S. public administration since the 1980s, for the most part they are written by academicians for academicians, with a modest nod at best to practitioner interests. Academic knowledge is valuable in itself. Accurate diagnosis is important even in the absence of prescription for intervention, stability, or change. Understanding administrative behavior is a worthy objective even when application does not follow. Research that shows association rather than causality or explains limited variance can be highly useful in building knowledge. However, it may not be immediately applicable to practice, especially when high stakes, high reliability, and high performance are involved. Accessing academic writing can also be difficult for practitioners operating with worldviews, units of analysis, cognitive approaches, time pressures, and professional vocabularies that differ from those of academicians. Contemporary interest in "evidence-based" public administration and policy is more likely to achieve positive results if the evidence includes practitioner knowledge and perspective. Pracademics, such as the book's contributors, who are steeped in academic theory and research as well as practice are ideally suited to base observation, interpretation, and prescription on operational evidence and knowledge. Pracademics also have much to teach academicians about what makes theory and research valuable to practitioners. The book's contributors cite a wide variety of theories, research findings, and sources. Why do they pull these out of a vast literature, while neglecting others? What makes academic theory and research useful to practitioners? For academicians interested in applied public administration, finding answers to these questions is crucial. This handbook is neither a beginning nor an end for such a search. However, by relying heavily on pracademic authors while comprehensively covering federal administration, it provides an unusual and valuable source for insights.

For the editors and contributing authors, producing this handbook has been an exciting venture and certainly a labor of love, momentary frustrations notwithstanding. We set out to produce a book that would use leading theory and research to guide federal administrative practice. But not just a book, *the book* to which career federal executives and political appointees will turn and continually return to gain better understandings of leadership and management in pursuit of stronger administrative performance in the national government. This has obviously been an ambitious goal, and like most books, ours is a step—a very substantial one, we hope—toward an objective, not the final word. We very much hope that it significantly contributes to an ongoing dialog on improving federal leadership and administration, and we welcome feedback from our readers.

Acknowledgments

As suggested earlier this *Handbook of Federal Government Leadership and Administration: Transforming, Performing, and Innovating in a Complex World* is a product of the Key Executive Leadership Programs in the School of Public Affairs at American University in Washington, DC. The book has benefited greatly from the University's intellectual, financial, and organizational resources as well as its collegial support and that of the community of faculty, coaches, and staff who are such an important component of the Key Programs. In particular we wish to thank Sheree Brand, who was instrumental in the early coordination of the authors. A special appreciation, along with the deep admiration of the editors, is extended to Samantha Tan for her tenacious copy editing, without which this book would not have been possible.

We also concretely express our thanks to the Key Executive Leadership Programs for providing the impetus for the book, the royalties received from which will be invested in the programs' passionate efforts to support those who lead in the federal government.

This book is dedicated to the men and women who have devoted their lives to the public service. Thank you for all you do to deliver democracy.

1 The Bureaucratic Landscape

Origin and Implications for the Federal Leader

Patrick S. Malone

It is getting harder to run a Constitution than to frame one.

—Woodrow Wilson

Federal leaders work in one of the most multifarious organizational environments of any kind—a bureaucracy. And the truth is, bureaucracy in and of itself is not a bad thing. In fact, it can provide a solid and predictable framework from which to deliver public services. Reporting chains are clear, processes are structured and followed as expected, and allegiance is owed not to irrational individuals, but to rational structured organizations and legally established positions of authority therein.

But the landscape upon which federal leadership treads is far different from Max Weber's bureaucratic haven. The environment is fraught with political, legal, and administrative forces all vying for control and influence. It's an atmosphere shaped by years of incremental adjustments based on political or popular will. Indeed, today's bureaucracy is one that demands extraordinary leadership skill in order to achieve agency objectives. And it began with the fight to build the U.S. Constitution.

The U.S. Constitution: The Source of the Problem?

When examining the structure of the U.S. government, a logical starting point is typically the United States Constitution itself. To familiar eyes, the preamble sets forth the reason for and scope of the Constitution—"to form a more perfect Union" and to "secure the blessings of liberty," for current and future generations of citizens (U.S. Constitution, Preamble). The subsequent seven original articles, along with 27 amendments, form the foundation of government as we know it today. Despite its brilliance, the U.S. Constitution is eerily silent on the issue of the delivery of public administration and policy. The Constitution is even more taciturn on the organizational mechanisms and structures necessary to make the business of the nation transpire. Nowhere in the entire document does the "how" exist.

Perhaps the closest one will get to guidance from the founding framers on how to administer the young nation is found in Article 2 (Table 1.1). But each of the four sections provides only the slightest glimpse of the mechanisms, structure, and requisite guidelines. Section 1 grants the president executive power and denotes the length of tenure to be served with the vice-president. Beyond this, the balance of Section 1 reflects guidance related to the election process, compensation, and terms of removal from office. Section 2 provides some level of executive clarity by appointing the chief executive as the commander of the military and giving authority to oversee the heads of the civilian departments. Section 2 also allows a lead role in negotiating treaties and nominating officials of the government, including officers of the executive branch and judges in the judicial branch. Reporting mechanisms are outlined in Section 3 where the president is directed to report to Congress, convene congressional sessions, receive ambassadors, and commission officers of the United States. Finally, Section 4 provides guidelines for removal from office. But what about the "how?" What these articles fail to tell us is what the organizations that exist to deliver our democracy look like, how they should be structured, what guidelines they should follow, and the operating principles to which they should subscribe. This is frightening considering these very organizations serve as the touch-points with the citizens the Constitution is designed to serve.

Table 1.1 United States Constitution—Article 2

Section 1

The executive power shall be vested in a President of the United States of America. He shall hold his office during the term of four years, and, together with the Vice President, chosen for the same term, be elected, as follows:

Each state shall appoint, in such manner as the Legislature thereof may direct, a number of electors, equal to the whole number of Senators and Representatives to which the State may be entitled in the Congress: but no Senator or Representative, or person holding an office of trust or profit under the United States, shall be appointed an elector.

The electors shall meet in their respective states, and vote by ballot for two persons, of whom one at least shall not be an inhabitant of the same state with themselves. And they shall make a list of all the persons voted for, and of the number of votes for each; which list they shall sign and certify, and transmit sealed to the seat of the government of the United States, directed to the President of the Senate. The President of the Senate shall, in the presence of the Senate and House of Representatives, open all the certificates, and the votes shall then be counted. The person having the greatest number of votes shall be the President, if such number be a majority of the whole number of electors appointed; and if there be more than one who have such majority, and have an equal number of votes, then the House of Representatives shall immediately choose by ballot one of them for President; and if no person have a majority, then from the five highest on the list the said House shall in like manner choose the President. But in choosing the President, the votes shall be taken by States, the representation from each state having one vote; A quorum for this purpose shall consist of a member or members from two thirds of the states, and a majority of all the states shall be necessary to a choice. In every case, after the choice of the President, the person having the greatest number of votes of the electors shall be the Vice President. But if there should remain two or more who have equal votes, the Senate shall choose from them by ballot the Vice President.

The Congress may determine the time of choosing the electors, and the day on which they shall give their votes; which day shall be the same throughout the United States.

No person except a natural born citizen, or a citizen of the United States, at the time of the adoption of this Constitution, shall be eligible to the office of President; neither shall any person be eligible to that office who shall not have attained to the age of thirty five years, and been fourteen Years a resident within the United States.

In case of the removal of the President from office, or of his death, resignation, or inability to discharge the powers and duties of the said office, the same shall devolve on the Vice President, and the Congress may by law provide for the case of removal, death, resignation or inability, both of the President and Vice President, declaring what officer shall then act as President, and such officer shall act accordingly, until the disability be removed, or a President shall be elected.

The President shall, at stated times, receive for his services, a compensation, which shall neither be increased nor diminished during the period for which he shall have been elected, and he shall not receive within that period any other emolument from the United States, or any of them.

Before he enter on the execution of his office, he shall take the following oath or affirmation:—"I do solemnly swear (or affirm) that I will faithfully execute the office of President of the United States, and will to the best of my ability, preserve, protect and defend the Constitution of the United States."

Section 2

The President shall be commander in chief of the Army and Navy of the United States, and of the militia of the several states, when called into the actual service of the United States; he may require the opinion, in writing, of the principal officer in each of the executive departments, upon any subject relating to the duties of their respective offices, and he shall have power to grant reprieves and pardons for offenses against the United States, except in cases of impeachment.

He shall have power, by and with the advice and consent of the Senate, to make treaties, provided two thirds of the Senators present concur; and *he shall nominate, and by and with the advice and consent of the Senate, shall appoint ambassadors, other public ministers and consuls, judges of the Supreme Court, and all other officers of the United States, whose appointments are not herein otherwise provided for, and which shall be established by law*: but the Congress may by law vest the appointment of such inferior officers, as they think proper, in the President alone, in the courts of law, or in the heads of departments.

The President shall have power to fill up all vacancies that may happen during the recess of the Senate, by granting commissions which shall expire at the end of their next session.

Section 3

He shall from time to time give to the Congress information of the state of the union, and recommend to their consideration such measures as he shall judge necessary and expedient; he may, on extraordinary occasions, convene both Houses, or either of them, and in case of disagreement between them, with respect to the time of adjournment, he may adjourn them to such time as he shall think proper; he shall receive ambassadors and other public ministers; he shall take care that the laws be faithfully executed, and shall commission all the officers of the United States.

Section 4

The President, Vice President and all civil officers of the United States, shall be removed from office on impeachment for, and conviction of, treason, bribery, or other high crimes and misdemeanors.

The Constitution, while a brilliantly crafted document with its broad language and separation of powers, perhaps was just what the founders intended to create—a mechanism to limit the dominance of any one faction. As designed, the U.S. government was not meant to be proficient or powerful but to be constrained. The founders were well aware the result of their work would be a government that would be restrained just enough to make it increasingly challenging to begin new programs and to establish institutions that would ultimately need to be supported by the citizens (Wilson, 1989).

When one observes the current structure of the U.S. government (Table 1.2), one sees an impressive organization made up of three branches, 15 departments, numerous independent agencies, with just over two million federal employees (Office of Personnel Management, 2015) serving a population of over 322 million, (U.S. Census Bureau, 2015) and spending about $3.5 trillion per year (Senate Budget Committee, 2014). But how did we get to where we are? And what kind of challenge does our current structure create for federal leaders?

How We Got Here: Seven Ironies Plus One

Evolution of the modern governance structure of our nation is best reflected in Michael Nelson's (1982) theories of the ironies of the American national bureaucracy. Nelson notes that our modern bureaucracy was shaped by significant events occurring in the period from 1775 to 1932, at a time that was marked by a number of incongruous happenings that led to the development of the administrative infrastructure we possess today.

During this time, there were seven notable ironies related to the historical, political, and cultural events of the time. These, combined with an eighth and final irony, have left us with what public policy analysts often refer to as a situation that is "rife with unanticipated consequences." Indeed, as Nelson (1982) suggests, political forces in the form of elected officials and organized political groups, in their effort to ensure control of government by the everyday citizen, unintentionally created the modern bureaucratic infrastructure we see today—the infrastructure in which our federal leaders must lead.

The First Irony: The Revolt Against the Old Administrative Order Planted the Seeds of a New Administrative Order

The Declaration of Independence (1775) is far better known for phrases beginning with "When in the course of human events ..." or "We hold these truths to be self-evident ..." than for its rebuttal of the administrative practices of the king of Great Britain. However, the colonists had nothing good to say about issues of administering the public good:

- He has forbidden his Governors to pass Laws of immediate and pressing importance, unless suspended in their operation till his Assent should be obtained; and when so suspended, he has utterly neglected to attend to them.

Table 1.2 The Government of the United States

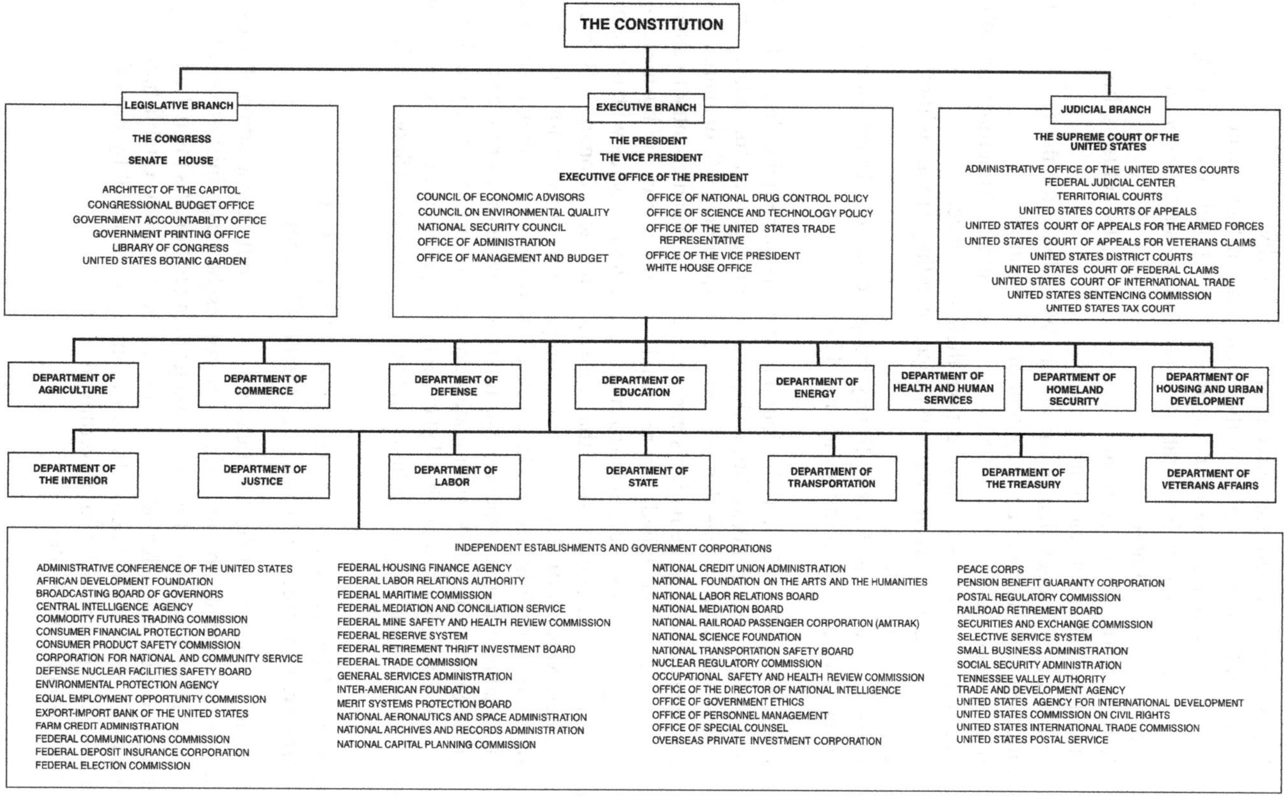

- He has refused to pass other Laws for the accommodation of large districts of people …
- He has dissolved Representative Houses repeatedly …
- He has endeavoured to prevent the population of these States; for that purpose obstructing the Laws for Naturalization of Foreigners; refusing to pass others to encourage their migrations hither, and raising the conditions of new Appropriations of Lands.
- He has obstructed the Administration of Justice, by refusing his Assent to Laws for establishing Judiciary powers.
- He has made Judges dependent on his Will alone, for the tenure of their offices, and the amount and payment of their salaries.
- He has erected a multitude of New Offices, and sent hither swarms of Officers to harrass our people, and eat out their substance.
- He has kept among us, in times of peace, Standing Armies without the Consent of our legislatures.
- He has affected to render the Military independent of and superior to the Civil power. (Declaration of Independence, 1775)

It is a fact that pre-revolution, the founding fathers were quite dissatisfied with many of the business practices of the ruling class. This fueled an anti-administrative tenor in the new nation—one that viewed such institutions with disdain.

After the revolution, the nation's early leaders still had a country to attend to, and there were several failed congressional attempts to run the business of the nation. Congress finally succumbed to creating a series of boards with outside officials, and in some cases executives, that were accountable to Congress. By creating these bodies, Nelson (1982) notes that Congress was responsible for the one of the first ironies of American history. In essence, the response to the uprising against the British administrative structure was to create new administrative structures in the United States. And while such bodies are compulsory to run any nation, "the adoption of a system of single-headed executive departments was a step distinctly in advance of formal English [administrative] development" (Short, 1923, p. 75).

The Second Irony: The System of Dual Control of Administration Became One of Limited Control

The events that followed the American Revolution reflected a nation at odds with its desire to repudiate former British control, eschew administrative infrastructures, and provide services for a new and growing nation. As the nation struggled with a suitable design for administrative capacity, newly established agencies found themselves in the unenviable position of dual control by both the legislative and executive branches of government.

As Nelson (1982) writes:

> The Constitutional Convention, in loosing the agencies from their old legislative moorings (politically necessary if the support of executive power adherents was to be won) without tying them securely to the presidency

> (equally politic if anti-federalist support was to be kept) forced agencies to find and exercise relatively independent power. Agencies began to learn to play one branch off against the other; if neither president nor Congress was supreme, then law was, and the agencies interpreted and implemented the law. (p. 755)

Thus, agencies began to recognize their vulnerability and mounted their own bases of power.

The Third Irony: Spoils Bred Bureaucracy

All was not well as agencies began their quest for power and survival. In fact, the election of Andrew Jackson to the presidency was driven by a sentiment among the citizenry that the developing administrative infrastructure was creating a system of the haves and have-nots and was fraught with corruption. Reminiscent of E.E. Schattschneider's (1960) claim that "the flaw in the pluralist heaven is that the heavenly chorus sings with a strong upper-class accent" (p. 35), members of government agencies at this time often came from positions of privilege.

It was in fact George Washington who considered one of his most important tasks was to appoint men with "fitness of character" (Kilpatrick, Cummings, and Jennings, 1964, p. 28). In an apparent effort to provide new meaning to the word nepotism, some 40% of Adams's high-level appointees were related to other appointees in his or George Washington's administration. Some civil servants claimed not only a property right to their offices, but a right of inheritance as well (Aronson, 1964; Fish, 1905; Rosenbloom, 1971).

Corruption also proved to be a problem. Government growth fueled by geographic expansion to the west opened the door for rampant corruption in federal agencies. Supervision of field personnel, well before the advent of telework, was exceptionally difficult due to the huge distances between supervisory authority and distant offices. Jackson's proposed solution to the issue of both corruption and privilege was to remedy the situation by creating federal jobs that were simple and uncomplicated.

He said the executive department would be organized as a "rationalized complex of offices, ordered by function, and defined by rules and regulations" (Marshall, 1967, p. 450). The philosophy was that individual civil servants could come and go, after election cycles were complete, without disturbing the existing infrastructure. "It was the administrative counterpart of the interchangeability of machine parts" (Marshall, 1967, pp. 455–56).

The Fourth Irony: Agencies Organized to Avoid Evil Became Less Able to Do Good

Organizational theory suggests that institutions should be organized with the end goal in mind. This focus allows for efficient and thoughtful placement of functions throughout the organization and avoids duplication and inefficiency as long as the mission of the organization remains at the forefront.

The reform system that Jackson proposed may have been the first step in addressing the issues of corruption and patronage, but it had a measurable impact on the performance of the bureaucracy. Interagency resources normally geared toward the organizational mission were strained as more efforts were directed toward internal controls. Processes became more complex and costly while agency efficiency and responsiveness suffered.

The Fifth Irony: Reformers' Efforts to Make the Civil Service More Responsive to the Political Branches Made It Less Responsive

One of the outcomes of reform efforts of the Jacksonian era was the focus on building a public service that was merit-based and eschewed political pressure from all sides. Such a civil service

> promoted the development of a professional, specialized bureaucracy whose expertise [could] not be matched either by president or Congress. Its emphasis on tenure and permanence in office built into the bureaucracy an insensitivity toward, and protection from, direct overhead political control.
>
> (Dodd & Schott, 1979, p. 25)

Civil servants, acting as tenured employees, were less apt to bend to the desires of elected officials, focusing more on their own interests. As the civil service grew in the years following the passage of the Pendleton Act in 1883, this behavior became more widespread.

The Sixth Irony: Client Agencies, Created to Enhance Political Representation in the Federal Government, Often Became Almost Independent from General Political Branch Control

Woodrow Wilson's description of the U.S. administrative state was an apt narrative of the growth of the government infrastructure following reform efforts. As Wilson noted, the administration had become a "lusty child" that "has expanded in nature and grown great in stature, but has also become awkward in movement. The vigor and increase of its life has been altogether out of proportion to its skill in living" (Wilson, 1887, p. 203). Growth among agencies, departments, divisions, bureaus, and commissions spiraled with no identifiable direction or strategic thought.

As a young and diverse nation grew, government struggled to keep up with the innumerable values and fluctuating attitudes of the American citizen. New interests emerged from industries from across the budding nation with the subsequent establishment of clientele agencies. Nelson's account of the process of creating these new agencies included the staffing of new organizations by supportive citizens. Legislative oversight committees would then seek membership from congressmen, loyal to their constituents and, by default, the mission of the agency. As a result, the strength of lobbying increased, enhancing agency power in Washington and back in home districts, where voter support fed the influence even more. The cyclical nature of the process of staffing, lobbying, and citizen support continued to feed the growth of the new agency (Nelson, 1979). The result was a primordial soup of various constituencies, agencies, and committees that found themselves hidden from the radar of busy elected political officials.

The Seventh Irony: Regulatory Agencies Created in Response to Popular Political Movements Often Became, in Effect, Client Agencies of the Regulated

The unfailing response to popular political movements over the years has been the creation of regulatory agencies. However, this often places our government agencies in the position of being client agencies of the regulated because professionals with unique skills find themselves moving from successful private sector positions to the public entity tasked with regulation.

This common occurrence manifests itself in many regulatory agencies in the federal government to this day. The Federal Aviation Administration has often shouldered the accusation of being too cozy with the airline industry. The Food and Drug Administration has been blamed for conflict of interests with major pharmaceutical companies. Finally, the Department of Defense must continually guard against claims of conflicts of interest with hundreds of defense contractors and subcontractors.

The Eighth Irony: Government Agencies Still Manage to Get the Job Done, Despite Their Ironic Evolution, at a Huge Cost

One reason for the somewhat the incongruous growth of the bureaucracy in United States is that the creation of democratic political institutions preceded the formation of administrative agencies as we know them today. This is in direct opposition to the history of traditional European rule where the authority of kings and princes has long been established. European rulers had already considered the potential problems of administering the needs of a nation because there was already something there to administer (Wilson, 1989).

But administrative institutions, which were not part of the founding fathers' vision or interest, were all but absent from the Constitution and have since been viewed with a mixture of cynicism and scorn (Nelson, 1979). This forced agency leaders to develop political skills in order to survive in the harsh political landscape where they found themselves (Rourke, 1976). Indeed, the challenge of leading a federal agency amidst political drama is a formidable one that remains with us today.

In truth, the eighth irony of the development of the U.S. administrative state is that the bureaucracy in general is somehow able to work well, with a price. Government leaders are generally able to deliver results. We live in a nation of clean air and water, with a safe interstate highway system, public health programs that protect our nation from rampant disease, one that has seen the implementation of civil rights laws that have leveled the playing field for so many, protection of commerce practices, safe food and pharmaceuticals, and the list goes on. And, federal public sector employees have been able to deliver these services with no real growth in the size of government in terms of the number of civil servants since 1965 (Dilulio, 2014).

But this doesn't mean we have an administrative infrastructure that is problem free. The legacy of the bureaucracy, born under a veil of anxiety toward anything resembling a fiefdom, and honed by political meddling for 245 years, has given birth to agencies, departments, bureaus, and any number of federal entities that must navigate a tumultuous political world to find relevance and survival. Federal leaders face an unbridled maze of procedures, requirements, and political pressures in order to lead successful policy implementation. Indeed, the legacy of the eight ironies has left leadership in the federal service with significant challenges, ranging from combatting the barriers created by endless bureaucracy to communication, to managing change in a volatile political landscape.

The Legacy of Bureaucracy: Weber and Beyond

The unharmonious development of the U.S. administrative state was the result of a series of events going back as far as the Constitutional Convention. However, other influences contributing to the growth of the current infrastructure came to bear as well. As the field of public administration developed, the exploration of organizational forms of the federal government was, in truth, not much more than an afterthought. Agencies, bureaus, offices, and divisions were added to an existing government palette based heavily on political, cultural, or societal forces. Further, when one examines the contributions among many scholars, politicians and practitioners, the evidence of influence emanating from a multitude of fields including science, politics, and humanist perspectives, along with a dependence on private business to chart the way to today's bureaucracy, emerges.

Max Weber (1864–1920), a German sociologist, provided us with the intellectual groundwork for bureaucracy in its current form. Sometimes referred to as "a man of the Renaissance who took all humanity for his province" (Bendix, 1978, p. 469), Weber's principles, developed at the turn of the 20th century, were instrumental in not only shaping the economic and political systems of today, but also creating the shape and feel of the modern federal bureaucracy. While other notable influences such as Wilson, Waldo, and White, would follow, each adding his own perspectives to federal organizations, it was Weber who laid the underpinning for modern bureaucratic states and had the most lasting impact on the bureaucracy we know today.

Weber's construct of bureaucracy began with his exploration of the common types of authority. Weber identified three types of legitimate authority: (a) Charismatic authority, based on the individual appeal of the leader; (b) Traditional authority, founded on the idea of customary or established practices; and (c) Legal authority, grounded in the legitimate ability to rule based on adherence to an accepted pattern of rules or regulations (Weber, 1947). It is the latter, legal authority, that formed the basis for which the modern bureaucratic state is best known.

Legal authority referred specifically to the establishment of agreed-upon regulations that would serve as the bedrock characteristics of the bureaucracy, and one not too different from what we see in the United States today. Several clearly evident components are present. First, the bureaucracy was centralized and hierarchical in nature. Each individual served as a cog in the wheel of the massive government machine, one that moved slowly, but kept moving. Federal workers who functioned within the bureaucracy worked under specific guidelines that included:

- organization in a clearly defined hierarchy of offices, each with a defined domain of skill and each filled through free choice;
- selection based on technical qualifications including testing by examination, diplomas, and/or technical training;
- promotion based on seniority, achievement, or both and with the approval of superiors; and
- subjection to firm and orderly discipline in the conduct of the office.

Weber's bureaucracy was also characterized by omnipresent rules, laws, and regulations that were meant to be adhered to. This standardized and impersonal approach based on legal authority ensured all citizens received the same treatment.

Other lines of thought regarding bureaucracy and organizational structure developed throughout the 20th century. Woodrow Wilson used his knowledge of the field of business to enhance administrative efficiency, responsibility, and agency accountability. His contention that politics and administration were inherently different, and should be approached as such, formed the basis for the all too familiar politics-administration dichotomy.

Indeed, Wilson (1887) argued that the field of administration was a field of business, outside of and exempt from politics. While this argument has captured the imagination of public administration scholars to this day, others took a different approach to institutions. Some sought more administrative efficiency by grouping departments with similar missions (Willoughby, 1927), or through attention to the division of labor and subsequent coordination and oversight of effort (Gulick, 1937). Mooney and Riley (1939) drew heavily upon military models of organization in their assessment of how organizations should be designed: unity of command, the vertical division of labor (along the lines of seniority), the horizontal division of labor (along functional lines); and the differences between line (authority) and staff (advisory) functions.

Chester Barnard (1938/1968) was among many taking a decidedly humanistic perspective, pointing out that the structure of organizations may not be so important after all, as long as one considers the underlying informal mechanisms existing underneath the formal structures. As Barnard noted, "Formal organizations arise out and are necessary to informal organization; but when formal organizations come into operation, they create and require informal organizations" (p. 120).

This perspective on the individual and his or her relationship to organizational structure was echoed in the examination of morality in organizations (Golembiewski, 1967), the presence of social and psychological rewards (Mayo, 1945), the ability to foresee and control human behavior (McGregor, 1960), and the somewhat dichotomous relationship of conventional management practice and individual growth and development (Argyris, 1962). Some went as far as to suggest that since workers make decisions based on bounded-rationality, they join organizations so they can attain efficiencies they could not garner alone (Simon, 1957).

As the academic field of public administration evolved, along with a nation's growing need to provide a larger administrative foundation, there were only occasional forays into the questions of the appropriate organizational and administrative structures of the executive branch. Many times this exploration was tangential to a deeper examination of decision-making studies, scientific models of public administration, and attempts to clearly define principles of the field of public administration. Still, there was some recognition of the role organizational structure plays in the implementation of public policy and proposals for restructuring government ultimately made their presence known. Such attention to organizations would usually be tied to efficiency or agency performance. However, many of the proposals set forth over the years (the Brownlow Commission, the Ash Commission, two Hoover Commissions, and others) were related more to power and politics than to organizational improvement (Seidman, 1975).

As Seidman (1975) penned:

> Organizational arrangements are not neutral. We do not organize in a vacuum. Organization is one way of expressing national commitment, influencing program direction, and ordering priorities. Organizational arrangements tend to give some interests, some perspectives, more effective access to those with decision-making authority, whether they be in Congress or in the Executive branch. (p. 14)

Political overtones related to administrative structure were also present with those arguing that by choosing efficiency as a mainstay in public administration, it would inadvertently lead to the evolution of bureaucratic infrastructure that was inconsistent with the tenets of democracy (Waldo, 1948/1984). Others echoed this argument, noting that democracy rests on the notions of equality, individuality, and subsequent participation. Participation included: access to information and forums of discussion, the practice of any issue being open for public debate, the ability to bring claims without fear of retribution, and due deliberation of all claims brought forth (Redford, 1969).

Even as the field of public administration trifled with the humanistic and political overtones of public organizations, it was the bureaucratic model of organization that continued to hold prominence. Leaders in the public sector, along with elected officials and scholars, mirrored organizational structures of private business that focused on hierarchical authority, unity of command, span of control, line-staff relations, and the division of labor (Denhardt, 1989). However, subsequent research findings tied to decision making opened the door to an examination of the external environment. The environment was an important consideration for not only organizational efficiency, but for adaptability and stability as well (Selznick, 1949).

Arguably, the federal structural existence of today does not reflect Weber's original thinking in the purest terms, but bureaucracy exists nonetheless, and it does so with great abandon. Despite the combination of political forces, humanist perspectives, morality and ethics, science, or allegiance to private sector organizational models, bureaucracy remains the most prominent organizational structure used to execute public policy. And the bureaucracy created by our forefathers remains a sardonic creation with unique challenges embedded for the federal leader.

Bureaucratic Nightmares of Running a Constitution

The trials of leading in the modern bureaucracy are no surprise to federal leaders. Bureaucratic organizations are harbingers of environments where strategy emanates from the senior levels, power filters to the lower levels, senior leadership makes appointment decisions for junior leaders, staff members battle one another for promotion opportunities, people are paid in accordance with seniority, jobs are allocated, managers evaluate individual performance, and rules limit discretion. The result is a confluence of military command-and-control structures and industrial engineering influences whose unchallenged principles can have a devastating impact on organizations (Hamel, 2014).

Sadly, rigidly authoritarian bureaucracies may even become coercive. Coercive bureaucracy, arguably a common presence on the federal landscape, is one reflective of the principles set forth by Fredrick Taylor (1911). Efficiency, control, and process are required in order to perform tasks. Coercive rules are generated to dictate obedience, rebuke those who violate established procedures, and enforce blind adherence to certain criteria (Adler & Boyrs, 1996). Employee autonomy is low, deviation from the established practices is frowned upon, and organizational trust is altogether absent.

Still another, and truly destructive, downside of bureaucracy is that it can result in trained incapacity (Merton, 1957). Since bureaucracy requires consistent and predictable actions combined with unquestioning adherence to regulations, public servants may find themselves viewing agency rules as absolutes. This blind adherence to guidelines spurns a common sense approach that takes into account the intent of the rule and the needs of the citizenry. Adaptation becomes unmanageable; organizational factors inherent in the bureaucracy, designed to create overarching efficiency, actually create inefficiency in unique circumstances. The public interest is ultimately unserved. Undeniably, the shortcomings of our ironically derived bureaucratic infrastructure are well documented. While the list is long, the major obstacles confronting the federal leader remain challenges of leadership, execution, communication, change, and innovation.

This handbook explores those challenges of leadership, execution, communication, change, and innovation. The following is a summary of how the handbook's authors view these challenges within the context of the modern executive branch.

Challenges of Leadership and Execution

The task of leadership and execution in our national bureaucracy is no small matter. Leaders in bureaucratic organizations are faced with the almost insurmountable challenge of demanding excellence, communicating the message of top leadership, motivating staff, and inspiring commitment toward a vision of the future. As recognizable as these tasks may seem, they are magnified extensively when viewed through the lens of the bureaucracy (Power, 2013).

Leaders in our federal government's executive branch must contend with some civil servants who follow rules for the sake of the rules and are content with the status quo. They must deal with an infrastructure that not only challenges any measure of individual autonomy, but also infuses the workforce with feelings of passivity, helplessness, and apathy. The outcome of such organizational indifference is of tremendous significance to the public. Government agencies may find themselves short on performance, inefficient, and potentially ineffective.

Noted scholar Robert Durant shows how the American political process creates challenges, choices, and opportunities for federal executive leadership. He writes that observers have often interpreted federal leadership challenges through the lens of hierarchical relationships within agencies, but the picture is far more complex. His chapter provides a detailed examination of how the political process affects federal executive leadership that has to be carried out in a networked state of public, private, and nonprofit actors.

As Durant suggests, the robust political force generated by a chorus of interest groups, political appointees, Congress, and the judiciary can limit leaders' discretion, complicate the administration of existing programs, and create problems of morale, recruitment, and retention. He explores various perspectives of this influence, including an instrumental view wherein the federal bureaucracy is simply a tool for carrying out the wishes of elected officials versus a constitutive view wherein the experts making up the bureaucracy inform, shape, implement, and evaluate policies. Durant concludes that in our Madisonian system, successful federal executive leaders must develop a specific set of skills to think analytically, systemically, strategically, technologically, legally, constitutionally, ethically, and institutionally.

Strategies for addressing these significant roadblocks to success are posited by retired senior executive Bill Valdez, who argues that a better understanding of both public administrative theory and practice would position federal leaders to be more effective in responding to today's unique challenges. Given the size, complexity, and impact on the daily lives of citizens, the executive branch is the perfect place to start.

He suggests the need for a renewed focus based on two assessments: first, the perpetual failure of the federal leadership to be prepared to develop a response that is appropriate to the scale of significant events (i.e., 9/11 terrorist attack). He advocates a more complete appreciation for the purpose of the executive branch (theory) and an in-depth knowledge of businesses' processes and organizational structures that, when combined, would position agencies for efficient and effective responses (practice).

Second, Valdez contends that federal leaders are not consistent in their ability to develop a coherent justification and implementation strategy for complex policy and funding decisions. He offers a number of practical steps, encompassed within a systems dynamics approach, to assist leaders when tackling complex societal challenges.

Andrew Rahaman builds on this focus on the federal leader by contending that what differentiates public administration from private industry are the inherent goals of the public side: providing service; regulation; and the depth of knowledge to keep government serving the citizenry. He notes that federal leaders are challenged if they are tied to leadership and decision making solely at the individual level which, while Weber-like and rewarded in many agencies, is hardly a recipe for success in a volatile and interconnected landscape.

Those mired in this paradigm of leadership are destined to miss the chance to harness communal power and influence. Rahaman challenges the reader to shy away from historical definitions of leadership and start conceiving of leadership at multiple levels within the organization, while weighing the subsequent outcomes as critical. His insightful perspective suggests that in today's society, responsibility is shared, and leaders must be prepared to lead with that in mind.

Robert Tobias acknowledges the complexity of the work to be done by the federal leader and presents a lucid argument for the leadership development required for efficient and effective public service. Successful leaders in the federal sector will succeed, but only if they first create quality relationships with those whom they lead, based on what they learn through a changed mindset and changed behavior. He strikes a cautionary note by asserting there remains a shortage of investment in developing leadership skills, and the cost is significant.

Tobias notes that in both the public and private sectors, it is common knowledge that employee engagement leads to improved organizational performance, but arming federal leaders with these tools has been slow in coming. This occurs amidst a cluttered landscape wherein the federal leader must clearly identify program and agency goals, formulate the related operational plan, involve stakeholders, and demonstrate results.

As Tobias writes, not only are federal leaders answerable for results, they are obliged to engage employees. But tackling this challenge requires leaders with skills sets that include the ability to identify new values, uncover underlying assumptions, understand and master emotional intelligence skills, and develop a leadership logic that builds a more interdependent collaborative organizational culture.

He concludes that for federal leaders to thrive in their volatile, uncertain, complex and ambiguous world, they must build a set of leadership competencies that reflect today's challenges. He calls on the Office of Personnel Management (OPM) to redefine existing Executive Core Qualifications (ECQs) for all federal managers, from aspiring leaders to current members of the Senior Executive Service that would reflect the need for greater employee engagement; more accurately assess whether the Fundamental ECQ leadership competencies are present in managers; require implementation of the recently redefined minimum leader competencies for selection, evaluation, and promotion; require competency recertification of existing leaders; and eradicate the present-day impediments to increasing employee engagement.

Ruth Zaplin and Bill Valdez extend Tobias' contention that federal leaders must exhibit leadership competencies that reflect the challenges of a volatile, uncertain, complex, and ambiguous world. Indeed, they suggest federal leaders must cultivate new mental capabilities in order to solve the dilemma of the adaptive challenges that plague the federal landscape. Zaplin and Valdez eschew the leaders' task of changing *what they know* in favor of leaders' discovering *how they know.*

They note that the 1993 Government Performance and Results Act, along with other reform measures, were passed in an attempt to inculcate a culture of restraint and answerability in government. But these attempts have fallen short. Zaplin and Valdez contend this shortfall is due to a failure on the part of the mind of the federal leaders to grasp intricate contexts and adaptive challenges. Falling prey to technical approaches to fixing complex problems, federal managers often depend on skillsets, not mindsets. The result is an inability to "see" the world they usually take for granted, surface their own assumptions, and challenge existing perceptual frameworks. They recommend an innovative approach to the training and development of executive branch political appointees and senior executives that extends beyond expertise toward an inner, more personal, transformation.

Emeritus professor Donald G. Zauderer provides deep insight into why integrity is essential for exemplary leadership. His introduction shines a light on breakdowns in integrity that exist in various branches of government. Zauderer harkens back to the work of James Madison and Alexander Hamilton in the *Federalist Papers,* where the authors demonstrate how humans pursue their self-interest—often to the detriment of others.

He follows with a thorough examination of six key questions that shine a light on different aspects of integrity: why are humans fallible in their ethical fitness?; what are the dimensions of character?; how does a leader build trust?; how does a leader exhibit civility and encourage it in others?; how and why should a leader exhibit courage?; and finally, how can a leader use ethical principles in making decisions?

Zauderer argues that all people face difficult decisions in their professional roles, but decisions should be made based on reflection and choice rather than on destructive impulse. He provides tools that leaders can use to appraise their level of integrity in light of universal ethical principles and concludes by encouraging readers to make integrity the foundation of their leadership practice.

Challenges of Communication and Change

A popular 1970s tune suggested that communication was the problem to the answer (Stewart & Goldman, 1976). Communication is indeed difficult, and interaction among individuals is often tainted with assumptions, unspoken cues, and misinterpretation. Within the modern bureaucracy, it can be even worse.

Rigid reporting structures, political limitations, and fragmented functional design create stovepipes, laughingly referred to by representatives from one agency as "cylinders of excellence." But the result of communication breakdowns is no laughing matter. Administrative hierarchy exacerbates problems of control and implementation. Information flow in both directions is thwarted as the hierarchical fabric filters and distorts data necessary for sound decision making. Lack of performance, inefficiency, ineffectiveness, and a soured organizational climate are bound to follow.

Angelo Ioffreda takes this concept to the decisive conclusion that in order to drive engagement and trust, federal leaders must communicate and do it well. Ioffreda concedes that much of the current circumstance surrounding communication problems is because of rapid technological change, globalization, the 24/7 news cycle, the rise of social media, and the speed at which organizations are being asked to communicate. To make matters worse, citizen expectations for how government should communicate have been fueled by expectations of Amazon, Google, and Apple-like performance.

When one considers the unique demands on governmental services, the communication picture becomes more intricate indeed. Citizens paying taxes demand results from their government agencies. As Ioffreda notes, the Postal Service, Food and Drug Administration, and the Internal Revenue Service serve all of the 360 million Americans. Indeed, the audience is not a small one. Political forces, a struggle to adapt to change at the organizational and technological levels, the often complex, jargon-laden nature of government information, and a general suspicion of government public relations/propaganda create a communication gap that can be felt institutionally and between civil servants and government leaders.

Ioffreda concludes that signs of progress are there, but will not succeed before federal leaders recommit themselves to improving government communications by leading with purpose, adopting a customer-centric perspective, focusing on organizational health, ensuring leaders lead and managers manage, and adopting best practices.

The very nature of bureaucracy, with its strict hierarchical and horizontal divisions, rarely encourages the flow of ideas, thoughts, and information in an open and organic fashion. So it indeed inhibits communication as Ioffreda suggests. But an ever-altering social and political landscape creates challenges on a grander scale. And while bureaucracies are not typically known for change—to think that change doesn't occur on the federal scene would be pure folly.

The challenges for federal leaders where change is concerned almost seem insurmountable, especially when one considers the volatile landscape, one fraught with one reform effort after another. Nancy Kingsbury notes that for the last 25 years there has been no shortage of reform initiatives put in place to improve government management and accountability, and it is under this cloak of repeated adjustment that federal leaders must continue to provide services to an ever-demanding citizenry.

Kingsbury informs readers that Congress and each presidential administration espouse management reform as a central initiative, and this trend is likely to continue. She notes that management reform initiatives have led to a number of good things: a focus on goal setting and performance measurement; improved program evaluation; financial information that is more accurate and readily available; a renewed focus on the importance of strategic human capital management; better acquisition practices; and the capacity to monitor cross-agency priorities.

But federal leaders face several hurdles to succeed in reform efforts, including dealing with the reality of political appointee turnover, which, as any federal executive knows, requires a balance of educating new appointees and simultaneously assimilating new approaches to existing program-management processes. Federal managers are also left to balance the numerous stakeholder perspectives, especially in a divided government, then operationalize new reform efforts with training and staff necessary for success. Kingsbury's discerning perspective challenges federal managers to embrace the challenges of reforms and cultivate the tools necessary to make reform efforts a success.

Compounding the difficulties surrounding federal government reform initiatives are those challenges inherent in change at the organizational level. Ruth Wagner begins her exploration into organizational change by suggesting change is a constant, and managing such change is a fundamental proficiency for the leaders of today. Her depiction of a multiplicity of simultaneous change initiatives as a "mazelike landscape" is sure to resonate with any federal leader.

She freely acknowledges that government leaders are generally rewarded for maintaining stability and reliability—not exactly consistent with the need for agile and malleable organizations existing in like environments. But that doesn't absolve leaders from their responsibility to strategically approach change at the organizational and human levels. Wagner's sensitivity to the unique challenges faced by public leaders is reflected in her exploration of the contextual fabric behind change, the drivers of change in public organizations, and the complicating factors often witnessed in the workplace. Her presentation of change models and theories proposed by experts such as Lewin, Kotter, and Bridges provide ample and applicable models from which to guide substantive and meaningful agency transitions.

Indeed, Wagner's "mazelike landscape" sets a cautionary tone for federal leaders in their efforts to introduce meaningful organizational change. And it takes not only federal leaders skilled in reading and assessing organizational dynamics, but also leaders knowledgeable of the limits under which they operate, especially where legal and fiscal constraints are concerned.

Joe Kaplan reminds us that being a federal employee is a mixed blessing. He writes that while protected by a wealth of rights that are encompassed in any number of laws enacted by Congress, government-wide regulations, agency-specific regulations, agency-specific policies, and rules, leaders in the federal sector have the sole responsibility to understand and arm themselves with knowledge of the legal bases of their actions. This is especially important in those cases when a subordinate's actions cause adverse consequences to the proficient realization of the agency's mission.

As Kaplan indicates, federal leaders possess constitutional competence not only because they took an oath, but because constitutional proficiency may help them avoid *personal* liability for violating an employee's constitutional rights. He leaves the reader with the dilemma of questions of conscience, which are always problematic to resolve. But he doesn't shy away from his belief that federal leaders must tackle the hard choices, as long as they do so responsibly, ethically, and legally.

Guidelines for sound decision-making do not involve legal components alone, and "following the money" is more than just a catchphrase. Neile Miller informs the reader that many government leaders see their responsibilities on the budget side of their programs as perfunctory associations at best. Since most initiatives introduced in a given presidential administration never become part of the funded agency baseline, federal leaders are left with the responsibility of being sensitive to the challenges of resource acquisition and sustainment.

As Miller writes, it is imperative that all aspiring federal executive leaders be accountable for understanding and actively pursuing the acquisition of funding, managing money, creating budgets, providing adequate supervision of the execution of appropriated funds, and working to influence those who will determine funding in the future. Her chapter provides a detailed examination of the pertinent budgetary concepts and rules, as well the process necessary for preparing the president's budget and allocating resources appropriated by Congress.

As Miller cautions, despite the procedural formalities, federal leaders must appreciate the political component—who's who, why they do what they do, and what to do about it. Her informative chapter concludes with five key points for leaders to know in order to navigate the budget process.

Managing Innovation in a Bureaucracy

While the tasks of leadership, the need for communication, and organizational readiness are formidable, one surprising aspect of administering the modern executive branch that goes largely unnoticed is the need to adopt innovations. As many of the handbook's authors argue, the executive branch is a constantly evolving organization that is currently responding to extraordinarily challenging national and international circumstances.

As a result, government reform and organizational change are a constant and are being driven by emerging trends already underway. This presents monumental challenges to the administrative state, especially in the areas of data management, resiliency, social media, transparency, and innovation. The authors in the final chapter wrestle with these issues.

Joyce Hunter, writing about "Big Data," warns that with the growth of data and the advanced technologies to analyze it, the accuracy of data collection becomes paramount. As Hunter notes, we often fail to collect and screen our data well. Second, our brains are simply not sophisticated enough to grasp the enormity of all the data we collect. Information system architecture has failed to keep up with the immense growth of data. And to no one's surprise, data security and privacy suffer. As a result, Hunter posits that agencies must abandon their command-and-control structures and processes and re-conceptualize their data management strategies to include investment in the appropriate solutions and skills.

Anita Blair builds on Hunter's recommendation on data management strategies by suggesting that workforce analytics advances agency human capital management not only by evaluating the performance of the human capital management function itself. She challenges human resource leaders to master the advanced employment rules in the public sector by focusing human resource performance as a value-added function for agencies. Blair provides numerous examples of how workforce analytics can not only inform and sustain existing programs, but also may be used to advance overall workforce performance.

Dr. David A. Bray and Charles R. Rath set the stage for the subject of resilience by noting that the world we live in is not experiencing linear change; rather it is experiencing exponential disruptive change, with implications for both the public and private sector and potentially for national sovereignty. They inform us that few catchphrases have been used as often in recent years as "resilience," but they note that all too often the word is misunderstood, especially in its application to modern-day public service.

Bray and Rath outline how public service regularly faces a volatile environment rife with societal challenges, including globalization, climate change, pandemics, increasing cybercrime, artificial intelligence, use of social media, rapidly emerging economies, aging populations, terrorism, and urbanism. With all due respect to the structural impediments of modern government (including legacy processes), this landscape nonetheless requires federal leaders to accept organizational resilience as a strategic imperative. A case study based on one of the author's own experiences in a public service organization provides clear direction for federal leaders wishing to improve resiliency in their organizations.

In her section on social media, Kim Mosser Knapp suggests federal leaders heed the advice of Oscar Wilde, who proposed that whoever controls the media controls the message. In today's backdrop of social media excess, this becomes more tantamount. Citing a 2015 study, Knapp presents astounding statistics that show in 1995, 35 million people used the Internet and 80 million people had mobile phones. But by 2014, 2.8 billion people, or almost 40% of the world's population was using the Internet (Meeker, 2015).

Knapp summarizes the current state of social media use in the federal government and informs federal leaders that "social media" is not a replacement for traditional media management; that different platforms have different audiences and different rules of the road and that federal leaders are well-advised to master them, that lessons learned the hard way provide usable tips for social media managers.

Finally, Dr. Avery Sen tackles what may be the biggest single challenge to bureaucracies: cultivating entrepreneurial leaders. Sen writes that complex problems require teams that are skilled in innovative and entrepreneurial thinking and that the leader plays the key role. He draws on the work of Hwang and Horowitt (2012) to describe the role of the entrepreneur as keeping concepts connected, bridging social distances, and reducing the transaction costs within an innovative system.

Sen's presentation of his island+bridge and bridge+island concept provides the federal leader with a framework for enhancing innovation at all levels. The latter, for example, describes a systematic approach to innovation that begins with the establishment of an infrastructure to assist many, versus few, with smaller scale innovations. The focus remains on places, practices, and people instead of programs.

Interestingly, Sen makes note of the fact that federal positions and their accompanying job security can actually foster exploration and risk-taking. Granted, political considerations must be taken into account, but the potential benefits of the island+bridge or bridge+island structures are very real indeed.

Conclusion

James Q. Wilson (1989) wrote:

> Our constitutional system so fragments authority and encourages intervention that it produces two opposing bureaucratic effects: citizen-serving agencies that are friendlier and more responsive, and citizen-regulating agencies that are more rigid and adversarial. (p. 377)

The twists and turns over 200-plus years of growth are puzzling in the fact that there are two seemingly opposing forces that co-exist quite happily in our governmental structure: the vast number of rules and the opportunity for access by the citizens.

Typically, a government with the number of the rules present in the U.S. system would be seen as arrogant and unapproachable and untouchable by the citizens. And in truth, our system has just that—a multitude of procedures. However this is combined with an elaborate system of citizen participation, including neighborhood councils, citizen advocacy assemblies, citizen oversight groups, advisory boards, and the like. So despite the complexity of the government, it's still reachable by the average citizen.

But the ultimate effectiveness of government to deliver democracy depends predominantly on the federal leader and his or her ability to communicate, inspire, and execute. In his exploration of administrative capacity some 80 years ago, E. Pendleton Herring (1936) wrote, "The bureaucrat … does not suffer so much from an inability to execute the law unhampered as from an uncertainty in direction" (p. 22).

Let the men and women of federal leadership, suffused with mindset change and cognizant of the complexity of leading in today's bureaucracy, provide that direction to public servants throughout the government.

References

Adler, P., & Borys, B. (1996). Two types of bureaucracy: Enabling and coercive. *Administrative Science Quarterly, 41*(1), 61–89.

Argyris, C. (1962). *Interpersonal competence and organizational effectiveness*. Homewood, IL: Dorsey.

Aronson, S. (1964). *Status and kinship ties in the higher civil service: Standards of selection in the administrations of John Adams, Thomas Jefferson, and Andrew Jackson.* Cambridge, MA: Harvard University Press.

Barnard, C. I. (1968). *The functions of the executive.* Cambridge, MA: Harvard University Press. (Original work published 1938).

Bendix, R. (1978). *Max Weber: An intellectual portrait.* Berkley: University of California Press.

Denhardt, R. B. (1989). Five great issues in organization theory. In J. Rabin, W. Hildreth & G. Miller (Eds.), *Handbook of public administration* (pp. 105–127). New York, NY: Marcel-Dekker, Inc.

DiIulio, J. J., Jr. (2014, August 29). Want better, smaller government? Hire another million federal bureaucrats. Retrieved from https://www.washingtonpost.com/opinions/want-better-smaller-governmenthire-1-million-more-federal-bureaucrats/2014/08/29/c0bc1480-2c72-11e4-994d-202962a9150c_story.html.

Dodd, L., & Schott, R. (1979). *Congress and the administrative state.* New York, NY: John Wiley & Sons.

Fish, C. R. (1905). *The civil service and the patronage.* New York, NY: Longmans.

Fredrickson, H. G. (1980). *The new public administration.* Tuscaloosa, AL: University of Alabama Press.

Golembiewski, R. T. (1967). *Men, management, and morality.* New York, NY: McGraw-Hill.

Gulick, L. (1937). Notes on the theory of organization. In L. Gulick & L. Urwick (Eds.) *Papers on the science of administration* (pp. 1–46). New York, NY: Institute of Public Administration.

Hamel, G. (2014, November 4). Bureaucracy must die. *Harvard Business Review.* Retrieved from https://hbr.org/2014/11/bureaucracy-must-die.

Herring, E. P. (1936). *Public administration and the public interest.* New York, NY: McGraw-Hill.

Hwang, V. W., & Horowitt, G. (2012). *The rainforest: The secret to building the next silicon valley.* Los Altos, CA: Regenwald.

Kilpatrick, F. P., Cummings, M. C., Jr., & Jennings, M. K. (1964). *The image of the federal executive.* Washington, DC: Brookings Institution.

Marshall, L. (1967). The strange stillbirth of the Whig party. *American Historical Review, LXXII* (January), 455–456.

Mayo, E. (1945). *Social problems of an industrial civilization.* Boston, MA: Harvard University Press.

McGregor, D. (1960). *The human side of enterprise.* New York, NY: McGraw-Hill.

Meeker, M. (2015). *Internet trends 2015 – code conference.* San Francisco, CA: Kleiner, Perkins, Caufield, Byers (KPCB). Retrieved from: https://kpcb.com/InternetTrends.

Merton, R. K. (1957). *Social theory and social structure.* Glencoe, IL: Free Press.

Mooney, J., & Riley, A. (1939). *The principles of organization.* New York, NY: Harper and Row.

Nelson, M. (1979). Power to the people: The crusade for direct democracy. *Saturday Review, 6*(23), 12–17.

Nelson, M. (1982). A short, ironic history of American national bureaucracy. *Journal of Politics, 44*(3), 747–778.

Office of Personnel Management. (2015). *Executive branch civilian employment since 1940.* Retrieved from https://www.opm.gov/policy-data-oversight/data-analysis-documentation/federal-employment-reports/historical-tables/executive-branch-civilian-employment-since-1940/.

Power, B. (2013, March 8). Innovating around a bureaucracy. *Harvard Business Review.* Retrieved from https://hbr.org/2013/03/innovating-around-a-bureaucracy.

Redford, E. S. (1969). *Democracy in the administrative state.* New York, NY: Oxford University Press.

Rosenbloom, D. H. (1971). *Federal service and the constitution: The development of the public employee relationship.* Ithaca, NY: Cornell University Press.

Rourke, F. E. (1976) *Bureaucracy, politics, and public policy.* Boston, MA: Little, Brown.

Schattschneider, E. E. (1960). *The semisovereign people: A realist's view of democracy in America.* New York, NY: Holt, Rinehart and Winston.

Seidman, H. (1975). *Politics, positions, and power.* New York, NY: Oxford University Press.

Selznick, P. (1949). *TVA and the grass roots.* New York, NY: Harper & Row.

Senate Budget Committee. (2014, October 15). Ten facts you may not know about the federal budget. *Budget Blog.* Retrieved from http://www.budget.senate.gov/democratic/public/index.cfm/2014/10/ten-facts-you-may-not-know-about-the-federal-budget.

Short, L. M. (1923). *The development of national administrative organization in the United States.* Baltimore, MD: Johns Hopkins University Press.

Simon, H. A. (1957). *Administrative behavior: A study of decision-making processes in administrative organization* (2nd ed.). New York, NY: Macmillan.

Stewart, E., & Gouldman, G. (1976). The things we do for love (recorded by 10CC). On *Deceptive Bands.* New York, NY: Mercury.

Taylor, F. W. (1911). *The principles of scientific management.* New York, NY: Harper Brothers.

United States Census Bureau. (2015). *U.S. and world population clock.* Retrieved December, 2015, from http://www.census.gov/popclock/.

Waldo, D. (1984). *The administrative state: A study of the political theory of American public administration* (2nd ed.). New York, NY: Holmes and Meier. (Original work published 1948).

Weber, M. (1947). *The theory of social and economic organization* (A. M. Henderson & T. Parsons, Trans.). New York, NY: Oxford University Press.

Willoughby, W. E. (1927). *Principles of public administration.* Baltimore, MD: Johns Hopkins University Press.

Wilson, J. Q. (1989). *Bureaucracy: What government agencies do and how they do it.* New York, NY: Basic Books.

Wilson, W. (1887). The study of administration. *Political Science Quarterly, 2*(2), 197–222.

2 Federal Administrative Leadership in the American Political System

Robert F. Durant

> [Public administration] is more than a lifeless pawn. It plans, it contrives, it philosophizes, it educates, it builds for the community as a whole.
>
> —Marshall E. Dimock

In his classic 1887 article, "The Study of Administration," then college professor and future Princeton University president, New Jersey governor, and U.S. president Woodrow Wilson wrote that "administrative questions are not political questions" (p. 210). If this were ever true, it is not so today, as administrative questions have clearly become the grist of national, state, and local politics in an era of divided government at all levels of the American political system. Not only do actors in the American political process monitor, raise questions about, and commence reforms of administration on a routine basis, they also pursue their policy preferences via administrative means. Moreover, the political process shapes the tasks and capacity of administrators to meet both their statutory and constitutional duties, especially in an era of what political scientists call "affective partisan polarization" (Iyengar, Sood, & Lelkes, 2012). In contrast to conventional partisanship where compromise is viewed as necessary and political opponents as still worthy of respect, affective partisan polarization occurs when compromise is seen as traitorous and opponents as villains to be vanquished.

Is the impact of the American political process on federal administration and administrative leadership advancing the nation's policy and constitutional interests, complicating their realization, or even fundamentally undermining them? Before answering this question, one has to understand that administrative leadership can occur at any level in an organization and that different forms of leadership exist. Michael Maccoby (2015) has identified three types of leaders: strategic, operational, and network. Strategic leaders define organizational purpose, vision, values, and partners. In comparison, operational leaders design, maintain, and continuously critique organizational processes for improvement in terms of their cost, productivity, and effectiveness. Network leaders, in contrast, may have no formal leadership role or title but are central to connecting experts, organizations, and other partners. For simplicity, this essay will use the term "administrative leadership" to connote each of these types of leaders.

That said, the classic framing of this issue in the academic field of public administration took place in the 1940s and rests on views of the proper role of bureaucracy in a democratic republic (Cook, 2015). Those taking an instrumental view of the federal bureaucracy—that is, who see it as a tool for carrying out the wishes of elected officials—find little to worry about in these developments. In this view, the political process affords a needed "external check" on the way bureaucrats exercise their policy discretion (Finer, 1941). In contrast, those who take a constitutive view of the federal bureaucracy—that is, those who see the bureaucracy as playing a critical role in informing, shaping, and evaluating policies, because the wishes of elected officials can be unclear, conflicting, or misguided absent the expertise of career civil servants—will find these developments disturbing. Their preference is for "inner checks" on the federal bureaucracy that involve their conscience, professional codes of ethics, counter-bureaucracies such as inspectors general, and professional competition (Friedrich, 1940).

Public administration scholars today also remain somewhat split on this question. Most worry that administration has become so negatively affected by the political process that their preferred Hamiltonian vision of "energy in the executive" is at risk (Light, 2002). More moderately, some argue that the "creative tension" between bureaucrats and elected officials that is needed to overcome the risk-aversion of the former and the impetuousness of the latter has swung too far in favor of elected officials. They see it as unnecessarily disruptive of agency operations, as compromising the role of expertise, and as morale-sapping for public employees (Durant, 2014). Rather than a bureaucracy problem, some in this "school" argue that we have a political problem that can be resolved by reducing political influence on agency operations (Meier, 1997). Others argue that a "legislative-centered" theory of bureaucracy cannot be ignored, as is explicitly done by advocates of energy in the executive (Rosenbloom, 2000). Congress has a constitutionally legitimate role to play in administration. Still others in both the "reinventing government" and "new public management" movements (Barzelay, 1992) have insisted that the appropriate role of the bureaucracy is to "row" (i.e., implement policy), while that of elected officials—primarily of chief executives and their political appointees—is to "steer" (i.e., develop policy). In reaction, a more citizen-centered view has emerged of the role of the federal bureaucracy and the leadership within it. Neither steering nor rowing is their primary role; rather, their oath is to serve citizens in a democracy (Denhardt & Denhardt, 2015).

For federal administrators trying to lead within this politicized context, however, the verdict is clear. The political process has pressured—and will continue to pressure—agencies for reforms that sorely test their leadership abilities. To see why this is the case, this chapter takes a broad view of federal administrative leadership that is more commensurate than traditional approaches with the realities of networked governance in the 21st century (Milward & Provan, 1993; O'Leary & Bingham, 2009). Traditionally, researchers view federal leadership challenges solely as they relate to hierarchical relationships within single agencies. But consistent with the dynamics of networked governance, this chapter examines how the political process affects federal administrative leadership across different levels of American government, as well as across the public, private, and not-for-profit sectors.

Such an approach also makes sense given the political climate in the United States today and its likely continuation for the foreseeable future. First, American's historical tendency to "hide" the visible size of government (Balogh, 2009) by working through or partnering with states, localities, and private and not-for-profit actors has spiraled since the 1980s. Second, the fate of federal policy initiatives increasingly is affected by state and local (as well as international) politics and administration. The interaction of these two dynamics, in turn, means that federal leaders need to think more than ever before about how to inspire, nurture, and hold accountable both their agency subordinates and those outside their agency with whom they are partnering.

The chapter begins by reviewing key elements of the evolution of public administrationists' thinking about the relationship among politics, policy, and administration (henceforth, PPA). It next reviews the current partisan context of the political process today and the unlikelihood that this context might change in the foreseeable future. Discussed are some of the tools that federal elected officials have used in responding to these dynamics—most notably to advance their policy agendas administratively—and the pressures they place on administrative leaders. The chapter concludes by reviewing what prior research suggests about the generic skills that administrative leaders need in these challenging times, as well as research gaps that need to be addressed to discern more robust lessons for them.

Partisanship, Administrative Leadership, and the Politics–Policy–Administration (PPA) Nexus

One of the most enduring concepts offered by the majority of the Progressive Era founders of public administration as a field of practice and study was the idea that politics could, and should, be separated from administration. They argued that the solutions to public problems at the turn of the 20th century were too complex for non-experts, a problem compounded by the amateurism and corruption of their elected officials. Elected officials in a democracy might rightly play politics when enacting policy agendas for action. However, carrying out these policies in the most efficient, economical, and effective way possible depended on shielding agency experts from politics as they implemented laws. Moreover, no danger to democracy existed in shielding experts from the political process. Applying the knowledge and standards of their professions, they would pursue the objectively "best way" to implement the desires of elected officials who were directly accountable to the public. In essence, careerists would be "neutrally competent" tools or instruments of elected officials.

This "separation" of politics from administration soon morphed into a "policy–administration" dichotomy premised on the same logic. It did so, first, because those funding early public administration research felt that figuring out how to "run government like a business" was politically less controversial and benign to their own interests (Lee, 2013; Roberts, 1994; Rosenbloom, 2008). Second, they felt that concentrating policy-making power in the executive branch would afford the nimbleness, cohesion of thinking, and durability of policy that legislatures could never afford and that modernity required. Finally, and more normatively, they believed that greater accountability for policy decisions would occur in a more hierarchically structured bureaucracy than in the less hierarchical structure of legislatures. Indeed, agency hierarchies meant that administrators could be given "broad powers and unhampered discretion" (W. Wilson, 1887) but be held responsible for their actions in ways that legislators could not.

Thus, the founders of public administration were not naïve when they spoke about a PPA dichotomy. They believed that politics *should* be separated from administration as much as possible, but they recognized that this separation could *never* be totally realized in practice. After all, "administration is policy," because the discretion public agencies wield *is* policy making and has political implications. Moreover, "politics follows discretion"; those affected by policy will seek to influence that discretion wherever it is exercised to advance their interests.

Their concern, then, was over *where* politics might better be played to advance the public interest—legislatures or the executive branch of governments. They came down strongly on the side of executive branch politics. Limiting the access to and influence on legislators of political party machines supported by surging immigration into the United States, as well as by corporations and other interest groups, would overcome the inefficiencies and corruption that in their day precluded energetic, effective, and coordinated policy making in the legislative branch. Shifting political pressures from the Congress to federal agencies would also produce more public interest-oriented policies, because presidents, governors, and mayors had to please a broader electoral constituency than legislators elected by districts or states.

The PPA dichotomy has had staying power in the minds of many federal agency employees and labor unions. It offers them a rhetorical device for trying to fend off political or policy interventions from the Congress or the White House. Likewise, the PPA dichotomy prevailed in academic circles until the late 1940s. Its Hamiltonian precepts for energy in the executive through application of the principles of business administration and shielded from congressional interference reached its apogee in the recommendations of President Franklin Roosevelt's Committee on Administrative Management for organizing the federal executive branch (also known as the Brownlow Committee). It also still surfaces implicitly in many of the reform recommendations that federal administrators are called upon to implement today. For instance, both the Clinton administration's "reinventing government" initiative during the 1990s and the more recent expansion of market-based and business-based reforms undertaken under the so-called "new public management" treated the Congress largely as if it did not exist. Indeed, the disappointments of these initiatives are directly traceable to pretending that politics are not a key ingredient in administration. Because of the discretion that agencies exercise, the federal bureaucracy becomes a battleground for control between the executive and legislative branches of government, with the courts often sorting out the winners and losers.

The academic undermining of the PPA dichotomy began in earnest in the late 1940s. Leading scholars who served in administrative or staff positions in the New Deal and World War II argued from their experiences that politics and policy were not severable from administration (e.g., Dahl, 1947; Simon, 1957; Waldo, 1948/1984). Elected officials passed legislation that was vague, ambiguous, or even contradictory. They did so, variously, to attain winning coalitions, because some problems are so complex that only experts can make judgments, or because elected officials wish to shift politically risky questions to the bureaucracy (Fiorina, 1989). Passing legislation was not the end of the political "race" but actually the starting gun.

Norton Long, for example, famously wrote in 1949 that the "lifeblood of administration is power" (p. 257). He defined power as agencies building and maintaining a favorable balance of external political actors who support their programs. Otherwise, these actors would jeopardize their programs and survival, or their interests would suffer in comparison to those with politically strong constituencies. Moreover, these political pressures would arise in Washington and in agency field offices.

Likewise, David Rosenbloom (2000) notes that, in 1946, Congress conceded that it was delegating its policy-making (rulemaking) authority to federal agencies. Consequently, it enacted the Administrative Procedure Act and the Legislative Reorganization Act to gain greater congressional oversight of agency decision making and operations. Among other things, the former created a deliberative process for agencies issuing rules and regulations that was subject to review by the courts. The latter created permanent oversight committees for agency programs. In doing so, Congress effectively offered a "legislative-centered theory" of administration predicated on the values of responsiveness and accountability to its membership, values that differed markedly from executive-centered administrative models focused on efficiency, economy, and effectiveness.

Also clear to scholars by the 1950s and 1960s was that those congressional oversight committees soon morphed into so-called "subsystems." Recognized, first, were so-called "iron triangles." These are comprised of cozy relationships that develop among agencies, interest groups affected by agency decisions, and legislative committee members charged with overseeing agencies (Freeman, 1965; James, 1969; Redford, 1969). Committee members oversee programs that affect their constituents, keeping an eye on them to acquire re-election benefits. Meanwhile, agencies need interest-group support in budget hearings, as sources of information to make decisions, and sometimes to help set policies (e.g., industry standards for chemical regulation) and enforce them (e.g., water quality standards and cleanup). Likewise, legislative committee members need campaign contributions and information from interest groups to counter agency claims. They also need agencies to allocate whatever resources they are giving out to the legislators' states or legislative districts. In turn, interest groups need agencies to make decisions in their favor. The stakes involved are material (e.g., funding) and, hence, divisible among interest groups. Thus, all actors share an interest in keeping policy conflict low and dividing the benefits.

For presidents and their political appointees, the lesson of iron triangles was that policy was captured by these interests, leaving the appointees little room to exercise leadership in directions other than those favored by interest groups and committee members. But by the late 1970s, the idea of "issue networks" began to replace iron triangles as the dominant metaphor capturing subsystem relationships (Heclo, 1977). Issue networks portray the reality that agencies are overseen by a number of congressional committees, often with diverse preferences, and that the interests surrounding various policy issues have both splintered and expanded exponentially during the 1960s. For example, although agricultural interest groups once dominated food stamps and farm subsidies, by the 1970s, these were also drawing the attention of health and nutrition groups that tried to influence agency discretion. Moreover, actors representing the pros and cons of various policy issues (e.g., pro-choice versus right-to-life groups) were motivated less by material stakes and more by normative or value issues. This made compromise among actors more difficult and sometimes impossible.

The concept of issue networks had major consequences for both the political and administrative leadership of federal agencies. For the career bureaucracy, the prior influence of mid-level public managers in closed subsystem politics was reduced significantly. Policy knowledge rather than pure administrative skill was now the coin of the realm in the legislative process. Moreover, policy knowledge extended beyond agencies to the growing number of policy think tanks in Washington. Thus, federal agencies no longer held as much of a monopoly on policy and program knowledge as they had in earlier decades, making them relatively less powerful actors in the policy process. This development also meant increased political pressures from members of Congress and presidents wielding often-contradictory results of think tank studies (often reflecting the interests of their funders).

Then, in the 1980s and 1990s, researchers began stressing the power of ideas, ideology, and knowledge in policy making and the political process. This brought in an even broader array of political actors who tried to influence and challenge administrative expertise. Political conservatives offered a new iron triangle, one comprised of: (1) agency program officials trying to expand their programs, (2) the print and electronic media with an economic stake in identifying policy and administrative problems, and (3) liberal interest groups bent on expanding the welfare state. Others described a "new partnership" comprised of congressional committee staff, agency program managers, and liberal-minded judges to protect and expand programs in the face of Reagan administration cuts (Melnick, 1985). Still others identified "advocacy coalitions" as the dominant drivers of agency programs and policy agendas (Sabatier & Jenkins-Smith, 1993). These were comprised of enduring networks of interacting interest groups, agency bureaucrats, journalists, academics, and public managers who, over time, would develop core beliefs and ways to approach problems. In these advocacy coalitions, actors were not willing to compromise their core political or policy beliefs, but they were open to compromise on the means to address problems.

Nor were these conceptualizations of the PPA relationship limited to any one level of government. Intergovernmental relations were analogized as a "picket fence." The vertical slats in the fence are best understood as like-minded experts in various fields—such as health, education, or welfare—developing rules and regulations and pushing grant money to each other through the federal system. They, too, were said to have interests in building new or expanding existing programs. The horizontal slats in the fence are elected officials at different levels of government trying to coordinate across different policy areas in their jurisdictions—and typically feeling quite frustrated by their exclusion from the vertical professional–bureaucratic complex (Beer, 1978).

Exercising leadership within these PPA relationships has since grown even more complex and difficult as networked government has expanded. The increasing turn to, and density of, contracting and cross-sectoral partnerships has occurred because of the downward pressures on the visible size and cost of the federal bureaucracy. This has occurred as federal budget deficits and the national debt have swollen, as the nature of what government is asked to do changes, and as economic globalization occurs. Elected officials, however, continue to pass legislation, but they hide the federal bureaucracy's visible size by shifting implementation costs to subnational governments and to the private and not-for-profit sectors through contracting, regulatory requirements, and partnerships. Put differently, they use these third-party actors to *compensate* for their unwillingness to build sufficient administrative capacity at the federal level to accommodate program expansion.

The mismatch between legislated demands on federal agencies and capacity restraints cannot be overcome simply by ferreting out waste, fraud, and abuse. Using constant 2013 dollars, John DiIulio (2014) reports that federal spending was four times larger than it was in 1960, but the federal workforce was about the same size as in 1960. Granted, much of this spending growth comes from entitlement programs such as Social Security, Medicare, Medicaid, and veterans' pensions. Including interest payments on the national debt, these comprise nearly 70% of the federal budget today. With entitlements so far deemed too politically risky to stop future rates of growth in expenditures, and with anti-tax increase pressures remaining supple, cuts in the rate of growth of federal programs fall repeatedly on the remaining 30% of discretionary defense and non-defense spending. These include spending on social programs, intergovernmental grants, and federal agency operations, which, in turn, have expanded reliance on third-party actors. Consider the magnitude of this "compensatory state" (Eisner, 2000). In 2012, approximately 56,000 not-for-profit organizations received about 350,000 contracts worth around $137 billion (DiIulio, 2014). Federal agencies also used "pass-through" grants from Washington through the states to not-for-profits. Together, these helped make not-for-profits the third largest employer in the United States. Meanwhile, federal funding of private contractors subsidized 26 million employees, or approximately 22% of the American workforce. In addition, federal grants to states, despite periods of cutbacks, increased in constant dollars more than ten-fold between 1960 and 2012, largely as a result of the Troubled Asset Relief Program and the Obama administration's $825 billion stimulus program in the wake of the 2007–09 Great Recession.

In the process, the nature of federal agency work shifted. In the 1960s, federal agencies were involved mostly in the direct delivery of goods, services, and opportunities. In contrast, today's federal civilian workforce functions in four major areas, in addition to tax collection: determining and allocating subsidies, transferring money to state and local governments, allocating and monitoring grants and contracts to private and not-for-profit actors, and regulating business (DiIulio, 2014).

Unchanged, however, is the duplication and stovepiping of agencies and programs across the federal government, intergovernmentally, and cross-sectorally that subsystem politics helped create, fortify, and sustain. For example, the political process has produced over 60 employment training programs located in different agencies. When presidents try to consolidate them or coordinate them by creating cross-cutting "czars" or "enterprise management" systems connected by information technology (IT), subsystems usually kick in to complicate, if not stymie, many of these efforts. Meanwhile, leaders in one agency are sometimes unaware of decisions made in other agencies that affect their programs. Like an assembly line, implementation is compromised by the weakest link in the chain, and leaders in one agency cannot order leaders in other agencies to correct these links. This also means that "policy" affecting target populations (e.g., single female-headed households) is not developed or implemented by any single agency. This is the result of a variety of uncoordinated actions taken by a variety of agencies, some of which may be inconsistent, offsetting, or counterproductive.

Thus, the challenges posed and pressures exerted by actors in the political process are multiple for both elected officials and agency administrative leaders. For example, both must learn how to navigate the political rapids of subsystem politics, taking time to understand the actors, what motivates them, and the opportunities and constraints they offer on agency goals. Administrative leaders must also figure out how best to let and oversee contracts and grants, as well as bring network actors together, keep them together and energized, and hold them accountable for their actions. These activities themselves are akin to a political campaign. At the same time, they must discern how best to motivate agency employees who work side-by-side in a "blended workforce" with contractors who may be receiving higher compensation.

In addition, administrative leaders must learn how best to hire, train, promote, and retain talented federal employees. Doing so means enhancing strategic human capital planning that embraces racial, gender, and ethnic diversity *and* millennials with very different work expectations than prior generations, doing both *amid* the upcoming "silver tsunami" of retiring federal, state, and local workers. Transitioning retirees as they leave in ways that maintain their institutional memory is critical in this regard (e.g., phased retirement programs). Gone, otherwise, will be the appropriate mix of skill sets for completing their agency's mission. Moreover, leaders must do so amid a political zeitgeist that demeans public service and favors such things as federal pay freezes, benefit cuts, restraints on collective bargaining, and at-will employment. All this makes the recruitment of talented millennials quite challenging for leaders who are competing with private business, a situation not helped by the inordinate delays in hiring new federal employees. Meanwhile, federal administrators working with partners in networks must deal with the stop-and-go nature, uncertainties, and disruptions of the congressional budgeting process. This is a process complicated further in recent years by repeated threats to shut down government for various political causes (e.g., over debt ceiling limits or Planned Parenthood funding).

Light at the End of the Political Tunnel?

Prospects also are not good for ending the dysfunctional affective partisanship that a shift to more ideological parties has occasioned in the political process and that currently challenges federal administrative leadership. In the early 1960s, political scientists called for more programmatic parties that, when elected, could govern as majorities to enact their policy agendas. Today, many despair the legislative gridlock that a de facto "responsible party" system has wrought. The development of ideological parties with distinct programs and priorities has occurred without a commensurate change in the institutional structure of our Madisonian system of separate institutions sharing power, checks and balances, bicameral legislatures, and federalism. As Thomas Mann and Norman Ornstein (2012) argue, we are left with European-style parliamentary parties unwilling to compromise on their defining issues but operating in a Madisonian system where compromise is usually necessary to get anything done.

Further reinforcing this tendency are residence patterns in the nation today. Researchers find that the American electorate has "sorted itself out" geographically, with those sharing social, political, and economic views clustering together (Bishop, 2009). Not only do they then vote in similarly striking ways, but they tend to avoid contact with others holding different opinions. Media segmentation (e.g., liberal and conservative "news" radio and TV stations and social media) that allows voters to avoid opinions differing from their own exacerbates this problem, thus reinforcing existing biases among voters and villainizing opponents.

Taking advantage of this residential sorting, both political parties use computer programs to draw favorable congressional districts for themselves after each decennial census when they control state legislatures. In effect, candidates can now choose reliably partisan districts to run in, thus nearly guaranteeing their election and re-election. Relatedly, polarization in Congress is further fomented by our primary election system. In these safe Democratic or Republican districts, primaries become more important than general elections, partly because the minority party often struggles to find quality candidates to run in general elections. Primary voters, in turn, tend to be the most committed voters politically and ideologically, meaning that those elected from safe districts need only play to their primary electoral base once in Congress. This also makes them less willing to compromise over issues in Congress, because compromise can jeopardize their chances with primary voters the next time around.

Although the media typically associates structural factors such as these with elections for national office, it is important in an era of networked governance to consider the structural features affecting electoral politics at all levels of government. When one does, the chances for less legislative gridlock and partisan polarization recede even further. Indeed, the old truism that "all politics is local" may need to be reconsidered. Recent research shows that a nationalization of state and local elections is occurring in many states, bringing with it the political polarization witnessed in Washington.

Prior to the 2016 elections, Democrats held the presidency, while Republicans held both houses of Congress. And although the national media is focused on the ethnic and generational demographic shifts facing Republicans in presidential elections (as one wit puts it, the majority of Republican supporters are "male, pale, and stale"), turnout among these voters is much lower than for other groups in society (with the exception of the 2008 and 2012 presidential contests with Barack Obama leading the ticket). Thus, this demographic shift had not hurt the Republican Party in congressional races and at the state government level.

Nor is it likely that turnout rates for these groups will rise appreciably in the near future at other levels of government. Voting registration rates have been lower, despite heavy Democratic outreach. Hispanics as a group are also likely to remain younger and, thus, less likely to vote. Moreover, even if they do, it is not clear that a sizeable proportion of ethnic and millennial voters are out of the reach of the Republican Party, at least if candidates (re)frame social issues and policies in ways that appeal to their family, economic, and religious or spiritual concerns. One also cannot rule out the possibility of Republicans taking the presidency in 2016 and holding on to majorities in both houses of Congress. Prior research suggests, however, that this could make intraparty rather than interparty rifts the basis for gridlock or polarization, although their prospects for doing so have grown dimmer due to stunning missteps by the Republican presidential candidate, Donald Trump.

In early 2016, Republicans held the second highest number of Senate seats (54), as well as the highest number of House seats (247) held since 1928 (Trende & Byler, 2015). At the state level, Republicans' share of governorships (31, with only 18 Democratic governors) was their third highest since the end of World War II, while their share of state legislative seats was their highest since 1920. Since President Obama took office, Democrats had lost 11 governorships. Republicans also controlled 67 state legislative chambers, five more than their previous record in the modern era, and had total control of 24 states (i.e., they held the governorship and majorities in both legislative chambers) (R. Wilson, 2014). Democrats held total control in only six states. Moreover, Republicans had supermajority status in 16 state legislative chambers. In the process, Democrats lost 910 legislative seats.

Basically, the Democratic Party went into the 2016 electoral cycle with a structural advantage in presidential and local elections in major cities, while the Republican Party started with a structural advantage in congressional and gubernatorial elections. Taking presidential elections first, and noting the 270 electoral college votes needed for victory, Democrats and Republicans started with approximately 247 and 206 electoral votes, respectively. These totals consisted of a solid base of "sure" states, states leaning toward each party, and swing states that the Republican Party has not won since the 1980s. This left Democrats needing only 23 swing-state electoral votes to win the presidency and Republicans needing nearly three times as many to win.

In contrast, Republicans held a solid, but not insurmountable, structural advantage in elections for the House of Representatives and a narrower one in the Senate. Two structural features brought this about: (a) the aforementioned clustering of likely Democratic voters in voting districts and (b) redistricting by Republican governors and legislatures that favored their candidates and disadvantaged Democrats. In terms of clustering, the problem for Democrats has been that their most likely voters are concentrated in urban areas (minority voters and younger voters). This makes all votes cast beyond a winning 51% for the Democratic candidate "wasted." If these voters were spread more evenly across districts, more competitive races in now Republican districts would be likely. Although not impossible, all this meant that the chances of a Democratic majority emerging to work with a Democratic president were slim. In contrast, regaining a Democratic majority in the Senate was much more plausible, because Republicans had to defend more seats than Democrats.

Likewise, with responsibilities for major federal programs having shifted over the years to the states, state elections and appointments have taken on new importance for federal administrative leaders. As the key executive officer in state governments, and with policy differences between Republican and Democratic governors so clear on many issues (e.g., welfare reform and global warming), governors' party identification matters in terms of priority setting, budgeting, and staffing for federal policy success or failure. Think, for example, about the effect of political partisanship on the adoption of climate change protocols in states, or state adoption of insurance exchanges and the expansion of Medicaid under the Patient Protection and Affordable Care Act.

Another structural feature of state politics going into the 2016 election cycle suggested Republican dominance was also likely in the future. Currently, 36 states hold gubernatorial elections in midterm (or nonpresidential) election cycles. With the presidential race not on the ballot to draw out a larger and more diverse electorate, Republicans held an advantage: older, white, and, thus, more Republican voters turn out. Moreover, term-limited Democratic governorships have been hard for the party to hold on to (e.g., in the 2014 elections in Arkansas, Maryland, and Massachusetts) (Greenblatt, 2015).

Finally, with so many federal policy and program implementation responsibilities assigned to local governments and their partners, the partisanship of mayors and city councils is also critical to federal program success. Going into 2016, very few of the nation's largest cities had Republican mayors. Moreover, these were clustered in cities with consolidated city–county governments (e.g., Miami–Dade) that make suburban voters eligible to vote, as well as Sun Belt cities such as Albuquerque, Oklahoma City, and San Diego. Also, as more millennial, ethnic, and LGBTQ voters move into cities as part of what Richard Florida (2002) calls "the creative class," they reinforce the economic and socially liberal values associated with minority voters and the Democratic Party. Consider how the "sustainable cities" movement in the United States has been led by mayors in democratic-leaning cities such as Baltimore, Boston, New York City, Portland, and Seattle (Portney, 2013), as has the controversial sanctuary city movement that defies federal policy.

Again, none of these structural advantages or disadvantages is insuperable or automatically determines election outcomes, such as those in the 2016 election cycle. As of this writing (July 2016), the unique dynamics at play in the 2016 presidential election may illustrate these points at all levels of government. They merely indicate the formidable structural forces faced by the two parties. Political campaigns—their candidates, their policies, their strategies and tactics—matter, as do court decisions. For instance, in 2016, at least four states had to revise their voting districts due to court challenges regarding their constitutionality. These states included the competitive and electoral college vote-rich states of Florida and Virginia (Greenblatt, 2015). Moreover, changes in the political zeitgeist can render structural features anachronistic in any given election. But the longer-term fundamentals of the electoral advantages enjoyed by the parties must be overcome for upsets to occur, as must the administrative leadership challenges brought by divided government and partisan polarization.

The Challenges of Institutional "Coevolution" for Federal Administrative Leadership

If the political dynamics just discussed were not challenging enough for federal administrative leadership, they are compounded by the responses of presidents and members of Congress to these developments. Researchers call this the "coevolution" of institutions, a term capturing how each reacts to others' actions. A similar coevolution of institutions has taken place at subnational levels of government. Most notable for federal administrative leadership are the steps that various presidents and the Congress have taken as they find themselves accountable to voters for actions taken by agencies in today's networked state. Elected officials who seek significant policy changes are also perplexed about their chances for successfully enacting them in the face of legislative challenges from actors in subsystems surrounding federal programs.

To combat this situation at the federal level, presidents have turned to the "administrative presidency" (Durant, 1992; Durant & Resh, 2012; Nathan, 1983). They see it as a means for controlling bureaucratic discretion and for advancing their policy agendas administratively rather than just legislatively. Administration is, after all, policy making in many instances. For example, nearly 4,000 rules are finalized each year by federal agencies and approximately 2,700 new regulations are issued by them annually. They also issue approximately 80 major new rules with an estimated economic impact of $100 million or more (Kosar, 2015). This has meant that agencies are often a battleground for control between the White House and congressional committees, with the courts serving as referee.

In the process, however, presidents have overturned the early progressives' ideal of a "neutrally competent" public workforce. Instead, using the enhanced authorities to evaluate and reward or punish the performance of career civil servants afforded by the Civil Service Reform Act of 1978, they seek "responsive competence" from agencies. Unlike neutral competence, responsive competence means that agency personnel should be responsive to the desires of their political superiors—even when what the latter want may be contrary to their professional values as experts—or else suffer the wrath of elected officials. In reaction, Congress has used its legal and constitutional powers to combat these initiatives.

Three primary sets of tools comprise the administrative presidency (Durant, 1992; Durant & Resh, 2012; Resh, 2015), can raise congressional scrutiny and ire, and can thus sorely complicate federal administrative leadership. First, presidents of both parties have pulled major policy-making priorities away from agencies and brought them into the White House—particularly, into the Executive Office of the President (EOP). Reminiscent of the PPA dichotomy, the federal bureaucracy is viewed merely as an instrument or tool to figure out how best to implement presidential priorities. Second, the administrative presidency relies on so-called "contextual tools" to try to create an agency environment suitable for advancing presidential policy goals. Third, administrative strategies rely on so-called "unilateral tools" such as executive orders, presidential signing statements, and national security directives to advance presidential agendas. These allow them to act without the formal consent of Congress.

Centralization of Policy Making into the White House Office

Research since the early 1970s has shown how presidents have centralized policy making related to their priorities into the EOP. They have tried to centralize agency rulemaking, for example, by creating clearance processes in the Office of Information and Regulatory Affairs (OIRA) in the Office of Management and Budget (OMB). They have also centralized personnel appointment decisions in the White House Office and developed domestic and national security policies in the EOP—often without departmental input. Researchers, however, find that this "institutional presidency" is now itself highly bureaucratized and laced with turf wars, information hoarding, and internecine conflicts (Warshaw, 2006). It also creates morale problems in the agencies along with tensions and resentments between the White House and departments, which administrative leaders must deal with on a regular basis.

Still, recent research suggests that claims of centralization, integration of initiatives, and strategic coherence in the White House are exaggerated, indicating that significant room still exists for administrative leadership. One analysis finds that only 17% and 11% of policy proposals, respectively, originated exclusively in the White House or the EOP rather than in Congress or the bureaucracy (Rudalevige, 2002). Instead, a contingency theory of policy development seemed more accurate: the greater the number of issues involved, the more novel the policy, and the more necessary reorganizations of agencies to implement them, the more likely presidents will opt for centralization of policy making (and even implementation) in the White House.

Likewise, recent research on OIRA regulatory review questions the conventional wisdom that presidents try to gain cohesiveness, coordination, and rationality of bureaucratic policy initiatives (West, 2006). Researchers find that "little if any effort is made in the review process to think about the implementation of different programs in a comprehensive and comparative way" (p. 445) or "to reduce conflicts [and] to ensure consistent application of the regulatory analysis process" (Comptroller General, 1982, p. 51). More recent research finds that presidents tend to use regulatory review in ways similar to what congressional scholars call "fire alarm" oversight of agencies (West, 2015). With time and personnel power scarce, it is more efficient for them to pick and choose when they use this tool, rather than apply it consistently across all policy initiatives. Moreover, when administrative initiatives are viewed from the grassroots where they interact, there is little evidence that a cohesive strategy either exists or is even possible (Durant, 1992, 2006). This situation also complicates agency management, as managers must somehow put "Humpty Dumpty" back together again.

Finally, as the stovepiping of agencies and programs has mushroomed over the decades and been buttressed by subsystems of actors, presidents have created White House "czars" for a variety of policy priorities. Since the 1970s, the United States has seen drug, energy, national security, climate change, and employment czars, among others, in the White House. But the Washington landscape is littered with the bodies of czars who typically lack formal authority to alter budgets and agency behaviors. Also, czars only have influence as long as their presidents pay attention to their policy areas. But the half-life of presidential attention is typically short given the competing claims on their time. As an alternative, the 2010 Government Performance and Results Act (GPRA) Modernization Act has fostered White House efforts to gain coordination across agencies, a collaborative effort facilitated partly by advances in information sharing through IT platforms.

The Contextual Tools of the Administrative Presidency

The contextual tools of the administrative presidency involve presidents' relying on presumably loyal political appointees in agencies to advance their policy agendas administratively. These appointees, in turn, work to align agency structures, decision rules, personnel policies and evaluations, and budgets with presidential goals (Durant, 1992; Maranto, 1993; Nathan, 1983). In efforts to gain loyalty to presidential agendas, appointees attempt to impose more limits on bureaucratic discretion, cut or increase program budgets or rates of spending, alter behavior through performance appraisals, reorganize agencies to give less authority to those opposing their policies, or leave program leadership positions vacant.

The straightforwardness of this strategy belies the hurdles that contextual tools encounter in practice, however. Researchers suggest that they are neither as powerful as their proponents hope nor as powerless as opponents predict. Collectively, they have found that bureaucratic responsiveness to contextual tools wielded by political appointees is contingent on a variety of factors (e.g., Durant, 1992; Golden, 2000; Maranto, 1993). Success in advancing presidential agendas is more difficult when: the extent of behavioral change required is high, presidential goals are less clear, the agency or program involved is more controversial, agency reward systems are more misaligned, the agency is less professionalized, and more opportunities exist for private-sector employment.

Unpacking these points, prior research shows that reorganizations can advance presidential goals (Lewis, 2008), but they are disruptive to agency operations and, thus, can delay or permanently foil presidential goals. At the same time, existing organizational structures are not efficiency or goal-related but, rather, are "treaties" reflecting the results of past agency battles over policies. Thus, when reorganizations are launched, the scars of past agency battles can occur once more, rallying subsystem actors who stand to lose access, influence, and power. In doing so, they can delay or derail implementation of presidential goals (Seidman, 1998), as well as other ongoing agency programs. Consequently, when appointees try to reorganize in order to implement presidential agendas administratively, they are, in effect, trying to reorganize congressional oversight systems as well. Hence, even if successful, reorganizations bring little behavioral change as long as congressional oversight committees remain the same, as they have since the massive reorganization that created the Department of Homeland Security after 9/11.

Moreover, although presidents have intensified efforts to politicize the career bureaucracy by placing greater numbers of political appointees as deep as possible in agencies to pursue their agendas, politicization is necessarily selective and can be problematic. Looking at number of appointees and their ratio to careerists, David Lewis (2008) finds that levels of politicization vary. Higher levels of politicization exist in agencies implementing social regulatory policies and policies where partisans differ most greatly, such as in the environmental policy arena. Moreover, greater numbers of appointees are found during a president's first term, when the same party controls the presidency and Congress, and when intraparty policy differences exist.

Also, as presidential loyalists are placed deeper into agencies, the relatively lower pay makes it likely that younger and more managerially inexperienced persons will be appointed. This, in turn, means that they will be vulnerable to the strategic and tactical mercies of more experienced civil servants in various programs, will turnover more quickly (as low as 12 to 14 months in positions) as they seek swift advancement up the hierarchy, and will want quick accomplishments to boost their chances of moving up the chain of command. These traits often reduce respect for appointees by careerists and cause additional resentment and frustration for program managers. This becomes an even bigger problem at the end of presidential terms, as the best and brightest of potential candidates are reluctant to "sign on" and disrupt their lives for a job that is not guaranteed beyond the end of the term.

Most researchers also question the wisdom of placing greater numbers of political appointees in federal agencies in the first place. They see it as a self-frustrating policy. Paul Light (1999), for example, argues that the greater the number of political appointees in an agency, the less direct control presidents and their appointees have over implementation of their policy preferences. Greater numbers of appointees mean greater layers of bureaucratic hierarchy. This means a greater chance for distortion of their goals or noncompliance with them as information moves slowly and strategically up and down the hierarchy.

Other researchers argue that the contextual tools of the administrative presidency have to be rethought in the networked state (Durant & Warber, 2001).

Contextual tools were designed for an era when government agencies were more directly involved in delivering goods, services, and opportunities to citizens. Agencies could thus be held accountable for presidential policy priorities through budget controls, personnel rules and regulations, decision rules, and reorganizations. Yet, today, government agencies and programs are more likely involved with state and local agencies, private contractors, and not-for-profit organizations whose activities are less susceptible to contextual hierarchical tools wielded from Washington.

But perhaps the most decisive constraint on the success of contextual tools is the reality that agencies have multiple actors overseeing agency structures, budgets, personnel regulations, and decision rules. Indeed, consonant with a legislative-centered theory of administration, Congress has substantial powers to check presidential agendas pursued administratively and legislatively. These include the power of the purse, normal oversight and investigations, legislative reports that stipulate congressional preferences rather than a president's agenda, and review of agency rulemaking. Additionally, were these powers not enough, the power of judicial review of agency regulations is omnipresent. Thus, researchers have at times found agencies more responsive, alternatively, to congressional direction (e.g., Chubb, 1985; Scholz & Wei, 1986); to multiple principals (including the courts) rather than to just presidents and their appointees (e.g., Wood & Waterman, 1994); to interest groups, subnational actors, and local contexts rather than to political appointees (e.g., Scholz, Twombly, & Headrick, 1991); and to either the Congress or presidents, depending on policy domain (e.g., Durant, 2006; Zegart, 1999).

Nor, in the wake of these presidential actions, has the Congress been shy about passing legislation to increase the transparency of agency operations. For example, the GPRA of 1993 and the GPRA Modernization Act of 2010 both require federal agencies and state and local recipients of federal funds to engage in strategic planning, review progress toward meeting agency goals, and report and make use of performance data. Policy-specific changes in areas such as welfare (the Personal Responsibility and Work Opportunity Reconciliation Act of 1996) and education (the No Child Left Behind Act of 2002 and the Race to the Top initiative of 2009) further encourage the use of performance measures that allow enhanced congressional oversight of presidential initiatives. To these must be added a variety of other congressional statutes that open up the actions of presidents to congressional scrutiny, including the Inspector General Act.

Regardless of their effectiveness in advancing presidential or congressional objectives, all these actions impose additional challenges for federal administrative leadership. But neither presidents nor members of Congress are continually involved in agency operations, and thus, the discretion that administrative leaders have varies. For instance, work done by David Epstein and Sharyn O'Halloran (1999) shows that Congress "trades off the internal policy production costs of the committee system against the external costs of delegation" (p. 7). The costs of detailed statutes include such things as whether or not Congress has the information to make well-informed decisions, whether institutional factors inhibit speedy action, and whether logrolling will drive up the costs of action. When the costs of conducting such oversight exceed the benefits anticipated by members of Congress, they try to write very detailed statutes that leave little discretion to the bureaucracy and, hence, to presidential appointees. Moreover, the discretion leaders have can vary across different dimensions of a statute. These include discretion over the goals of the legislation, its objectives, what agents use in carrying out the law, the specific tools to use (regulations, subsidies, guaranteed loans), the rules that must be followed (e.g., consider risks to health but not costs), and the assumptions to work under (normative, behavioral, and instrumental).

The Unilateral Tools of the Administrative Presidency

With affective partisan polarization rising in Washington since the 1980s, the power of presidents to bargain has diminished. Some scholars even argue that a president's need to do so has diminished as well, if a president uses the unilateral powers of the presidency wisely (Campbell, 2008). The second term of the Obama presidency, for example, has seen a major, albeit controversial, application of this principle in action (e.g., regarding immigration and climate change). Controversy notwithstanding, the president's actions are consistent in many ways (but not all) with the way his recent predecessors have relied on unilateral tools to advance their policy agendas. What is different is the way he has urged agencies to look for opportunities to advance his priorities within the confines of their existing authorizing statutes and in controversial interpretations of their authority to act that have found their way to courts for resolution.

As noted, the unilateral tools of the administrative presidency include executive orders, presidential signing statements, national security directives, and (less so) presidential proclamations. These are said to give presidents the ability to change policy without congressional acquiescence "with a stroke of the pen" (Mayer, 2001). Proponents also claim that unilateral tools give "first-mover" advantages to presidents over a Congress facing collective-action problems in reacting to them (Howell, 2003).

As applied, researchers do find strong evidence for first-mover advantages for presidents, suggesting that power advantages actually do shift to presidents. Only 3% of all unilateral actions (e.g., executive orders and presidential signing statements) ever receive immediate legislative scrutiny, and most efforts to overturn them fail (Howell, 2003). Researchers also find the federal judiciary similarly passive in accepting these initiatives without declaring them invalid (Howell, 2003).

The advantages of unilateral tools for policy adoption notwithstanding, the absence of repealing unilateral actions is hardly a sufficient measure of success. Researchers find that implementing them can be quite difficult. For example, executive orders may require a reprogramming of funds that may be politically difficult and may harm other programs that members of Congress or the president value more. They also can gain resistance from members of Congress on key oversight committees by means of ex post monitoring and sanctions (e.g., budget cuts for implementation). Moreover, executive orders can be reversed by their successors with a stroke of the same presidential pen.

Especially controversial is the justification often given for the use of unilateral tools: the so-called "unitary executive theory" of the presidency. This problematic theory effectively denies Congress a role in executive branch operations. As such, attendant actions are frequently challenged as giving inordinate—and even unconstitutional shifts in—power to presidents (Cooper, 2002; Pfiffner, 2008; Pious, 2007; Rozell, 1994). In addition, these actions can pose significant challenges for administrative leadership because of: (a) their tendency to bring about disruptive stops-and-starts in policy implementation, (b) the heavier congressional and interest group scrutiny they attract, and (c) White House scrutiny when they are not implemented expeditiously.

Conclusion: Some Ways Out of "No Way!"

As the preceding indicates, the political process impacts federal administrative leadership in multiple, extensive, and challenging ways. The responsive competence that elected officials seek from the career service can limit leaders' discretion, complicate management of existing programs, and create capacity and morale problems that they must navigate. Were these not challenging enough for administrative leadership, they are compounded by the multiple signals sent by various congressional, presidential, and judicial overseers when it comes to agency direction, policies, and programs. Indeed, leaders living with the results of today's political process can certainly identify with Francis Rourke's (1993) evocative question, "Whose Bureaucracy Is This, Anyway?"

It is important to note that experience and prior research suggest that, at times, political appointees will involve career executives in defining the specifics and implementation of presidential initiatives, but at other times, they will not. Some political appointees are "bureauphobes" (Durant, 1992) who fear that careerists will resist or undermine presidential goals. Thus, they practice "jigsaw puzzle" or "mushroom house" management. The former style involves appointees giving pieces of information about an initiative to different actors in an agency but reserving the whole picture for themselves. In the vernacular, the latter style "keeps careerists totally in the dark and feeds them manure." Other appointees try to work closely with career executives, realizing that they can be quite helpful because of their institutional memories and political skills. In any case, federal administrative leaders must be prepared to work with any type of appointee, starting from a position of "conditional cooperation" (Heclo, 1977). That is, they must assume collaboration, try to work closely with appointees in affording expertise, and do so at least until the appointee's behavior suggests otherwise.

What We Do Not Know and Why

As the preceding also indicates, we know quite a bit from prior research about the impacts of the political process on the challenges confronting federal administrative leadership today and in the near future. But there is much that we do not know about those challenges and how leaders can deal with them to advance their agencies' effectiveness. Central to these gaps is an appreciation of power—how to gain, maintain, and use it, as well as how to avoid losing or dissipating it (Long, 1949). Moreover, much of what we know is premised on anecdotes or academic research that fails to engage in comparisons of success and failure in different settings over time (for a notable exception, see Riccucci, 1995).

Basically, this means that what we know about administrative leadership comes from viewing it at different points in time, rather than across time, in order to see how leaders gain, increase, maintain, lose, or dissipate the ability to lead and work with political appointees and subordinates over time (Durant, 2015). These longitudinal studies could be done across leaders in the same political circumstances, in different political circumstances, or in cases of successful or unsuccessful leaders in the same or different political circumstances.

A variety of other questions exists that would benefit from comparative analyses of administrative leadership over time and across settings. For example, we know:

- how and why top-down control efforts have spiraled, but we still do not know how leaders marshal horizontal sources of power (e.g., interest groups or supporters in OMB or other agencies) to cope with or combat these efforts at top-down control.
- the administrative presidency is a major component of politicizing federal agencies, but we still do not know how and why leaders produce initiatives that succeed while others fail over time, using what strategies alone or in combination, and provoking what kinds of effects and strategies by careerists.
- power varies across agencies, but we remain unsure how the power of administrative leaders is affected over time by politicization and whether or not the ebb and flow of appointees have disruptive or positive effects on their power.
- agency structures matter in defining power, access, and influence, but questions remain unanswered about if, how, and why continuities or discontinuities in leadership affect power relationships with the White House or Congress because of agency reorganizations.
- bureaucratic control is a "two-way street" wherein agencies are strategic actors who sometimes seek and other times avoid additional increments of power, but we still need further longitudinal research designs to find out more about how administrative leadership shapes those decisions for legislators over time.
- strategic planning is a major tool of agency control, but we are not sure how it affects the strategies of administrative leaders in defining countermeasures to maintain needed agency discretion and agency integrity.
- the courts play a major role in agency operations, but we still lack a clear understanding of how these affect administrative leaders—and their strategies and tactics—over time.
- variation in agency discretion occurs, but we do not know if and how discretion wielded by agency administrative leaders shifts the relative power of agencies or programs over time, or if discretion is dissipated or lost over time because of controversies and how it is regained, if it is.

- think tanks have exploded in Washington and state capitals to diminish the near-monopoly on expertise that agency leaders have had historically, but we are unsure of how various administrative leaders garner, increase, dissipate, or lose influence and power over time because of these trends.

What We Do Know and Why

Still, prior research does illustrate that effective administrative leadership relies on several general sets of "literacies." Many other chapters in this volume offer detailed discussions of the specific knowledge, skills, and values that are needed in various aspects of administrative leadership. Thus, it suffices presently to talk about them in generic terms. Overall, an effective leader understands factors in themselves (e.g., their adaptability, their comfort level with different leadership and motivational styles, and their level of emotional intelligence); factors in others (e.g., their maturity, skill, and needs for self-actualization); and factors in the situation (e.g., the nature of the tasks involved, the political environment generally, and the configuration of political interests surrounding a program; Tannenbaum & Schmidt, 1958). As Maccoby (2015) insists, they must also operate with a strong sense of purpose, convey that purpose to their colleagues, and have the courage to act.

These, in turn, require six interrelated but analytically distinct sets of skills that help leaders to think:

- analytically;
- systemically;
- strategically;
- technologically;
- legally, constitutionally, and ethically; and
- institutionally (see Durant, 2014).

Thinking Analytically

Thinking *analytically* means that leaders must have methodological, econometric, performance measurement, and statistical skills. These are imperative to interpret accurately the quality and utility of research, data analytics, and performance measures presented to them in an era where evidence-based analyses are expected to inform policy and program design and implementation. But analytical skills go far beyond leaders being critical consumers of data-based research. An "argumentative turn" has occurred in policy analysis as a field. This turn sees the policy process as often informed by technical analysis but driven by participants' critical thinking, communication, and interpersonal skills. That is, administrative leaders must be able to engage skillfully in "evidence, argument, and persuasion" within their agency, with immediate agency stakeholders, and with the public more generally.

These skills, in turn, depend on the ability of leaders to think historically, contextually, and contingently about the agencies, programs, and policies with which they are involved. History does not repeat, but it does rhyme. As such, it can inform present policy and administrative decisions, and it can be an excellent diagnostic tool. Understanding the immediate context—especially the political, social, technological, and macroeconomic contexts—helps leaders to identify opportunities and constraints for advancing what their agencies or partners are trying to accomplish. Advice and decision making predicated on econometric analysis that ignores or misunderstands organizational, interorganizational, or bureaucratic politics are a prescription for leadership failure. Equally important is understanding how contingencies—that is, unexpected events such as 9/11 or the Ebola outbreak—can make possible what historically has not been possible or disrupt what was possible.

Thinking Systemically

Persistently honing and refining their ability to think *systemically* can give leaders a competitive edge in the policy and administrative marketplace—especially in today's networked state. Indeed, in complex organizations with multiple stakeholders, leadership is less about discerning simple cause–effect relationships and more about pattern recognition (Barnard, 1938/1968). This means asking themselves, "Who has to do what, in what ways, with what resources (human and financial capital), under what political or economic constraints, and with success measured in what way(s)?" They must do so for a variety of reasons, including pressures placed upon them for sharing resources, acquiring resources or skills that their agency does not have, sharing information with other agencies or programs as political pressures mount for "enterprise management," or simply because they are mandated by elected officials to partner with other agencies. Leaders must have skills for identifying or participating in opportunities for partnering, negotiating over the terms of a partnership, holding the partnership together (due to a tendency for them to atrophy over time), and keeping partners and subordinates focused on goals.

Leaders must do all this while keeping in mind what implementation researchers call the "complexity of joint action" (Pressman & Wildavsky, 1984). They find that the greater the number of actors involved in carrying out a policy, the more difficult implementation is likely to be. This means leaders must engage in the design of implementation structures that cut back on the number of actors involved in the process. If they feel that certain actors are unlikely to support policy initiatives or do not have the right skill mix to do what is required of them, they should try to find alternative routes (i.e., actors) to achieve their goals. Researchers also find that implementation success is more likely if leaders engage in "pre-mortem" analyses by asking, "What can go wrong and are there ways—typically, more direct ways—to accomplish the task?" Another way to phrase this question is to ask, "Five years from now, what will people say prevented policy or program success?"

Research also indicates that leaders benefit from thinking systemically from the "bottom up" rather than the "top down" (Elmore, 1979–80). Rather than start their analysis with those systems currently addressing needs (what is called "forward mapping"), effective leaders focus on identifying what behaviors, exhibited by whom, and for what reasons need to be changed in order for policy or program success. In the process of using this "backward-mapping" approach, they may be able to discern a more direct approach than that of navigating all the existing actors in the system (e.g., with vouchers or subsidies). The key question is: "Who closest to a problem (e.g., local churches, synagogues, or mosques) has the most ability to positively affect bad behavioral choices (e.g., choosing IV drug use)?" The answers to this question may suggest ways to re-engage or even save resources by directing them to actors who can more directly influence individuals to make better behavioral choices.

Thinking Technologically

As alluded to earlier, leaders must have a working knowledge of the opportunities and challenges afforded their agencies by today's *technological* revolution. For example, data-mining and data analytics can reveal patterns of needs or administrative shortcomings previously unknown or unspoken of in agencies, provide greater efficiencies and effectiveness in service delivery, and garner greater levels of accountability. But more than technical familiarity is needed; leaders must understand the strategic and tactical advantages and caveats of these technologies, as well as the challenges in training subordinates to cope with them and citizens to navigate them easily.

The use of information-age technology—such as social media, smartphone apps, tablets, and geographical information systems—is rapidly expanding in the public, private, and not-for-profit sectors. It is doing so, however, with variations in usage, data availability and quality, and cybersecurity across agencies and jurisdictions. Common problems include a lack of user training by agencies, internal agency acquisition processes preventing full realization of IT capabilities, and work–life imbalances caused by supervisors expecting immediate responses at all hours of the day and night.

Public agencies have also found themselves embarrassed and potentially liable for data breaches involving employee information, as well as for "Tweets" and other social media comments made by public employees. The social media age comes replete with training and coaching needs that leaders need to supply their subordinates. Administrative leadership also means ensuring that cybersecurity processes are up-to-date, threats to privacy are attenuated, and so-called "data poverty" is prevented by ensuring the representation of the needs of low-income persons whose data are hard to collect, incomplete, or nonexistent.

Administrative leaders quickly understand that foundational IT work still awaits completion in federal agencies and in their partners' organizations. For instance, the Federal Information Technology Acquisition Reform Act (FITARA) requires agencies to do self-assessments of implementation and submit them to OMB. However, a recent survey found that only 22% of agencies had sufficient resources to implement the needed FITARA acquisition reforms (FCW Staff, 2015).

But underfunding is only one of several factors that prevent agencies from implementing IT reforms effectively and that require administrative leadership to overcome. Agencies need strategic information resources management that is integrated with agency strategic planning efforts. For example, too often, faulty acquisition decisions have been made, such as those at the Internal Revenue Service and during implementation of President Obama's health care reforms. Also, redundancies exist in IT acquisition for different agencies and programs that are unnecessary, facilitate data hoarding, and cry out for leadership.

To be sure, the costs of remedying interoperability issues among fragmented databases and systems are large and technologically challenging. Thus, the Departments of Defense and Veterans Affairs shut down a recent $1 billion attempt to integrate their databases in an effort to expedite veterans' claims and services. But the Obama administration has been very active in addressing IT reforms and cybersecurity issues, and his fiscal year 2016 budget allocates nearly $87 billion to acquisition. Despite the administration's strong push to move agencies away from their multiple legacy systems and onto cloud-based systems, however, only 4% of that budget is allocated to cloud computing. In addition, agencies have delayed because they fear cloud computing may be more vulnerable to cyberattacks.

Likewise, federal leaders face serious implementation challenges when it comes to responding to pressures for performance management. As one researcher summarizes the literature on performance measurement:

> Best-practice case stories can be found, and are repeated, but systematic studies of the impact of these approaches give little ground for optimism. For example, a meta-analysis of 49 empirical studies of performance reforms between 2000 and 2014 concluded that performance reforms generally have a small impact. A study of U.S. federal managers concluded that those exposed to Clinton and Bush-era performance reforms were no more likely to use performance data than managers who had not encountered these reforms. Historical case-based studies are similarly discouraging.
>
> (Moynihan, 2015, p. 3)

Finally, effective leaders must be aware of several caveats that apply to IT, social media, and their application to agency decision making. First, a great deal has been written about the potential of "evidence-based" decision making; for example, for improving the allocation of resources. However, leaders must also keep Carl Sagan's warning in mind: "absence of evidence is not evidence of absence." Not everything has or can be measured or translated into bytes, and part of the art and science of management is debunking unwarranted assumptions.

Second, under these political pressures, effective leadership involves being cautious when hearing claims that evidence-based analytical techniques can reveal "best practices" applicable to all settings. In reality, context always matters, and the policy and program world is littered with failures to transplant successes from one setting to another (e.g., recent failed efforts to replicate the success of social impact bonds in social science studies of recidivism rates at Rikers Island prison in New York and in the United Kingdom). Relatedly, effective leaders are not lured into complacency when best practices *do* produce positive results. The evolving nature of both the law and our policy problems requires a focus on "next practices"; that is, on innovation. Best practices focus on the past and are often based on research that lacks methodological rigor.

Similarly, effective leaders understand that although measurement is typically touted as "objective," it really is not. Thus, they must have skills to protect the integrity of the performance measurement process. Good measures are not objective entities waiting "out there" to be discerned by agencies. Rather, they are the product of social choices made by fallible, sometimes calculating, and frequently self-interested individuals in agencies. "What gets measured gets done," and thus, winners and losers are created within organizations and among stakeholders. Even if done properly, using them may cause agencies to ignore other, sometimes more important, problems simply because they are less measurable.

Thinking Strategically

All of which leads to a need for administrative leaders who continually refine their ability to think *strategically*. Acting strategically involves an adroit linking of all the other skills discussed, as well as skills in strategic planning and strategic management. It also means having the skills—amid all the political and administrative constraints facing them—to align the activities of their business (e.g., central budgeting and personnel offices), program (e.g., drug enforcement), and technology units (e.g., IT acquisition office) so that they reinforce each other in ways that advance agency goals. Likewise, they must work to ensure that existing incentive structures reinforce these goals. Finally, in adopting new strategic policies or using administrative strategies from the private sector, a strategy of "trust but verify" must always be kept in mind.

In dealing with these issues, prior research suggests that administrative leaders treat all newly proposed policy, program, and management reforms as "hypotheses." These are propositions stating that if we do X, then Y will result (Bardach, 1977). Every proposal or mandate—explicitly or implicitly—is based on assumptions. Thus, treating them as hypotheses can reveal valid, invalid, or dubious assumptions that need challenging, amending, or finessing.

For instance, welfare reform in the 1990s might be understood by proponents as follows: "If we make welfare harder to obtain, then the culture of dependency that welfare has created among recipients will decline and welfare recipients will seek employment more aggressively." Likewise, an underlying hypothesis of the Patient Protection and Affordable Care Act is that if we provide health insurance to the uninsured, they will make less use of emergency rooms and, thus, cut health care costs in the United States. By treating new policies or administrative reforms as "hypotheses," leaders may not stop mandates to implement them from elected officials. However, such a perspective can allow them to see what gaps exist in their logic. This, in turn, can allow them to discern other elements needed for success and prepare political appointees for disappointing results unless these are addressed.

Finally, skilled administrative leaders must understand the shortcomings of traditional approaches to strategic planning. For starters, prior research suggests that the strategic planning mandates typically imposed by elected officials on their agencies are unrealistic. They envision a "straight-ahead," heroic, transformative leader who brooks no hesitation (to change), takes no prisoners, and does not suffer fools gladly (Nadler, 1998). Yet, effective leaders know that building and implementing a strategic plan involves transactional leadership: the ability to bargain, cut deals, trim sails, and pursue more patiently a set of changes over time while remaining goal-oriented.

Relatedly, studies also show that effective leadership means not thinking of strategic planning and strategic management (i.e., implementing the plan) as a two-step process. Both must be considered together during the formulation process. Too many strategic plans sit on the shelf or disappoint when implemented, because they are based on unrealistic expectations, are based on faulty "hypotheses," or fail to consider the realpolitik of organizational change (who wins and who loses). When implementation moves slowly or seems to have derailed, cynicism increases among employees already cynical due to the shortcomings of previous planning efforts they have experienced. In effect, they are waiting for glitches, slowdowns, or failures that will "confirm" their cynicism.

In turn, prior research suggests that top-down, one-time only, and comprehensive strategic planning are neither useful nor necessary. Instead, researchers find that truly innovative companies rely on what is called "time-paced evolution" of plans that slowly roll out goals and changes. Moreover, they rely on an "assertive patience" approach to strategic thinking (Durant & Marshak, 2014). Unlike traditional strategic planning efforts, aggressive patience strategies assume that organizations behave more like diffuse bureaucratic systems than hierarchical ones. Public agencies are not "machines"; they have internal and external political and economic bases of power and support that strategic planning typically challenges.

Thus, effective leadership involves accepting progress on parts of one's goals or strategy while still keeping the whole in mind. It also means knowing how to create and watch for windows of opportunity to make progress and setting benchmarks and celebrating accomplishments as they occur rather than awaiting total success. In addition, it means being alert to possibilities for change while maintaining a multiyear timeframe for action, communicating this to employees, and reminding them constantly of how short-term actions relate to long-term goals. Finally, it means making short-term tactical retreats calculated to placate the opposition in order to meet longer-term strategic goals, as well as explaining these detours to subordinates who champion the reform effort.

Thinking Legally, Constitutionally, and Ethically

Even if administrative leaders hone the preceding literacies to perfection, their success also depends upon a strong sense of their *legal*, *constitutional*, and *ethical* obligations as public servants. When calls for change arise, they must know that public agencies cannot do what they are not legally authorized to do. Moreover, agency employees might even be held personally liable for failing to follow the laws and rules derived from them. Consequently, leadership also involves understanding the substantive and due process rights of subordinates and citizens working in or affected by public agencies or programs (see Rosenbloom, 2015). Failure to protect civil liberties, civil rights, or due process is unacceptable in the public sector.

However, leaders must do more than this. They must leaven their activities with a sense of ethics. Ethics does not mean merely following the rules; one can follow all the organizational rules and still do harm. Louis Gawthrop (1998) argues that such an approach results in a dysfunctional attitude where public servants, in effect, say, "Tell me what is right, what is wrong, what is legal, what is permissible … so that I can be judged an ethical public servant" (p. 153). History is replete with examples where what was legal was not ethical (e.g., the states' role in creating and sustaining Jim Crow laws in the South), and where public servants used noncompliance to correct policy and societal wrongs ordered by political appointees (e.g., members of the Civil Rights division of the U.S. Justice Department refusing to carry out a discriminatory policy during the Nixon administration). Also illustrative of the mission-threatening and reputation-squandering consequences of ethical and legal improprieties are recent scandals involving the Department of Veterans Affairs, the U.S. Drug Enforcement Agency, and the Secret Service.

Thinking Institutionally

Lastly, thinking *institutionally* means that, amid the rush of political pressures, leaders understand that not all change is good or serves the public interest. This is especially true when change undermines the organizational essence of their agency or program. Political pressures for change often imply that the legacy inherited by current employees has no redeeming value. To the contrary, effective leadership means maintaining the institutional integrity of one's organization in the face of threats or explaining to subordinates how change will still protect that integrity.

Institutional thinking is a leadership mindset that embraces "faithful reception" of the past and the bountiful institutional inheritance bequeathed to current employees by their predecessors (Heclo, 2008). But it also means leaders taking what they have inherited from their predecessors, adapting it to new and evolving challenges, and ensuring that the essence of that heritage is not lost. As Heclo writes, "Innovation is not meant to change the [policy or administrative] game. Legitimate innovation is meant to realize, with greater skill and fidelity, the larger potential of what the game is" (p. 99). Take baseball, football, or basketball. These sports, respectively, have raised and lowered the pitcher's mound to benefit hitters or pitchers, changed rules for rushing passers and defending receivers to protect the quarterback and enhance the excitement of the passing game, and introduced the three-point shot. But the essence—the nature and aims of each sport—has remained the same.

Similarly, the astute administrative leader "seeks to understand what has been received in light of new circumstances. … Without appropriate adaptations, the legacy cannot be preserved" (Heclo, 2008, pp. 99–100). Thinking institutionally thus requires leadership that considers the long-term implications of changes for agencies and society at large, advances what protects and nurtures an agency's essence, and finds ways to slow down or resist changes (passively or actively) that undermine the agency's statutory mission.

In sum, prior research suggests that these six sets of literacies for coping with the impact of the political process on administration are not optional for federal administrative leaders today—or as far as the eye can see. The dynamics of the political process are not separate from administration, if they ever were. Whether for good or ill, the impact of the political process on administrative leadership of the federal bureaucracy at whatever level of an agency it is practiced is profound and perdurable. Thus, administrative leaders must embrace the sentiments expressed by Marshall Dimock (1936) in the epigraph introducing this chapter. And in doing so, they can either understand and acclimate strategically and tactically to these realities or fail to make a positive difference in the lives of the citizens they serve.

References

Balogh, B. (2009). *A government out of sight: The mystery of national authority in nineteenth-century America*. New York, NY: Cambridge University Press.

Bardach, E. (1977). *The implementation game: What happens after a bill becomes a law*. Cambridge, MA: MIT Press.

Barnard, C. I. (1968). *The functions of the executive*. Cambridge, MA: Harvard University Press. (Original work published 1938).

Barzelay, M. (1992). *Breaking through bureaucracy: A new vision for managing in government*. Berkeley, CA: University of California Press.

Beer, S. H. (1978). Federalism, nationalism, and democracy in America. *American Political Science Review, 72*(1), 9–21.

Bishop, B. (2009). *The big sort: Why the clustering of like-minded America is tearing us apart*. New York, NY: Mariner Books.

Campbell, J. E. (2008). Presidential politics in a polarized nation: The reelection of George W. Bush. In C. Campbell, B. A. Rockman, & A. Rudalevige (Eds.), *The George W. Bush legacy* (pp. 21–44). Washington, DC: CQ Press.

Chubb, J. E. (1985). The political economy of federalism. *American Political Science Review, 79*(4), 994–1015.

Cook, B. J. (2015). *Bureaucracy and self-government: Reconsidering the role of public administration in American politics* (2nd ed.). Baltimore, MD: Johns Hopkins University Press.

Cooper, P. J. (2002). *By order of the president: The use and abuse of executive direct action*. Lawrence, KS: University Press of Kansas.

Dahl, R. A. (1947). The science of public administration: Three problems. *Public Administration Review, 7*(1), 1–11.

Denhardt, J. V., & Denhardt, R. B. (2015). *The new public service: Serving not steering* (4th ed.). New York, NY: Routledge.

DiIulio, J. J., Jr. (2014). *Bring back the bureaucrats: Why more federal workers will lead to better (and smaller!) government*. West Conshohocken, PA: Templeton Press.

Dimock, M. E. (1936). Criteria and objectives of public administration. In J. M. Gaus, L. D. White, & M. E. Dimock (Eds.), *Frontiers of public administration* (pp.116–134). Chicago, Il: University of Chicago Press.

Durant, R. F. (1992). *The administrative presidency revisited: Public lands, the BLM, and the Reagan revolution.* Albany, NY: State University of New York Press.

Durant, R. F. (2006). Agency evolution, the new institutionalism, and "hybrid" policy domains: Lessons from the "greening" of the U.S. military. *Policy Studies Journal, 34*(4), 469–490.

Durant, R. F. (2014). *Why public service matters: Public managers, public policy, and democracy.* New York, NY: Palgrave Macmillan.

Durant, R. F. (2015). Whither power in public administration? Attainment, dissipation, and loss. *Public Administration Review, 75*(2), 206–218.

Durant, R. F., & Marshak, R. M. (2014). Rethinking strategic leadership in public agencies. Working paper, American University, Washington, DC.

Durant, R. F., & Resh, W. G. (2012). "Presidentializing" the bureaucracy. In R. F. Durant (Ed.), *The Oxford Handbook of American Bureaucracy* (pp. 545–568). Oxford, England: Oxford University Press.

Durant, R. F., & Warber, A. (2001). Networking in the shadow of hierarchy: Public policy, the administrative presidency, and the neoadministrative state. *Presidential Studies Quarterly, 31*(2), 221–244.

Eisner, M. A. (2000). *From warfare state to welfare state: World War I, compensatory state-building, and the limits of the modern order.* University Park, PA: Pennsylvania State University Press.

Elmore, R. F. (1979–80). Backward mapping: Implementation research and policy decisions. *Political Science Quarterly, 94*(4), 601–616.

Epstein, D., & O'Halloran, S. (1999). *Delegating powers: A transaction cost politics approach to policy making under separate powers*. Cambridge, England: Cambridge University Press.

FCW Staff. (2015, August 3). FITARA good and bad, US-CERT warns of spear phishing and more. *FCW: The Business of Federal Technology*. Retrieved from http://fcw.com/articles/2015/08/03/news-in-brief-august-3.aspx.

Finer, H. (1941). Administrative responsibility in democratic government. *Public Administration Review, 1*(4), 335–350.

Fiorina, M. P. (1989). *Congress: Keystone of the Washington establishment* (2nd ed.). New Haven, CT: Yale University Press.

Florida, R. (2002). *The rise of the creative class: And how it's transforming work, leisure, community, and everyday life*. New York, NY: Basic Books.

Freeman, J. L. (1965). *The political process; executive bureau-legislative committee relations.* New York, NY: Random House.

Friedrich, C. J. 1940. Public policy and the nature of administrative responsibility. In C. J. Friedrich & E. S. Mason (Eds.), *Public policy* (pp. 3–24). Cambridge, MA: Harvard University Press.

Gawthrop, L. C. (1998). *Public service and democracy: Ethical imperatives for the 21st century*. New York, NY: Chatham House.

Golden, M. M. (2000). *What motivates bureaucrats? Politics and administration during the Reagan years.* New York, NY: Columbia University Press.

Government Accountability Office. (1982). *Improved quality, adequate resources, and consistent oversight needed if regulatory analysis is to help control the cost of regulations* (GAO/PAD-83-6). Washington, DC: U.S. Government Printing Office.

Greenblatt, A. (2015, August). Kentucky governor's race: A battle for the future of the South. *Governing*. Retrieved from: http://www.governing.com/topics/elections/gov-kentucky-governors-race-bevin-conway.html.

Heclo, H. (1977). *A government of strangers: Executive politics in Washington.* Washington, DC: Brookings Institution Press.

Heclo, H. (2008). *On thinking institutionally.* Boulder, CO: Paradigm Publishers.

Howell, W. G. (2003). *Power without persuasion: The politics of direct presidential action.* Princeton, NJ: Princeton University Press.

Iyengar, S., Sood, G., & Lelkes, Y. (2012). Affect, not ideology: A social identity perspective on polarization. *Public Opinion Quarterly, 76*(3), 405–431.

James, D. B. (1969). *The contemporary presidency.* New York, NY: Pegasus.

Kosar, K. R. (2015, August 5). Federal agencies missed 1,400 regulatory deadlines. *Roll Call*. Retrieved from: http://blogs.rollcall.com/beltway-insiders/federal-agencies-missed-1400-regulatory-deadlines-commentary/?dcz=.

Lee, M. (2013). Glimpsing an alternate construction of American public administration: The later life of William Allen, cofounder of the New York Bureau of Municipal Research. *Administration & Society, 45*(5), 522–562.

Lewis, D. E. (2008). *The politics of presidential appointments: Political control and bureaucratic performance*. Princeton, NJ: Princeton University Press.

Light, P. (1999). *The true size of government.* Washington, DC: Brookings Institution.

Light, P. (2002). *Government's greatest achievements: From civil rights to homeland security*. Washington, DC: Brookings Institution.

Long, N. E. (1949). Power and administration. *Public Administration Review, 9*(4), 257–264.

Maccoby, M. (2015). *Strategic intelligence: Conceptual tools for leading change*. Oxford, England: Oxford University Press.

Mann, T. E., & Ornstein, N. J. (2012). *It's even worse than it looks: How the American constitutional system collided with the new politics of extremism.* New York, NY: Basic Books.

Maranto, R. A. (1993). *Politics and bureaucracy in the modern presidency: Careerists and appointees in the Reagan administration.* Westport, CT: Greenwood Press.

Mayer, K. R. (2001). *With the stroke of a pen: Executive orders and presidential power*. Princeton, NJ: Princeton University Press.

Meier, K. J. (1997). Bureaucracy and democracy: The case for more bureaucracy and less democracy. *Public Administration Review, 57*(3), 193–199.

Melnick, R. S. (1985). The politics of partnership. *Public Administration Review, 45*(Special Issue: Law and Public Affairs), 653–660.

Milward, H., & Provan, K. (1993). The hollow state: Private provision of public services. In H. Ingram & S. R. Smith (Eds.), *Public policy for democracy* (pp. 222–237). Washington, DC: Brookings Institution Press.

Moynihan, D. P. (2015, June). Performance principles for regulator. Paper prepared for *Penn Program on Regulation's Best-in-Class Regulator Initiative*, Philadelphia, PA.

Nadler, D. A. (1998). *Champions of change: How CEOs and their companies are mastering the skills of radical change.* San Francisco, CA: Jossey-Bass.

Nathan, R. P. (1983). *The administrative presidency*. New York, NY: John Wiley & Sons.

O'Leary, R., & Bingham, L. B. (2009). Surprising findings, paradoxes, and thoughts on the future of collaborative public management research. In R. O'Leary & L. B. Bingham (Eds.), *The collaborative public manager: New ideas for the twenty-first century* (pp. 255–269). Washington, DC: Georgetown University Press.

Pfiffner, J. P. (2008). *Power play: The Bush presidency and the Constitution*. Washington, DC: Brookings Institution Press.

Pious, R. M. (2007). Inherent war and executive powers and prerogative politics. *Presidential Studies Quarterly, 37*(1), 66–84.

Portney, K. E. (2013). *Taking sustainable cities seriously: Economic development, the environment, and quality of life in American cities* (2nd ed.). Cambridge, MA: MIT Press.

Pressman, J. L., & Wildavsky, A. (1984). *Implementation: How great expectations in Washington are dashed in Oakland: Or, why it's amazing that federal programs work at all, this being a saga of the economic development administration as told by two sympathetic observers who seek to build morals on a foundation of ruined hopes* (3rd ed.). Berkeley, CA: University of California Press.

Redford, E. S. (1969). *Democracy in the administrative state*. New York, NY: Oxford University Press.

Resh, W. G. (2015). *Rethinking the administrative presidency: Trust, intellectual capital, and appointee–careerist relations in the George W. Bush administration*. Baltimore, MD: John Hopkins University Press.

Riccucci, N. (1995). *Unsung heroes: Federal execucrats making a difference*. Washington, DC: Georgetown University Press.

Roberts, A. (1994). Demonstrating neutrality: The Rockefeller philanthropies and the evolution of public administration, 1927–1936. *Public Administration Review, 54*(3), 221–228.

Rosenbloom, D. H. (2000). *Building a legislative-centered public administration: Congress and the administrative state, 1946–1999*. Tuscaloosa, AL: University of Alabama Press.

Rosenbloom, D. H. (2008). The politics–administration dichotomy in U.S. historical context. *Public Administration Review, 68*(1), 57–60.

Rosenbloom, D. H. (2015). *Administrative law for public managers* (2nd ed.). Boulder, CO: Westview Press.

Rourke, F. E. (1993). Whose bureaucracy is this, anyway? Congress, the president and public administration. *PS: Political Science and Politics, 26*(4), 687–692.

Rozell, M. J. (1994). *Executive privilege: The dilemma of secrecy and democratic accountability*. Baltimore, MD: Johns Hopkins University Press.

Rudalevige, A. (2002). *Managing the president's program: Presidential leadership and legislative policy formulation*. Princeton, NJ: Princeton University Press.

Sabatier, P. A., & Jenkins-Smith, H. C. (1993). *Policy change and learning: An advocacy coalition approach*. Boulder, CO: Westview Press.

Scholz, J. T., & Wei, F. H. (1986). Regulatory enforcement in a federalist system. *American Political Science Review, 80*(4), 1249–1270.

Scholz, J., Twombly, T., J., & Headrick, B. (1991). Street-level political controls over federal bureaucracy. *American Political Science Review, 85*(3), 829–850.

Seidman, H. (1998). *Politics, position, and power: The dynamics of federal organization* (5th ed.). New York, NY: Oxford University Press.

Simon, H. A. (1957). *Administrative behavior: A study of decision-making processes in administrative organization* (2nd ed.). New York, NY: Macmillan.

Tannenbaum, R., & Schmidt, W. H. (1958). How to choose a leadership pattern. *Harvard Business Review,* (36), 95–101.

Trende, S., & Byler, D. (2015, May 19). The GOP is the strongest it's been in decades. *Real Clear Politics*. Retrieved from: http://www.realclearpolitics.com/articles/2015/05/19/the_gop_is_the_strongest_its_been_in_decades_126633.html.

Waldo, D. (1984). *The administrative state: A study of the political theory of American public administration* (2nd ed.). New York, NY: Holmes and Meier. (Original work published 1948).

Warshaw, S. A. 2006. The administrative strategies of President George W. Bush. *Extensions,* (Spring), 19–23.

West, W. F. (2006). Presidential leadership and administrative coordination: Examining the theory of a unified executive. *Presidential Studies Quarterly, 36*(3), 433–456.

West, W. F. (2015). The administrative presidency as reactive oversight: Implications for positive and normative theory. *Public Administration Review, 75*(4), 523–533.

Wilson, R. (2014, November 5). Republican sweep extends to state level. *Washington Post*. Retrieved from: http://www.washingtonpost.com/blogs/govbeat/wp/2014/11/05/republican-sweep-extends-to-state-level/.

Wilson, W. (1887). The study of administration. *Political Science Quarterly, 2*(2), 197–222.

Wood, B. D., & Waterman, R. W. (1994). *Bureaucratic dynamics: The role of bureaucracy in a democracy*. Boulder, CO: Westview Press.

Zegart, A. B. (1999). *Flawed by design: The evolution of the CIA, JCS, and NSC.* Stanford, CA: Stanford University Press.

3 Theory and Practice in Federal Government Executive Branch Leadership and Administration

Developing Rigorous Approaches to Effective Government

Bill Valdez

> The disappointment surrounding recent presidents is not due (mainly) to defects in their leadership qualities but to their failure to address the structural paralysis of modern government. George Washington couldn't run the government today.
>
> —Phillip K. Howard

The intersection between theory and practice in federal government executive branch leadership and administration has great relevance to public perceptions about the role and purpose of the U.S. federal government. If appropriately studied and understood, improved theory and practice would enable executive branch leaders to develop more effective responses to 21st-century challenges and would increase confidence that the executive branch is delivering on the great public trust it has been given.

The federal government is composed of three branches: executive, judiciary, and legislative. This chapter will focus on executive branch leadership and administration, which, as will be argued, has become increasingly associated with public perceptions about the *overall* performance of the federal government. Congress establishes the laws of our nation and approves the federal government's budget, and the courts adjudicate interpretations of those laws on a daily basis, but it is left to the executive branch to implement those laws and budgets.

As a result, the executive branch is primarily responsible for responding to the challenges that impact the daily lives of all U.S. citizens. Disruptive change—such as the rise of international terrorism, the repudiation of communism as a national governance system, corporate and financial globalization, societal shifts originating from social media and big data, and rapid cycle technology advances in energy, environment and information technologies—has become the norm in the 21st century. This disruptive change has its greatest impact on those organizations that are not resilient and do not have the structures and processes in place for nimble and adaptive change, whether agencies within the executive branch of the federal government or private sector companies.

Economists have been increasingly influenced by Joseph Schumpeter's view of capitalism as a process of "creative destruction," with an "endless succession of cycles of disturbance and new growth" (Nordhaus, Shellenberger, & Caine, 2014, p. 10). Nowhere is this cycle of disturbance and new growth felt more acutely than in the executive branch, which is subject to a quadrennial change in political leadership and the annual dictates of Congress through the federal budget process, and yet, it is a poorly understood phenomenon that has tremendous public policy consequences.

It will be argued that executive branch leadership and administration should be a distinct field of study and a national priority given the out-sized impact the executive branch has on the U.S. economy and daily lives of all Americans. Lessons learned from discrete studies of public administration systems, such as other national governments or state and local governments, will provide insights into this field of study, but the U.S. federal government's executive branch is deserving of special consideration given its uniqueness, evolution, and complexity/scope. A theory of public administration has emerged largely due to the work of Rosenbloom (1983, 2013), but no comparable theory has emerged for leadership practices in the executive branch. And, perhaps most importantly, there has been no work done to merge the two theories and turn theory into practice.

The public policy consequences of these gaps in knowledge fall into two general categories. First, when the federal government is called upon to respond to a disruptive event, such as the 9/11 terrorist attacks, federal leaders *are ill prepared to develop a response that is appropriate to the scale of the event.* This is a direct result of a poor understanding of the purpose of the executive branch (theory) and the business processes and structures that could be created/adapted to respond to the event (practice). Executive branch leaders typically operate in the moment, and their responses—reorganize, consolidate, provide more funding and people—are not grounded in an understanding of how the complexity of the unfolding situation impacts current executive branch administration and leadership practices.

Second, federal leaders *are unable to develop a coherent justification and implementation strategy for complex policy and funding decisions.* Paul Light (2014) has documented a "cascade of failures" from 2001 to 2014 that include Hurricane Katrina and 40 other "failures" that will be familiar to most Americans. Light identifies five causes for these failures: policy, resources, structure, leadership, and culture. Light's analysis underscores the argument in this chapter that federal executive branch leadership and administration theory and practice have not matured rapidly enough to assuage concerns about the ability of the federal government to meet 21st century challenges. The American Customer Satisfaction Index (ASCI) (2014), for example, has measured a steady decrease in public trust in the executive branch to deliver on essential public services—a perception that is only enhanced when highly prominent "failures" come to the attention of the Congress and the general public.

A generation of presidential candidates, starting with Ronald Reagan, has promised to "fix" Washington. These critics are typically responding to perceptions of executive branch performance relative to slow or inappropriate responses to the failures Light has documented. These perceptions contribute to a vicious circle of recriminations that undermine public trust in the ability of the federal leaders to effectively and efficiently deliver on the great public trust the federal executive branch has been given.

This chapter will make the argument that perceptions about the role and purpose of the federal government are closely linked to the gap between theory and practice in executive branch administration and leadership and that this gap is an understandable phenomenon that could be remedied. This argument is based on the following:

1 A full understanding of the complexity, scope, and evolution of the modern U.S. federal government would enable the development of improved theory and practice.
2 Executive branch administration and leadership are operationalized in an extraordinarily complex environment that is poorly understood but requires greater analysis before theory and practice can be improved.
3 The current state of social/economic science—particularly the development of data, tools, and methods required to characterize the federal government ecosystem—are in need of improvement before rigorous analyses can be performed.
4 It is possible to develop a coherent theory of executive branch leadership and administration, with a concurrent increase in the federal government's performance, particularly during disruptive events.

Understanding the Complexity, Scope, and Evolution of the Modern U.S. Federal Government

The U.S. federal government has evolved since the founding period in a manner that has significantly impacted the administration and leadership of the executive branch. An ever-increasing complexity and scope of operations due to the emergence of the United States as a world leader following World War II has contributed to the challenges the executive branch encounters when responding to disruptive changes.

Consider these characteristics of the modern U.S. federal government and how it evolved to become the world's largest and most complex organization to administer and lead:

- 2 million federal employees who belong to the career federal civil service (Office of Personnel Management [OPM], 2015) and 7 million contract employees (Light, 2011) who work directly with the federal government in support positions or manage key federal resources such as the U.S. Department of Energy's national laboratory system.
- A $3.8 trillion annual budget (Office of Management and Budget [OMB], 2016) composed of $1.11 trillion in discretionary spending (research and development, infrastructure improvements, national defense, etc.), $2.45 trillion in mandatory spending (Medicare, Social Security, veteran's benefits, etc.), and payment on debt ($240 billion).

- Over 1,500 major operating units (OMB, 2015) that range in size from a million dollar commission that regulates agriculture products to the $900 billion centers for Medicare and Medicaid.
- Agency missions that touch the lives of all 360 million Americans on a daily basis through thousands of vital services and products that enhance the quality of life for all Americans, including research and development into new energy systems and medical treatments; crop management programs that have made the U.S. a leading exporter of grains to the world; national defense at home and abroad; national parks management and preservation; Social Security administration for 65 million Americans; and infrastructure projects such as roads and court houses.
- Deep ties through diplomacy and military obligations to nations throughout the world, which require executive branch employees to understand complex issues such as foreign commercial markets, maritime laws, and improvements to international health systems.
- A governance system within the executive branch that has evolved from the 1780s with ever-increasing rules, regulations, and responsibilities that often are in conflict and/or create operating environments that favor risk aversion and caution.

Effects of Scope and Complexity

Compare the scope and complexity of the federal executive branch to other public administration systems or private corporations, and the challenge becomes evident. Administering and leading a company such as Apple, with its public valuation of $700 billion and 150,000 employees, is a major undertaking, but it does not begin to approach the complexity and scope of the federal government. The National Institutes of Health's (NIH) FY16 $31.3 billion budget (Department of Health and Human Services, 2015) is greater than the GDP of more than 90 sovereign nations; and the mission responsibilities of the Department of Homeland Security (DHS)—with its 250,000 employees, $51.8 billion FY16 budget (OMB, 2016), and 22 sub-agencies ranging from the Coast Guard to the federal Emergency Management Agency to the Immigration Service—has few peers in the world.

Current executive branch leaders, Congress, and the general public at large share a fundamental misunderstanding about how to lead and administer what is among the largest and most complex organizations in the world. The popular assumption is that the executive branch is a slow moving, highly structured organization that is impervious to change. Newly minted presidents and their management gurus typically offer that "government should be run like a business" with performance metrics, accountability, and consequences for poor performance.

These attitudes toward executive branch administration and leadership are often reflective of executive branch leaders' experiences from state and local government or corporate America. The working assumption is: "If what worked in those sectors could be successfully transferred to the federal sector, improvements would be immediate." The best example of this mindset is the 1993 Government Performance & Results Act (GPRA), which originated from the experience of a small town California mayor who became an influential staff member for a senator. The staff member persuaded congressional reformers that creating performance metrics, strategic plans, and accountability structures would improve the effectiveness and efficiency of executive branch operations.

During the 24 years since GPRA (1993) was passed, however, little or no evidence has emerged that GPRA or its successor, the GPRA Modernization Act of 2010, have had its intended effects (Ho, 2007). Subsequent presidential administrations tried other reform measures but with similarly negligible impacts. It will be argued in this chapter that an absence of understanding about the theory and practice of executive branch leadership and administration is the root cause for these failures.

Characterizing Executive Branch Operating Guidelines

Contributing to this absence of understanding of how the executive branch operates is a failure to rationally characterize the operating guidelines behind executive branch administration and leadership. The federal government suffers from construction by committee, with all of the chaos that implies. As the popular metaphor goes, "a camel is a horse designed by a committee."

In the case of the executive branch, Congress is the committee, which passes the laws that provide the authorities and funding required to administer and to lead the executive branch of the federal government. There are currently more than 200 congressional committees and subcommittees that annually approve a bewildering series of laws and rules that beleaguered federal bureaucrats must implement. Executive branch lawyers and policy makers have developed many processes and procedures to assess "congressional intent," but those processes allow a great deal of discretion when determining what Congress actually intended when it passed a law or a budget.

By delegating so much authority to the executive branch, Chief Justice Clarence Thomas argued in four opinions that Congress has contributed to the growth of an executive branch "that concentrates the power to make laws to enforce them in the hands of a vast and unaccountable administrative apparatus that finds no comfortable home in our constitutional structure" (Will, 2015, p. A25).

This process has been ongoing since the birth of the United States, and the accretion of rules, regulations, laws, and organizational structures has had a profound impact on the ability of federal government leaders to respond to disruptive change. An examination of Light's 41 examples of executive branch "failures" since 2001 indicates that the typical response of Congress and the president to perceived failures is either to create new organizations or to develop new oversight processes. The creation of the Department of Homeland Security is an example of this accretion process, which ultimately paralyzes executive branch leaders as they attempt to unravel the implications of yet another major addition to the rules and regulations that underpin how it operates (Light, 2014).

A five-year Brookings Institution project (Galston & McElvein, 2015) examined federal agencies with a goal of understanding how to improve institutional innovation. They found that institutional innovation followed one of two courses: "acute" innovation resulting from crises such as the creation of the Federal Deposit Insurance Corporation (FDIC) to avert the collapse of the U.S. banking system, and "institutional" innovation that led to the creation of the Environmental Protection Agency (EPA). Two primary characteristics emerge from their analysis: crisis-driven innovation is hugely disruptive and expensive; and all innovation is difficult because overcoming resistance and simple inertia is impossible due to the complexity of the executive branch operating environment.

Evolution of Executive Branch Leadership

The 1883 Pendleton Civil Service Act remains one of the most influential pieces of legislation in terms of executive branch leadership and administration. The Pendleton Act resulted from a series of political patronage scandals in the 1870s and cemented in place a civil service that is premised on the twin notions of merit-based competition and freedom from political influence. The Pendleton Act created a professional class of executive branch leaders who would follow 1880s-era "modern" notions of corporate governance, such as "policy-free" decision making and reliance on metrics such as dollars spent and projects completed.

Today's executive branch struggles with this legacy in many ways. Two recent examples of highly publicized challenges point to an endemic inability by career leaders in the executive branch to interpret political leadership direction. The first was the inability of the Internal Revenue Service to interpret Congress' intent regarding the status of non-profits, which led to congressional investigations alleging political suppression of non-profits associated with the Republican Party. The second was the operationalization by the Department of Veterans Affairs of directives from political leaders to improve the delivery of hospital services for veterans, which created a culture that favored reduced waiting times over actual patient care (Light, 2014).

In both cases, executive branch career leaders were ill equipped to respond to extremely complex operating environments that had been strongly influenced by political considerations. The failure to respond effectively to these and other challenges, it could be argued, is due in part to a lack of training and knowledge, which in turn can be traced to the absence of an understanding of theory and practice in the executive branch (National Academy of Public Administration [NAPA], 2009).

A tremendous amount of academic scholarship has been devoted to leadership theory and practice (van Wart, 2015), with portions of that research focused on the federal government executive branch, notably Larry Terry's work to develop a theory of "administrative conservatorship" (2002). Terry and van Wart both acknowledge that not enough attention has been paid to leadership in the federal government, resulting in theories that are too abstract and practices that are complex and typically too specific, i.e., are only relevant to one agency within a given period of time. Cuervo (2015, p. v) notes that "more than 1,500 different definitions of the term *leadership*" exist.

In addition, little work has been done to meld Rosenbloom's "three perspectives model" of public administration with theories and the practice of leadership in the executive branch. Rosenbloom's three perspectives model argues persuasively that the "collapsing of the separation of powers (into the executive branch) has been well recognized," which requires executive branch leaders "to integrate the three approaches (legal, managerial and political) to public administration" (Rosenbloom, 1983, p. 454). Rosenbloom and others (Zalmanovitch, 2014) argue that the evolution of executive branch leadership has been strongly influenced over the past 35 years by legislation and presidential executive orders that have increased political influence in the executive branch, with a diminution in the traditional managerial role played by career executive branch leaders.

President Kennedy had the authority to appoint less than 300 individuals to "political appointments," primarily high-level cabinet positions and his closest aides in the Executive Office of the President (Volcker Commission, 2003). Judicial appointments and "honorary" appointments to commissions and study groups are not considered to be presidential political appointees for the purposes of this analysis.

In 2009, President Obama had the authority to appoint more than 3,000 "political appointees" to Senate-confirmed cabinet agency positions such as secretary of state and assistant secretary of housing, and "Schedule C" appointees who could range from the director of a major sub-agency of the Department of Interior to a senior advisor at the White House. In addition, there are other non-competitive hiring authorities that can be used by presidents to bring in the talent they need to run the sprawling federal bureaucracy, including "Schedule A" appointments, temporary consultant positions, and "Limited Term Senior Executive Service" appointments.

This expansion in the number of appointees has seen a concurrent rise in the responsibilities of political appointees. In JFK's administration, the 300 individuals were in very senior positions sitting atop the bureaucracy. Those appointees relied upon career civil service leaders to provide day-to-day implementation of the president's policies. Starting with the Reagan administration in the 1980s, however, there has been a steadily growing substitution of career civil service leadership in the day-to-day administration of programs by political leadership (Light, 1999; Lewis, 2008).

Hannah Sistare, former director of the Volcker National Commission on the Public Service said,

> The (Volcker) Commission, among others, was concerned about the layering at the top of government. ... What gets lost is that we have gotten into a situation where the secretary of a department is far removed from the top civil servants who have knowledge and experience and a lot to offer.
>
> (National Academy of Public Administration [NAPA], 2006, p. 79)

This accretion of political influence in the administration of the executive branch has influenced public perceptions about the federal government's performance in two ways. First, the public at large and most critics of the executive branch, including many members of Congress, do not understand that political leaders are the ultimate decision makers at federal agencies and bear the responsibility for "failures" that are typically ascribed to career civil servants. Career employees are required by law to follow the direction of political leadership and may not supervise a political appointee. Thus, the vast majority of policy decisions that impact the lives of Americans are made by political leaders, not career leaders. Light's analysis of the 41 "failures" of the executive branch indicates that policy decisions made by executive branch leaders were the key contributors to the failures (2014).

Second, the expansion of the number of political appointees has meant that the expertise of career leaders is often absent when major policy decisions are made. Career leaders, particularly the 7,200 career members of the Senior Executive Service (SES), are expected to implement an administration's policy decisions through procurement, human resources, and other key business operations. Increasingly, however, temporary political appointees are leading these vital operational positions or have a major influence over their direction, which often requires an in-depth knowledge of federal business process. For example, development of the federal budget at most agencies is considered to be the primary responsibility of political leadership. Career leadership is often involved, particularly at the onset of the budget process, but when final decisions are made, they are made by political leaders.

This problem is particularly acute during presidential transitions. "High turnover among politically appointed leaders in federal agencies can make it difficult to follow through with organizational transformation because of the length of time often needed to provide meaningful and sustainable results," noted a Government Accountability Office report (GAO0 (2007, p. 8).

GAO proposed the creation of career Chief Operating Officer/Chief Management Officer positions that would ensure that career leaders experienced in the functions and responsibilities of the agency would be in place during those transitions. A letter to the Senate accompanying the 2007 report noted:

> As agencies across the federal government embark on large-scale organizational change to address 21st-century challenges, there is a compelling need for leadership to provide the continuing, focused attention essential to completing the multiyear transformations. … These long-term responsibilities are professional and non-partisan in nature. (p. 1)

Effectiveness of Career and Political Leadership

The 21st-century executive branch is not free from political influence and has never achieved the Pendleton Act ideal of managing by merit. Since 1958, an increasing level of political influence has been infused into the executive branch through a number of mechanisms that have fundamentally altered how the 21st-century executive branch is administered and led.

Primary among these were the 1958 Executive Order by President Dwight Eisenhower, which created the "Schedule C" category of political appointments, and the 1978 Civil Service Reform Act, which created "Limited-Term Senior Executive Service" authorities. Evidence is abundant that these authorities have been increasingly utilized by presidents since Ronald Reagan to bring senior political appointees into their administrations without Senate confirmation.

David Lewis has documented the pattern of politicization in the executive branch and some of the consequences of that politicization. "A ... reason why studying politicization is (important is) that it is a vital tool for controlling the bureaucracy," Lewis (2008) writes. "It follows, then, that whoever controls the bureaucracy controls a key part of the policy process" (p. 6). Lewis noted that his study of the difference between career and political leaders in the executive branch demonstrated that "the historical justification for the merit system, current debates about reducing the number of appointees, and democratic theory ... is generalizable to other programs and agencies." These results, Lewis concludes, validate the 1880s Pendleton Act merit-based civil service reforms and could lead to "lower turnover in the federal workforce and the cultivation of useful administrative expertise" (2007, p. 25).

Lewis's (2008) analysis included a study of the performance of political and career leaders. His conclusion was that political leaders are more effective at "translating political wishes into a clear program purpose and design" (p. 189) but that in all other aspects career leaders "have negative effects on management" (p. 188) at federal agencies. This dynamic, Lewis concludes, underscores the delicate balance between political and career leadership and the effect that a president's choice has on the administration of the executive branch.

James Pfiffner (2015) notes that the average lifetime of a political appointee is 2.5 years and that while many of the more senior appointees are competent, "the large number of positions that are filled with political appointees result in lower levels of competence in the leadership of executive branch agencies" (p. 2).

Legislative Leadership: The Need for a New Paradigm

This chapter argues that a theory of administration has emerged but that leadership theory for the executive branch has not similarly benefited. Some academic work has been done, for example, Carolyn Ban's *How Do Public Managers Manage?* (1995), but the focus is on management and not leadership. Training programs in the public and private sector have not caught up with this emerging requirement, thus the need for new theories and practices that explore the intersection of executive branch leadership and administration.

As Collins (2005) argues, 21st century organizations will likely be led by "Legislative Leaders" who combine the characteristics and skill sets of what are traditionally thought of as "Executive Leaders" and "Political Leaders." Modern administrative and leadership practices, according to Collins, require a mix of management and political skills that are not often found in either the public or private sector. In addition, modern leadership theory requires a blend of disciplined, accountable leaders who also have political sensibilities (Arbinger Institute, 2010).

From this viewpoint, the evident increase in political leadership in the executive branch if properly balanced in theory and practice with career leadership could produce a net benefit to the federal government. The constant churn of political leadership, it could be argued, brings a dynamic element to the federal government that balances the inherent conservatism of the modern administrative state (Rosenbloom, 1983). Without an influx of fresh ideas and political leadership that is reflective of the electorate as embodied by presidential administrations, federal career leaders would have very little incentive to change or adapt. Political leadership also has the potential, in the words of Supreme Court Justice Brandeis, "to preclude the exercise of arbitrary power" (Rosenbloom, 1983, p. 448).

The lack of study in this field—Collins acknowledges that his concept of "Legislative Leaders" is based on observation, not theory or study—is telling. The current state of executive branch leadership training is based on a wide assortment of methods and tools that generally aim to provide managers with the skills required to be effective in government—dealing with difficult employees, improving emotional intelligence, managing complex programs, etc. Legislative skills—such as "persuasion," and developing "political currency, and shared interests to create the conditions for the right decisions to happen" (Collins, 2005, p. 11)—are not typically taught to executive branch leaders.

In addition, few executive branch leaders, career or political, study the federal government as an organizational entity, and all have varied levels of expertise in the underlying business processes that are vital to effectively administering the executive branch's complex agencies. As discussed previously, the federal government is a vast ecosystem made up of many individual parts, but most federal leaders are only expert in limited aspects of that complex ecosystem. This leads to the "design by committee" phenomenon and the creation of bureaucratic behemoths like the Department of Homeland Security or the inability of career leaders to remove their agencies from Government Accountability Office (GAO) watch lists for project/program management failures.

Political leaders, who typically serve two years or less in the executive branch, are rarely provided an opportunity to learn the legislative skills and in-depth business processes required for the 21st-century executive branch. This explains why there is such a steep learning curve for many executive branch political leaders and why many bureaucratic leaders cite new Administrations and their political appointees as part of a "hostile takeover" every four years of the federal government, with all of the disruption that the term "hostile takeover" implies.

Operationalization of the Modern Federal Government

Each successive president and Congress since George Washington has added new responsibilities to the executive branch, with that process accelerating after World

War II when the United States became a dominant world power and then moving into hyper-acceleration since the fall of the Soviet Union and the advent of the Internet Age. And, yet, the operations of the current executive branch remain mired in the past because of a lack of an understanding about how to transform existing executive branch administrative and leadership structures into an organization that is responsive to 21st-century rapid disruptive change (Galston & McElvein, 2015).

The federal government of the 21st-century bears little resemblance to the government that President John F. Kennedy led in 1961. Three major trends since 1961 have had an outsized impact on the operational ability of the federal government to respond to disruptive change: the "hollowing out" of the federal bureaucracy (Milward, Provan, & Else, 1993); an increase in "mission extrinsic" responsibilities at agencies (Rosenbloom, 2014); and an enormous increase in the role of the federal government in the daily lives of all Americans.

The "Hollowing Out" of the Federal Government

The federal government of 1962 had an annual budget of $107 billion (OMB, 2016) and employed 1.8 million career civil servants (OPM, 2015). In real terms (adjusted for inflation with the gross domestic product price index), the FY16 $3.9 trillion federal budget is 5 times larger than that of 1961, but the number of executive branch employees has stayed relatively the same at 2 million in 2015. The major difference between 1961 and 2015 appears to be the use of third parties who provide services and products for the federal government, a process that Milward, Provan, and Else (1993) describe as the "hollowing out" of the executive branch.

Reliable estimates of the scale of third-party providers prior to the early 1990s do not exist (Peck, 2011; CBO, 2015), but the Congressional Budget Office (2015) found that "federal spending on contracts grew by 87 percent ... from 2000 to 2012. ... The category that rose the most ... was contracts for professional, administrative and management services" (p. 4). This outsourcing of professional services is a strong indicator that the "hollowing out" of the executive branch is a continuing phenomenon.

As noted previously, the executive branch's responsibilities have increased exponentially since 1961. The executive branch has coped with this expansion in roles and responsibilities through the use of third parties to operationalize programs and projects. In the last detailed study done on the number of executive branch third-party providers, it was estimated that up to 17 million third parties provided goods and services for the federal government if state and local government officials who spend federal block grant funds are included (Light, 1999).

While Light's accounting has come under criticism for being "astronomically high" (Peck, 2011), the phenomenon of the growth in third-party providers and its effects on the administration of the executive branch are undisputed. Senator David Pryor called this "a very large, invisible, unelected bureaucracy of consultants who perform an enormous portion of the basic work of and set the policy for the Government" (Light, 1999, p. 13). The "hollowing out" of the executive branch helps explain a primary difference between 1961 and 2015 and the need for further study of the phenomenon. "What is so astonishing about this worldwide movement away from government provision to government procurement is that there is little evidence that governments or academics know much about how to govern or manage networks" (Milward & Provan, 2000, p. 361).

The hollow state arises due to the complexity and scope of modern governments and results in a devolution of power to local and state governments and to third-party agents such as non-profits, universities, and for-profit contractors. This devolution of power, no doubt, has an impact on the administration and leadership practices of the executive branch, but sufficient study has not been done on the issue, and the executive branch lacks the tools and data to do the analysis (Frederickson & Frederickson, 2007).

The Increase in "Mission-Extrinsic Public Values"

Rosenbloom (2014) documents 37 examples of "mission-extrinsic public values" that have been assigned to executive branch agencies through court rulings, legislation, and presidential executive orders. Mission-extrinsic public values are defined as responsibilities that are not directly related to the core mission of the agency. For example, the Department of Energy (DOE) is primarily a science and technology agency but states in its strategic plan that "diversity" is a core value and that all departmental elements should work toward increasing the diversity of DOE's workforce.

Two schools of thought exist about mission-extrinsic public values: either they are viewed as important drivers of social equity, or they are seen as distractions that divert resources and attention away from core missions. In the former, an agency such as the DOE has a social equity responsibility to ensure that its programs benefit all Americans, not just the majority white scientific research community. In the latter case, the argument is that the DOE's efforts to ensure energy independence for the United States are undermined by social equity programs.

Reconciling these two schools of thought is within the province of academics, but the consequences of the clash between them are deeply felt in all federal agencies. Collins writes that "great" organizations have a "relentless culture of discipline" that focuses on mission accomplishment as the primary way to drive employee performance and ultimately create value for an organization (Collins, 2005). Without this mission focus, Collins argues, organizations lose their way and begin the decline to mediocrity.

Increased Role of the Federal Government

The accretion of responsibilities within the federal government accelerated during the Johnson administration with "great society" initiatives, which led to the expansion of social services agencies (Departments of Housing and Urban Development, Health and Human Services, primarily), and continued unabated through the energy crises of the 1970s that led to the creation of the Department of Energy and the rise of state-sponsored terrorism in the 1990s that led to the creation of the Department of Homeland Security.

During those three major increases in executive branch responsibilities, the "old line" agencies such as the Departments of Defense, Agriculture, State, Treasury, and Interior were also given new roles and responsibilities concomitant with the United States' status as the dominant world power.

This ever increasing evolution in the responsibilities of the federal government does not have an analog in the private sector for two reasons. First, federal agencies do not have the option of "declining" a new mission. Once Congress and the president decide that Agency X is now responsible for widget development, Agency X has no choice but to develop programs to accomplish that mission. Second, agencies are burdened with business processes that were adapted for other purposes and eras but must be used for the new mission.

Successful corporations such as AT&T or DuPont can trace their lineage over 100 years and have been able to adapt to new circumstances. When new technologies, market conditions, or demographic changes required changes in business processes, private corporations were able to adapt or were forced out of the market. For example, Kodak collapsed when digital photography killed the market for instant and film photography.

In the private sector, holding company structures that contain different entities with different business processes and missions have proven to be failures as organizational structures. "Silo busting" to create nimble and flexible organizations is currently a hot research topic, and corporations are turning to university researchers to help solve the problem. "Economists are trying to do a better job of predicting market movements by calling on experts in areas like biology, psychology, and the humanities. Major brain-science initiatives now routinely bring together researchers across many fields to share data," writes Rana Foroohar (2014, p. 24).

But it is virtually impossible to do "silo busting" within major agencies, and as might be expected, the increased roles and responsibilities of the executive branch did not proceed from an orderly process or plan. Phillip K. Howard said that Congress "did not deliberately create this bureaucratic jungle. The jungle just grew, like kudzu" (2015, p. A19).

This crisis/opportunity-driven increase resulted in a hodgepodge of business processes and structures that created layers of rules and regulations that had one primary purpose: sustain a deliberative process of implementing federal programs that has integrity, is open to all, and discharges the public trust in the most efficient and effective manner possible.

This deliberative process, however, is undermined by laws and business practices, many originating in the 1800s, such as procurement or human resources, which are still in force today. This accretion of congressionally mandated rules limits the ability of federal managers and leaders to be "nimble and flexible." Change management literature underscores the challenges that arise due to this accretion. Solutions to the problems experienced during one administration are exactly what breeds new problems as organizations continue to grow and mature. Organizations frequently have difficulty letting go of previously successful strategies, even when they are no longer useful (Greiner, 1998; Skarke, Rogers, Holland, & Landon, 1995).

Thus, risk aversion and caution have been hardwired into the federal system. Procurement processes became complex and daunting for anyone without decades of training and experience with the Federal Acquisition Regulation (FAR), while human resource processes were designed to meet the mutually incompatible goals of ensuring competition while adapting to social equity goals that created special rules for veterans and disadvantaged communities.

Collins (2005) has referred to this paralysis and caution as a familiar challenge confronting many large and complex organizations. Faced with seemingly insurmountable "systemic constraints," leaders believe they are powerless to create "great organizations." His solution is to promote "pockets of greatness," such as reforming the procurement process of a grants-making agency or tackling environmental regulatory oversight processes that can add up to 10 years in the life of a major federal project. "This is perhaps the single most important point in all of *Good to Great.* Greatness is not a function of circumstance. Greatness it turns out, is largely a matter of conscious choice, and discipline" (pp. 28–31).

The congressional and Bush administration responses to the 9/11 terrorist attack in relationship to the visa and immigration system for scientists and engineers is an example of the unintended negative consequences of crisis-inspired change management in the executive branch. A hallmark of the U.S. science and technology system is that it allows gifted scientists and engineers to enter the United States to study and work, but after 9/11 new policies and regulations were imposed that significantly curtailed the ability of foreign students to enter the United States. The issue, writes Al Teich (2014), is that while the United States is discouraging the best and the brightest from coming to the United States, "other countries are creating incentives to attract talented scientists to their universities and laboratories" (p. 56) with potentially negative results for the United States in the international competition for innovation and economic growth.

A full understanding of the federal government ecosystem and how various feedback loops of processes and interactions related to the operations of the executive branch could mitigate those unintended consequences.

Current State of Social and Economic Sciences

The social/economic sciences are increasingly viewed by the executive branch and Corporate America as vital tools to improve management, evaluation, and leadership. This chapter argues that understanding executive branch leadership/administration theory and practice is an academic and national challenge on the order of string theory in physics and genomics in systems biology and should have a priority equal to the Manhattan Project that led to the development of nuclear weapons and JFK's goal of putting a man on the moon.

The primary challenge confronting the social/economic sciences is that the "natural sciences" (physics, biology, chemistry, etc.) have the advantage of highly advanced theories, tools, and methods that have been honed over millennia. By comparison, the concept that the social/economic sciences could be approached in a rigorous and evidence-based manner, with accepted theories, methodologies and practices, is less than 200 years old.

This relative lack of social/economic science maturity has strong implications for executive branch leadership and administration. In the natural sciences, theory and practice go hand in hand and result in new technologies, processes and general improvements in knowledge that benefit society at large. It is well understood in the natural sciences that absent theory, practices could emerge that could be oppositional to the intended outcome. Thus, to produce a better light bulb, the study of existing processes and theories must be conducted before improvements can be made.

The Power of Theories, Data, Tools, and Methods

Lisa Dilling and Maria Carmen Lemos recently noted that "decision makers in the United States have increasingly called upon publicly funded science to provide 'usable' information for policy making, whether in the case of acid rain, famine prevention or climate change policy" (Dilling & Lemos, 2009, p. 680). This is a recognition, particularly in the natural sciences community, that evidence-based policy making is important for highly complex and vitally important national issues. The goal of science-based policy decision making is to lead to more effective resource allocation and successful outcomes, such as determining that fossil-fuel consumption is a primary cause of climate change and that mitigation strategies by the federal government should develop to encompass not just technology solutions, but legal, regulatory, and policy considerations.

Dr. John Marburger, who served as President George W. Bush's science advisor, was a world-class physicist who decided that it was impossible to lead and administer the federal government's $140 billion annual research and development budget without improvements to the "science of science policy," which he defined as using evidence-based tools to inform policy making. In 2006, Marburger commissioned an inter-agency working group to study the problem, which resulted in a roadmap (National Science and Technology Council [NSTC], 2008); an $8 million/year social sciences research program at the National Science Foundation that has produced new theories, data, tools, and methods now being used by federal agencies to better manage their programs; and the development of a "community of practice" that actively promotes new theories and practices used in the public and private sectors.

Marburger's decision was based on his experience as a member of the physics community, which uses advanced decision-support tools and data sources to perform analyses and develop new theories and practices. He understood that the social and economic sciences could be a powerful tool for executive branch leaders.

Marburger, however, was dealing with a subset of the larger problem confronting the executive branch: how to develop the data, tools, and methods that would lead to the creation of theories and practices to improve the overall administration and leadership of the executive branch. As noted previously, the scope and complexity of the federal government presents a daunting challenge to researchers seeking to understand the federal ecosystem. This scope and complexity prohibits benchmarks and longitudinal analyses because no comparable organizations currently exist. Whereas Germany might reasonably compare its system of government to France given their historical ties and evolution as nations, the United States because of its size, complexity, and evolution is singular in the world.

In addition, whereas the natural sciences community has had millennia to develop data sources and benchmarks for the phenomena that they observe (chemical reactions, plant growth, evolution of the universe, etc.), the theories they construct (the Theory of Relativity, Darwinism, etc.), and the tools/methods/data that they have evolved (bioinformatics, computers, internal combustion engine, Internet, etc.), the social/economic sciences community by comparison is still developing testable theories and practices.

Zalmanovitch ponders this problem in relationship to developing an "identity" for the study of public administration "that is urgently required to encompass the vast range of public administration configurations" that currently exists (Zalmanovitch, 2014, p. 14). This paucity of support for academic research into theory and practice in executive branch administration and leadership results in a great deal of experimentation and academic debates that do not generally lead to successful outcomes.

For example, the current GPRA Modernization Act implementation strategy of the Obama administration is based on developing agency pilots that do not have a coherent theoretical basis and will likely result in one-off results that cannot be replicated. The administration has also made it a priority to increase "employee engagement" based on the results of the annual Federal Employee Viewpoint Survey (FEVS). This effort, however, is not grounded in a full understanding of what "employee engagement" actually means and is based on misleading data from the FEVS that does not distinguish between career and political leadership practices.

The Rise of Business Schools

Corporate America has wrestled with the challenge of developing new administrative and leadership structures for many decades, with a concomitant proliferation of business schools at major universities. These schools have increasingly been well funded by their key stakeholder—Corporate America. This funding would not have been so generous if they had not seen benefits to their bottom line.

These benefits came in two forms. First, business schools are sharply focused on the research questions of interest to corporations, such as improving return-on-investment, infusing disruptive information technologies into legacy business practices and processes, or developing risk strategies for environmental compliance.

Second, as the modern era of disruptive change has exploded into the public consciousness, corporations with the assistance of academia evolved from rigid "command-and-control" entities that followed the IBM- and U.S. military-structured business model into the more free-flowing structures that Google, Apple, and other social media behemoths have adopted. This has enabled nimble and flexible corporations to sweep up available talent. Millennials and Gen-X'ers, in particular, have been eager to engage with corporate America to "green the economy" or create added value to social institutions.

Current State of Schools of Public Administration

By contrast, public administration schools have also sprung up at major universities, but they have lacked the corporate or federal funding required to match the research results coming out of business schools. The key stakeholder that might provide such support for public administration schools is the executive branch of the federal government, but an examination of the National Science Foundation's (NSF) annual budget is telling.

Those areas of the NSF budget that most directly benefit corporate America (the "natural sciences" such as chemistry, physics, engineering, and biology) had a total budget of $5.8 billion in FY16 (NSF, 2015), while those areas of science that most directly benefit the study of public administration—NSF's annual support for the social/economic sciences—is less than $300 million. And that funding is spread widely among programs in state, local, federal government administration, psychology, economics, and neuro-science.

This mismatch in funding has two primary consequences. First, current perceptions of the federal government as a career destination for Millennials and Gen-X'ers is at an all-time low despite the fact that "public service" is a core value of these new generations of workers (Kim, 2015). Second, criticisms of the "bloated" and "corrupt" federal government go unanswered because the executive branch has not had the benefit of an energetic scholarly community attuned to its needs and ready to rise to its defense.

Analyses that demonstrate the contributions of the executive branch to economic prosperity and increases in the standards of living for all Americans would be beneficial to public perceptions of the overall federal government. For example, Nordhaus et al. (2014) write: "Thanks to the work of a generation of neo-Schumpeterian scholars, it is now widely accepted that the U.S. government" was responsible for the development of the Internet, cell phones, MRIs, the civilian nuclear power industry and other transformational technologies (p. 8).

Most Americans think these innovations were created by entrepreneurs working in an unfettered free market economy and would likely be shocked that federal bureaucrats contribute so heavily to the innovation economy on a daily and continuing basis.

The Need for More Social and Economic Support

A major justification of federal intervention in the U.S. banking, automotive, and housing industries during the 2007 recession was the idea that those industries were "too big to fail" and could result in the economy crashing even harder than it did. If those industries were "too big to fail," it would seem that the executive branch is *prima facie* too big to fail and is worthy of greater support for studies that would improve the executive branch's ability to lead and administer the federal government.

President Obama's science advisor, John Holdren, recognized the need for increased use of social science through the creation of the interagency "Social and Behavioral Science Team" in 2014 and issuing what is intended to be an annual report on best practices in the executive branch. "When *behavioral insights*—research findings from behavioral economics and psychology about how people make decisions and act on them—are brought into policy, the returns are significant," the report concluded (NSTC, 2015, p. 1).

As Elizabeth McElvein (2015) wrote in a Brookings Institution brief: "In an era of waning public confidence in the U.S. government and a need among agencies to do more with shrinking appropriations, there is no better time to apply to apply the insights of behavioral economics to public administration and public policy."

Developing a Coherent Theory and Practice of Federal Government Leadership and Administration

Administering and leading the modern federal government requires a clear understanding of theory and practice. Rosenbloom has made a significant contribution to the theory of executive branch public administration with his 1983 treatise on the three pillars of public administration. There has been no comparable theoretical approach to executive branch leadership, and certainly there has been no attempt to tie executive branch administration theory and practices with executive branch leadership theory and practices.

Rosenbloom argues that "the main contributor to the impact" of his 1983 article "has been to anchor its framework in the functions (and institutional structures) of government" (2014, p. 386). If this could be extended to leadership practices and anchoring both frameworks in the functions and structure of government, then clarity and cohesion could be improved in overall theory and practice.

This chapter argues that the study of executive branch leadership and administration should be distinct from other public administration study given the unique standing of the U.S. federal government. The absence of such a theory is a tremendous missed opportunity because responsibility for the administration of a $3.8 trillion organization is routinely handed to career and political leaders who have no formal training in theory and practice about that organization, with predictable results.

This is analogous to asking a corporate executive to become the captain of an ocean liner. Our mythical CEO knows generally how to run organizations and lead people but in the event of a crisis, say hitting an iceberg, has no understanding of how the ocean liner was built and operates, particularly during an emergency. With no time for hesitation, crucial mistakes, such as relying on engineering reports that flooded compartments will hold, delays the launching of lifeboats and the sending of distress signals.

The iceberg analogy was made real to the George W. Bush administration in the aftermath of the Hurricane Katrina disaster and to the Barack Obama administration as it tried to respond to questions from the veteran's community about its handling of the Veterans Administration hospital system. In both cases, the responses by the administrations were halting, ill timed, and eventually the subject of congressional hearings and many corrective actions.

Three Key Questions

The answers to the following three questions are fundamental to developing a theory of executive branch administration and leadership that would improve the ability of federal government leaders to effectively administer the federal government during periods of disruptive change:

- *How does the constitutional structure of three distinct branches of government—legislative, judiciary, and executive—impact the daily functioning of the executive branch?* The federal ecosystem is complex and constantly evolving. A general theory of administration and leadership that takes into account the interactions and feedback loops inherent in this ecosystem would provide insights and solutions to executive branch and congressional leaders seeking to create an executive branch that is responsive to 21st-century disruptive changes.
- *What is the impact of the quadrennial presidential election on the operations of the executive branch?* The shift in the balance of power between career leaders and political leadership is arguably the key dynamic creating dissonance among career leadership, political leadership, and congressional leadership. An ability to study this phenomenon and develop more effective administrative and leadership practices could reduce political polarization between administrations and the Congress and increase public faith in the competence of the U.S. federal government.
- *Is it possible to develop a unified theory of public administration/leadership that enables the creation of a more flexible and nimble executive branch response to 21st-century disruptive challenges and takes into account factors such as the hollowing out of the executive branch and the addition of mission-extrinsic public values?* A primary criticism of the current executive branch is that it is constrained by 19th- and 20th-century practices. The modern federal government is increasingly called upon to solve societal challenges that defy easy solutions, such as ensuring energy security or implementing complex immigration policies. A system-dynamics approach to this challenge could lead to insights that would improve the efficiency and effectiveness of the executive branch.

Conclusions and Next Steps

This chapter has argued that developing improved theories and practices for executive branch leadership and administration should be a national priority. This argument is based on the following observations:

- The executive branch, through its programs, impacts the daily lives of all Americans.
- Current perceptions of executive branch leadership and administration are hindered by a lack of understanding of the evolution, scope, and complexity of the modern federal government.
- Social/economic sciences have not matured quickly enough to meet the real-world demands of executive branch leaders, who must respond to rapidly accelerating disruptive changes.

The following steps could lead to an improvement in the ability of executive branch leadership to effectively administer the federal government during a time of accelerated disruptive change:

1 *Devote more resources to the study of executive branch leadership and administrative theory and practices.* The Obama administration in 2014 announced an initiative designed to increase the use of social/economic sciences by federal agencies, but no additional funding was provided. Consideration should be given to providing agencies with resources in this area.

2 *In the short-term, focus efforts on ways to improve transitions between presidential administrations and better prepare political and career leaders to manage that change.* Numerous commissions have been established over the years to study presidential transitions, but these typically arise during the year prior to a presidential election and are not sustained, long-term efforts. Transitions and their impact on the executive branch arguably have the strongest impact on administration and leadership, and focusing on them could provide immediate benefits.

3 *Identify "pockets of greatness" within the executive branch that could serve as exemplars for other agencies in terms of flexible and nimble leadership and administration practices responsive to 21st-century challenges.* Collins argues that organizations should focus on what is within their control and build pockets of greatness that eventually will proliferate through the system. Within the executive branch, examples would include sub-agencies within a major department, such as the Department of Health and Human Services, striving toward greatness.

4 *Develop training programs for executive branch leaders that focus on creating "legislative leaders" capable of adapting to disruptive change.* Schools of public administration and the many training institutes that focus on the executive branch should create training programs that produce "legislative leaders."

5 *Create a "community of practice" of academics and practitioners focused on the specific challenges of the executive branch.* The executive branch routinely establishes "communities of practice" in specific areas of need. For example, the federal scientific community formed a community of practice around climate change issues, and federal business operation professionals have communities of practice in procurement and human resources. These communities of practice are forums for discussions about new processes and procedures and for the resolution of issues that confront the community, such as a lack of data to perform analyses. A "community of practice" of academics and practitioners focused on the administration and leadership of the executive branch could serve as the advocate for effective and modern executive branch leadership and administration.

References

American Customer Satisfaction Index (2014). *ACSI federal government report 2014.* Ann Arbor: University of Michigan. Retrieved from https://www.theacsi.org/news-and-resources/customer-satisfaction-reports/reports-2014.

Arbinger Institute (2010). *Leadership and self-deception: Getting out of the box.* San Francisco, CA: Berrett-Koehler Publishers.

Ban, C. (1995). *How do public managers manage? Bureaucratic constraints, organizational culture, and the potential for reform.* Hoboken, NJ: Jossey-Bass.

Collins, J. (2005). *Good to great and the social sectors: A monograph to accompany Good to Great.* Boulder, CO: HarperCollins.

Congressional Budget Office. (2015, March 11). *Re: Federal contracts and the contracted workforce* [Letter to Rep. Chris Van Hollen]. Retrieved from https://www.cbo.gov/publication/49931.

Cuervo, J. (2015). *Leaders don't command: Inspire growth, ingenuity, and collaboration.* Alexandria, VA: ATD Press.

Department of Health and Human Services. (2015). *HHS FY2016 budget in brief.* HHS.gov. Retrieved from http://www.hhs.gov/about/budget/budget-in-brief/nih/index.html#.

Dilling, L., & Lemos, M. C. (2010). Creating usable science: Opportunities and constraints for climate knowledge use and their implications for science policy. *Journal of Global Environmental Change, 21*(2011) 680–689.

Foroohar, R. (2014, June 23). We've all got GM problems. *Time Magazine, 183*(24), 24.

Frederickson, D. G., & Frederickson, H. G. (2007). *Measuring the performance of the hollow state.* Washington, DC: Georgetown University Press.

Galston, W.A., & McElvein, E. (2015). *Institutional innovation: How it happens and why it matters.* Washington, DC: The Brookings Institution.

Government Accountability Office. (2007). *Organizational transformation: Implementing chief operating officer/chief management officer positions in federal agencies* (GAO-08-34). Retrieved from http://www.gao.gov/products/GAO-08-34.

Greiner, L. E. (1998). Evolution and revolution as organizations grow. *Harvard Business Review, 76*(3), 55–68.

Ho, A. (2007). GPRA after a decade: Lessons from the Government Performance and Results Act and related federal reforms. *Public Performance & Management Review, 30*(3), 307–311.

Howard, P. K. (2015, May 15). The high cost of red tape. *The Washington Post,* p. A19.

Howard, P. K. (2015, October 2). "You're fired!" won't fix government. *The Washington Post,* p. 21.

Kim, A. (2015, April). The federal government's worsening millennial talent gap. *Republic 3.0.* Retrieved from http://republic3-0.com/federal-government-millennials-talent-gap/.

Lewis, D. E. (2007). Testing Pendleton's premise: Do political appointees make worse bureaucrats? (forthcoming) *Journal of Politics.* Retrieved from https://my.vanderbilt.edu/davidlewis/files/2011/12/newpamgt17.pdf.

Lewis, D. E. (2008). *The politics of presidential appointments: Political control and bureaucratic performance.* Princeton, NJ: Princeton University Press.

Light, P. (1999). *The true size of government.* Washington, DC: Brookings Institution.

Light, P. (2011). *Creating high performance government: A once in a generation opportunity.* Retrieved from http://wagner.nyu.edu/news/newsStory/report-shows-ways-create-high-performance-government/.

Light, P. (2014). *A cascade of failures: Why government fails and how to stop it.* Washington, DC: Brookings Institution. Retrieved from http://www.brookings.edu/research/papers/2014/07/14-cascade-failures-why-government-fails-light.

McElvein, E. (2015, October 6). *A nudge toward better governance.* Washington, DC: Brookings Institute. Retrieved from http://www.brookings.edu/blogs/fixgov/posts/2015/10/06-nudge-better-governance-mcelvein.

Milward, H., & Provan, K. (2000). Governing the hollow state. *Journal of Public Administration Research and Theory, 10*(2), 359–379.

Milward, H., Provan, K., & Else, B. (1993). What does the hollow state look like? In B. Bozeman (Ed.), *Public Management: The State of the Art* (pp. 309–22), San Francisco, CA: Jossey-Bass.

National Academy of Public Administration. (2006). *Forum: Managing the workforce of the future* (Issue 1). Retrieved from http://www.thoughtleadershipinc.com/about/napa_magazine.pdf.

National Academy of Public Administration. (2009). *Agencies in transition: A report on the views of the members of the federal executive service.* Washington, DC: Author. Retrieved from http://www.napawash.org/wp-content/uploads/2009/09-05.pdf.

National Science Foundation. (2015). *Summary table: FY 2016 request to Congress.* Retrieved from http://www.nsf.gov/about/budget/fy2016/pdf/03_fy2016.pdf.

National Science and Technology Council (2008). *The science of science policy: A federal research roadmap.* Retrieved from http://cssip.org/docs/meeting/science_of_science_policy_roadmap_2008.pdf.

National Science and Technology Council (2015). *Social and behavioral sciences team annual report.* Retrieved from https://www.whitehouse.gov/sites/default/files/microsites/ostp/sbst_2015_annual_report_final_9_14_15.pdf.

Nordhaus, T., Shellenberger, M., & Caine, M. (2014). Embracing creative destruction: Hopeful pragmatism for a disruptive world. *The Breakthrough Journal, 4,* 7–12.

Office of Management and Budget. (2015). *Making performance information more accessible.* Retrieved from http://www.performance.gov/federalprograminventory.

Office of Personnel Management. (2015). *Executive branch civilian employment since 1940.* Retrieved from https://www.opm.gov/policy-data-oversight/data-analysis-documentation/federal-employment-reports/historical-tables/executive-branch-civilian-employment-since-1940/.

Office of Management and Budget. (2016). *Table 4.1, OMB Budget outlays by agency: 1962–2021.* Retrieved from https://www.whitehouse.gov/omb/budget/historicals.

Peck, L. (2011, September 28). America's $320 billion shadow government. *The Fiscal Times.* Retrieved from http://www.thefiscaltimes.com/articles/2011/09/28/Americas-320-billion-shadow-government.

Pfiffner, J. P. (2015). *Presidential appointments and managing the executive branch.* The Political Appointee Project. Retrieved from http://www.politicalappointeeproject.org/commentary/appointments-and-managing-executive-branch.

Rosenbloom, D. H. (1983). Public administrative theory and the separation of powers. *Public Administration Review, 43*(3), 219–227.

Rosenbloom, D. H. (2013). Reflections on "public administrative theory and the separation of powers." *The American Review of Public Administration, 43*(4), 381–396. doi:10.1177/0275074013483167.

Rosenbloom, D. H. (2014). Attending to mission-extrinsic public values in performance-oriented administrative management: A view from the United States. In J. P. Lehrke, E. Bohne, J. D. Graham, & J. C. Raadschelders (Eds.), *Public administration and the modern state: Assessing trends and impact.* Hampshire, England: Palgrave Macmillan.

Skarke, G., Rogers, B., Holland, D., & Landon, D. (1995). *The change management toolkit for reengineering.* Houston, TX: WorthingtonBrighton Press.

Teich, A. (2014). Streamlining the visa and immigration systems for scientists and engineers. *Issues in Science and Technology, 31*(1), 55–64.

Terry, L. (2002). *Leadership of public bureaucracies: The administrator as conservator* (2nd ed.). New York, NY: Routledge Press.

Van Wart, M. (2015). *Dynamics of leadership for public service: Theory and practice* (2nd ed.). New York, NY: Routledge Press.

Volcker Commission. (2003). *Urgent business for America: Revitalizing the federal government for the 21st century.* Washington, DC: Partnership for Public Service. Retrieved from https://ourpublicservice.org/publications/viewcontentdetails.php?id=314.

Will, G. F. (2015, November 29). A fix to our unbalanced government. *The Washington Post*, p. A25.

Zalmanovitch, Y. (2014). *Don't reinvent the wheel: The search for an identity for public administration.* International Review of Administrative Sciences, *80*(4), 808–826.

4 Leadership and Management

The Use of Distributed Power and Influence in a Changing Federal Government

Andrew Rahaman

> Always, it seems, the concept of leadership eludes us or turns up in another form to taunt us again with its slipperiness and complexity.
>
> —Warren G. Bennis

What makes public administration leadership different from leadership in private industry? This chapter will argue that what is distinguishing are the overall goals of public administration, which are to provide service, regulation, and depth of knowledge; to keep the bureaucracy working in service to the people of our nation, to organize that work; and to provide the leadership necessary in a changing workplace. We see those changes reflected in "reinventing the government" and the new public management (NPM) as an organizational outcome in contrast to organizational governance. We see it in the changes of how leadership is conceptualized and how decisions are made.

While this chapter does not identify the best method of leadership and managership for public administrators, it provides a roadmap. Section 1 identifies the changing context of the government and consequently leadership. The second and third sections move the reader toward integrated leadership definitions and theories. This discussion explains how leadership has changed with the social system through time and is meant to challenge you to think about how you should lead now and into the future.

Important to this understanding is how we view leaders in making decisions. For those that adhere in the Weberian form of bureaucracy, leadership, authority, and decision making are largely vested in the individual. Those from the emerging school of "new governance," the NPM, consider the need for leadership distributed among a flatter, more nimble organization that is interconnected, flexible, and constantly adapting. As social system eras have changed over the last 120 years, so have our corresponding leadership theories and definitions. That begs the question of how leaders will use the collective power and influence of the group to make decisions, in lieu of decisions made by individuals vested with authority.

Perhaps our target of opportunity is to stop defining "leadership" as it has been done over the last century and to start to consider its outcome. Hence, the fourth part of this chapter introduces the notion that while the leader and leadership are important, what may be more important is how leadership is shared at different levels of the organization and that the outcome and process are distinct. This discussion addresses a question I have asked well over 300 federal executive branch civil servants at all levels of the organization and in different government departments and agencies: *What kind of leader and leadership skills and traits do we need now and into the future?*

The Government Context

The Changing Paradigms of Government

Bureaucracy is not a "bad word"; in fact, we need it, and we need leaders who can work in a bureaucracy and know how to influence others with or without formal authority. Max Weber provided the historical roots of bureaucracy in his treatise, *Ideal Bureaucracy:*

> It is superior to any other form in precision, in stability, in the stringency of its discipline and in its reliability. It thus makes possible a particularly high degree of results for the heads of the organization and for those acting in relation to it. ... The primary source of the superiority of bureaucratic administration lies in the role of technical knowledge.
>
> (As cited in Matteson & Ivancevich, 1993)

Hence, bureaucratic administration is fundamentally control on the basis of knowledge. Administration and management are rational as the organizational systems are large, and the work must be divided "because the same man cannot be at two places at the same time; because the range of knowledge and skill is so great that a man cannot within his lifespan know more than a small fraction of it" (Gulick & Urwick, 1993/1937, p. 3).

Consequently, in large bureaucracies, we need organization, a way to coordinate the central purpose—the objective of the work—into a reality through the consolidated efforts of the many specialists. All of the efforts must be coordinated efficiently and effectively. Organizations are viewed as the vehicle to accomplish the goals and objectives of the policies and programs, which make up the bureaucracy. One definition of the organization is:

> [A] system of structural interpersonal relations. ... Individuals are differentiated in terms of authority, status, and role with the result that personal interaction is prescribed. ... Anticipated reactions tend to occur while ambiguity and spontaneity are decreased.
>
> (Presthus, 1958, p. 50)

The question is "who controls all of the tasks in the organization and how these tasks are led and decisions made in an evolving world with external and internal pressures, globalization, matrixed organizations, cultural expectations, different mindsets and paradigms, and the speed of information." Part of the answer lies in how the changing paradigm of public administration and governance have evolved through time.

Public Administration

Public administration involves almost every facet of American life and embodies the economic, political, social, managerial, legal, medical, and financial fields. The skills encompass all levels of educational development, from scientist to layman. Public administrators are conceptualized as managers, political appointees, civil servants, legal and regulatory overseers, enforcers, policy writers, and every day "bureaucrats." We know who they are, but what is public administration? Public administration is the action part of the three branches of government responsible for implementing the business functions of statues, rules, and regulations (as cited in Rosenbloom, Kravchuk, & Clerkin, 2009, p. 4).

Rosenbloom et al. (2009) then defined public administration as "the use of managerial, political, and legal theories, practices, and processes to fulfill legislative, executive, and judicial mandates for the provision of governmental regulatory and service functions" (p. 5). These and other definitions of public administration show the complexity of defining the term. There have been three distinct approaches to public administration: (a) a managerial approach, that it is the purview of the executive branch to implement the law; (b) the political approach, with a focus on legislative policy making; and (c) the legal approach, involving a "focus on the government's adjudicatory function, commitment to maintaining constitutional rights—the blessings of liberty and the rule of law" (Rosenbloom et al., 2009, p. 15).

How we view public administration and public administrators is becoming bifurcated. The traditional view is the role of oversight. Woodrow Wilson wrote, "It is the object of administrative study to discover, first, what government can properly and successfully do, and, secondly, how it can do these proper things with the utmost possible efficiency and at the least possible cost either of money or of energy" (as cited in Rosenbloom et al., 2009, p. 16).

Therefore, public administration was viewed as a field of business to maximize efficiency, effectiveness, and service to the public and economy. Then came the rise of Frederick Taylor's scientific management, which promoted the idea that efficiency and effectiveness in products and services could be produced by a set of intractable procedures, processes, and specialization. The organizational structure to achieve efficiency included bureaucracy to maximize output; the specialization of skills; hierarchy to manage and integrate specific work products; and linear, rational input and output of products. The decision making of the government is rooted in the paradigms of efficiency where they started. Max Weber believed that efficiency was best achieved by a division of labor with tasks and duties for each level, a chain of command or hierarchy with a decision maker and specialized skills.

Neoliberalism in public administration considers government bureaucracy as a broken system of outdated formalized processes that stop innovation and creativity. It has taken areas of focus from mainstream private business, focusing on results, customers, a needs orientation, employee empowerment, working across boundaries, and a culture of innovation, to name a few (Larbi, 1999).

The New Public Management Approach

If Weber were to appear today, he would probably not recognize some of the public administration entities in our government. The functionally uniform, hierarchical organizations overseen by strong leaders have given way to public managers who at times coordinate through multilevel stakeholders, both internal and external to the government, to provide governance, not government (Hjern & Porter, 1981).

New Public Management (NPM) represents a shift from traditional public administration to public management. This shift occurred as public service entities were faced with internal and external challenges at the local, national, and global level related to economics, social expectations, politics, and technology, as well as neoliberal ideas of less government resulting in "right sizing," "the need for agility," "structural reorganizations," "decentralization," and "reform" (Ferlie, Pettigrew, Ashburner, & Fitzgerald, 1996; Hood, 1991). The view is that the free market with competition for services is the lens society should be looking through to determine the governance of public administration, given the increasing debts of many departments and the government as whole, the need to counteract the Keynesian welfare state, and the need for responsiveness to customers and responsive leadership.

Public choice theory, as Jordan (1995) argued, holds that the reward system in the public sector does not promote effective performance, and bureaucrats have no incentives to control costs, which leads to waste. At the same time, there have been changes in the political landscape and the explosion of information technology, which has made access to information easier, decision making easier and faster, and feedback loops more readily available (Greer, 1994).

Public choice theory promotes accountability of good governance through improved budgeting, accounting, and rooting out inefficiencies. As NPM has evolved, "its central feature is the attempt to introduce or simulate, within those sections of public services that are not privatized, the performance incentives and the disciplines that exist in a market environment" (Pollitt, 1993, p. 13). Philosophically, NPM is seen as public service managerial governance through which the benefits of the private sector are imported (Ferlie et al., 1996, p. 9; Hood, 1991, 1995).

The traditional model of organization, the delivery of public services and decision making, based on the longstanding philosophies of bureaucratic hierarchy, planning, centralization, direct control, and self-sufficiency, is undergoing a paradigm shift to market-based public service management (Flynn, 1993; Stewart & Walsh, 1992; Walsh, 1995), or to a system of looking at the totality of the market as an enterprise culture (Mascarenhas, 1993).

As Dixon, Kouzmin, and Korac-Kakabadse (1998, p. 170) argued, "The managerialist approach appears to seek to shift public agencies from an allegiance of the bureaucratic (hierarchy and control) paradigm to an acceptance of a post-bureaucratic (innovation and support) paradigm." The assumption is that the private market can expose public service to the benefits of efficiency and effectiveness in response to market pressures (Metcalfe & Richards, 1990, p. 155; see also Barzalay, 1992; Odom, Boxx, & Dunn, 1990).

NPM is conceptualized as a future of interconnected, fast-moving, and responsive service-provider organizations kept lean by the pressures of market competition. These organizations would develop flatter internal structures (i.e., fewer layers) and devolve operational authority to frontline managers with the skills and capacity to make decisions, network with others, be flexible, and adapt to market conditions. With fewer, more flexible staff members, many services would be contracted as performance related and assume that the market, not in-house staff, knew better. Staff would be more generalist to reflect the market, and there would be fewer specialists in lieu of cost-effective mixes of staff.

The supporters of NPM view the existing Weberian bureaucratic paradigm as moribund, slow moving, and rule bound resulting in inefficient, unresponsive, and costly services to their users. The public service bureaucracy providers, such as health care, education, and public housing, are powerful, autonomous professions that defend their interests and, importantly, are not held accountable for the inefficiencies (Day & Klein, 1987; Pollitt, 1993).

This author would contend that both models are needed and both are right. Modern theories reflect the changes from the past in social systems and theories and definitions of leadership, whether they be in private or public practice. To understand what leadership is in public administration is to understand the changing concept of leadership in a changing social system. These have moved in tandem with one another throughout four distinct eras over the last 120 years or so.

Leaders and Managers in the Public Sector

The study of leadership is well over a hundred years old, and we believe the success and failure of organizations of all sizes has been ascribed to leadership. Its definition has ranged from being the unitary "boss" to being an aggregator of ideas, from having specific elements to having a more holistic meaning. To identify how public administrators should influence the inner workings of the federal government, finish this sentence, "Leadership is…"

In fact, the number of differing interpretations led Roger Stogdill (1974) to write, "There are as many definitions of leadership as there are persons who have attempted to define the concept" (p. 259). Leadership is complex and influenced by the dimensions of power, authority, context, individual and group followership, goals, and so forth. We seem to know what it means when we experience it or don't experience it. Fleishman, Mumford, Zaccaro, Levin, Korotkin, & Hein (1991) identified more than 60 ways to classify leadership, including by traits, behaviors, influence, relationships to individuals and groups, skills, and whether it is hierarchical or emergent, to name a few. Similarly, Yukl (2010) identified 17 separate authors from 1953 to 2002 who have provided leadership behavioral taxonomies, each with 2 to 14 different categories.

This bewildering number of categories ensures no one common definition of leadership. Leaders in public administration, like those in the private sector, have an important impact on our social institutions and even our personal lives. Leadership is highly sought after, a commodity of sorts, a demonstrated skill as identified by the U.S. Office of Personnel Management's 28 core competencies. Amazon.com lists no less than 189,000 books on the topic of leadership. The costs for training and development on leadership topics range in the billions of dollars within the government.

Leadership is subjective because it is defined by theorists based on their assumptions, outcomes, and focus areas. It has been conceptualized as a group process with the leader being at the center of the group activity; as dependent on personality, with the idea that leaders have traits and characteristics that enable them to influence others; as behaviors that inspire others to act; as a power relationship between followers and leaders, who can effect change through power; as a transformational process where leaders and followers support and develop in unison; as a transactional process of the leader exchanging rights and benefits with followers; and as dependent on the individual leader's skills and knowledge (Bass, 1990, pp. 11–20). In addition, leadership has changed with time. Bennis and Nanus (1985, p. 4) stated, "Multiple interpretations of leadership exist, each providing a sliver of insight but each remaining an incomplete and wholly inadequate explanation."

Hence, it is important to recognize as a public manager the different types of leadership, the strengths and shortcomings of each, the competencies needed to excel, and the characteristics of leadership most needed now in our public institutions. It is also important to grasp that public administration is the work of both leadership and management; involves the use of different forms of power; employs personality traits as well as learned skills; has different styles of leadership, such as transactional and leader-member exchange as well as transformational; and embodies both process and an outcome.

Leadership Defined

For the purpose of this chapter, leadership is defined as "the process of influencing others to understand and agree about what needs to be done and how to do it, and the process of facilitating individual and collective efforts to accomplish shared objectives" (Yukl, 2010, p. 8). This definition includes accomplishing meaningful tasks but is not limited to one person within the organization. Leaders and followers are engaged in a mutual process. Peter Northouse (2010) defined leadership as a process that occurs between leaders and followers, involves cooperation and mutual influence between leaders and followers, and is directed toward a common goal.

Both Yukl's definition and Northouse's definition are important in public administration because they conceptualize leadership as moving from individual to collaborative and from *transactional leadership*, that is, an exchange between the leader and follower through a set of requirements, rewards, conditions, etc., to *transformational leadership,* which engages followers to create conditions that raise the level of motivation and morality, improve those around them, and change organizational culture (Avolio, 1999; Burns, 1978; Schein, 1992). In both definitions, relationships, influence, and a common goal are used to mobilize people, there is no single best style, and input and different perspectives are needed to meet the goals.

Leadership is a process. Process infers that both leaders and followers are affected in an interactive, reciprocal relationship that involves influence, collaboration, and engagement, and this can happen at any level in an organization. Influence is how the leaders affect followers or have a compelling force on the actions, behaviors, or opinions of others. Collaboration is the process in which two or more people work together to realize a shared goal, and engagement is getting others involved.

Leadership occurs in groups and involves individuals influencing others in the group. Leadership involves common goals of the leader and follower; they have a mutual purpose. Mutuality decreases the possibility of leaders acting in ways followers believe to be unethical. Mutuality increases the possibility that leaders and followers will work together (Rost, 1991). Social influence, collaboration, and engagement can occur at any level of the organization, whether horizontally or vertically, with the senior team or the implementers. Implicit in the process is that organizational leadership is "the influential increment over and above mechanical compliance with the routine directives of the organization" (Katz & Kahn, 1978, p. 528).

The Difference Between Leadership and Management

Much has been written on distinguishing management from leadership. In many ways, the two complement each other. Both leaders and managers influence others, work with others, and create organizational success. There is much that also distinguishes them from each other.

Leadership can be traced back to antiquity, while management is a function of the 20th century and the rise of the industrial revolution. Management was created to complement bureaucracies to reduce chaos and bring order. The primary functions of management, according to Fayol (1949), are planning, organizing, staffing, and controlling. Thematically, management is about bringing order and consistency to the organization to meet objectives and be effective.

In contrast, leadership is about creating vision, producing change and movement that align the organization's resources and people, and motivating individuals and inspiring them to do more than they believe they are capable of, while creating a deep sense of commitment to the organization by harnessing their enthusiasm and collective intelligence (Bennis & Nanus, 1985; Kotter, 1990). These differences are summarized in Table 4.1.

Table 4.1 Elements of Management and Leadership

Management	*Leadership*
Planning and budgeting • Establishing agendas • Planning needed resources • Creating schedules and timelines	Establishing direction • Creating the vision • Setting the course
Organizing and staffing • Establishing roles and responsibilities • Developing rules • Providing training • Monitoring staff abilities	Ensuring alignment • Developing buy-in for goals • Gaining commitment • Configuring for optimum performance • Optimizing resources
Controlling, problem solving, executing • Identifying milestones • Creating solutions	Motivating • Inspiring others • Sharing ownership • Empowering others • Connecting to and attending to others' needs

Mintzberg (1973) asserted that leaders are in short supply and that many executives are actually managers. To lead means to influence and to manage means to accomplish activities and routines. Bennis and Nanus (1985) said, "Managers are people who do things right and leaders are people who do the right things" (p. 221). Rost (1991) offered that leadership is multidirectional-influence relationships to develop mutual purposes, whereas management is unilateral-authority relationships to coordinate activities to accomplish a task. Leaders create the change; managers implement the change. Sanders (1998) argued that leadership is essential in the transformation of the government. Similarly, Behn (1998) opined that leadership in the way of initiative, motivation, and inspiring others is needed now in the government to solve its deficiencies and to craft a path forward into tomorrow.

Yet, public administrators have both leadership and management functions. If the organization has strong leadership without management, it is possible that work may be not be directed and results oriented, as managers are needed to budget, plan, organize, and execute. Likewise, if there is management without leadership, work may not be innovative and may lack vision. Public administrators cannot focus on creating organizational change without being able to focus on organizational alignment. Likewise, they cannot focus on managerial tasks of budgeting and project management without being able to empower, motivate, and create a sense of direction.

The focus of this chapter is on the organizational member who supervises employees, focuses on development and implementation of policies, manages projects, and conducts the day-to-day business in public institutions. This work occurs in different settings, and context is important to determining the style and competencies of leadership needed at the time. In each case, leadership at all levels embodies core characteristics of being able to set direction, align resources, and create commitment. This is achieved either through formal roles and power vested in the position or through informal roles where direction, alignment, and commitment are achieved through influence, expertise, or referential position.

Leadership and Power

Influence is at the root of leadership. Effective leaders influence others to carry out requests, innovate, and implement decisions. At all levels in public organizations, the effectiveness of civil servants depends on being able to influence others vertically and horizontally.

The movement from the rational reductionist approach to a focus on operational efficiency and effectiveness through social systems has led to an interest in the creation, use, and distribution of power as distinct from authority. Power, as defined by Buckley (1967), is "control or influence over the actions of others to promote one's goals without their consent, against their will or without their knowledge or understanding." Authority is related to the rights, prerogatives, duties, and obligations associated with a particular position (Yukl, 2010).

The scope of authority differs in organizations and can be dependent on the amount of influence needed to accomplish a task (Barnard, 1952). Buckley (1967) defined authority as "the direction or control of the behavior of others for the promotion of collective goals, based on some ascertainable form of knowledge consent" (p. 186). It is the leader's right to make particular types of decisions, such as work rules and assignments, that affect a follower.

The most widely cited work on the different types of power is the taxonomy of French and Raven (1959), which includes five types of power coming from dyadic relationships of personal or positional basis (Table 4.2). Positional power

Table 4.2 The Power Taxonomy of French and Raven (1959)

Positional power		*Personal power*	
Type	*Description*	*Type*	*Description*
Legitimate	Targets are influenced because they believe the person (agent) has the right to make the request and therefore they have an obligation to comply.	Referent	Targets are influenced by their liking and identifying with the Agent and may also want to gain approval from the Agent.
Reward	Targets are influenced because they believe the Agent controls and can administer rewards.	Expert	Targets are influenced by the Agent's specialized knowledge.
Coercive	Targets are influenced because they believe the Agent has the capacity to dispense penalties or punishment.		

is the power derived from rank, status, or more formal positions. Personal power is the ability to influence others because of being seen as likeable, a role model, or highly knowledgeable, such as a subject matter expert.

Two additional forms of positional power have entered the mainstream literature to reflect the evolution of social systems: informational power and ecological power. Informational power is power over the control of information that one acquires and distributes to others. Those that have information can interpret the information for others and hence influence them (Mintzberg, 1983; Pettigrew, 1972). This power is especially important now, as social systems are highly networked and this power has to be cultivated (Kotter, 1982).

Ecological power is the control over physical aspects, technological aspects, and the organization of work. It can be thought of as social engineering or cultural engineering. The culture of an organization consists of implicit and explicit values that are manifested in sanctioned behaviors (Schein, 1992). By establishing strong norms, individuals in positional authority can influence the attitudes and behaviors of others.

The conceptualization of bureaucracy and scientific management laid power in the hands of the authority (Taylor, 1911; Weber, 1930). Today, the ability to have influence in the working halls of public administration also depends on building coalitions and being evaluated as one able to reciprocate influence to others. This has been a pivotal point in the changing conceptualizations of power and authority and is embedded in the definitions of leadership and the descriptions of the social system.

Major Leadership Theories

The concept of "leadership" is a large and unwieldy social complex given the multiplicity of leadership scenarios, types of followers, and work to be done. We can, however, begin to understand leadership in the hallways of public administration by first understanding the evolution of leadership over the past century. Through the lens of the social system, we see the evolution of the leader and of leadership practice based on what was needed then and what is needed now (Table 4.3). This section reviews the major leadership theories beginning with the traditional "great man" theory, which stipulates that leaders are born and not made, and ending with a more holistic view of leadership as emergent, shared, and collaborative.

Period 1: Great Man Theory, Classical Management Approach, and Traits, 1890s–1930s/1940s

The study of management theory and leadership started around the turn of the 20th century with the understanding of the "great man" theories best put forth by historian Thomas Carlyle, who said in 1910, "The history of the world is but the biography of great men." A reductionary approach, this statement conceptualizes leadership as an innate trait residing in one hierarchical person. Galton in 1871

Table 4.3 Major Theories of Leadership from the 1890s to the Present

Period	*Social system characterization*	*Leadership*
1 Great man theories and classic management traits (1890s–1940)	Social arrangements are characterized in formal and recurring processes that involve individual and groups. The efficiency of the system is dependent on control, design, administration, and human factors (Fayol, 1949; Gantt, 1919; Taylor, 1911; Weber, 1930).	Leadership is "the relation between an individual [manager] and the group built around some common interest and behaving in a manner directed or determined by him" (Schmidt, 1933, p. 282).
2 The leader-centered (person-role) approach: The skills, style, situational, and contingency approach (1940s–1960s/ 1970s)	Social systems are made up of relationships, with groups of individuals focused on a problem. Fundamental to the social system are the elements that determine relationships around goal attainment, integration, and maintaining the system (Parsons, 1951; Parsons & Shils, 1952). A system is open to information, capable of feedback, and has interlocking chains of causation that produce goal-seeking and self-controlling behavior (Bertalanffy, 1968; Burrell & Morgan, 1979; Wiener, 1954).	Leadership "is the result of an ability to persuade or direct men, apart from the prestige of power that comes from office or other external circumstances" (Reuter, 1941, p. 133). Leadership is "acts by persons which influence other persons' shared direction" (Seeman, 1960, p. 127). The essence of leadership is the "influential increment of and above mechanical compliance with the routine directives of the organization" (Katz & Kahn, 1966, p. 528).
3 Learning systems, interaction, and complex systems (1970–2000)	Social systems are produced relationships between actors and collectives where integration is produced through reciprocity. The structure of the system is to influence action and be influenced by the action to change (Giddens, 1979, p. 66). Society is composed of a social system that is made and remade through routine practices (Habermas, 1984).	Leadership is exercised when "persons with certain motives and purposes mobilize in competition or conflict with others … as to arouse, engage and satisfy the motives of followers in order to realize goals mutually held by both leaders and followers" (Burns, 1978, p. 18).

Period	*Social system characterization*	*Leadership*
	Complex systems ask "how changes in the agent's decisions, rules, the interconnectedness among peers … produce different aggregate outcomes" (Anderson, 1999, p. 220).	Leadership is "pulling rather than pushing; inspiring rather than ordering; creating achievable though challenging expectations and rewarding progress …; by enabling people to use their own initiative and experience" (Bennis & Nanus, 1985, p. 225). Leadership is the leaders, "as the designer of living systems … strategic thinkers … teachers … responsible for building organizations where people continually expand their capacities to understand complexity, clarify vision and improve shared mental models, that is, they are responsible for [organizational] learning" (Senge, 1990, p. 340).
4 Beyond definitions of process to outcomes (2000s)	Social systems are highly interactive and adaptive to the feedback loops.	Conceptualized as an output of coordinated direction, that is, a shared common vision, alignment of resources to meet the common vision, and commitment of leaders at all levels taking ownership for the outcome and their own development. (Van Velsor et al., 2010)

Source: Adapted from Schwandt & Salzba (2007).

believed that man was born with natural abilities that are derived by inheritance; similar to what was found organically and naturally in the world.

A number of later authors also identified traits of effective leadership, including being commanding and controlling, intelligence, alertness, insight, masculinity, achievement, persistence, dominance, drive, integrity, motivation, openness, and social intelligence, to name a few (Bass, 1990, p. 75). This discourse positioned the leader as apart from and directing the behaviors of the group. The leadership studies of the early 1900s then focused on finding the traits that made them great. The underlying assumption was that a list of traits would make them successful by guiding their behavior. Classical management was looking for a universal prescript of practices, and leadership looked for a unifying potpourri of traits.

Simultaneously, this was a time characterized by movement from rural areas to urban centers, the need for the control of production, a growing factory worker workforce, and a growing economy. A systems approach identified elements of people, material, time, and control with social engineers, such as Frederick Taylor, applying linear cause-and-effect models so management could control the workflow and workforce. Scientific management became the model for efficiency and effectiveness, in contrast with the predecessor cottage industries that were poorly organized. Taylor (1911), Gantt (1919), and Gilbreth (1917) advocated analytical tools to derive management practices by looking at efficient practices to organizing and coordinating people and machines. These were the decision makers with influence vested in the power of the position.

Among the common leadership definitions of the time was that of Moore (1927, p. 134), "the ability to impress the will of the leader on those led and induce obedience, respect, loyalty, and cooperation." Bundel (1939) posited leadership as "the art of inducing others to do what you want them to do." Leadership was characterized by the control and centralization of power, not necessarily the ethics of doing what was right for all. This led Bogardus (1934) to opine that leadership is "the interaction between specific traits of one person and the other traits of the many, in such a way that the course of action of the many is changed by the one" (p. 3).

Period 2: The Leader-Centered (Person-Role) Approach: The Skills, Style, Situational, and Contingency Approach (1940s–1960s/1970s)

By the 1930s, trait theory was still strong, although questions were starting to be raised. Based on evidence of how leadership traits led to success in some and not in others given the situation and the function, the idea was formed that it took learned knowledge and skills to effectively lead. Cowley (1928) asked, "Is there a difference between leadership in a particular situation and the ability to be a leader in several or any situation?" (p. 149). Sociologists entered the discussion of leadership, and group dynamics became a lens to look through when addressing leadership in public administration. The idea of leadership by rank was replaced with new paradigms and definitions. One such definition was that of Reuter (1941): "Leadership is the result of an ability to persuade or direct men, apart from the prestige or power that comes from office or external circumstances" (p. 133).

Organizations still needed structure to control the flow of information and to respond to both external market stakeholder forces and the relationships between followers and leaders. However, leadership was moving away from the reductionary period of scientific methods and Taylorism toward subjective judgment, the recognition of open systems (Katz & Kahn, 1966), and cybernetics or feedback loops to include social communication so systems or organizations could retain a sense of homeostasis (Wiener, 1954). "For all these forms of behavior … we must have central decision organs which determine what the machine is to do next on the basis of information fed back to it, which stores by means analogous to the memory of a living organism" (Wiener, 1954, p. 33).

Clearly, different contexts required different levels of engagement, skills, and traits, and the group itself needed to be a moderating factor in the leader's style. Simplistic cause-and-effect models of scientific management were no longer adequate to improve productivity. The major shift from trait to leadership behaviors—what leaders do in lieu of who they are—led to research that is still evident in today's never-ending quest to define leadership. The Hawthorne studies of Elton Mayo (1946) moved the pendulum from scientific methods to a model that placed relationships and process in equilibrium; this new model balanced the system's influence on the people with the people's influence on the system. The administration and management of the organizational entity became a system involving not just workers and the work, but the roles of the workers and the interaction of the workers and management in the hierarchy of the work (Weber, 1930). This shift emphasized that an organization needed the balance of rational control processes imposed on workers as much as it needed the mutual action of the people in social roles who created norms and had choice, and this was, in part, dependent on the leader's abilities.

Hence, the evolution of leadership moved beyond what is inherent in the person to the social process of the leader and those being led, the followers, in context. The *Encyclopedia of Social Sciences* from the 1930s asserted that "leadership appears only where a group follows an individual from free choice and not under command or coercion, and secondly, not in response to blind drives, but on positive or more or less rational grounds" (Schmidt, 1933, p. 282).

The skills approach to leadership, while still leader-centered, shifted the thinking from innate personality characteristics to skills and abilities that can be learned. Hence, the recognition of the importance of how traits, skills, knowledge, groups, and context influenced followers to interact with each other to achieve goals led researchers such as Tead (1935) to write that leadership is "the ability to influence people to cooperate toward some goal, which they find to be desirable" (p. 20). Katz's (1955) article attested that skills transcend traits; leaders needed to develop skills; and the three necessary skills were technical, human, and conceptual. Technical skills were those related to the work. Human skills were people skills that allowed the leader to work with others. Conceptual skills were the ability to work with ideas. Several leadership definitions reflected the skills approach, including that of Ralph Stogdill who asserted that leadership is a process of influencing a group toward goal setting and achievement (1948, 1974).

Another major distinction from the prior era was the acknowledgment of the open system referred to by Katz and Kahn (1966). The open system recognized the growing complexity of leadership, with the importance of relationships and the influence of collective norms, control, communication, and individual cognitive and emotional patterns (Parsons & Shils, 1952). The social discourse of leadership moved beyond the focus on work processes alone to include social concerns of power and authority (March & Simon, 1958; Simon, 1947), growing commitment and participation of followers, the understanding of personalities in the workplace (McClelland, 1961), and leadership styles and their effects on followers (Blake & Mouton, 1964; Fiedler, 1964). Gibb (1954) stressed that an understanding of leadership required an understanding of the characteristics of leaders in groups; "leadership is what leaders do in groups" (p. 882). Leaders achieved rank not because of birthright traits or position, but because they could develop effective relationships with followers through which organizations performed and met goals.

The leader was now conceptualized as *part of* the working group, not *apart from* the working group. This concept in public administration could be conveyed that: (a) "any member of a group may be a leader in the sense that he may take action which serves group functions" and (b) a given function by different people in a group may be served by many different behaviors (Cartwright & Zander, 1953). In essence, anyone in the group could take on the functions of leadership without having to be the formal, hierarchical leader.

The Ohio State leadership studies established that behavior can explain leadership (Fleishman, 1953) and assessed leadership success based on the action of the leader toward the individual and the group by two independent behaviors: initiating structures and consideration. Initiating structure is the degree to which a leader defines and structures his or her role and that of the group toward achieving a goal. Consideration is the degree to which a leader acts friendly toward direct reports. The University of Michigan was also exploring leadership from the perspective of leadership behaviors, identifying two constructs: employee orientation and production orientation. Employee orientation is similar to consideration and includes leaders taking an interest in the followers, valuing them as individuals, valuing their feedback, and giving them attention. The production orientation, which is similar to initiating structure, consists of behaviors for getting the work done and viewing workers as resources.

The best-known model for the two constructs is known as the managerial grid (Blake & Mouton, 1964), which explains how leaders help organizations reach their goals through concern for production and concern for employees. The manager takes a self-assessment and plots his or her scores on a grid from 1 to 9 on two axes, with the horizontal axis representing concern for results or the task and the vertical axis representing concern for the employee. From there, managers can determine where they might need to improve.

These two constructs, initiating structure and consideration, led to research on maintaining the social system of organizations. Berrien (1961) argued that a leader's role was to satisfy group needs so as to achieve organizational performance. In addition to the leader's behavior, other factors were researched, such as the conditions that influence how leaders behave.

Further development of the behavioral theory recognized that the managers' "style" of being either task or relationship focused needed to include the situation. Effective leaders altered their style based on the situation; both directive and supportive behaviors were needed depending on the changing needs of the follower. Situational leadership theory postulated that task and relationship behaviors of the leader are best moderated by the followers' development style and willingness to perform a task (Hersey & Blanchard, 1977). Thus, based on the followers' skill, will, and maturity level, leaders adapt to either a directing, coaching, supporting, or delegating style. Both the style and situational approaches remain leader centric and prescriptive.

Fiedler's (1964, 1967) contingency theory represented a shift to focus on the leader operating within the situation. This is a leader-match theory, which means that the effectiveness of the leader is contingent on matching the leader's style to the context. The leadership styles are described as task motivated, which is concerned with reaching the goal, or relationship motivated, which is concerned with developing close interpersonal relationships. The situation is characterized by the leader-member relations, such as group atmosphere, degree of confidence, and loyalty that followers feel toward the leader; task structure, which relates to the clarity of task requirements and follower response to high or low degrees of structure; and position power, which is the amount of authority a leader has to punish or reward followers, indicative of legitimate power.

In summary, this era described social systems as needing feedback and being open to external forces. In this era, leadership was beginning to be explained as both an adaptation to the external environment and a reaction to internal variables. Consequently, leadership theories and definitions advanced to incorporate behaviors that recognized followers as part of the open system and included their needs and impact on the organizational climate and culture (Hoy & Miskel, 2007).

Period 3: Learning Systems, Interaction, and Complex Systems, 1970–2000

This period saw the augmentation of functionalism with an emphasis on individual and collective interpretation of the social system that acted as a force to maintain and/or change the structure through information control, decision making, strategic thinking, and organizational learning (Schwandt & Szabla, 2007). Meaning became interpretive in the last part of the century, and sensemaking within an organization relied on collective values supported by a culture (Schein, 1992; Weick & Roberts, 1993).

In this era, public administration entities as social systems incorporated self-generation or the understanding that bureaucratic structures are emergent at the local operating level based on shared, ongoing social interactions. The view of administrative bureaucracies imposing structure on social interactions and people was rejected in favor of seeing people (employees) as active incubators of knowledge. Their behavior may be constrained, though not determined (Baert, 1998). Bureaucracies inherently create structures for information control.

Giddens's (1979) structuration theory for organizations recognizes the dual nature of social structures as both guiding the action of those within it and giving power to them to change the structure and the interactions. Hence, social systems within the formal bureaucracies become self-sustaining and pliable through interaction and communication of work products to produce emergent ideas and be self-organizing. This structure requires a different leadership style than formal command and control; it recognizes leadership as having processes across multiple layers and a shared outcome. Second, the organization not only focuses on production; it is equally driven by creating organizational knowledge through systems learning (Senge, 1994) and linking the leader and follower to each other and to the organizational purpose.

To create emergent knowledge, the employees within the system have to interact, share information, and have the operational flexibility to experiment across levels, receive feedback, and see themselves as part of the organization's purpose and values. The nature of exploration and exploitation for the sake of emergent knowledge changes how leadership is viewed. It also leads one to recognize the importance of creating cultural conditions where the social systems can generate and regenerate as an open system (Archer, 1988; Schein, 1992; Senge, 1994).

Leadership theories morphed with the interaction of the social systems within public administration entities, and new theories emerged about public- and private-sector leadership. Until this time, leadership had been defined from the viewpoint of the leader (trait, skills, style theories) or the follower and context (situational, contingency theories). These definitions embodied what the leader did to the follower, implying that followers were a collective.

Building on social exchange theory, leadership began to be defined and conceptualized with leaders as resources in dyadic relations, either directly or indirectly, by promoting networks, helping achieve organizational goals, and retaining their own legitimacy. Group members, at all levels of the organization, needed to experience achievement for leaders to be "leaders." Leadership became known as a process, not a person (Hollandeer & Julian, 1978) that involves ongoing work between leaders and followers. To that end, followers had some power, given how the interaction took place with the leader and the degree to which the leader helped them become successful.

House's (1971) path-goal theory posited that leaders' behavior is influenced by the characteristics of the task, the environment, and the subordinates. Building on and contrasting with situational leadership, which suggests that leadership adapts to the will and skill of the employee, and with contingency theory, which emphasizes matching a leader's style to the specific situational variables, path-goal theory has as its theoretical underpinning both social exchange theory and expectancy theory. Kracke (1979), an anthropologist, supported the idea that leadership is key in developing social structures and that leadership as a social phenomenon finds its genesis in the deeper motives of leaders and followers, "the interplay of personalities" (p. 252).

Expectancy theory suggests that employees are motivated if they believe they can do the job, their efforts will result in a good outcome, and they will be rewarded for their efforts. The theory's goal is to enhance the performance and satisfaction of the employee by focusing on the employee's motivation, and doing so requires interaction and linking the employee and leader to the organization. It is the leader's responsibility to align worker and organizational goals and then to ensure that the employees' path to goal attainment is clear.

In essence, leadership is identifying the right behaviors (directive, supportive, participative, or achievement oriented) to motivate the employee based on his or her characteristics (need for affiliation, preference for structure, desire for control, and self-perceived level of task ability) and the task characteristics (ambiguous, complex, repetitive, structured, or unstructured). Hence, a supportive leadership behavior may be needed when a subordinate needs affiliation and the task is unchallenging. A participative leadership style may be needed when the subordinate has an external locus of control and a need for clarity when the task is unstructured. It is important to note that leadership is not always needed. The leader supplies what is needed or missing at that time. For highly trained, motivated followers, little "leadership" is needed, in contrast to followers that need more.

Leader-member exchange conceptualized leadership as a process, an interaction that occurs between the leader, the follower, and the collective as dyads. It is an ongoing relationship between leaders and members of the group as they negotiate and exchange mutual perceptions, influences, and types and amount of work. Leaders' relationship to the group is viewed as a long-term reciprocal interaction of leaders with followers and followers with followers, and the quality of these exchanges leads to higher performance at the individual, group, and organizational levels (Graen & Uhl-Bien, 1995). The result is lower turnover, more positive performance evaluations, greater organizational commitment, better attitudes, higher degrees of interaction, and creative work as positive feelings for each other are nurtured.

Leader-member exchange is a descriptive approach to explain leaders' focus on the leader-member relationship and how that relationship leads to networks throughout an organization to create high-quality partnerships that solve organizational goals at multiple levels (Graen & Scandura, 1987). The theory does not focus on how to produce the high exchange relationships, which tend to be more fluid and based on equally shared trust, respect, and supportive behaviors.

The 1980s witnessed a marked difference in leadership theories, as notable writers such as Bennis and Nanus (1985) noted the lack of decisive leadership that could harness the power of the organization: "The problem with many organizations and especially the ones that are failing is that that they tend to be over managed and under-led" (p. 21). Similarly, Zaleznik (1977) penned an article for *Harvard Business Review* titled "Managers and Leaders: Are They Different?"

Interestingly, Weber (1904/1930), the German sociologist who wrote on personality-based leadership, had earlier used the word *charisma* to mean breathing fire back into life. Conger and Kanungo (1987) proposed a theory of charismatic leadership in which they contend that charisma is prominent when leaders dissatisfied with the status quo idealize a vision of a future that is different from the current state. These leaders are bold in their opposition to the status quo and "because of their emphasis on deficiencies in the system and their high levels of intolerance for them, charismatic leaders are always seen as organizational reformers or entrepreneurs" (Conger & Kanungo, 1998, p. 53). Charismatic leadership is based on the passion, confidence, and ability of the leader to persuade and sway other people. These same abilities are also traits of dysfunctional leaders.

The 1980s to 1990s was a time of globalization and matrixed organizations, requiring leaders to form alliances; respond quickly to internal and external feedback; adapt, use, and share information quickly; and expand their capabilities into different countries and cultures. Tichy and Devanna (1986) posited that the key to global competitiveness will be the ability of institutions to consciously transform. To transform means to change, and to change it must be a learning organization (Senge, 1994). Additionally, they stated that "increasing excellence is a condition not just for dominance but for survival," and their transformational theory, building on traits, behaviors, and interaction, was about "change, innovation and entrepreneurship" (Tichy & Devanna, 1986, p. xii).

Tichy and Devanna (1986) asserted that managers are common, but transformational leaders are critical to change and learning. Transformational leaders set out "to create new approaches, and imagine new areas to explore; they relate to people in more intuitive and empathetic ways, seek risk where opportunity and reward are high and project ideas into images to excite people" (p. xiii).

Burns (1978) identified the importance of transformational leadership and discussed the value of leaders and followers working together toward mutual benefit and organizational benefit. He defined a transformational leader as one who looks "for motives in followers, seeks to satisfy higher needs and engages the full person of the follower" (p. 4). This approach defines leadership as the ability to understand, adapt, and partner with followers to meet their needs and motives as well as those of the leader in concert with organizational goals.

Transformational leaders set a clear vision, are change agents and role models, empower others to meet higher standards, motivate them to create meaning with the organization's goals, and act in ways that engender two-way trust (Bass, 1985; Bennis & Nanus, 1985; Burns, 1978; Kouzes & Posner, 2002). Kouzes and Posner surveyed 1330 individuals and identified five leadership practices of transformational leaders: challenging the process; inspiring a shared vision for all; enabling others to act and to participate; modeling the way by being an example for others; and encouraging the heart.

Bass (1985) asserted that transformational leadership should be present across organizational levels if organizations are to be competitive. He identified four discrete elements of transformational leadership: inspirational motivation, communicating high standards and empowering others to the shared vision to achieve more than they would by themselves; intellectual stimulation, challenging status quo beliefs and encouraging followers to be creative and extend themselves throughout the organization; individualized consideration, acting as coaches by assisting followers to actualize their personal goals; and idealized influence, acting in ways that followers want to emulate, to include moral and ethical standards (Bass & Avolio, 1994).

Strategic thinking emerged as a leadership style that broadened behavior-based definitions to cognitive power. As Jacques and Clement (1991) explained, "Leadership is a process in which one person sets the purpose or direction of one or more persons and gets them to move along together with him or her and with each other in that direction with full competence and full commitment" (p. 4). The focus on strategy also happened as public administration organizations "right sized" in the 1990s and organizations saw themselves more as open systems interacting with the external and internal environment to create emergent change.

Peter Senge (1990) brought systems thinking, asserting that leaders at all levels should be able to see the organization as an interacting system both externally and internally. He conceptualized leaders as being "responsible for building organizations where people continually expand their capabilities to understand complexity, clarify vision, and improve shared mental models—that is they are responsible for learning" (p. 340). They were able to see the entire system and how decisions made in one part affected all parts.

Authentic leadership emerged to meet the needs of society and public administration entities on the heels of 9/11, Enron, Worldcom, and large-scale financial failures that affected not only the individual organizational workers but society as a whole. Chan (2005) conceptualized an authentic leadership view that focuses on the leader's self-knowledge, self-regulation, and self-concept. Leadership has also been viewed from a developmental perspective. Walumbwa, Avolio, Gardner, Wernsing, and Peterson (2008) identified authentic leadership as something that is nurtured rather than a fixed trait and that is grounded in the leader's positive psychological qualities and strong ethics.

From an interpersonal definition, authentic leadership is relational, that is, created by leaders and followers together (Eagly, 2005). From a practical approach, George (2003) identified five dimensions of authentic leaders: (a) leaders have passion around their purpose and ignite it in others; (b) they demonstrate their values through their behavior toward others; (c) they build relationships and connect with people by being available and trusting and engaging in high-level communication; (d) they have self-discipline, are focused, have energy, and hold themselves and others accountable; and (e) they have compassion and heart, that is, they are sensitive to other cultures, backgrounds, and living situations. This era can be summed up as interactive leadership and the growing knowledge that information was rapidly making centralized decision-making ineffective.

Period 4: Beyond Definitions of Process to Outputs: Networks and Emergence (Beyond 2000)

Toward the close of the decade, leadership again evolved due to the explosion of technology interfaced with the rise of differing societal norms of "ready-now" information and a highly networked society. The discourse recognized the necessary exchanges between leaders and followers as dynamic interactions in the context of the culture and structure, which now were malleable and permeable at all levels of the organization. Leadership became an organizational phenomenon as "leaders' roles overlapped, complemented each other and shifted from time to time and from person to person" (Barnes & Kriger, 1986, p. 16).

Hence, a more inclusive form of leadership was apparent, and it was recognized that all of those within organizations are leaders operating in an interacting open system that has structure but is not defined by the structure, which can change based on the interactions and needs of the organization. The fact that the organization needs all to be leaders gave rise to the concepts of *distributed leadership,* characterized by "conjoint agency" for the organization (Gronn, 2002), and *shared leadership,* defined as a "dynamic interactive influence process among individuals in groups for which the objective is to lead one another to the achievement of group or organizational goals" (Pearce & Conger, 2003, p. 1).

The Meaning of Leadership Evolution and the Public Administrator

In these eras with their intertwined social systems and leadership theories, there has been both movement away from and integration of the concepts of each preceding historical period. It was necessary to have reductionism and Taylorism to create efficiency in a growing production-era economy. Weber's précis on bureaucratic administration came to be the fundamental exercise of control on the basis of knowledge (Matteson & Ivancevich, 1993).

It can be argued that bureaucracy was developed to bring efficiency and coordination within a well-defined chain of command, a system of rules and procedures to ensure fairness with an operating system, a division of specialized labor, and the need for consistency. It is not fair to say that bureaucracy is dead, although there are threats to it, including the speed of technological change, the readily available sources of information, the diversity of experiences and occupations, the cultural expectations of those leading and following, the concept of power and authority, and globalization, to name a few. There has been a movement away from a mechanical focus on one leader's traits and actions as the mechanism for efficiency and decision making to a more holistic approach of collective meaning-making and to how decisions were being made.

In the second period, there was recognition of collective action and a flow of information to act as feedback to respond to a changing environment. From a leadership perspective, there was acknowledgment that traits alone do not make the leader and that leadership includes behavior and the integration of both leader's and followers' actions.

In the third period, the understanding of the social and leadership systems incorporated emergent change and knowledge vis-à-vis interacting networks. Organizational structure, while necessary for reporting chains, became permeable at the working level to respond to the complexity of events, recognizing that meaning making is crucial within the operating context. Hence, the leader's role expanded to include the behavioral theories of the second period and integrated systems thinking and complexity theory from the third period.

In the fourth period, the rapid pace of change, the integration of networks, and the emergence of ideas incorporated the notion that internal and external forces are constantly changing and fluid, with numerous touchpoints that make adaptation necessary. Consequently, the leadership process required everyone to be able to influence, collaborate, and engage, with an integrated leadership output at all levels of activity for a common direction, alignment, and commitment. Leadership was influenced by information flow, multiple levels of causation, and emergence. Thus, as summarized in Table 4.4, traits, behaviors, cognition, and interactions have been incorporated over time within a context of organizational values and culture.

Table 4.5 provides the context for these changes. Lastly, Figure 4.1 shows the existing understanding of leadership based on these eras.

Table 4.4 Overview of Leadership Theories and Social Systems from 1890 to the Present

Decade	*Leadership theory*	*Social systems*	*Social system era*
1890 1900 1910	• Great man theory	• Bureaucracy, • Scientific management • Henry Ford	*Period 1* The classical approach and traits
1920 1930	• Trait theory	• Human relations	
1940	• Skills theory		*Period 2* The leader-centered approach
1950	• Behavior theory	• Cybernetics • Open systems	
1960	• Style theory • Situation theory		
1970	• Contingency theory	• Self-regulating systems	
	• Path-goal theory • Servant leadership		*Period 3* Learning systems, interaction and complexity approach
1980 1990	• Leader-member exchange theory • Transaction theory • Transformational theory	• Interaction • Organizational learning	
2000	• Strategic theory • Cognitive theory • Authentic and ethical leadership	• Complexity	
2010 2020	• Shared theory • Distributed • Focus on direction, alignment and commitment	• Complexity • Networked • Shared	*Period 4* Beyond process to outputs: Networks and emergence

Table 4.5 Comparisons of Evolving Views of Leadership

	Classical approach person-role	*Leader-centered approach leader-follower*	*Leadership as process learning systems and interaction*	*New perspectives complexity, emergent approach*
Initiated	1900–1940s	1940s–1970/1980s	1970s/1980s–2000s	2000–now
Focus	Heroes	Liberation	Entrepreneurs	Complexity
Relationship	Leader	Leader-follower	Leader in organizational culture	Leader-follower culture context
Knowledge base/ paradigms	Natural sciences/rational objective	Behavioral and psychological/rational subjective		Sociological complexity/ interactive reciprocation
Political environment	Military industrial	Cold War/global dominance	Engagement social input	Terrorist networks
Social-economic environment	Industrial Revolution	Civil rights	Small business revolution matrix organizations	dot.com boom globalization
Societal changes	Prescriptive	Individual differences	Team dynamics	Networks
Technology	Industry/factory	Corporate culture	Globalization/computing	Performance computing and networks
Studies/theories	Trait, (Stogdill, 1974); skill (Katz, 1955; Mumford, et al., 2000)	Style (Blake & Mouton, 1964); contingency (Fiedler, 1964); situational (Hershey & Blanchard, 1984); Path-goal (House, 1971).	Leader-member exchange (Graen & Uhl-Bien, 1995); transactional and transformational (Avolio, 1999; Bass, 1985; Burns, 1978); shared leadership (Pearce & Conger, 2003; Yukl, 2010, Bennis, 1959); distributed leadership (Jacques & Clement, 1991); authentic (Bass & Avolio, 1994).	Emergent (Marion & Uhl-Bien, 2001); complexity (Hazy, 2006); adaptive leadership (Heifetz, Grashow, & Linsky (2009) direction, alignment, and commitment (Drath, McCauley, Paulus, Van Velsor 2008)

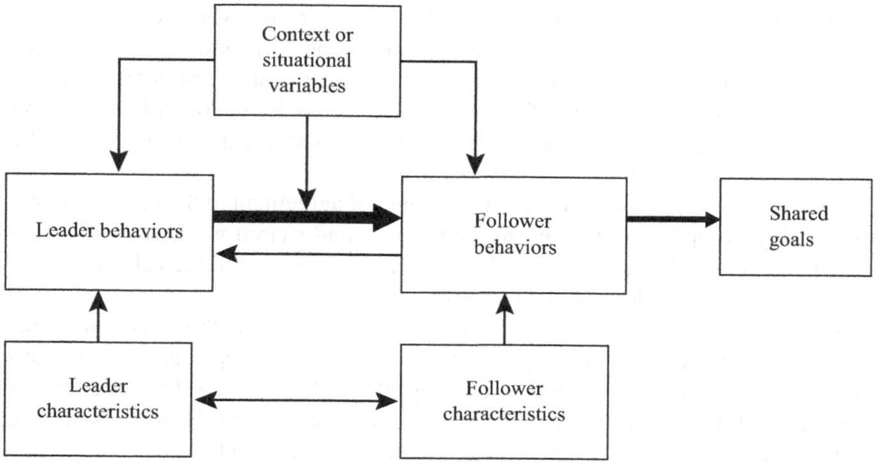

Figure 4.1 Framework of the Existing Definition of Leadership
Source: Reprinted with permission from Drath, McCauley, Palus, Van Veslor, O'Conner, & McGuire (2008).

Leadership as an Outcome, Not a Definition, for Public Administrators

Accepted in the vast array of leadership definitions are the unifying notions that leadership includes leaders, followers, goals, and context, and the interaction has to be understood as a process, as does the style of leadership. For the public administrator in a leadership role, one size does not fit all.

Leadership is experienced in numerous ways: the "leader" may be working remotely and connecting virtually; organizations have become flatter with no one person being able simply to "lead" the group; and more people are working on teams or working groups that cut across organizational boundaries both vertically and horizontally. In addition, culturally diverse workforces present challenges with nuanced differences in values, traditions, customs, and beliefs; the changes in technology create networks that impede or cause followers to shape their own development (Chan & Dasgrow, 2001); generational differences shape how leaders and followers reach organizational objectives while attending to the needs of the individual; and the context of the organization plays an important role (Mischel, 1973).

Furthermore, leadership in public entities has become more collaborative and peer-like. Although the reporting hierarchy is in place, the *process* of influence, collaboration, and engagement occurs at all levels. Hence, for the public administrator, it may be more beneficial to go beyond defining leadership and start *defining the outcomes* of leadership, such as direction (vision), alignment, and commitment (Van Velsor, McCauley, & Ruderman, 2010).

Direction, Alignment, and Commitment

Kotter (1996) defined leadership as entailing: (a) establishing direction (developing a vision) for the future and the strategies to create it, (b) aligning people (communicating direction in words and deeds to everyone whose cooperation is needed to create the vision), and (c) motivating and inspiring (energizing people to overcome major political, bureaucratic, and resource barriers to change by satisfying basic but often unfulfilled human needs). Direction, alignment, and commitment help define the skills, characteristics, and talents needed within the leader-follower relationship.

Direction is shared direction and is the level of agreement to the organization's or working group's aim, vision, mission, goals, and shared work products. This goes beyond knowing about the goal; it involves subscribing to the value of reaching the goal as individuals and the collective.

Alignment refers to the coordination of resources to meet the direction. Commonly, bureaucracies initiate alignment through structure, reporting changes and hierarchies, or what is referred to as a tightly knit or loosely knit operational structure. Ultimately, it is the coordination and integration of resources so that they fit together efficiently and effectively. In collectives, individuals and groups coordinate work with other individuals and groups.

Commitment is the willingness of individuals to take ownership for their work, understanding that it is subsumed into the larger portrait of the collective's vision. Commitment takes place through a variety of modalities. Table 4.6 shows

Table 4.6 Evidence of Direction, Alignment, and Commitment

	It's working	*It's not working*
Direction	• A clear vision is articulated by everyone. The collective can articulate what it is trying to achieve individually and collectively. • A desired future state can be envisioned with a set of goals and objectives that tie into the vision. • There is agreement on success.	• There is a lack of agreement on priorities. • People are pulled in different directions, with inertia, working in circles. • There is competition for the vision.
Alignment	• Everyone's roles and responsibilities are clear. • The work of individuals and the collective fits with the overall vision. • There is a sense of organization and coordination and synchronization.	• Deadlines are missed, rework is required, and effort is duplicated. • Silos of work are present, with isolation from the shared vision. • There is competition for resources.
Commitment	• People give the extra effort needed for the group to succeed. • There is a sense of trust and mutual accountability and responsibility. • There is an expressed passion and motivation for work.	• Easy things are accomplished. • People ask, "What's in it for me?"

Source: Van Velsor et al. (2010).

examples of the outcomes of direction, alignment, and commitment in a diverse workforce.

Each outcome can be produced by itself, but the greatest effect is when the three are synthesized. An organization can have direction without alignment or commitment, such as when the collective agrees on the goal but cannot agree on how to organize and subsequently does not have the backing of the collective. Likewise, organizations can agree on alignment without sharing the same vision or being committed to the project, as seen when organizations continue to expend resources for which no one wants to take ownership. This is exemplified in the Abilene paradox, in which a group pursues a collective end, though no individuals would have done so themselves (Harvey, 1996). Finally, there can be commitment to a course of action, without a commonly agreed integrated approach.

The direction, alignment, and commitment framework assumes that in public administration entities where work is collective, there are both individual beliefs and collective beliefs about each other's work, the direction, and how work is organized, and people are motivated to commit themselves, connected by the context of the work and ongoing interaction. These individual and collective leadership beliefs are determinants for the process of influence, collaboration, and engagement (Figure 4.2). The outcome of direction, alignment, and commitment is a *means for obtaining a shared goal,* which moves beyond the traditional thinking that leaders create shared goals (Drath et al., 2008).

There are three reasons for the public administrator to expand the definition of leadership from a process to include an outcome of direction, alignment, and commitment.

First, public administrators are not only managers and/or leaders, they also do the work. Existing managerial paradigms characterized by "a single leader in a formal position wielding power and influence over multiple followers who had relatively little influence on upper management decision making" (Seers,

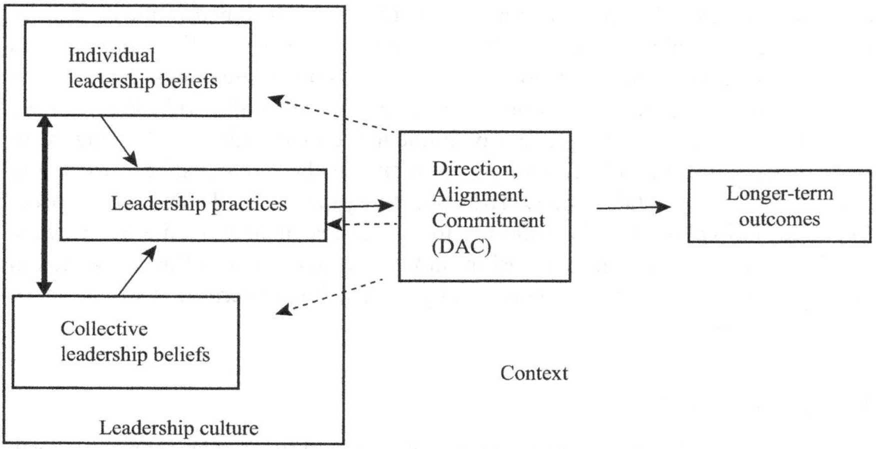

Figure 4.2 A Framework Based on the Direction, Alignment, Commitment Ontology
Source: Reprinted with permission from Drath et al. (2008).

Keller, & Wilkerson, 2003, p. 77) have become outdated in public administration entities as different generations, technology, and social expectations have entered the workforce.

Hence, responsibility for projects and programs is shared more and more among members who each must use the process of influence, collaboration, and engagement to reach organizational objectives. Shared leadership is inherently an exchange of lateral influence among peers. Teams are influenced either traditionally, by the vertical leader, or holistically, by the team itself, which is a powerful source of influence on the group. Shared leadership then becomes a "collaborative, emergent process of group condition in which teams collectively exert influence … that occurs through an unfolding series of fluid, situational exchanges of lateral influence … as team members negotiate shared understandings of how to navigate decision and exercise authority" (Cox, Pearce, & Perry, 2003, p. 53).

This is a social competency that includes an expectation of one's own performance and its link to others' performance, accepting responsibility to provide influence and respond to the influence of others and therefore develop skills needed for an integrated public administration setting. The employee's sense of purpose and focused energy is evident to others through the display of personal initiative, adaptability, effort, and persistence directed toward the organization's goals (Macey & Schneider, 2008).

Second, the workplace has become more complex and connected to larger systems. In a complex work environment, the interaction of internal and external stakeholders acts as a catalyst for emergent ideas. The catalysts are the people, ideas, and behaviors that increase the need for adaptive tension, foster interdependence, and speed up the dynamics of the work itself (Marion & Uhl-Bien, 2001). Consequently, the needs to influence, collaborate, and engage others is left not to one individual, but to all. The outcome is creating alignment within the system.

Third, in public administration entities, where for the most part decisions are made by consensus, relational theory finds its roots in the constructionist approach, which holds that meaning is generated and sustained in the context of ongoing relationships (Gergen, 1994). An implication for public administrators is that through influence, collaboration, and engagement, meanings are reframed from one context to another as perspectives are shared and novel ideas emerge. From this perspective, the process of influence, collaboration, and engagement is distributed and negotiated among the many in the context of the work and culture (Uhl-Bien, 2006, p. 665). The collective practice of "leadership" evolves from one individual and the follower to exchanges of mutual interdependence and influence. Consequently, decision making means shared influence vested in any layer of the hierarchy as expressed by knowledge, expertise, information, or referential power

What's Needed Now

This leads us to the question of how we should lead in an ever-changing world as public administrators. The discussion of social system eras showed that one era has not replaced another. Simply said, older eras, theories, and definitions become the bedrock for newer ones. Kuhn (1970) wrote, "In the development of any science, the first received paradigm is usually felt to account quite successfully for most of the observations" (p. 64). When phenomena are not explained by an existing theory, new theories emerge. The literature on leadership offers different theoretical perspectives regarding the understanding of leaders (Bass, 1990; Yukl, 2010) and how they use their power and influence to make decisions.

As public administrators, we will find uses for the different leadership theories and definitions in our day-to-day work. Yes, having traits that other people can relate to and admire (Era 1) is as important as creating the conditions for all staff members to take ownership and create self-actualizing commitment to their work as it's nestled in the larger vision of the organization (Era 4). Bureaucratic intuitions are closely tied to Taylorism and scientific management. These concepts hold partial truths today in public administration, as rational logic is needed to design, develop, and create outputs. However, we also need the social constructionist approach to ensuring emergent, novel solutions to harness the power of technology and the speed of information.

Until the proposal to see leadership as an output rather than a process, leadership theory differentiated between leaders and followers, task and people orientations to leadership, differences in managers and leaders, transactional and transformational. In more recent years and propelled by the changing nature of society and technology, we are reshaping our thinking to include emergence and complexity from networked people.

In essence, we are constantly learning and emerging. John Dewey (1938) believed our lives were concentric circles interacting with the past and moving to the future, reflecting both reflective action and progress. We find this dualism in public administration as we seek new ways of being, such as reinventing government, and connect to where we've arrived from, such as the traditional role of management and leadership. What is becoming clear is that in our current and rapidly changing society, responsibility for organizational life, developing ourselves and others, creating the culture, and meeting individual and organizational goals is distributed to all members. As leaders in public administration, we can use that principle to lead our own teams.

The older rational conceptions of roles, power, and social structure are giving way to a subjective, socially constructed social era. There is an inherent tension between traditional knowledge and constructed knowledge in situ given the changing context. Our role is to harness this with leadership that uses the "process" of influence, collaboration, and engagement to reach an end of commonly shared direction, alignment, and commitment. To do so, we have to have interaction among people in multiple roles; learning that integrates the experience of activities into sensemaking; and an understanding, if not creation, of context that provides meaning to be adaptive, whether it be from the bottom up or top down.

Over the last several years, I have asked close to 300 civil servants representing different departments and agencies and different levels one question: *What*

Figure 4.3 Responses to the Question: What Kind of Leader and Leadership Skills and Traits Do We Need Now and into the Future?

kind of leader and leadership skills and traits do we need now and into the future? (Figure 4.3).

When we look at the skills, abilities, and traits of what is needed we can determine that leadership can be conceptualized as communicating a vision and aligning people to bring their perspective, developing others and to being a role model, getting things done through others by being actively engaged.

For the public administrator, the lines blur between leading and managing as we know the functions are varied. Subsequently, the social era and the evolving nature of the external and internal environment require decisions to be made in a fluid environment, and "leadership" cannot be vested into one positon. True "leaders" do not limit themselves by being the only decision maker. Decisions require different frameworks: political, legal, democratic, cooperative and security to name a few. Very few hierarchical leaders have broad expertise coupled with the changing paradigm of reinventing government. Leaders can establish a common direction, align the resources and objectives, and create commitment so that decisions are made connected to the whole.

The top 10 words accounted for 121 of the votes, and those were: vision (20); communicator (18), flexible (14); active listener (12); collaborator (11); heart (10); perspective (9); accountability (9); trust (9), and integrity (9).

Conclusion

"Always, it seems, the concept of leadership eludes us or turns up in another form to taunt us again with its slipperiness and complexity" (Bennis, 1959, pp. 259–260). Inherent in this timeless quote is the notion that context changes—although the outcome remains the same, which is to create direction, alignment, and commitment. There is an inherent tension when paradigms shift, and in this case leaders and leadership in public administration are being re-conceptualized to make room for the benefits of Weber's form of bureaucratic accountability, Woodrow Wilson's separation of politics and public administration for the civil servant, and the NPM of looser structures and shared leadership. All have their place, and all have leadership styles that reflect what is needed now.

References

Anderson, P. (1999). Complexity theory and organizational science. *Organizational Science, 10*(3), 216–232.

Archer, M. (1988). *Cultural agency: The place of culture in social theory*. Cambridge, England: University Press.

Avolio, B. (1999). *Full leadership development: Building the vital forces in organizations*. Thousand Oaks, CA: Sage.

Barzelay, M. (1992). *Breaking through bureaucracy: A new vision for managing in government*. Berkeley, CA: University of California Press.

Baert, P. (1998). *Social theory in the twentieth century*. Cambridge, England: Polity.

Barnard, C. I. (1952). A definition of authority. In R. K. Merton, A. P. Gray, B. Hockey, & H. C. Selven (Eds.), *Reader in bureaucracy* (pp. 180–184). New York, NY: Free Press.

Barnes, L. B., & Kriger, M. P. (1986). The hidden side of organizational leadership. *Sloan Management Review, 28*(1), 15–25.

Bass, B. M. (1985). *Leadership and performance beyond expectations*. New York, NY: Free Press.

Bass, B. M. (1990). *Bass and Stogdill's handbook of leadership: A survey of theory and research*. New York, NY: Free Press.

Bass, B. M., & Avolio, B. J. (1994). *Improving organizational effectiveness through transformational leadership*. Thousand Oaks, CA: Sage.

Behn, R. (1998). What right do public managers have to lead? *Public Administration Review, 58*(3), 209–225.

Bennis, W., & Nanus, B. (1985). *Leaders: The strategies for taking charge*. New York, NY: Harper & Row.

Bennis, W. G. (1959). Leadership theory and administrative behavior: The problem of authority. *Administrative Science Quarterly, 4,* 259–301.

Berrien, F. K. (1961). Homeostasis theory of groups: Implications for leadership. In L. Petrullo and B. Bass (Eds.), *Leadership and interpersonal behavior* (pp. 82–100). New York, NY: Holt, Rinehart & Winston.

Bertalanffy, L. (1968). *General system theory: Foundations, development and application*. New York, NY: George Braziller.

Blake, R. R. & Mouton, J. (1964). *The managerial grid*. Houston, TX: Gulf Publishing.

Bogardus, E. S. (1934). *Leaders and leadership*. New York, NY: Appleton-Century-Crofts.

Buckley, W. (1967). *Sociology and modern systems theory*. Upper Saddle River, NJ: Prentice Hall.

Bundel, C. M. (1939). Is leadership losing its importance? *Infantry Journal, 36,* 339–349.

Burns, J. M. (1978). *Leadership*. New York, NY: Harper & Row.

Burrell, G., & Morgan, G. (1979). *Sociological paradigms and organizational analysis*. Burlington, VT: Ashgate.

Carlyle, T. (1840). The hero as divinity. In *Heroes and hero-worship*.

Cartwright, D. & Zander, A. F. (1953). *Group dynamics*. Evanston, IL: Harper and Row.

Chan, A. (2005). Authentic leadership measurement and development: Challenges and suggestions. In W. L. Gargner, B. J. Avoko, & F. O. Walumbwa (Eds.), *Authentic leadership theory and practice: Origins, effects and development* (pp. 227–251). Oxford, England: Elsevier Science.

Chan, Y. Y., & Drasgow, F. (2001). Toward a theory of individual differences in leadership: Towards a more realistic view of top managers. *Journal of Management, 23,* 213–238.

Conger, J. A., & Kanungo, R. N. (1987). Toward a behavioral theory of charismatic leadership in organizational settings. *Academy of Management Review, 12,* 637–647.

Conger, J. A., & Kanungo, R. N. (1988). *Charismatic leadership in organizations.* Thousand Oaks, CA: Sage.

Cowley, W. H., (1928). Three distinctions in the study of leaders. *Journal of Abnormal and Social Psychology, 23,* 144–157.

Cox, J. F., Pearce, C. L., & Perry, M. L. (2003). Toward a model of shared leadership and distributed influence in the innovation process: How shared leadership can enhance new product development team dynamics and effectiveness. In C. L. Pearce & J. A. Conger (Eds.), *Shared leadership: Reframing the how's and why's of leadership* (pp. 48–76). Thousand Oaks, CA: Sage.

Day, P., & Klein, R. (1987). *Accountabilities: Five public services.* London, England: Tavistock.

Dewey, J. (1938). *Experience and education.* New York, NY: Collier.

Dixon, J., Kouzmin, A., & Korac-Kakabadse, N. (1998). Managerialism. Something old, something borrowed, little new: Economic prescriptions versus effective organizational change in public agencies. *International Journal of Public Sector Management, 11*(2/3), 164–187.

Drath, W. H., McCauley, C., Palus, C., Van Veslor, E., O'Conner, P., & McGuire, J. (2008). Direction, alignment and commitment: Toward a more integrative ontology of leadership. *Leadership Quarterly, 19,* 635–653.

Eagly, A. H. (2005). Achieving relational authenticity in leadership: Does gender matter? *Leadership Quarterly, 16,* 459–474.

Fayol, H. (1949). *General and industrial management.* London, UK: Pitman.

Ferlie, E., Pettigrew, A., Ashburner, L., & Fitzgerald, L. (1996). *The new public management in action.* Oxford, UK: Oxford University Press.

Fiedler, F. E. (1964). A contingency model of leadership effectiveness. In L. Berkowitz (Ed.), *Advances in experimental and social psychology* (Vol. 1, pp. 149–190). New York, NY: Academic Press.

Fiedler, F. E. (1967). *A theory of leadership effectiveness.* New York, NY: McGraw-Hill.

Fleishman, E. A. (1953). The description of supervisory behavior. *Personnel Psychology, 37,* 1–6.

Fleishman, E. A., Mumford, M. D., Zaccaro, S.J., Levin, K.Y., Korotkin, A.L., Hein, M. B. (1991). Taxonomic efforts in the description of leader behavior: A synthesis and functional interpretation. *Leadership Quarterly, 2,* 245–287.

Flynn, N. (1993). *Public sector management.* London, England: Harvester Wheatsheaf.

French, J., & Raven, B. H. (1959). The bases of social power. In D. Cartwright (Ed.), *Studies of social power* (pp. 150–167). Ann Arbor, MI: Institute for Social Research.

Gantt, H. L. (1919). *Organizing for work.* New York, NY: Harcourt, Brace and Howe.

George, B. (2003). *Authentic leadership: Rediscovering the secrets of creating lasting value.* San Francisco, CA: Jossey-Bass.

Gergen, K. J. (1994). *Realities and relationships: Soundings in social construction.* Cambridge, MA: Harvard University Press.

Gibb, C.A. (1954). Leadership. In G. Linzey (Ed.), *Handbook of social psychology* (Vol. 2, pp. 877–920). Reading, MA: Addison-Wesley.

Giddens, A. (1979). *Central problems in social theory: Action, structuration and contradiction in social analysis.* Cambridge, England: Polity.

Gilbreth, F. B., & Gilbreth, L. (1919). Fatigue study: The elimination of humanity's greatest waste; a first step in motion study. New York; 1st edition, New York, 1916.

Graen, G. B., & Scandura, T. A. (1987). Toward a psychology of dyadic organizing. In B. Staw & L. L. Cummings (Eds.), *Research in organizational behavior* (Vol. 9, pp. 175–208). Greenwich, CT: JAI.

Graen, G. B., & Uhl-Bien, M. (1995). Relationship-based approach to leadership: Development of leader-member exchange (LMX) theory of leadership over 25 years: Applying a multi-level, multi-domain perspective. *Leadership Quarterly*, *6*(2), 219–247.

Greer, P. (1994). *Transforming central government: The next steps initiative*. Philadelphia, PA: Buckingham and Open University Press.

Gronn, P. (2002). Distributed leadership as a unit of analysis. *Leadership Quarterly*, *13*, 423–451.

Gulick, L., & Urwick, L. (1993). Notes on the theory of organization. In M. T. Matteson & J. V. Ivancevich (Eds.), *Management and organizational behaviors classics* (5th ed., pp. 3–13). New York, NY: McGraw-Hill. (Originally published in 1937).

Habermas, J. (1984). The theory of communicative action. In T. McCarthy (Trans.), *Reason and the rationalization of society* (Vol. 1). Boston, MA: Beacon Press.

Harvey, J. B. (1996). *The Abilene paradox and other meditations on management.* San Francisco, CA: Jossey-Bass.

Hazy, J. K. (2006). Measuring leadership effectiveness in complex socio-technical systems, *Emergence: Complexity and Organization*, *8*(3) 58–77.

Heifetz, R. A., Grashow, A., & Linsky, M. (2009). *The practice of adaptive leadership: Tools and tactics for changing your organization and the world.* Boston, MA: Harvard Business Press.

Hersey, P., & Blanchard, K. H. (1984) *The management of organizational behavior* (4th ed.). Englewood Cliffs, NJ: Prentice Hall.

Hjern, B., & Porter, D. (1981). Implementation structures: A new unit of administrative analysis. *Organization Studies*, *2*(3), 211–227.

Hollandeer, E. P. & Julian, J. W. (1978). A further look at leader legitimacy, influence and innovation. In L. Berkowitz (Ed.), *Group processes: Papers from Advances in Experimental Social Psychology* (pp. 153–165). New York, NY: Academic Press.

Hood, C. (1991). A public management for all seasons. *Public Administration*, *69*, 3–19.

Hood, C. (1995). Contemporary public management: A new global paradigm. *Public Policy and Administration*, *10*(2), 104–117.

House, R. J. (1971). A path-goal theory of leader effectiveness. *Administrative Science Quarterly*, *16*, 321–328.

Hoy, W. K. and Miskel, G. (2007). *Educational administration: Theory, research and practice* (8th ed.). New York, NY: McGraw Hill.

Jacques, E. & Clement, S. (1991). *Executive leadership. A practical guide to managing complexity*. Arlington, VA: Cason Hall and Company.

Jordan, B. (1995). Are new right policies sustainable? Back to basics and public choice. *Journal of Social Policy*, *24*(3), 363–384.

Katz, D., & Kahn, R. L. (1978). *The social psychology of organizations* (2nd ed.). New York, NY: Wiley.

Katz, R. L. (1955) Skills of an effective administrator. *Harvard Business Review*, *33*(1), 33–42.

Kotter, J. P. (1982). *The general managers.* New York, NY: Free Press

Kotter, J. P. (1990). *A force for change.* New York, NY: Free Press.

Kotter, J. P. (1996). *Leading change.* Boston, MA: Harvard Business School Press.

Kouzes, J. M., & Posner, B. Z. (2002). *The leadership challenge* (3rd ed.). San Francisco, CA: Jossey-Bass.

Kracke, W. H. (1979). *Force and persuasion: Leadership in an Amazonian society*. Chicago, IL: University of Chicago Press.

Kuhn, T. S. (1970). *The structure of scientific revolutions* (2nd ed.). Chicago, IL: University of Chicago Press.

Larbi, G. (1999). *The new public management approach and crisis states* (Discussion Paper No. 112). Geneva, Switzerland: United Nations Research Institute for Social Development.

Macey, W. H., & Schneider, B. (2008). The meaning of employee engagement. *Industrial and Organizational Psychology: Perspectives on Science and Practice, 1*, 3–30.

March, J. G., & Simon, H. A. (1958). *Organizations*. New York, NY: John Wiley.

Marion, R., & Uhl-Bien, M. (2001). Leadership in complex organizations. *Leadership Quarterly, 12,* 389–418.

Mascarenhas, R. C. (1993). Building an enterprise culture in the public sector: Reforms in Australia, New Zealand and Great Britain. *Public Administration Review, 53*(4), 319–328.

Matteson M. T. & Ivancevich, J. M. (Eds.). (1993). *Management and organizational behavior classics* (5th ed.). Boston, MA: Irwin.

Mayo, E. (1946). *The human problems of an industrial civilization* (2nd ed.). Cambridge, MA: Harvard University.

McClelland, D. C. (1961). *The achieving society*. New York, NY: The Free Press.

Metcalfe, L., & Richards, S. (1990). *Improving public management* (2nd ed.). London, England: Sage.

Mintzberg, H. (1973). *The nature of managerial work.* Englewood Cliffs, NJ: Prentice Hall.

Mintzberg, H. (1983). *Power in and around organizations*. Englewood Cliffs, NJ: Prentice Hall.

Mischel, W. (1973). Toward a cognitive social learning reconceptualization of personality. *Psychological Review, 80,* 252–283.

Moore, B. V. (1927). The May conference on leadership. *Personnel Journal, 6,* 124–128.

Mumford, M. D., Zaccaro, S. J., Connelly, M. S. & Marks, M. A. (2000), Leadership skills: Conclusions and future directions. *Leadership Quarterly, 11*(1), 155–170.

Northouse, P. G. (2010). *Leadership: Theory and practice* (5th ed.). Los Angeles, CA: Sage.

Odom, R. Y., Boxx, W. R., & Dunn, M. G. (1990). Organizational cultures, commitment, satisfaction and cohesion. *Public Productivity and Management Review, 13*(2), 157–169.

Parsons, T. (1951). *The social system*. New York, NY: Free Press.

Parsons, T., & Shils, E. A. (1952). *Toward a general theory of action.* New York, NY: Harper Books.

Pearce, C. L., & Conger, J. A. (Eds.). (2003). *Shared leadership: Reframing the how's and why's of leadership*. Thousand Oaks, CA: Sage.

Pettigrew, A. M. (1972). Information control as power resource. *Sociology, 6,* 187–204.

Pollitt, C. (1993). *Managerialism and the public services: The Anglo-American experience* (2nd ed.). Oxford, England: Blackwell.

Presthus, R. (1958). Toward a theory of organizational behavior. *Administrative Science Quarterly, 3*, 48–72.

Reuter, E. B. (1941). *Handbook of social psychology*. New York, NY: Dryden.

Rosenbloom, D., Kravchuk, R., & Clerkin, R. (2009). *Public administration: Understanding management, politics and law in the public sector* (7th ed.). Boston, MA: McGraw-Hill Higher Education.

Rost, J. C. (1991). *Leadership for the twenty-first century*. New York, NY: Praeger.

Sanders, R. (1998). Heroes of the revolution: Characteristics and strategies of reinvention leaders. In P. Ingraham, R. Sanders, & J. Thompson (Eds.), *Transforming government: Lessons from the reinvention laboratories* (pp. 29–57). San Francisco, CA: Jossey-Bass.

Schein, E. H. (1992). The role of the CEO in the management of change. In T. A. Kochan & M. Useem (Eds.), *Transforming organizations* (pp. 80–96). New York, NY: Oxford University Press.

Schmidt, R. (1933). Leadership. In E. R. A. Seligman (Ed.), *Encyclopedia of the social sciences* (pp. 282–286). New York, NY: Macmillan.

Schwandt, D., & Szabla, D. (2007). Systems and leadership: Coevolution or mutual evolution towards complexity. In J. Hazy, J. Goldstein, & B. Lichtenstein (Eds.), *Complex systems and leadership theory* (pp.35–60). Mansfield, MA: ISCE.

Seeman, M. (1960). *Social status and leadership*. Columbus, OH: Ohio State University, Bureaus of Business Leadership.

Seers, A., Keller, T., & Wilkerson, J. M. (2003). Can team members share leadership? Foundations in research and theory. In C. L. Pearce & J. A. Conger (Eds.), *Shared leadership: Reframing the how's and whys of leadership* (pp. 77–102). Thousand Oaks, CA: Sage.

Senge, P. (1990). *The fifth discipline: The art and practice of the learning organization*. New York, NY: Doubleday.

Senge, P. (1994). Creating quality communities. *Executive excellence*, *11*(6), 11–13.

Simon, H. A. (1947). *Administrative behavior: A study of decision-making processes in administrative organization* (2nd ed.). New York, NY: Macmillan.

Stewart, J., & Walsh, K. (1992). Change in the management of public services. *Public Administration*, *70*(4), 499–518.

Stogdill, R. M. (1948). Personal factors associated with leadership: A survey of the literature. *Journal of Psychology: Interdisciplinary and Applied*, *25*(1), 35–71.

Stogdill, R. M. (1974). *Handbook of leadership: A survey of theory and research*. New York, NY: Free Press.

Taylor, F. W. (1911). *The principles of scientific management*. New York, NY: Harper Brothers.

Tead, O. (1935) *The art of leadership*. New York, NY: McGraw-Hill.

Tichy, N. M., & Devanna, M. A. (1986). *The transformational leader*. New York, NY: John Wiley.

Uhl-Bien, M. (2006). Relational leadership theory: Exploring the social processes of leadership and organizing. *Leadership Quarterly*, *17*, 654–676.

Van Velsor, E., McCauley, C. D., & Ruderman, M. N. (Eds.). (2010). *The Center for Creative Leadership handbook of leadership development* (3rd ed.). San Francisco, CA: Jossey-Bass.

Walsh, K. (1995). *Public services and market mechanisms: Competition, contracting and the new public management*. London, England: Macmillan.

Walumbwa, F. O., Avolio, B. J., Gardner, W. L., Wernsing, T. S., & Peterson, S. J. (2008). Authentic leadership: Development and validation of a theory based measure. *Journal of Management*, *34*(1), 89–126.

Weber, M. (1930). *The protestant ethic and the spirit of capitalism.* (T. Parsons, Trans.). Australia: Allen and Unwin. (Original work published 1904).

Weick, K. E., & Roberts, K. (1993). Collective mind in organizations: Heedful inter-relating on flight decks. *Administrative Science Quarterly, 38*(3), 357–381

Wiener, N. (1954). *The human use of human beings*. Boston, MA: Houghton Mifflin.

Yukl, G. (2010). *Leadership in organizations* (7th ed.). Englewood Cliffs, NJ: Prentice Hall.

Zaleznik, A. (1977). Managers and leaders: Are they different? *Harvard Business Review, 55*(5), 67–78.

5 Leadership Development

An Investment Necessary to Increase Federal Employee Engagement and Federal Government Productivity

Robert M. Tobias

Leadership and learning are indispensable to each other.

—John F. Kennedy, 1963

Successful leaders learn how to create the quality relationships that are necessary to engage those they lead and how to implement what they learn through a changed mindset and changed behavior. Successful leaders do this while keeping in mind the need to increase individual and organizational performance. "Learning how to learn" requires will, time, discipline, and an employer's investment in their leadership's success.

It will be argued in this chapter that greater investment is needed to help train federal sector leaders to "learn how to learn," particularly as this relates to employee engagement. In both the public and private sectors, there is a broad consensus that employee engagement leads to improved organizational performance. In the federal government, it is now accepted that the more workers are involved with their employment, improved personal and organizational performance will result.

Encouraging employee engagement by leaders runs counter to the "command and control" management style that has traditionally dominated federal government executive branch leadership practices. This requires 21st-century leaders to be more fully engaged with their staff, particularly Millennials and Gen-Xers, who do not respond well to "take it or leave it" leadership styles. Learning to learn is a necessary prerequisite for leaders who wish to be successful in the modern federal workplace.

The first president to take responsibility for increasing executive branch employee performance was President Bill Clinton, who linked improved individual and organizational performance to increased employee motivation. Eight years later, President Barack Obama reignited President Clinton's effort to tie improved government performance to increase employee engagement. While organizations have traditionally attempted to increase employee motivation by increasing personal employee gain through salary and benefits, engagement is based on an employee's connection to the organization and results in an employee's working harder. Although President Clinton used the term "employee motivation," the intended "employee gain" was "inclusion and involvement," very similar to the concept of employee engagement.

This renewed emphasis on motivating employees has demanded that managers significantly change their behavior. Federal leaders are now required to: specify program and agency goals; devise processes for achieving the goals; include and involve employees in the processes; ensure that their reports are providing effort "above and beyond" the norm; and, finally, be responsible for the results (Donovan, Corbert, Archuleta, & McLaughlin, 2014).

Not only are federal leaders being held accountable for results, they are also required to "engage" employees to assist them in reaching organizational goals. This approach is 180 degrees contrary to the traditional hierarchical command-and-control leadership style of the past. However, despite demands that government leaders change behavior, little personal leadership development training has been offered to support them. To master the arts involved in engaging their employees—and to assume their new responsibilities—leaders must be trained and coached as they take on new roles.

Federal managers and supervisors must develop a skill set including the ability to identify new values and assumptions, understand the role of emotional intelligence in creating the relationships they now need to be successful, and develop a leadership logic to create a more collaborative work culture. But too often leaders have not been taught these skills. Frustration on the part of both leaders and those they lead has been the inevitable result, which is reflected in the basically flat employee engagement in recent years.

To function in the volatile, uncertain, complex, and ambiguous world federal leaders face, there must be a broader set of leadership competencies than those currently outlined in the Executive Core Qualifications (ECQs) (Reinhold, 2015). Specifically, the U.S. Office of Personnel Management (OPM) must redefine and supplement existing ECQs for all federal managers, from aspiring leaders to current members of the Senior Executive Service (SES). That would require OPM to:

- add new ECQs necessary to increase employee engagement and organization success;
- evaluate whether the fundamental ECQ leadership competencies are present in managers;
- mandate that the recently redefined minimum leader competencies for selection, evaluation, and promotion be mandatorily implemented;
- require existing leaders to regularly recertify those leadership competencies critical to employee engagement; and
- remove the current barriers to increasing employee engagement.

What Is Employee Engagement?

There is no one common definition of employee engagement, but there seems to be common agreement that engagement is based in part on an emotional connection between an employee and his or her organization that stimulates increased performance.

The private sector has long accepted that engaged employees work better and produce better results. The Corporate Leadership Council (2004), based on an extensive survey, concluded that employees who "derive pride, inspiration, and enjoyment from their job and organization" expend the highest levels of effort to achieve their goals and objectives (p. 36).

The U.S. Merit Systems Protection Board (MSPB) (2008) came to the same conclusion about employees in the federal sector. It found that employee engagement "is vital to the continued success of agency missions" (p. i). MSPB found not only a direct correlation between employee engagement and higher organizational productivity, but also that engaged employees:

- are less likely to leave,
- use fewer sick days,
- file fewer Equal Employee Opportunity complaints, and
- file fewer work-related injury cases.

Equally important, those employees who report they are likely to leave and are unengaged have the highest performance ratings on their latest evaluation: agencies risk losing high-performing employees because they are unengaged (MSPB, 2008, p. iv).

William Kahn (1990) provided the first formal definition of personal engagement to include a commitment of physical, intellectual, and emotional energy. Such engagement represents "the harnessing of organization members' selves to their work roles; in engagement, people employ and express themselves physically, cognitively, and emotionally during role performances" (p. 694).

Gallup (2015) provides a definition of engagement that includes the passion to accomplish the organization's mission: "When employees are engaged, they are passionate, creative, and entrepreneurial, and their enthusiasm fuels growth. These employees are emotionally connected to the mission and purpose of their work" (para. 6). Similar to the MSPB, Gallup (2015) found the consequences of non-engagement significant: "When employees are not engaged, they are indifferent toward their jobs—or worse, outright hate their work, supervisor, and organization—and they will destroy a work unit and a business" (para. 6).

American University's Key Executive Leadership Certificate Program defines employee engagement as the willingness of an employee to choose to give his or her discretionary energy to accomplish the boss's goals and objectives. The assumption is that an employee will not make that choice without an emotional connection to the boss and the organization.

The Office of Management and Budget (OMB) and OPM have adopted the commonly accepted definition of employee engagement by linking "employees' sense of purpose" to the organization's mission to stimulate a "display of dedication, persistence, and effort in their work" (Donovan et al., 2014, p. 1; OPM, 2015a, p. 6).

Similar to Kahn, the OPM's definition is linked to three components:

> A *behavioral component,* represented by the willingness to give discretionary effort, to go above and beyond, and an *attitudinal component*, represented by passion for the job or task, and a *cognitive component* reflecting each employee's understanding of the job demands and the work group's strategy.
>
> (Emphasis in original; OPM, 2015b, p. 6)

Using Employee Engagement to Increase Organizational Performance

Reinforcement of the link between employee engagement and organizational productivity is contained in a December 23, 2014, Memorandum for Heads of Departments and Agencies, signed by those officials most responsible for leading executive branch employees: Shaun Donovan, Director of the Office of Management and Budget; Catherine Archuleta, Director of the Office of Personnel Management; and Meg McLaughlin, Deputy Director of the White House Office of Personnel. These officials stated, "The most critical factor necessary for increasing federal employee productivity is increased employee engagement and should be the focus for all levels of an agency—from the front line employee to the agency head" (Donovan et al., 2014, p. 2).

OPM's most recent statement reiterates that employee engagement is "a positive condition that benefits the organization. The focus for agencies, therefore, is to implement and foster conditions that increase engagement, and ultimately, impact key organizational drivers of success" (OPM, 2015b, p. 6).

Early Employee Engagement Efforts

President Bill Clinton was the first to reject the heretofore commonly accepted belief that a president should focus only on public policy creation and not on the effective and efficient implementation of public policy. He recognized that a president and cabinet secretaries must provide the leadership necessary to increase government results (Gore, 1993b, p. 8). That focus led to the attention on improving employee engagement.

The strategy to increase government performance was preceded by an NPR announced on March 3, 1993. The review, headed by Vice President Al Gore, aimed to reform the way the government worked. Six months later Vice President Gore delivered a report to the president titled "Creating a Government that Works Better and Costs Less" (Gore, 1993a), and offering some "380 major recommendations concerning management reform, reorganization, and government downsizing" of 225,00 employees (Relyea, Cornejo, Riemann, &, Hogue, 2001, para. summary). The strategy for implementation was to identify goals and then hold leaders accountable for goal achievement. Implementing NPR recommendations for structural change, including significant downsizing of the federal workforce, were achieved (Relyea et al., 2001).

NPR's basic strategy for changing leadership behavior was to delegate responsibility for "maintaining an environment for workforce excellence that increases worker involvement" to managers and supervisors (Gore, 1993a, p. 67). Maintaining an environment of excellence "rewrites the relationship between managers and the managed. The bright line that separates the two vanishes as everyone is given greater authority over how to get their job done" (Gore, 1993a, p. 67).

President Bill Clinton decided that Labor Management Partnerships would be the best vehicle for implementing his vision for creating an engaged workforce. Issuing Executive Order 12871, the president commented that the "involvement of federal Government employees and their union representatives is essential to achieving the National Performance Review's government reform objectives" (Exec. Order No. 12871, 1993, p. 1955).

The newly created labor management partnerships were tasked to:

- help reform government;
- involve employees and their union representatives as full partners with management representatives;
- identify problems and craft solutions to better serve the agency's customers and mission; and
- evaluate progress and improvements in organizational performance resulting from the labor-management partnerships (Exec. Order No. 12871, 1993, p. 1955).

This ground-breaking executive order envisioned significant changes in the relationships between leaders and those they led. This was the first time a president had attempted to improve work processes by linking non-manager workplace knowledge, union leaders, and agency decision makers to increase organizational results (Gore, 1993a, p. 87). To say the least, the effort was difficult to implement.

Difficulty Maintaining Partnerships

The whole idea of workers partnering with their bosses ran headfirst into the existing labor-management culture of adversarialism. Collaboration had not historically been the modus operandi in government, nor was it necessarily welcomed by management and labor.

For union leaders, it was high risk to give up winning grievance arbitrations, lawsuits, and unfair labor practice charges in the hope that sometime in the future they would actually be meaningfully involved. Nor were managers interested in investing the time necessary to create the trust needed, on the unproven hope that the inclusion of employees would actually yield results (Tobias, 2010).

Leading in a collaborative environment requires leadership development competencies that include trust-building skills, which are necessary to lead a significant organizational change effort. However, there were no leadership development programs for either union leaders or managers. NPR overlooked the need for systemic leadership development training to aid leaders struggling to change their behavior, and lead others to change their behavior in a delayered, less hierarchical environment.

The NPR recognized the need for "skill training so employees could perform their job more effectively" (Gore, 1993b, p. 68), but leadership development training was limited to training in "consensual methods of dispute resolution, such as alternative dispute resolution techniques and interest-based bargaining approaches" (Gore, 1993b, p. 1).

The results of the NPR effort to increase employee engagement were mixed. There is evidence that employee involvement through their unions led to increased government performance (Defense Partnership Council, 1999; Masters, 2001;

U.S. Government Accountability Office [GAO], 2001). But the lack of fundamental leader competencies—aimed to help develop the abilities necessary to lead differently—limited NPR success. For example, Donald Kettl (1998) pointed out that federal employee motivation increased or decreased based on whether leaders specifically identified NPR goals, a fundamental leader competency.

> The NPR succeeded in motivating employees, quite predictably, to the degree to which top government officials made this an important goal. Where they did not—and the [MSPB] survey suggests that the NPR deeply penetrated only about a third of all federal agencies—the NPR became known principally for its downsizing focus and consequently motivation lagged. (p. 9)

James Carroll (1995) also pointed out the adverse impact on motivation resulting from laying off frontline federal employees but not middle managers. Since NPR did not "propose a systemic agenda for rebuilding the career service," the "overall message of the NPR on the career civil service [was] ambivalent or negative" (p. 309).

In 2001, President George W. Bush issued Executive Order 13203, rescinding President Clinton's employee motivation efforts by eliminating any focus on employee involvement/engagement as a tool for improving government performance. Many federal workers, both leaders and employees, breathed a sigh of relief. They were free to revert to comfortable adversarialism, providing evidence that the successful partnering labor management relationships had not taken root in institutionalized changed behavior (Masters, Sickles, & Tobias, 2010). But President Bush did continue a presidential focus on increasing government performance.

Although Bush's executive order eliminated Clinton's effort to link employee engagement to increased productivity, he continued the focus on improving executive branch performance through a new performance measurement instrument: the Program Assessment and Rating Tool (PART). PART required agencies to answer 25 questions describing the processes used, and the results achieved, for each major program under their jurisdictions. The goal was to use the PART information to allow OMB to make funding and management decisions, conduct internal program and budget analysis, and hold agency leaders accountable for increasing the PART scores (GAO, 2004a).

To increase PART scores, OMB instituted regular discussions with agencies to develop processes for increasing PART scores and made the PART public so as to create competition to increase the scores. While this was meant to drive leader behavior necessary to fulfill the goals of PART, no leadership development training was suggested or offered. This was somewhat like holding a swim meet before teaching participants to swim.

The Obama administration reinstated an emphasis on employee motivation (now called employee engagement), while continuing to focus on goal definition, processes to be used, and leaders' accountability. The Obama administration's first budget eliminated the PART process for measuring performance and instead required agency leaders "to set priority goals, demonstrate progress in achieving goals, and explain performance trends" (OMB, 2009, p. 9). In addition, the Fiscal Year (FY) 2011 budget identified employee engagement as an administration priority (OMB, 2010, pp. 104–105).

The following year, the FY 2012 Budget recognized the need to increase employee engagement in the interest of improving agency performance: "A high-performing government depends on an engaged, well-prepared, and well-trained workforce with the right set of skills appropriate to the situation" (OMB, 2011, p. 103). OPM also announced creation of the current employee engagement index (Table 5.1) based on the 2012 Federal Employee Viewpoint Survey (FEVS; OPM, 2012a, p. 34) and published the Department and agency results (OPM, 2012a, pp. 50–57).

In 2015, OPM recognized the role leaders must play to increase engagement:

> The degree to which one feels a connection to the job being performed can be enhanced or diminished by the leader's ability to effectively communicate job expectation, give performance feedback, and/or provide for employees to be involved in decisions that impact their work.
>
> (OPM, 2015c, p. 13)

It was not until 2015 that the Obama administration recognized the link between increasing employee engagement and providing leadership development training.

Mark Reinhold (2015), Associate Director of Employee Services and Chief Human Capital Officer at OPM, says it is not enough for agencies to describe *what* leaders must do, they must provide the *how*. Agencies must "focus on developing effective leaders if they are to move the needle on employee engagement and retention" (p. 2).

Because existing leadership competencies have not been successful, he defines a new set of competencies for every level of government, from emerging leaders to SES to increase employee engagement (Reinhold, 2015). Implementation may be limited because training to achieve the competencies is "recommended," no funding is provided to conduct what is described as needed, and no leadership competency changes are recommended for members of the SES.

Table 5.1 Government-Wide Employee Engagement Scores (%)

	2010	*2011*	*2012*	*2013*	*2014*	*2015*
Leaders lead	55	56	54	53	50	51
Supervisors	71	72	70	70	71	71
Intrinsic work experience	72	72	71	69	68	69
Government-wide index score	66	67	65	64	63	64

Note: Values reflect % of respondents who answered the question with a 5 or 4 on a 5-point Likert scale.

Source: 2010 data are from OPM (2012, pp. 52–55), 2011–2015 data are from OPM (2015, pp. 44–58).

How Is Employee Engagement Measured?

To calculate employee engagement, OPM created an index in 2010 based on three factors—Leaders, Supervisors, and Intrinsic Work Experience (*Federal Workforce*, 2015, pp. 4–5). The Intrinsic Work Experience factor seeks to gauge the level of emotional connection between the employee and his or her work; the Leaders and Supervisors factors pinpoint the role played by leaders and supervisors in creating that emotional connection. Five questions from the Federal Employee Viewpoint Survey are assigned to each factor.

Answers to the Intrinsic Work Experience Category questions "reflect the employees' feelings of motivation and competency relating to their role in the workplace" (OPM, 2015d, p. 11). The goal is to find how emotionally connected workers are to achieving the organization's mission (Table 5.2).

The Supervisors' Category questions (Table 5.3) "reflect the quality of the interpersonal relationship between employee and supervisor, including the trust, respect, and support" necessary to generate intrinsic engagement (OPM, 2015d, p. 11). Finally, the Leaders Lead Category (Table 5.4) "reflects the employees' perceptions of the integrity of leadership, as well as leadership behaviors such as communication and workforce motivation necessary to generate intrinsic workforce motivation" (OPM, 2015d, p. 11).

Table 5.2 Intrinsic Work Experience Questions (%)

Intrinsic Work Experience	*2010*	*2011*	*2012*	*2013*	*2014*	*2015*
3 I feel encouraged to come up with new and better ways of doing things.	65	59	58	56	55	57
4 My work gives me a feeling of personal accomplishment.	74	74	72	70	70	70
6 I know what is expected of me on the job.	80	80	80	79	79	79
11 My talents are used well in the workplace.	60	61	60	58	56	58
12 I know how my work relates to the agency's goals and priorities.	84	85	83	83	82	83
Total	72	72	71	69	68	69

Note: Values reflect % of respondents who answered the question with a 5 or 4 on a 5-point Likert scale.

Source: 2010 data are from OPM (2012, pp. 52–55), 2011–2015 data are from OPM (2015, pp. 44–58).

Table 5.3 Supervisors Lead Questions (%)

Supervisors Lead	*2010*	*2011*	*2012*	*2013*	*2014*	*2015*
47 Supervisors in my work unit support employee development.	66	67	65	64	63	64
48 My supervisor listens to what I have to say.	75	75	74	74	75	76
49 My supervisor treats me with respect.	80	80	80	80	80	81
51 I have trust and confidence in my supervisor.	67	67	66	66	65	66
52 Overall, how good a job do you feel is being done by your immediate supervisor?	68	69	68	69	70	70
Total	71	72	71	70	71	71

Note: Values reflect % of respondents who answered the question with a 5 or 4 on a 5-point Likert scale.

Source: 2010 data are from OPM (2012, pp. 52–55), 2011–2015 data are from OPM (2015, pp. 44–58).

OPM (2015b) points out in *Engaging the Federal Workforce: How to Do It and Prove It* that the employee engagement index focuses on leaders' behavior in the workplace because "strong leaders" posses

> the ability to communicate goals and priorities motivate employees (behavior component of engagement), establish trust, enforce contingencies for exceptional and unacceptable behaviors, and generate commitment. Leadership can also influence intrinsic work experiences by gathering ideas and communicating expectations and providing feedback. The degree to which one feels a connection to the job being performed can be enhanced or diminished by the leader's ability to effectively communicate job expectations, give performance feedback, and/or provide the opportunity for employees to be involved in decision that impact their work. (p. 13)

The question is whether we have enough "strong leaders" in the federal workplace.

Federal Employee Engagement Scores

Federal leaders are facing a time when it is critical to increase employee engagement. The normal extrinsic motivators of pay increases, promotions, and awards are not available in today's environment of declining revenue, pay freezes, and limited promotions. Add the extrinsic demotivators of furloughs, government shutdowns, and continued attacks on federal employees, and the need for leaders to identify intrinsic motivators (engaging in behavior because it is personally rewarding) to increase employee engagement and agency productivity is critical.

In the face of the increased need, the government-wide employee engagement scores declined three percent from 2010 to 2015 (Table 5.1).

It is not surprising that leaders are generating a declining level of engagement from those they lead. Question 53 of the survey ("In my organization, leaders generate high levels of motivation and commitment in the workforce") with an already low base score declined 13% from 2010 to 2015 (Table 5.4). Similarly, without the ability to create a motivating work environment, employees have less respect for federal sector senior leaders: Question 61 ("I have a high level of respect for my organization's senior leaders") lost 7 percent between 2010 and 2015 (Table 5.4).

In an effort to place a poultice on the declining federal employee engagement index, Donovan, Corbert, Archuleta, and McLaughlin in December 2014 mandated an aggressive process to increase employee engagement:

- Agencies were required to identify a Senior Accountable Official (SAO) to lead the effort;
- Agencies were told that each Deputy Secretary would review the 2014 engagement results;
- Chief Human Capital Officers were directed to identify metrics and targets for improvement, using the "HRStat" quarterly meetings; and
- Each "component head" was ordered to review plans for increasing the employee engagement score, including by sending scores "to each manager with breakout results."

Table 5.4 Leaders Lead Questions (%)

Leaders lead	*2010*	*2011*	*2012*	*2013*	*2014*	*2015*
53 In my organization, senior leaders generate high levels of motivation and commitment in the workforce.	45	45	43	41	38	39
54 My organization's senior leaders maintain high standards of honesty and integrity.	58	57	55	54	50	50
56 Managers communicate the goals and priorities of the organization.	64	64	62	61	58	59
60 Overall, how good a job do you feel is being done by the manager directly above your immediate supervisor?	57	58	58	57	56	57
61 I have a high level of respect for my organization's senior leaders.	56	57	54	52	50	51
Total	55	56	54	53	50	51

Note: Values reflect % of respondents who answered the question with a five or four on a 5-point Likert scale.

Source: 2010 data are from OPM (2012, pp. 52–55), 2011–2015 data are from OPM (2015, pp. 44–58).

At the same time, Performance Improvement Officers and SAOs were directed to collaborate to identify "percent change" targets and include them in the "FY16/17" Annual Performance Plans and Performance Reports (Donovan et al., 2014).

The focused attention by the highest levels of government—down through the leadership chain of political appointees to first level supervisors—emphasized how important the issue was and that action must be taken. The results were positive. OPM (2015d) described the 1.5% increase from 2014 to 2015 in the government-wide employee engagement index (Table 5.1) as a "highlight" of the 2015 FEVS survey results. Acting OPM Director Beth Cobert is quoted as linking the success to how "agency leaders and managers have responded to the president's management agenda" (Corton, 2015).

Setting a goal and requiring leadership accountability are important first steps in leading behavior change. However, as with previous attempts to increase employee engagement, the 2015 process contains no attempt to evaluate whether those assigned to execute tasks had the leadership competencies required to be successful. As Reinhold (2015) pointed out, an increase in employee engagement will come only with developing the leadership competencies represented in Tables 5.2, 5.3, and 5.4, combined with the leaders' ability to implement the competencies. One without the other will not increase employee engagement scores on a sustained basis.

J. Peter Leeds (2015) in "Investment in Senior Executive Training Pays Off" used a 2011 OPM SES survey (OPM, 2011) to determine the amount of leadership development training members of the SES had received since becoming a member of the SES and links the results to increased employee engagement (Leeds, 2015).

The five categories of leadership training created by Leeds (2015) are based on the amount of leadership training received by members of the SES (Table 5.5). Category 5, which comprises 22.8% of those surveyed, contains the group with the highest level of leadership development training. For example, 100% of the most trained participated in a residential leadership development program. In contrast, only 16% of the least trained had a similar experience (Leeds, 2015). Leeds then compared the five categories to the FEVS scores in 2011 and 2012. He found that the more Category 4 and 5 SES leaders were in a federal agency, the higher the employee engagement scores, perceptions of the quality of SES leadership, and perceptions of how agencies manage talent (Leeds, 2015).

Leeds' results are a strong indicator that leadership development training works.

Notwithstanding the fact that leadership development training works, the MSPB (2015), in *Training and Development for the Senior Executive Service: A Necessary Investment*, found no systemic development efforts for members of the SES. The MSPB reviewed questionnaires received from 22 federal agencies requesting information describing SES training and development practices, analyzed the OPM 2011 SES Survey (OPM, 2011) and concluded that even though "(t)raining and development can improve individual and organizational performance … [there] appears to be no systematic way senior executives are trained and developed" (MSPB, 2015, p. i).

Table 5.5 Training Provided to Members of the SES (%)

Since becoming a member of the SES have you ...	*Participated in fewest training opportunities*				*Participated in most training opportunities*
	Category 1: (n=1011, 23% of total respondents)	*Category 2:* (n=1111, 24% of total respondents)	*Category 3:* (n=537, 11.6% of percent total respondents)	*Category 4:* (n=861, 18.6% of total respondents)	*Category 5:* (n=1055, 22.8% of total respondents)
Attended a residential executive development program	16	20	18	0	100
Taken a sabbatical	1	1	1	1	2
Been on a developmental assignment lasting more than 30 days	7	8	5	26	41
Participated in action learning	3	14	7	32	42
Had a mentor advising you for developmental purposes	9	14	10	57	57
Attended a short-term training program for executives	24	94	30	89	89
Completed an executive development plan	10	55	21	70	79
Taken an online training course	22	89	88	79	84
Received formal executive coaching	5	5	36	78	69
Received a 360 degree type assessment	35	29	50	89	91
Served as a mentor	60	69	2	90	88

Source: Leeds (2015, p. 2).

It is not that federal leaders lack motivation to increase government performance: "Public servants are motivated more by mission than financial or other extrinsic rewards and therefore [are] predisposed to respond to public service missions goals, and motives" (Lavigna, 2013, p. 94). But motivation must be supported with leadership development opportunities to increase leadership competencies.

A Plan for Success

The following five recommendations propose a long-term strategic commitment to providing federal leaders with enhanced leadership competencies and opportunities for leadership development required to increase employee engagement and organizational performance over an entire career.

Add ECQs that Increase Employee Engagement and Organizational Success

OPM (2010) describes five Executive Core Qualifications (ECQs)—leading change, leading people, results driven, business acumen, and building coalitions—and 22 interdependent leadership competencies successful executives need to bring "to bear when providing service to the nation" (p. 1).

OPM (2012) developed the ECQs after "extensive research" in the public and private sectors on the attributes of successful executives in both the private and public. The ECQs were reviewed and revalidated "with a few modifications" in 2006 sectors (Introduction). The ECQs are considered the "gold standard" for leadership development because agencies and departments use them not only to set minimum qualifications for eligibility when selecting members of the Senior Executive Service, but also to evaluate managers and leaders at all levels for selection, as factors in performance evaluations, and when designing leadership development programs.

OPM (2015c) states, "The executive core qualifications define the competencies needed to build a federal corporate culture that drives for results, serves customers, and builds successful teams and coalitions within and outside the organization" (p. 1).

Table 5.1, however, shows that since 2010, the existing ECQs have not resulted in increased employee engagement. Additional ECQs should be added to the existing Leadership Framework (Reinhold, 2015) to identify the leadership competencies needed to create a more collaborative, interdependent learning environment that grows employee engagement and productivity at every leader level, including members of the SES. If additional ECQs are adopted, candidates for the SES would have to show evidence of the existing and new leadership competencies to the Qualifications Review Board (QRB), the group convened by OPM to determine if a candidate meets the ECQ requirements necessary to be eligible for selection into the SES (OPM, 2010, p. 6).

The following are suggested additional ECQ leadership competencies to be met by candidates seeking to be certified as eligible for selection into the SES and infused into the Leader Framework (Reinhold, 2015):

- ***Exhibits a commitment to learn about self through feedback and self-reflection, identifies the need to change behavior, and displays the discipline to achieve the changed behavior goal.*** A continuing commitment to learn about self in the context of relating to those led is a basic leadership competency because increasing understanding about self is necessary for increasing engagement with others. Are leaders challenged to continue learning about themselves in relation to those they lead? Based on what they discover, are they willing to learn about their mindset and change their behavior? Do they exhibit the discipline to change their behavior?

Before engaging those led, leaders must first understand the impact of their behavior on followers. This can be accomplished through a 360-degree evaluation, but even more effectively by creating a safe environment where those led are willing to provide truthful feedback. Leaders who hear negative feedback, engage in self-reflection, and determine a need to change their behavior have a higher probability of being successful. Changing behavior is difficult. Leaders who have the willingness to learn and the discipline to change are the types of flexible, resilient leaders needed to increase employee engagement.

- ***Exhibits authentic leadership behavior.*** We make instantaneous decisions concerning whether a leader is behaving authentically or inauthentically. We create distance between ourselves and a leader based on the level of inauthenticity we discern; the greater the level of inauthenticity, the greater the distance. Followers create distance in order to feel safe from a leader hidden behind the mask of inauthenticity. Inauthenticity is antithetical to leaders engaging with those they lead. Without the ability to behave authentically, all other efforts to increase employee engagement will fail. The path to authentic leader behavior, according to Northouse (2016), includes exhibiting:
    - Personal self-awareness, the ability to reflect "on your core values, identity, emotions, motives, and goals, and coming to grips with who really are at the deepest level."
    - A "self-regulatory process whereby individuals use their use their internal moral standards and values to guide their behavior rather than allow outside pressures to control them."
    - A self-regulatory process that refers to an individual's "ability to analyze information objectively and explore other people's opinions."
    - A self-regulatory capacity for "relational transparency": being "open and honest in presenting one's true self to others" (pp. 202–203).
- ***Exhibits a commitment to increase his or her level of emotional intelligence.*** Emotional intelligence is defined as the leadership competency required to create an emotional connection between oneself and those led. This connection leads to employee engagement. As Goleman, Boyatzis, and McKee (2002) point out in *Primal Leadership: Learning to Lead with Emotional Intelligence,* "Great leadership works through the emotions" (p. 1).

  According to Goleman et al. (2002), when leaders are able to resonate with the emotions of those led, they are able to amplify "and prolong the emotional impact of leadership" (p. 20). Resonance "means that people's emotional centers are in sync" (p. 33) and in any "resonant human group, people find meaning in their connection and in their attunement with one another" (p. 218).

  Emotional intelligence comprises both domains in Personal Competence—how we manage ourselves; and domains in Social Competence—how we manage relationships. Personal Competence embraces aspects of self-awareness: emotional self-awareness, accurate self-assessment of one's strengths and weaknesses, and a sound sense of one's self-worth. Self-management incorporates keeping disruptive emotions under control; displaying honesty and integrity; trustworthiness; flexibility in adapting to changing situations; drive to improve performance; readiness to act and seize opportunities; and seeing the upside in events (p. 39).

Social Competence includes social awareness and relationship management. Social awareness revolves around empathy; organizational awareness; and recognizing and meeting follower, client, or customer needs. Relationship management involves inspirational leadership achieved through a compelling vision; influence; developing others; resolving disputes; building bonds; and building teams through collaboration (Goleman et al., 2002, p. 39).

Goleman et al. (2002) believe that the emotional intelligence competencies "can be learned by any leader at any point" (p. 101). By including the acquisition of emotional intelligence by experienced managers in the Managerial Training Framework (Reinhold, 2015), OPM seems to agree with Goleman et al.; but inexplicably, OPM fails to identify the need for supervisors, new managers, current senior managers, applicants to the SES, or current members of the SES to acquire emotional intelligence.

The ability to connect emotionally with those led is particularly important to the Leaders Lead category (Table 5.4) and to Supervisors (Table 5.3). Adding emotional intelligence to the ECQs and expanding the need for its acquisition to every leader at every level could have a positive impact on the employee engagement score.

- ***Exhibits an ability to create a collaborative learning culture.*** Horizontal skill development (thinking and behaving at one's basic comfort level) is not enough to become an effective leader, according to McGuire and Rhodes (2009) in *Transforming Your Leadership Culture.* Leaders need vertical development, or the increased ability to make sense of the world and to create an organizational culture where leaders successfully engage those they lead through collaboration and learning (Berger & Johnston, 2015; McGuire & Rhodes, 2009).

McGuire and Rhodes (2009) describe three stages of organizational culture:

- *Dependent-Conformer:* Command-and-control structure, success depends on "obedience to authority and loyalty, mastery is equated to technical expertise, mistakes are treated as a weakness, and feedback tends to be negative" (p. 22).
- *Independent-Achiever:* Authority and control are distributed. A culture focused on success by adapting faster and better than the competition. Engagement focuses on individual performance, self-interest, and a primary group (p. 88).
- *Interdependent-Collaborator:* A culture where "engagement gets beyond individual achievement to a point where successes and failures are shared

because both are equally regarded as knowledge." An individual's competency is viewed as "talent, skills, knowledge, and behaviors that make the individual and organization successful simultaneously." Further, "group interaction centers on opening up the subject at hand and reaching multiple right answers that can be advocated, integrated, and prioritized" (pp. 88–89).

Developing a leader's ability to develop a leader logic that reflects a phase of adult development necessary for the creation of an interdependent-collaborator culture that relies on respect, trust, group problem-solving and goal achievement would create enhanced employee engagement and increased organizational success.

- ***Exhibits a "corporate" view of government linked to the U.S. Constitution.*** To sufficiently understand public administration, one must view it from the perspective of the three functions of government: management, politics, and law, as David Rosenbloom (1986) posited 30 years ago in *Public Administration: Understanding Management, Politics, and Law in the Public Sector*. OPM (2010) recognized the need for understanding the interrelationship of law, management and politics in its "Guide to Senior Executive Service Qualifications," which states that as they execute the laws of the United States, federal executive decisions should reflect the values of the Constitution:

  > Executives with a "corporate" view of Government share values that are grounded in the fundamental Government ideals of the Constitution: they embrace the dynamics of American Democracy, an approach to governance that provides a continuing vehicle for change within the Federal Government. (p. 1)

  Yet no existing ECQ competency includes knowledge about how the US Constitution can and should influence executive decision making. It should be added.

Separately Evaluate Whether SES Applicants Possess ECQ Leadership Competencies

The six fundamental ECQ competencies—interpersonal skills, oral communication, integrity/honesty, written communication, continual learning, and public service motivation—are the "foundation for each of the Executive Core Qualifications" (OPM, 2010, p. 3).

It is hard to imagine how anyone could be successful as a leader without the fundamental ECQ competencies. Without them, a leader might be a mathematician, scientist, or other subject-matter expert who is able to be successful when acting alone, but could not be successful if any interconnectedness with others in any form is required.

Yet the fundamental ECQs are not separately evaluated to determine whether a person is eligible to be certified for selection into the SES by OPM's Quality

Review Board (QRB). The QRB merely seeks to recognize the fundamental ECQs as portrayed in the five core ECQs.

It is not enough to determine the "foundation" of the ECQs inferentially. They should be separately identified by SES candidates and separately reviewed by the QRB to ensure that these most fundamental competencies have been acquired prior to certification as eligible to be selected into the SES.

Mandate Implementation of Redefined Minimum Leadership Competencies for Aspiring Leaders to SES Selection, Evaluation, and Promotion and Require Training for Those Who Lack It

An integrated training framework, starting with aspiring leaders and leading up to SES selections, was recently designed and published by OPM Chief Human Capital Officer Mark Reinhold (2015). The framework is training that is merely recommended be provided when a promotion occurs. It is based on the sequential acquisition of the leadership competencies defined by ECQs. New supervisors receive HR-related technical knowledge training together with organizational and performance management training. New and experienced managers receive sequential training on managing self and managing others. The experienced manager learns about emotional intelligence, adaptability, fostering employee engagement, and developmental coaching together with managing organizational systems (Reinhold, 2015, pp. 8–9).

Providing the framework training when promotions occur, however, is currently optional. It should be required to ensure that leaders have the leadership competencies necessary to increase employee engagement. In addition, the framework is silent on providing leadership development training to those leaders in leadership positions who have not received the framework training.

To guarantee an increase in organizational performance, OPM, using its statutory authority in 5 USC 4118(a) to "prescribe regulations containing the principles, standards, and related requirements for the programs, and plans thereunder, for the training of employees under this chapter," should mandate the described training to every person who is promoted and to every person at every level who did not receive the training when promoted.

Require SES to Regularly Recertify Employee Engagement Leadership Competencies

It is not enough to provide training when leaders are promoted. A person may be promoted to the supervisory level, receive all framework-suggested training, and retire 25 years later having received no additional training. Or a person selected may have all 28 leadership competencies certified by a Qualifications Review Board prior to selection into the SES but never receive additional training and personal leadership development.

Leader competencies are not static. Once learned, they need to be maintained and expanded. The assumption that a leader who is once exposed to a leader development concept will change behavior consistent with the desired outcome, and fully maintain that change, is to ignore reality.

For example, leaders who want to change after learning to create interdependent collaborator cultures are often fully entrenched in their current culture, which may be command-and-control or dependent-conformer. Because command-and-control is pervasive, particularly in the federal sector, most leaders are acclimatized to organizations and leaders who exhibit command-and-control behavior or conform to dependent-conformer cultures (Schwarz, 2013).

Rewiring our brain is not easy. Despite good intentions, leaders lose their focus on learning because of stress in the workplace or at home. They forget what they learned or find it too difficult to change. Leaders need a regular opportunity to reconnect with the material they've learned in the past, a chance to further their learning with new material, and an environment conducive to recommitting to the change they seek.

The existing process for SES leadership development is not working. Members of the SES are required by 5 C.F.R. § 412.401 to annually create an Executive Development Plan (EDP) and submit it to the agencies' Executive Review Board to help improve their performance. However, a 2011 survey of SES members indicated only half actually completed their EDP (OPM, 2011).

In a recent study of the value of providing training and development to members of the SES, MSPB (2015) concluded "an investment in executive training and development can yield substantial returns in the form of higher performance" (p. i). As the MSPB (2015) stated, "it is imperative that SES have access to relevant training and development opportunities so that they can be in the best position to achieve optimal performance" (p. 7).

OPM should exercise its statutory authority in 5 U.S.C. § 3131(12) to "[p]rovide for the initial and continuing systematic development of highly competent senior executives" by mandating members of the SES to participate in an annual recertification of the material in the existing framework together with the suggested additional ECQs.

As a society, we recognize the need for regular training and updated certification of competencies in many professions (e.g., doctors, lawyers, accountants, program managers). We should require no less of those who are "to provide more effective management of agencies and their functions, the more expeditious administration of the public business" (5 U.S.C. § 1101). The investment will pay off (MSPB, 2015).

Remove the Barriers Necessary to Increasing Employee Engagement

At least three major barriers must be removed before leaders will improve their employee engagement practices.

- ***"Absence of Context" as an excuse for doing nothing.*** OPM (2015b) points out that there are better measures of employee engagement than the identified questions in the Federal Employee Viewpoint Survey, and "consideration of contextual factors within and outside the organization, such as the recent

Federal pay freezes, will help determine how such conditions might differentially affect levels of engagement and where to focus efforts" (p. 17). Robert Lavigna, (2015) in a *Public Administration Review* article, "Public Service Motivation and Employee Engagement," also notes that broad-scale attacks on government create barriers to employee engagement (p. 733).

Seeking more comprehensive measures, or understanding the contextual factors better, does not absolve the president and political leaders in OMB and OPM from the duty to provide leadership development opportunities to create the "strong leaders" required to improve the federal employee engagement index (OPM, 2015d, p. 13). Nor does it absolve federal leaders from accountability for identifying behavior they can change to increase employee engagement.

- ***Reexamine the balance between mandatory technical qualifications and ECQs for selection into the SES.*** When the SES was created in the Civil Service Reform Act of 1978, leadership skills were envisioned as the primary qualifications for entry. When developing the ECQs, OPM also made clear that the ECQs were "designed to assess executive experience and potential—not technical expertise" (OPM, 2015a).

  MSPB recently reviewed all permanent career SES vacancies on USAJobs.gov for 2014. They found "[a]pproximately 80% of the announcements required applicants to describe at least one technical competency in addition to the ECQs to be considered qualified for the position" (OPM 2015c, p. 12).

  The technical qualification requirement raises the question of the impact they have on selection and whether they are more important than the ECQ leadership competencies to selection. As the Partnership for Public Service (PPS, 2014) pointed out in *Building the Enterprise: A New Civil Service Framework*, the SES as originally conceived would comprise individuals with highly developed leadership competencies, who could move from agency to agency to solve difficult problems.

  But that goal has not been realized. PPS (2014) found from recent data that 81% of promotions into the SES came from the same agency; only eight percent came from a different agency (p. 35). It would appear that the technical qualifications are the culprit.

  Technical qualifications are not linked to creating employee engagement. Of the 15 selected questions in the FEVS that measure employee engagement, not one is related to technical expertise. Similarly, in an exercise conducted in American University's Key Executive Leadership Program with close to 3,000 students since 2002, not one has identified technical expertise as the basis for willingness to give discretionary energy to accomplish his or her boss's goals and objectives. It is not technical expertise that creates the emotional connection of employee engagement.

  OPM should be examining the role of technical qualifications as factors in selection of SES candidates to determine if they are defeating the need for leaders with enhanced leadership competencies to engage those they lead to increase government performance.

- ***Funding leadership development training to increase employee engagement and organizational success.*** When Congress cuts agency budgets, leaders are quick to slash leadership development training, notwithstanding the proven link of leadership development to improved organizational results (Donovan et al., 2014; MSPB, 2015; OPM, 2015d).

The quick budget fix to cut leadership development training may occur because of the presumption that leaders do not change their mindsets and behaviors as a result of participating in a leadership development program. It is true that leadership programs limited to observation or conversations with successful leaders, or pep talks and inspirational messages, do not challenge participants to change their behavior. There is ample evidence, however, that leadership programs that challenge leaders to change, and support them as they struggle to change, actually achieve changed behavior (Leeds, 2015; MSPB, 2015). This reduction in spending may also occur because agencies are unwilling to budget a "fully funded, full time equivalent (FTE)" federal position that includes training necessary for skill and leadership development. The normally budgeted FTE cost includes only current salary, expected promotions, within-grade and necessary salary increases, and benefit increase calculations. Training is separately funded, not a cost made part of funding every federal employee.

If an agency budget needs to be reduced and fully funded FTEs are cut, or fully funded FTE positions are not filled, the remaining employees continue to be trained. If an agency budget needs to be reduced and training is separately funded, FTEs are the first to be reduced or eliminated. The short-term advantage of separately funding training is more FTEs may be maintained on the roles, but in the median term there are fewer FTEs who have the position skills and leadership development training necessary to be successful. As a result, the delivery of public service gradually deteriorates over time, destroying public confidence.

The most ardent practitioner of the importance of employee training and leadership development in the face of budget cuts is IRS Commissioner John Koskinen, who promised increased skill and leadership development training while cutting IRS FTEs to pay for the training. On February 3, 2015, in a testimony to the Senate Finance Committee on IRS Budget and Current Operations, Commissioner Koskinen pointed out that the IRS budget had been cut by $1.2 billion over the previous five years. Considering inflation, he stated, the IRS budget was equivalent to the 1998 budget. As a result, he told Congress, he was putting off information technology investment, conducting fewer audits and collection activities, delaying refunds to taxpayers, and answering only 50% of the taxpayer calls for assistance because of FTE reductions (*IRS Budget and Current Operations*, 2015).

Koskinen (*IRS Budget and Current Operations*, 2015) chose to cut additional FTEs to pay for an investment in employee training:

> Our determination to protect the core operations of the agency has led us to the decision that we need to continue to invest in our workforce.

> The ability of the IRS to fulfill its mission depends on the experience, skills and dedication of our employees. We need to do everything we can to ensure that every employee has the leadership, systems and training to help us retain good employees, to support them in their work and to allow them to perform at the highest levels, whether they are involved in customer service, compliance programs or information technology (IT) infrastructure and operational support. (p. 2)

Conclusion

The world is more complex, the federal employee workplace is more unstable, because of budget cuts and external political attacks, and employee engagement is at a lower level now than in 2010 (Table 5.1). New "work processes" and more "leadership accountability" will only whip the dead horse. Providing new life requires adopting the recommended ECQs and providing the leadership development training necessary for continuous learning. Leeds (2015) has shown that an investment in leader development yields an increase in employee engagement. More investment will substantially move the employee engagement index and increase employee and agency organizational results.

References

Berger, J. G. & Johnston, K. (2015). *Simple habits for complex times.* Stanford, CA: Stanford University Press.

Carroll, J. D. (1995, May–June). The rhetoric of reform and political reality in the national performance review. *Public Administration Review, 55*, 302–312.

Corporate Leadership Council. (2004). *Driving employee performance and retention through engagement: A quantitative analysis of the effectiveness of employee engagement strategies.* Washington, DC: Corporate Executive Board.

Corton, C. (2015, October 6). FEVS: Satisfaction edges up; leadership stays low. *Federal Times*. Retrieved from http://www.federaltimes.com/story/government/management/agency/2015/10/06/f evs-satisfaction-edges-up-leadership-stays-low/73475388.

Defense Partnership Council. (1999, December). *Report on the examination of partnership and labor relations in the Department of Defense.*

Donovan, S., Corbert, B., Archuleta, C., & McLaughlin, M. (2014). *Strengthening employee engagement and organizational performance.* [Memorandum for heads of executive departments and agencies, M-15-04]. Washington, DC: Office of Personnel Management. Retrieved from https://www.whitehouse.gov/sites/default/files/omb/memoranda/2015/m-15-04.pdf.

Executive Order No. 12871. 3 C.F.R. 1955–1957 (1993). *Labor-management partnerships.*

Executive Order No. 13203. 3 C.F.R. 761. (2002). *Revocation of executive order and presidential memorandum concerning labor-management partnerships.*

Federal workforce: Preliminary observations on strengthening employee engagement during challenging times: Hearings before the Subcommittee on Government Relations, House Committee on Oversight and Government Reform, 114th Cong. (2015). (Testimony of Robert Goldenkoff, Director of Strategic Issues, Government Accountability Office, GAO-15-529T).

Gallup. (2015). *Q 12 employee engagement.* Retrieved October 27, 2015 from http://www.gallup.com/services/169328/q12-employee-engagement.aspx.

Goleman, D., Boyatzis, R., & McKee, A. (2002). *Primal leadership: Learning to lead with emotional intelligence.* Boston, MA: Harvard University Press.

Gore, A. (1993a). *From red tape to results, creating a government that works better and costs less* [third report of the National Performance Review]. Washington, DC: U.S. Government Printing Office. Retrieved from http://www.nsf.gov/pubs/stis1993/npr93a/npr93a.txt.

Gore, A. (1993b). *From red tape to results, creating a government that works better and costs less: Creating quality leadership and management* [accompanying report of the National Performance Review]. Washington, DC: U.S. Government Printing Office.

Government Accountability Office. (2001, September). *Human capital: Practices that empower and involve employees* (GAO-01-1070). Washington, DC: Author.

Government Accountability Office. (2004a). *Performance budgeting, observations on the use of OMB's program assessment rating tool for the fiscal year 2004 budget* (GAO 04–174). Washington, DC: Author.

IRS budget and current operations: Hearings before the Senate Committee on Finance, 114th Cong. (2015). (Written testimony of John A. Koskinen, Commissioner, Internal Revenue Service). Retrieved November 24, 2015 from https://www.irs.gov/PUP/newsroom/Written_Testimony_of_Commissioner_Koskinen_before_the_Senate_Finance_Committee_on_IRS_Budget_and_Current_Operations.pdf.

Kahn, W. A. (1990). Psychological conditions of personal engagement and disengagement at work. *Academy of Management Journal, 33*(4), 692–724.

Kennedy, J. F. (1963). Undelivered remarks for Dallas Citizens Council, Trade Mart, Dallas, Texas. *Presidential Papers.*

Kettl, D. (1998). *Reinventing government: A fifth-year report card.* Washington, DC: The Brookings Institution.

Lavigna, R. (2013). *Engaging government employees: Motivate and inspire your people to achieve superior performance.* New York, NY: American Management Association.

Lavigna, R. (2015). Public service motivation and employee engagement. *Public Administration Review, 75*(5), 732–733.

Leeds, J. P. (2015, November 24). Investment in senior executive training pays off. *GovExec.Com.* Retrieved from http://www.govexec.com/management/2015/11/investment-senior-executive-training-pays/123956.

Masters, M. (2001). *A final report to the National Partnership Council on evaluating progress and improvements in agencies' organizational performance resulting from labor-management partnerships.* Washington, DC: Office of Personnel Management.

Masters, M., Sickles, C., & Tobias, R. (2010, February 2). *Engaging federal employees through their union representatives to improve agency performance.* Retrieved from http://www.govexec.com/pdfs/021010ar1.pdf.

McGuire, J. B. & Rhodes, G. B. (2009). *Transforming your leadership culture.* San Francisco, CA: Jossey-Bass.

Merit Systems Protection Board. (2008). *The power of federal employee engagement.* Washington, DC: Author.

Merit Systems Protection Board. (2015). Training and development for the senior executive service: A necessary investment. Washington, DC: Author.

Northouse, P. G. (2016). *Leadership: Theory and practice* (7th ed.). Los Angeles, CA: Sage.

Office of Management and Budget. (2009). *Analytical perspectives, budget of the U.S. government, FY2010.* Washington, DC: US Government Printing Office.

Office of Management and Budget. (2010). *Analytical perspectives, budget of the U.S. government, FY2011.* Washington, DC: US Government Printing Office.

Office of Management and Budget. (2011). *Analytical perspectives, budget of the U.S. Government, FY2012.* Washington, DC: US Government Printing Office.

Office of Personnel Management. (2010). *Guide to senior executive service qualifications.* Washington, DC: Office of Personnel Management. Retrieved September 20, 2015 from https://www.opm.gov/policy-data-oversight/senior-executive-service/reference-materials/guidetosesquals_2010.pdf.

Office of Personnel Management. (2011). *Senior executive survey results for fiscal year 2011.* Washington, DC: Office of Personnel Management.

Office of Personnel Management. (2012). *Federal employee viewpoint survey: Employees influencing change.* Washington, DC: Author.

Office of Personnel Management. (2015a). *Senior executive service: Executive core qualifications.* Retrieved September 20, 2015 from https://www.opm.gov/policy-data-oversight/senior-executive-service/executive-core-qualifications.

Office of Personnel Management. (2015b, September 28). OPM releases government-wide FEVS scores and UnlockTalent.gov [Press Release]. Retrieved from https://www.opm.gov/news/releases/2015/09/fevs-press-release-92815.

Office of Personnel Management. (2015c). *Federal employee viewpoint survey results: Employees influencing change.* Retrieved from http://www.fedview.opm.gov/2015FILES/2015_FEVS_Gwide_Final_Report.PDF.

Office of Personnel Management. (2015d). *Engaging the federal workforce: How to do it & prove it.* Retrieved from https://admin.govexec.com/media/gbc/docs/pdfs_edit/engaging_the_federal_workforce_white_paper.pdf.

Partnership for Pubic Service. (2014). *Building the enterprise: A new civil service framework.* Washington, DC: Author.

Reinhold, M. D. (2015). *Federal supervisory and managerial frameworks and guidance* [Memorandum for human resources directors].Washington, DC: Office of Personnel Management. Retrieved from https://www.chcoc.gov/content/federal-supervisory-and-managerial-frameworks-and-guidance.

Relyea, H., Cornejo Riemann, M. J., & Hogue, H. B. (2001). *The national performance review and other government reform initiatives: An overview, 1993–2001* (CRS Report No. RL30596). Washington, DC: Congressional Research Service.

Rosenbloom, D. H. & Rosenbloom, D. D. (1986) *Public administration: Understanding management, politics, and law in the public sector.* New York, NY: Random House.

Schwarz, R. (2013). *Smart leaders, smarter teams: How you and your team get unstuck to achieve results.* San Francisco, CA: Jossey-Bass.

Tobias, R. M. (2010). Working with employee unions. In S. Condrey (Ed.), *Human resource management in government* (3rd ed.). San Francisco, CA: Jossey:Bass.

6 Administering and Leading in the Federal Government

The Need for an Adaptive Leadership Approach for 21st-Century Leaders

Ruth Zaplin and Bill Valdez

> The most common cause of failure in leadership is produced by treating adaptive challenges as if they were technical problems.
>
> —Ronald Heifetz, Alexander Grashow, and Marty Linsky

In today's globalized world of permanent white water change, administering and leading within the federal government's executive branch is arguably one of the most daunting assignments any executive, public or private, could undertake. More and more, leading in the public service is about handling challenges characterized by volatility, uncertainty, complexity, and ambiguity (VUCA). And, in this context, the typical career federal executive must deal with hundreds, if not thousands, of staff and millions, if not billions, of dollars in budget that deliver extraordinarily diverse products and services to the American taxpayer. All of this is done within a highly charged and transparent political environment that punishes failures and rarely rewards quiet and steady success.

The Office of Personnel Management (OPM) identified the Executive Core Qualifications (ECQs) as the general set of leadership skills/attributes required to successfully administer federal programs (Merit Systems Protection Board [MSPB], 2015). The ECQs fall into two general categories:

- Leadership Skills: Leading change (creativity and innovation, external awareness, flexibility, resilience, strategic thinking, vision), leading people (conflict management, leveraging diversity, developing others, team building), and building coalitions (partnering, political savvy, influencing/negotiating).
- Business Skills: Results driven (accountability, customer service, decisiveness, entrepreneurship, problem solving, technical credibility) and business acumen (human capital management, technology management, financial management).

In addition, OPM identified six fundamental competencies that serve as the foundation for the ECQs: (a) interpersonal skills; (b) oral communication; (c) integrity/honesty; (d) written communications; (e) continual learning; and (f) public service motivation. Collectively, the ECQs and the fundamental competencies are also the basis for selection into the Senior Executive Service (SES).

Currently, executive branch leaders, at all levels, learn their craft, in large part, through trial and error and an array of agency and OPM training and development programs. We argue this is a failed model and make the case that the federal government should adopt more rigorous, systematic, and continuous training and development programs for both political and career leaders to improve their ability to better respond to the unfolding challenges they will increasingly encounter in a VUCA world. We provide examples of these challenges and contend they require a new paradigm of federal leader training and development that focuses on developing, not only the ECQs and the fundamental competencies but the mental capacity to handle VUCA challenges.

As a framework for discussion, we use adaptive leadership theory, a preeminent 21st century leadership theory. We first present a brief overview of the adaptive leadership approach with selected examples of adaptive challenges faced by federal executives. Next, we discuss the roles of political appointees and career SES, where we are now in terms of their training and development, and the far-ranging impacts of the prevailing command-and-control organizational cultures that result largely from the dynamic of the relationship between political appointees and career SES. The chapter concludes with a discussion of the Cynefin framework, a decision-making model particularly useful for facing today's challenges and high-level training and development recommendations.

The Adaptive Leadership Approach

The adaptive leadership approach rests on the assumption that there are two broad categories of leadership—technical and adaptive. According to Heifetz and Linsky (2002):

> Leadership would be a safe undertaking if your organizations and communities only faced problems for which they already knew the solutions. … We call these technical problems. But there is a whole host of problems that are not amenable to authoritative expertise or standard operating procedures. … We call these adaptive challenges because they require experiments, new discoveries, and adjustments from numerous places in the organization or community. Without learning new ways—changing attitudes, values, and behaviors—people cannot make the adaptive leap necessary to thrive in the new environment. The sustainability of change depends on having the people with the problem internalize the change itself. (p. 13)

Heifetz, Grashow, and Linksy (2009) state:

> While technical problems may be very complex and critically important (like replacing a faulty heart valve during cardiac surgery), they have known solutions that can be implemented by current know-how. They can

> be resolved through the application of authoritative expertise and through the organization's current structures, procedures, and ways of doing things. (p. 19)

Adaptive challenges, on the other hand, cannot be dealt with by following established knowledge, proven guidelines, and methods known to experts. Adaptive challenges are those for which the necessary knowledge to respond does not yet exist, so training in "best practices" inevitably falls short (Heifetz et al., 2009). Both the problems and the solutions are unclear.

As illustrated in the examples presented, problems do not always come neatly packaged as either technical or adaptive; most problems/challenges come mixed, with the technical and adaptive elements intertwined (Heifetz et al., 2009). Developing business processes, for example monitoring systems that predict potential failures in project governance or workforce analytics to identify trends that impact major national occupation gaps, such as cyber security workers, are technical challenges. Dealing with the system dynamics of the "hollow state," in the example given below, is an adaptive challenge.

"Hollowing Out" of the Modern Federal Government

In 1962, when John F. Kennedy was president, the federal government's executive branch had an annual budget of $107 billion (Office of Management and Budget [OMB], 2016) and employed 1.8 million career civil servants (OPM, 2015b). In real terms (adjusted for inflation with the gross domestic product price index), the FY16 $3.9 trillion federal budget is five times larger than that of 1962, but the number of executive branch employees in 2016 has stayed relatively the same at two million. A major difference over the past 56 years is the use of third parties (primarily contractors and state and local officials) to administer government programs, a process that Milward, Provan, and Else (1993) describe as the "hollowing out" of the executive branch.

Whereas a federal government manager in 1962 would have had direct control over budgets and federal staff, in 2016 that same manager has much less direct control and must use different administrative processes to successfully manage taxpayer and deficit dollars. Executive branch leaders "oversee an extended chain of grants and contracts with little real leverage over contractor behavior," which results in government "by remote control" (Frederickson & Frederickson, 2007, pp. 18–21). Because there has been little or no traction expanding the capacity of leaders to manage these extended networks of providers, this appears to be an adaptive challenge.

Accretion of "Mission-Extrinsic Public Values"

Rosenbloom (2014) documents 37 examples of "mission-extrinsic public values"—defined as those responsibilities assigned to a government agency that are not directly related to the agency's core mission—that have been delegated to executive branch agencies through court rulings, legislation, and presidential executive orders. Mission-extrinsic public values, ranging from ensuring diversity at an agency to implementing small business goals, are focused on achieving important societal goals, but they greatly increase the complexity of administering the modern federal government.

Federal executives prior to the 1960s were not expected to manage their programs in ways that provided an "added value" to society. Rosenbloom notes that the "new public administration" movement of the 1960s and 1970s led to calls for "public administrators to use their positions to promote social equity" (Rosenbloom, 2014, p. 24) such as ensuring that disabled workers could be accommodated or that environmental justice was factored into decisions about infrastructure projects.

This accretion in responsibilities has impacted the modern federal bureaucracy in subtle and not-so-subtle ways. Whereas a federal executive in the 1960s could focus on the mission of the agency to the exclusion of social equity requirements, executives in 2016 must balance a myriad of social equity requirements in every decision they make. This results in a shift from strictly addressing technical problems (transactional considerations), e.g., building a project on time and on budget, to adaptive considerations, e.g., the environmental implications of a project and the role of stakeholders in the project approval processes.

A Constantly Evolving Dynamic Federal Ecosystem Requires Adaptive Solutions

In the scientific world, the biology community has discovered that complex external influences (drought, disease, pollution, etc.) significantly impact not just entire ecosystems (such as the Earth), but also individual ecosystems (people). This has led the biology community to map the human genome to understand the full effects of the genome on disease and aging, while the physics community has developed engineering and data systems that enable the biology community to develop bioinformatics to parse out the complexities of the system.

The federal government is a prime example of a dynamic ecosystem that has evolved over time through interactions with other systems (state governments, other nations, private sector) and has developed its own processes, rules, and regulations to manage itself and survive/prosper. Dynamic feedback loops affect the administration of the U.S. federal government's executive branch on a daily basis—whether it is a Supreme Court ruling that might require a new regulatory policy or a collapse in oil prices that leads to a reconsideration of how to structure national energy security programs. These interactions and feedback loops have accelerated because the responsibilities of the executive branch have enlarged due to an accretion of mission-extrinsic public values and the evolution of the "hollow state."

Rosenbloom has identified competition for resources as a key driver of agency behavior and administrative processes ("Agency becomes adversary of agency";

Rosenbloom, 2014, p. 449) and noted that post-World War II, the executive branch grew by leaps and bounds in size and authorities. Rosenbloom describes the evolution of the five key elements of the executive branch (boundaries, rules, processes, participants, and resources) as having resulted in a "three perspectives model" of public administration that has collapsed many of the traditional judicial and legislative functions envisioned by the framers into the executive branch.

Rosenbloom (1983, 2014) has concluded that the modern federal government is increasingly moving to a business model that emphasizes a strong executive branch that must be capable of administering highly complex programs and projects. Executive branch leaders must "integrate the three approaches (legal, managerial and political) to public administration" (Rosenbloom, 1983, p. 226). Zalmanovitch (2014) argues that the evolution of executive branch leadership has been strongly influenced over the past 35 years by legislation and presidential executive orders that have increased political influence in the executive branch, with a diminution in the traditional managerial role played by career executive branch leaders.

Rosenbloom's and Zalmanovitch's analyses provide insights into the complicated mix of both technical and adaptive challenges faced by many federal managers, who feel under siege from two directions—the demand from Congress and the president to manage increasingly complex programs and having their decision-making authorities assumed by political leaders. Moreover, career civil service leaders are asked by Congress and the president to be "accountable" for their actions, but the majority of policy decisions made within the executive branch are made by political leaders who rely on career leaders for advice but ultimately make the final decision, a state of affairs that seems ripe for adaptive change.

Roles of Executive Branch Senior Leaders

There are two categories of executive branch senior leaders: the 3,000 political appointees who have an average tenure of 2.5 years in office and serve at the pleasure of the president and the 7,200 career SES who are selected in a rigorous competitive process. Political leaders cannot be supervised or evaluated by career federal employees. In addition, career executives are required to follow the direction of political leaders and are generally in support roles to political leaders (Lewis, 2008). This distinction between career and political leadership is important to understand before career training and development programs can be successfully developed.

Role of Political Appointees

The role of the political appointee is to provide essential leadership and policy direction for the civil and military services that run the daily machinery of the federal government. According to a study conducted by the National Academy of Public Administration (2009, p. 13), SES members view the role of the political appointee as the person who sets the tone for the administration, engages with key people both within and outside the organization, and communicates his or her vision and goals. In this role, the appointee:

- articulates an understanding of the administration's policies;
- is responsible for quickly getting a sense of the organization and setting a positive tone by reaching out and acknowledging the value of the career workforce;
- needs to let the workforce get to know who he or she is in the first 30 days of the appointment; and
- engages with external stakeholders and interest groups, with particular attention paid to Congress.

Political appointees are placed into management and leadership positions of organizations such as the Department of Homeland Security, which has 22 separate operating units, an FY16 budget of $48 billion, and 250,000 employees scattered across the US and abroad (OMB, 2016). They rarely have experience with that agency and generally do not have the time to understand the culture and learn the business processes of the agency before being "thrown" into the maelstrom of fire drills and crises that seem to dominate the time and attention of leaders at major federal agencies.

Role of Career SES

As originally conceived in the Civil Service Reform Act (CSRA) of 1978 that established the SES, the SES was envisioned as a corps of executives who possess a broad government perspective and are capable of serving in multiple leadership positions across government agencies. The purpose of the SES was "to ensure that the executive management of the Government of the United States is responsive to the needs, policies, and goals of the Nation and otherwise is of the highest quality" (The Senior Executive Service, 1978) and "to create a stronger link and facilitate a better working relationship between political appointees and federal employees" (Carey, 2012, p. 4).

Career SES advise political appointees about what is and what is not possible for an agency to do within its legal authority and tend to focus on program operations (National Academy of Public Administration, 2009). As new political appointees arrive, the SES must help them quickly understand the agency and build good working relationships to advance the goals set for their organization.

During presidential transitions, which can take several months before a new administration is installed, the consistency and guidance for maintaining government operations provided by the career SES is especially important. The SES must maintain the flow of work in support of the agency's mission, while simultaneously preparing for the arrival of new leadership.

As described in the MSPB report (2015), the SES insignia of a keystone—the center stone that holds all the stones on an arch in place—signifies that career SES serve as the connection between politically appointed agency leadership and civil servants. Once the new administration is in place, the SES continues to serve in a variety of roles including:

- providing guidance and recommendations to top leadership in areas of the SES member's expertise;
- managing the federal workforce fairly and effectively;
- promoting workplace improvements, innovations, and creativity;
- ensuring that business processes (procurement, HR, IT systems, etc.) are effectively and efficiently run;
- evaluating agency performance and programs to determine if the desired outcomes are achieved; and
- building and maintaining partnerships with other stakeholder groups.

The broad criteria common to all senior executive jobs as established by the CSRA are that the individual:

- directs the work of an organizational unit;
- is responsible for the success of one or more specific programs or projects;
- monitors progress toward meeting organizational goals and periodically evaluates and makes appropriate adjustments to such goals;
- supervises the work of employees other than personal assistants at least 25% of the time; or
- otherwise exercises important policy making, policy determining, or other executive functions.

A 2011 survey of SES indicated that only 21% of career SES members agreed that their positions did not require technical skills, indicating a divide between the original vision for SES and the realities that SES face in their daily jobs (OPM, 2012). This has led the MSPB to conclude that "it may be time to examine what the executive's roles, duties, and responsibilities should be to meet present and future challenges" (MSPB, 2015, p. 12).

Consistent with the MSPB report (2015), we argue that the fundamental differences between the original vision of how the SES was to function and how the SES functions today only underscores the urgency of re-examining their training and development needs. It further begs the question related to the ECQs: should even the baseline training of the ECQs be differentially taught?

Training and Development of Political Appointees and Career SES: Where We Are Now

Political appointees seldom have federal government executive branch experience. They receive little, if any, training before they begin managing the vast organizations they have been selected by the president to lead notwithstanding the fact that at the start of each new administration studies are done about the need to train new political appointees in the basics of administering and leading the executive branch (Volcker Commission, 2003) and new administrations always work with OPM to "orient" their new political appointees in a series of workshops that go over the basics of federal government administration.

By the time a new crop of political appointees learns the names of the direct reports and the acronyms used for each of the operating units (FEMA, USCC, etc.) they are likely to be on their way out of the building. Appointees rarely receive training related to mastering the ECQs. And, as the examples further below illustrate, even when they do receive this training, their executive positions require much more than mastery of the ECQs.

Related to the training and development of the career SES, the basic premise is that to perform their broad functions well, the SES must possess high proficiency levels in the two broad categories of ECQs and the six fundamental competencies. As discussed in the 2015 MSPB report, this requires a commitment on their part to: (a) place a high priority on their continued self-development; (b) allocate the time needed for continued training and development; and (c) have the resources to obtain the needed training and development on an ongoing basis. According to the MSPB report (2015), these conditions are not often met.

In practice, only half of career senior executives have completed Executive Development Plans (EDPs). According to the MSPB report (2015), the absence of completed EDPs indicates that there may not be written documentation to identify training needs and possible activities to address them. Further, only seven out of 23 agencies surveyed for the MSPB report state that SES employees frequently receive the training and development activities identified in the EDPs (p. 17).

In summary, according to the report, "there is no systematic way that career senior executives are trained and developed" because training and development practices vary across and possibly within organizations and, further, "[t]o achieve continuous systematic development of senior executives, a more planned and methodical approach is needed" (MSPB, 2015, p. 18). We contend that even if training of the ECQs were taught more systematically and differentially to address the changing role of the SES, this would still not be sufficient to prepare them to lead in a VUCA world. At present, the absence of rigorous, systematic, and continuous training and development programs for political appointees and career SES serving in the executive branch results in federal government executives who are ill prepared to meet the increasingly complex challenges of the 21st century.

Consequences of Inadequate Training and Development Programs

Paul Light (2014) has analyzed a "cascade of failures" in the federal government between 2001 and 2014, including Hurricane Katrina, the Obama health care launch, and food safety recalls. Among the top reasons for these failures, Light said, were inept policy choices and leadership failures. In most cases, the circumstances were so fast moving and complex that leaders were overwhelmed.

Indeed, scholars agree that few public service leaders around the world—East, West, North, or South—have been able to handle the overwhelming cognitive and emotional stresses of the challenges that face them—economic dislocation, large-scale migration, global financial crises, environmental degradation, law-and-order problems and other looming threats. And, facing the mental and physical challenges of running faster and faster on a 24/7 treadmill, public service leaders find themselves on the verge of emotional burnout and physical exhaustion. In private, many candidly admit that they are "in over their heads," as suggested by the provocative title of a book by Robert Kegan (1994).

Signs of More Rigor, But Still Not Enough

On a more positive note, the Chief Human Capital Officers Council on September 28, 2015, issued a memorandum with information about the *Federal Supervisory and Managerial Frameworks and Guidance* (Reinhold, 2015). Consistent with the recommendations of the MSPB report for training and developing members of the SES, the *Federal Supervisory and Managerial Frameworks and Guidance* (*Frameworks and Guidance*) provides a proactive development approach targeting the training and development of the following levels of federal employees: aspiring leader/team leader, new supervisor (first three months), new supervisor (first year), new leader (first year), experienced leader, and senior leader (Reinhold, 2015).

Targeted toward developing high potential employees to become SES eligible, the document also incorporates training and development recommendations as well as leadership competencies and human resources technical knowledge needed to administer federal programs. Intended to assist senior leaders with succession planning, the *Frameworks and Guidance:*

- bridges strategic, tactical, and operational perspectives;
- aligns with federal regulations;
- provides for accountable and measurable objectives; and
- incorporates diverse learning delivery approaches.

In short, the *Frameworks and Guidance* is intended to help execute OPM's Federal Supervisory and Managerial Training Framework of 2012 *(Frameworks and Guidance,* 2015*)*. In the long run, the *Frameworks and Guidance* should go a long way toward ensuring systematic and continuous training and development of the ECQs, the fundamental competencies, and human resource "essentials."

Consistent with our argument, however, we believe the training and development now recommended in the *Frameworks and Guidance* is not sufficient to adequately prepare leaders to face adaptive challenges. We contend that federal employees, at all levels, will increasingly be required to deal with adaptive challenges where, in the words of Heifetz and his colleagues, prior knowledge no longer works and expert solutions are often contradictory, inapplicable, or nowhere to be found (2009).

Command and Control Organizational Cultures

The dynamic of the relationship of political appointees and career SES is, we believe, an adaptive challenge in and of itself given the nature of their roles as presently defined. Consider that new political appointees must rely on senior civil servants to help them fulfill election promises. As articulated by the Public Sector Consortium in their classic article entitled, "The Leadership Dilemma in a Democratic Society: Re-energizing the Practice of Leadership for the Public Good" (2003), this reliance creates a need for short-term results quickly achieved in a micro-managed environment and the need to reward senior leaders for achieving "results" in spite of the long-term impact on the employees or the organization.

Further, with an average tenure of 2.5 years in government, a political appointee will not be accountable for the failure of a program that is implemented over 5 to 10 years, but the bureaucrats remaining at the agency will be held responsible by Congress and the general public for program failures. This was made evident to the Obama administration, which inherited a Department of Homeland Security that was created in the aftermath of 9/11 but did not have the organizational structures and business processes sufficient to respond to disasters that occurred after President Bush left office, such as the BP Gulf oil spill in 2010.

The result of this relationship dynamic is the further institutionalization of command-and-control organizational cultures with a short-term focus. When the focus is on the short term, leaders start micromanaging and applying a command-and-control leadership style. This leadership style is also conducive to treating everything as a technical problem (if you are a hammer, everything looks like a nail). This leadership style is deeply entrenched in the federal government and has a long history.

Evolution of Command and Control Leadership

The "command-and-control" leadership style was embedded in the civil service through the 1883 Pendleton Civil Service Act and has remained the dominant leadership model for over 130 years. The Pendleton Act originated from political patronage scandals in the 1870s and created a career civil service that is premised on merit-based competition and freedom from political influence (Lewis, 2008).

The Pendleton Act also fostered the creation of a professional class of executive branch leaders who were primarily business managers and were charged with administering the federal government as efficiently and effectively as possible. Thus, a broad knowledge of key business processes was assumed to be a critical skill required of career federal executives (Rosenbloom, 1983).

This highly structured business model for the federal government executive branch remained in place through World War II, but the emergence of the U.S. as a world power created the need for new administrative processes within the federal government's executive branch. As the executive branch's budget and authorities grew, the business processes used to administer programs were also expanded, resulting in a complex set of laws, regulations, presidential executive orders, and directives that now serve as the codex for administering the federal government.

Dealing with this complexity is a critically important challenge faced by both political appointees and members of the SES. The 1978 Civil Service Reform Act was a partial response to the changing nature of executive branch leadership and administration. And, as stated, at present, very few SES receive rigorous, systematic, and continuous training and development for the ECQs; again, even if they did, this training and development would not be sufficient to enable them to effectively anticipate or respond to complex challenges.

Whenever a natural disaster occurs, such as Hurricane Katrina or the 2013 Texas fertilizer plant explosion, coordination among federal agencies is inevitability halting and indecisive (Light, 2014), despite the fact that agencies such as the Department of Homeland Security and the Environmental Protection Agency know with certainty that something bad will happen sometime in the near future.

Why does this uncertainty and indecision occur? We believe the root cause is that senior executives have failed to develop the capacity to see things from new viewpoints, assimilate complex concepts, and address real-world opportunities using tools that fit the complexity of the circumstances they face (Snowden & Boone, 2007) One such tool is the Cynefin framework (pronounced ku-*nev*-in), a leader's framework for decision making in a VUCA world.

The Cynefin Framework

The Cynefin decision making framework has implications for current federal government leaders. It is an approach to leadership and decision making based on complexity science (Snowden & Boone, 2007). Snowden and Boone (2007) describe the five domains of the Cynefin framework as follows:

> The Cynefin framework helps leaders determine the prevailing operative context so that they can make appropriate choices. Each domain requires different actions. *Simple* and *complicated* contexts assume an ordered universe, where cause-and-effect relationships are perceptible, and right answers can be determined based on the facts. *Complex* and *chaotic* contexts are unordered—there is no immediately apparent relationship between cause and effect, and the way forward is determined based on emerging patterns. The ordered world is the world of fact-based management; the unordered world represents pattern-based management. The very nature of the fifth context—*disorder*—makes it particularly difficult to recognize when one is in it. Here, multiple perspectives jostle for prominence, factional leaders argue with one another, and cacophony rules. The way out of this realm is to break down the situation into constituent parts and assign each to one of the other four realms. Leaders can then make decisions and intervene in contextually appropriate ways. (p. 4)

To elaborate further, in complex situations in a disordered world, there are so many variables and so many things that might happen that they require not only a different way of *acting* in the world but also a whole different way of *seeing* the world. Garvey Berger and Johnston, (2015) call this the world of the possible rather than the probable. They state, "coping with the probable is what humans and human systems are most oriented toward. Dealing with the nearly endless numbers of things that are possible is beyond our easy reckoning and requires new approaches" (p. 42). Adaptive challenges occur in the world of the possible.

In chaotic situations in a disordered world, there is a temporary dissolution into a random state in which things need to be stabilized and moved into another domain for longer-term work (Garvey Berger & Johnston, 2015, p. 42). The other domain is disorder, when we don't make a thoughtful decision about what sorts of actions the situation might require and we instead just act out of our preferences (Garvey Berger & Johnston, 2015). Of primary concern to us, given the deeply embedded command-and-control organizational cultures in the federal government, is, we believe, the temptation of federal leaders to use the traditional command-and-control management style they are familiar with as a fallback position which mostly takes them into the realms of the probable (simple and complicated), and rarely into the complex realm where adaptive challenges occur. In other words, we contend that federal leaders, given the nature of the cultures that they operate in, treat adaptive (complex) challenges as technical problems in the simple and complicated domains of an ordered world.

Related to the complicated domain, in the words of Garvey Berger and Johnston (2015);

> In a complicated system, we search for likely cause and effect. We try to understand the variables and figure out which are most important. We try to create processes and procedures that are repeatable and scalable, and that lead to predictable outcomes. ... We do not tend to wonder whether our basic assumptions about the predictability of the world are themselves flawed. (p. 45)

A simple domain is characterized by stability and clear cause-and-effect relationships that are easily discernable by everyone (Snowden & Boone, 2007). This is the only context that, when properly assessed, requires straightforward management and monitoring, i.e., simple problems are well-suited to being addressed in a command and control culture. It is no wonder that, in high-pressure contexts to get short-term results, federal leaders "favor" operating in a simple domain. Garvey Berger and Johnston (2015), describe the typical way organizational problems, e.g., not enough leadership-bench strength, is solved when operating in the simple domain:

> We see a current problem (not enough leadership-bench strength), we see the hoped-for solution (more leaders), and we connect a fairly simple cause-and-effect line to get us what we want (a talent management system that

> we have seen in another organization with great leadership-bench-strength). Our resources get poured into the solution, and soon enough implementing the solution becomes its own challenge. (p. 45)

In summary, adaptive challenges require leaders to have not only a different way of acting in the world, but also an entirely different way of seeing the world (Garvey Berger & Johnston, 2015). Technical problem solving is *not* helpful in complex situations. In the words of Garvey Berger and Johnston (2015):

> There's too much emphasis on the narrowing of the problems and the implementing of a crisp and clean solution. If things weren't so interconnected, if they weren't so volatile, if they weren't so messy, this might work. But as it is, these sorts of cause-and-effect solutions rarely work for complex problems. (p. 46)

It follows that collaboration, not hierarchy, will become a more important skill to leaders in the future.

Conclusion

Our core conclusion is that public service leaders will have to develop new mental capabilities—new ways of seeing—in real time, moment by moment, during the process of working on the leadership challenge. To address adaptive challenges successfully, they must be able to create new knowledge on the spot, not merely apply existing knowledge or past practices.

When no one knows what is going on or what to do, new ways of thinking are necessary. This involves changing *how leaders know*, not changing *what they know*. The structure of a leader's mind is more important for executive functioning and decision making than the content of a leader's mind. Mindset, not skillset, should now be the determining factor in how well top public leaders perform.

If the paradigm of leadership development were to shift from skillset to mindset, leaders would become more conscious of what they usually take for granted—how they see the world and how they should pay attention to what is usually invisible to them. They would begin to learn how to surface and examine their own taken-for-granted assumptions, beliefs, and perceptual frameworks—in other words, how they see the world through their prevailing "prism" (Marshak, 2006), and the narratives they construct about what they see.

Adaptive leaders have learned how to update their mental models on the spot—see with new eyes—and ferret out meaning in fresh, unfiltered ways to respond effectively to challenges (Heifetz et al., 2009). When necessary, they create new mental maps, revise old ones, and think anew. They have the courage and wisdom to drop or "unlearn" unproductive ways of thinking and acting. They are not locked into only one way of seeing, one interpretation, one solution, one narrative. They leverage paradoxes and polarities rather than choose one pole at the expense of the other. Understanding the polarities and paradoxes of a chosen direction helps leaders draw the right sort of boundary—the boundary that attempts to deal with the complexity inside the system rather than trying to solve it away (Garvey Berger & Johnston, 2015, p. 95).

As we have argued, modern federal government executive branch leaders, political or career, simply have not had the training and development required to understand and deal effectively with adaptive challenges given their level of complexity. That is the reason they experience what is commonly referred to in bureaucracy as "paralysis by analysis" and what Snowden and Boone (2007) call the "entrained thinking" that occurs when "a group of experts hits a stalemate, unable to agree on any answers because of each individual's entrained thinking—or ego" (p. 71).

The passage of the 1993 Government Performance and Results Act (GPRA) and other "government reform" efforts (including the 2010 GPRA Modernization Act) can be viewed as attempts to bring order to an unordered world, freeing the bureaucracy from paralysis by analysis (OMB, 2015b). Congress and past administrations have tried to instill a culture of discipline and accountability to achieve national objectives by effectively implementing accountability projects and training executives in the use of GPRA tools. This effort has largely failed to produce results (Groszyk, 1995).

The reason for this failure is that when operating in complex contexts, faced with adaptive challenges, federal leaders are likely to experience what Jim Collins (2015) describes as an obsession "on systemic constraints" (p. 9). Without understanding the unique requirements of the system they are operating within as well as the environmental factors that are impacting them, executive branch leaders, in an effort to get results, attempt to solve adaptive challenges as technical problems or get distracted to such an extent that they cannot achieve the primary mandates of their organization and deliver on its mission.

The epigraph at the beginning of this chapter is, "the most common cause of failure in leadership is produced by treating adaptive challenges as if they were technical problems" (Heifetz et al., 2009, p. 19). The structure of the modern administrative state—with its frequent turnover in political leadership and turf rivalries within and among agencies created by overlapping authorities and responsibilities—guarantees, we conjecture, indecision and slow movement. Better preparing leaders to anticipate these barriers and work around them may create more effective governance, but only in the short term. What is ultimately needed for the long term is a leadership-focused "government reform" effort that trains and develops executive branch leaders to lead adaptive change in an increasingly complex world.

Recommendations

We recommend an approach to the career training and development of executive branch political appointees and senior executives that goes beyond merely increasing the content of their expert knowledge or adding to their repertoire of behaviors. We have made the case that an inner, more personal, transformation is necessary; a transformational path that develops, more than anything else, senior executives' ability to see with new eyes.

Ultimately, the effectiveness of executive branch senior leaders can only be assessed by how well they respond in real time under conditions of permanent white water when no one knows what to do but immediate action is essential. No single set of skill-based or behavioral competencies (e.g., planning, listening, deciding, managing conflict, etc.) is sufficient for making a high-performing leader (Cook-Greuter, 2004, p. 276).

Therefore, we make the following recommendations:

- ***Create training and development programs that differentiate between the needs of political and career leaders.*** Political leaders require a crash course in the fundamentals of executive branch governance and continuous development to deal with adaptive change. Career leaders also require both governance and adaptive skills developed over their careers. In addition, both leadership cadres require training and development to understand how to share the burdens of administering the modern executive branch.
- ***Develop a new paradigm for leadership development of the senior civil service and political leaders based on developing mindsets not skillsets.*** What senior leaders need to learn most is how to radically transform their current mental models when they are out-of-date or no longer useful.
- ***Strengthen existing technical and behavioral skills training and development.*** Senior leaders must acquire the skills and behaviors, especially those involving emotional intelligence competencies, needed to build trusting, mutually respectful, results-oriented relationships with others. This training and development must be systematic and rigorous.
- ***Equip leaders to operate in ordered and unordered contexts.*** Senior executives must learn to differentiate technical problems from adaptive challenges. They must develop their capacity and use of tools, e.g., the Cynefin framework, to operate in ordered (simple and complicated) and unordered contexts (complex and chaotic) to deal with the often "mixed" (technical and adaptive) challenges they are increasingly faced with.

Given the fact that the federal government touches the lives of every U.S. citizen on a daily basis and is the greatest influencer of the world economy, we must, as a nation, develop a 21st century executive branch leadership cadre that is capable of delivering on the great public trust they have been given.

References

Carey, M. P. (2012). *The senior executive service: Background and options for reform.* (CRS Report No. R41801). Retrieved from http://fas.org/sgp/crs/misc/R41801.pdf.

Collins, J. (2005). *Good to Great and the social sectors: A monograph to accompany Good to Great.* Boulder, CO: HarperCollins.

Cook-Greuter, S. R. (2004). Making the case for a developmental perspective. *Industrial and Commercial Training, 36,* 275–281.

Frederickson, D. G., & Frederickson, H. G. (2007). *Measuring the performance of the hollow state.* Washington, DC: Georgetown University Press.

Garvey Berger, J., & Johnston, K. (2015). *Simple habits for complex times: Powerful practices for leaders.* Stanford, CA: Stanford Business Books.

Groszyk, W. (1995). *Implementation of the Government Performance and Results Act of 1993.* Washington, DC: Office of Management and Budget. Retrieved from http://govinfo.library.unt.edu/npr/library/omb/gpra.html/.

Heifetz, R. A., & Linsky, M. (2002). *Leadership on the line: Staying alive through the dangers of leading.* Boston, MA: Harvard Business School Publishing.

Heifetz, R. A., Grashow, A., & Linsky, M. (2009). *The practice of adaptive leadership: Tools and tactics for changing your organization and the world.* Boston, MA: Harvard Business Press.

Kegan, R. (1994). *In over our heads: The mental demands of modern life.* Cambridge, MA: Harvard University Press.

Lewis, D. E. (2008). *The politics of presidential appointments: Political control and bureaucratic performance.* Princeton, NJ: Princeton University Press.

Light, P. (2014). *A cascade of failures: Why government fails and how to stop it. Washington, DC: Brookings Institution.* Retrieved from http://www.brookings.edu/research/papers/2014/07/14-cascade-failures-why-government-fails-light.

Marshak, R. J. (2006). *Covert processes at work: Managing the five hidden dimensions of organizational change.* San Francisco, CA: Berrett-Koehler Publishers.

Merit Systems Protection Board. (2015). *Training and development for the senior executive service: A necessary investment.* Washington, DC: Author.

Milward, H., Provan, K., & Else, B. (1993). What does the Hollow State look like? In Barry Bozeman (Ed.), *Public management: The state of the art* (pp. 309–22). San Francisco, CA: Jossey-Bass.

National Academy of Public Administration. (2009). *Agencies in transition: A report on the views of the members of the federal executive service.* Washington, DC: Author. Retrieved from http://www.napawash.org/wp-content/uploads/2009/09-05.pdf.

Office of Management and Budget. (2015). *Making performance information more accessible.* Retrieved from http://www.performance.gov/federalprograminventory.

Office of Management and Budget. (2016). *Table 4.1, OMB budget outlays by agency: 1962–2021.* Retrieved from https://www.whitehouse.gov/omb/budget/historicals.

Office of Personnel Management. (2012). *Senior executive service survey results for fiscal year 2011.* Washington, DC: Author.

Reinhold, M. D. (2015). *Federal supervisory and managerial frameworks and guidance* [Memorandum for human resources directors].Washington DC: Office of Personnel Management. Retrieved from https://www.chcoc.gov/content/federal-supervisory-and-managerial-frameworks-and-guidance.

Rosenbloom, D. H. (1983). Public administrative theory and the separation of powers. *Public Administration Review, 43*(3), 219–227.

Rosenbloom, D. H. (2013). Reflections on "public administrative theory and the separation of powers." *The American Review of Public Administration, 43*(4), 381–396. doi:10.1177/0275074013483167.

Rosenbloom, D. H. (2014). "Attending to mission-extrinsic public values in performance-oriented administrative management: A view from the United States." In J. P. Lehrke, E. Bohne, J. D. Graham, & J. C. Raadschelders (Eds.), *Public administration and the modern state: Assessing trends and impact.* Hampshire, England: Palgrave Macmillan.

Snowden, D. J., & Boone, M. E. (2007). A leader's framework for decision making. *Harvard Business Review*, *85*(11), 68–76.

The Public Sector Consortium. (2003). The leadership dilemma in a democratic society: Re-energizing the practice of leadership for the public good. Retrieved November 30, 2015 from http://govleaders.org/leadership-dilemma.htm.

The Senior Executive Service, 5 U.S. Code § 3131. (1978).

Volcker Commission. (2003). *Urgent business for America: Revitalizing the federal government for the 21st century.* Washington, DC: Partnership for Public Service. Retrieved from https://ourpublicservice.org/publications/viewcontentdetails.php?id=314.

Zalmanovitch, Y. (2014). Don't reinvent the wheel: The search for an identity for public administration. *International Review of Administrative Sciences*, *80*(4), 808–826.

7 Leading with Integrity

Donald G. Zauderer

> In looking for people to hire, you look for three qualities: integrity, intelligence, and energy. And if you don't have the first, the other two will kill you.
>
> —Warren Buffet

When citizens send their taxes to Washington, they would like to trust that the money will be used for the common good. A review of *Washington Post* headlines, however, reveals that that there are many examples in which this trust is violated. The following are just a few of these headlines:

"The Altering of Wait Time Statistics at the VA"
"GSA Rocked by Spending Scandal"
"NIH Scientist Pleads Guilty in Accepting $285,000"
"Teachers Cheating on Test in 11 DC Schools"
"Seventh Official Suspended in Navy Corruption Probe"
"Former Governor McDonnell and His Wife Maureen Convicted of Corruption Charges"
"The Pentagon Spent 9 Million to Professional Sports Franchises to Stage Phony Paid Patriotism Events"

Some of these ethical transgressions, such as Navy corruption, were clearly illegal. "Paid patriotism," however, is legal, but would be considered unethical by many reasonable observers. Honoring soldiers in uniform should not be a profit-making venture for sports teams. All these headlines, however, shine a light on one undeniable reality: People often pursue their self-interest without regard to ethical propriety or social consequences. For this reason, transgressions of integrity are fodder for the media. In this chapter, I will be exploring the dimensions of integrity as it relates to leadership in the public sector.

The word integrity evolves from the Latin adjective integer, which means whole or complete. From a leadership perspective, a person of integrity maintains steadfast adherence to a code of ethical values and uses the ethical code as a guide in determining the right thing to do in given circumstances. In exploring the dimensions of integrity, I hope to provide information that will help individuals assess and improve their ethical fitness and gauge the ethical fitness of candidates for promotion and employment. The following six questions will be the subject of this chapter:

- Why are humans fallible in their ethical fitness?
- What are the dimensions of character?
- How does a leader build trust?
- How does a leader exhibit civility and encourage it in others?
- How and why should a leader exhibit courage?
- How can a leader use ethical principles in making decisions?

These ideas, if adhered to, will enhance a leader's reputation, promote followership, and enable sustainable partnerships in the service of organizational mission.

The Fallible Nature of Humans

The flawed nature of humans was discussed extensively by James Madison and Alexander Hamilton in the *Federalist Papers* written in 1787. These 85 essays were written to encourage the 13 states to ratify the revised Constitution of the United States. They explain the foundation of thought that went into the separation of powers and checks and balance framework of governance.

Why did the founders choose to fragment power among Congress, the presidency, and the judiciary? Some quotes from these papers will shine a light on this question. Madison, for example, wrote in Federalist Paper No. 1 that "In every political institution, a power to advance the public happiness involves a discretion which may be misapplied and abused." Alexander Hamilton, in Federalist No. 6, states that "Has it not, on the contrary, invariably been found that momentary passions, and immediate interests, have a more active and imperious control over human conduct than general or remote considerations of policy, utility, or justice." In Federalist No. 10, Madison expressed concern about the formation of factions of citizens "who are united and actuated by some common impulse of pass*ion*, or of interest, adverse to the rights of other citizens, or to the permanent and aggregate interests of the community?" In Federalist No. 47 Madison asserted that the "accumulation of powers … in the same hands whether of one, a few, or many, and whether hereditary, self-appointed or elective, will lead to tyranny" (Ostrom, 2008, p. 85).

The founders possessed a deep fear of the misuse and abuse of power by officials pursuing their self-interest to the detriment of others. In their view, justice can best be achieved only when ambition can be made to counteract ambition; when there are multiple access and veto centers to place constraint on the excesses of special interests. The ratification of Amendment X to the Constitution fragmented power even further. Amendment X specified that "The powers not delegated to the United States by the Constitution, nor prohibited by it to the States are reserved to the States respectively, or to the people." This opened another avenue to allow people to pursue a redress of grievance at the state or federal level. In addition, The First Amendment guaranteeing free speech, the right to assemble and petition to redress grievances, and a free press provides yet other avenues to bring issues before the American people. While this structure provides opportunities to redress grievances, it comes with a cost—policy formation and decision making are often painfully slow and incremental. The Founders believed that our country would be better off in the long run if more emphasis were placed on constraining the abuse of power than in creating a governance structure that promotes expeditious decision making.

Examples of Abuse and Misuse of Power

Even with a structure of fragmented power, the founders were quite prophetic in their concern for the abuse and misuse of power. Between 1932 and 1972, the Public Health Service in Alabama conducted a study of the natural disease progression of syphilis among 600 impoverished black males. They provided no treatment despite the fact that penicillin had proven to be a cure by 1940. In another case of abuse, President Roosevelt, shortly after Pearl Harbor, ordered all people with Japanese ancestry on the Pacific Coast to be forcibly relocated into camps. In yet another example, Jim Crow laws were enacted in the southern confederate states from 1890 to 1965 mandating that schools, housing, and transportation and all public places were to be segregated. The Civil Rights Act of 1964 and the Voting Rights Act of 1965 forbid racial segregation and discrimination in voting. The harsh remnants of Jim Crow exist as some policeman have used excessive and lethal force against black Americans. Many jurisdictions are still using voter suppression techniques aimed at weakening the impact of minority voters on election outcomes.

Richard Nixon, our 37th president, couldn't constrain the impulse to "get even" with his critics. The Watergate break-in of the Democratic National Committee exemplified on how negative emotions can be employed to weaken adversaries. Similarly, in 2003 Lewis Libby, Vice President Cheney's chief of staff, disclosed to Robert Novak, a *Washington Post* columnist, that Joseph Wilson's wife was an undercover CIA operative. One week earlier, Valerie Plame's husband, Joseph Wilson (2003) wrote in a *New York Times* op-ed piece that it was highly doubtful that Saddam Hussein purchased yellowcake uranium in Niger, Africa. This conclusion ran counter to President's Bush's attempts to emphasize the seriousness of the Iraqi threat. Dick Cheney and Lewis Libby couldn't constrain the urge to "get even" with critics. They may also have wanted to send a message to other critics that they can expect a retaliatory response should they speak against the goals of the Bush administration. Libby ultimately was convicted of obstructing justice in the following investigation and received a 30-month prison term. Hamilton and Madison's concern about human fallibility and the potential for the abuse of power were compelling reflections on the human condition.

Examples of human fallibility also exist within public agencies. Lawrence M. Small was secretary of the Smithsonian from January 2000 to March 2007. He was responsible for 18 museums and the National Zoo. He earned 5.7 million dollars in outside fees while secretary. He took 10 weeks of yearly vacations;

he spent 1.5 million dollars for home maintenance costs, utilities, and cleaning for his home. This included $12,000 to repair the pool. The expectation was that he would use his home to entertain potential donors, but there were only four events in the last four years of his tenure when he utilized his home for such purposes. He also spent $90,000 in unauthorized expenses. Among the expenses was a chartered air flight trip that his wife took to Cambodia. She stayed in a luxury hotel and utilized a luxury car service. Finally, a sharply critical Inspector General report, pressure from Congress, and articles in the *Washington Post* led to his resignation (Trescott & Grimaldi, 2007). Lawrence Small allowed his flawed humanity to control his behavior.

David Brooks (2015) contends that some people are firmly committed to "Big Me" values that represent the drive for wealth, fame, and status. Brooks encourages leaders to focus more of their energy on values such as kindness, service, courage, honesty, faithfulness, and understanding—"to [in essence,] sacrifice self in the service of others." He describes these as eulogy values, suggesting that we choose behaviors that represent what we would like people to say about us at the conclusion of our lives (p. xii).

The 2015 Federal Employment Viewpoint Survey conducted by the Office of Personnel Management (OPM, 2015) suggests that many leaders could benefit by paying more attention to eulogy values. For example, 67% of respondents said they have "trust and confidence in their supervisor." On face value, this doesn't appear to be a particularly regrettable percentage. But if you think about it, one out of every three employees does not feel his or her supervisor is trustworthy. Things get a little worse as you go up the chain of command. Only 50% of respondents believe that "the organization's senior leaders maintain high standards of honesty and integrity." It is not unreasonable to assume that the low trust scores are associated with managers who give little attention to eulogy values in their daily practice as leaders. The flawed character of these managers may help explain these discouraging numbers (OPM, 2015).

Dimensions of Character

Executive selection committees often specify that they are looking for candidates with good character. Core value statements on the walls of offices often refer to the importance of "character" as a standard of behavior. Candidates for public office attempt to demonstrate how the quality of their character separates them from rivals. Rarely, however, is there any specific discussion of what the word means in practice.

The word "character" refers to the moral or ethical quality of a person. Nancy Sherman (1991) writes that "people of character are contemplative, just, and decent in ways of living as social beings." She further specifies that people of character "use both emotion and reason to ground the moral response" (pp. 1–2). Thus, people of character aren't enslaved by their impulses and consult their thoughts and feelings before making decisions. In an article titled "Leading with Character," I attempted to define and clarify a character framework from which leaders can assess themselves and make better hiring and promotion decisions (Zauderer, 2005). The framework is as follows:

1) Exhibiting Deputyship

Dietrich Bonhoeffer, the distinguished German theologian who died at the hands of the Nazi Regime, postulated that people in authority are obligated to act in the place of others "much like a father acts for his children, working for them, caring for them, interceding, fighting and suffering for them." In short, deputyship requires a "selfless commitment" that transcends the ordinary commitment to personal self-interest (Bonhoeffer, 1955, pp. 221–223).

Every organization has a formal and/or operational mission or overarching purpose. This might be to improve public health or public safety, enhance the appreciation of art, protect America from foreign threats, or reduce greenhouse gasses in the environment. People of character express fidelity to mission by exhibiting an "intense commitment" to understanding the needs of those they serve, establish bold goals to meet those needs, overcome resistance to make those goals turn into reality, and consistently search for new and innovative ideas on how to better fulfill the mission over time. Work is not simply a job; rather, it's an "all in" commitment to create something larger than yourself. This distinguishes the average from the extraordinary leader.

2) Keeping Core Values Alive

The second dimension of character is closely aligned with deputyship. Deputyship is about motive, focus, and direction. Keeping core values alive involves identifying and reinforcing behaviors that build coordinated commitment to the achievement of goals. John Gardner (1990), the distinguished statesman, social entrepreneur, and intellectual wrote that: "We must hope for leaders who will help us keep alive values that are not so easy to embed in laws—our feeling about individual moral responsibility, about caring for others, about honor and integrity, about tolerance and mutual respect, and about individual fulfillment within a framework of values" (p. 77). Extraordinary leaders shine a light on these values, model the behavior, and use various means to bring about a collective commitment to practice these values on a consistent basis.

3) Focusing on Self-Awareness and Self-Development

If a leader is truly committed to creating something larger than oneself, he or she may have to change certain personality characteristics that are undermining effectiveness. Daniel Goleman has led a movement to help leaders better manage their emotions and moderate dysfunctional behaviors. Emotions can drive many dysfunctional behaviors; among them are narcissism, excessive controlling, unconstrained anger, the impulse to get even, bullying, difficulty feeling and expressing empathy, and the unconstrained urge to hoard information. Goleman

(1998) encourages people to gain, "A candid sense of their personal strengths and limits, a clear vision of where they need to improve, and the ability to learn from experience" (p. 66). It takes courage to seek a better understanding of your imperfections, but those who are committed to personal growth overcome their resistance to personal change by seeking the help of coaches, requesting feedback from colleagues, reading books and articles, and following up on 360 feedback instruments, and may even avail themselves of a therapist who may be able to uncover some root causes of dysfunctional behavior. It takes courage to get honest with yourself. Yet those who engage in such activity earn the opportunity to experience more satisfying relationships and enhanced effectiveness as a leader.

4) Exhibiting Personal Humility and Fierce Resolve

The fourth dimension of character is to "exhibit humility and fierce resolve" in the service of a larger purpose. This is exactly what Jim Collins (2002) found in his classic study of companies that shifted from good performance to great performance and sustained it. He found that the one common factor that explained the transformation into greatness was a leader who possessed a paradoxical mix of personal humility and fierce resolve (p. 13). These personal attributes can be applied at any organizational level in the private, public, or non-profit sectors of the economy. When facing adversity, these leaders find a way to push forward with great tenacity to bring their vision into reality. This is true in corporate life, the non-profit sector, and government. In the non-profit sector, there is usually one person who identifies a need and then builds an organization that provides services such as the distribution of food to the homeless, providing work opportunities for disabled people, teaching documentary skills to junior high students, or preserving the history of the Underground Railroad. It all starts with passion and commitment. But they can't do it alone. And that is where humility plays a role. A humble person respects people, pays attention to their interests, listens carefully, engages in respectful dialogue, and integrates perspectives from diverse sources. This helps to fully engage people in the vision of service.

5) Exhibiting Caring and Concern

People of character exhibit care and concern for staff, partners, customers, and citizens. Exhibiting active concern for the welfare of others finds many expressions in organizational life. When Sherrie Smith revealed that her husband was fighting a very serious form of cancer, her boss called her into his office and said, "I want you to know that we are here to support you. If you need to take time off, we will find a way to cover your work. If you need to come in here and cry, I will be here for you. We are all here for you. We are a family." Afterward she told a colleague, "I cannot even describe how important these words were to me."

There are many other ways that leaders can express caring at the work place: They can coach their staff to higher levels of effectiveness; work to remove impediments that are blocking a staff member's progress on projects; provide both positive and negative feedback in a caring manner; provide talented staff with an opportunity to make presentations in front of senior managers; provide awards for deserving staff; and express appreciation for the small and large things they do every day to add value; and advocate for additional resources to enhance staff productivity. Caring leaders also seek to build trust with partners by designing mutually satisfactory collaborative practices. Another expression of caring for the organization is ensuring that the right people are promoted and hired.

6) Hiring People of Character

How does a leader discern whether a candidate for hire or promotion possesses these virtuous qualities? If the candidate is internal, the leader can assess him or her based on what has been observed. If external, the leader may be able to talk to others who have worked with the candidate. Well-designed interview questions may also give clues to a person's character. Dana Telford and Adrian Gostick, in their book *Integrity Works* (2005), provide a variety of such questions. Among them are:

- Who has had the greatest influence on you and why?
- Who is the best boss you've worked for and why?
- Tell me about your worst boss?
- If you were the leader of your previous unit, what would you change?
- What values did your parents teach you?
- Tell me about a time when you let someone down?
- What is your greatest accomplishment, personal or professional?
- Tell me about a time when you were asked to compromise your integrity?
- How have you dealt with adversity? (p. 101)

Answers to these questions can expose the degree to which an individual thinks and acts with an integrity mindset. Another virtuous quality is the intent and ability to establishing trusting relationships—the next subject to be examined.

Developing Trust

Webster's Dictionary defines a trusted person as: "One in which confidence is placed;" and as "one to whom something is entrusted to be used or cared for in the interest of another" (Trust, n.d.). Unfortunately, there are many individuals and organizations that are not considered trustworthy. We cannot trust that many pharmaceutical companies will charge reasonable prices for specialty drugs; we cannot trust that large financial institutions will not use our money for risky ventures; we cannot trust that Congress will make laws based on the long-term interests of American citizens; we cannot trust that media reporting is accurate; we cannot trust that politicians won't disguise their true motives behind lofty misleading rhetoric; and we cannot trust that children will not be abused in some religious organizations.

Mistrust extends to life in the bureaucracy as well. The 2015 Federal Employee Viewpoint Survey (OPM, 2015) reveals that only 40% of employees believe that awards depend on job performance. Only 33% believe that differences in performance are recognized in a meaningful way. My executive students at American University have also indicated that some of their supervisors maintain defensive routines to block out unfavorable information; distort information; limit the visibility of talented subordinates; diminish the reputation of potential rivals; take credit for the achievements of others; punish and isolate risk taking; and cater to the interests of supervisors while neglecting the interests of subordinates. Behaviors such as these evoke skepticism and low motivation. Employees may wonder whether they should "lean in" heavily on their jobs when their interests are totally neglected.

Even though these defensive behaviors exist in some places, a leader with integrity will consciously choose behaviors that transcend his/her base nature. But, what are these leadership behaviors? David Maister, in his book *True Professionalism* (1997), writes that: "Before a leader can be accepted, let alone succeed, autonomous professionals must agree to be led or managed ..." (p. 65). He then posits four tests that determine whether professionals will follow a leader (i.e., motives, values, competence, and style).

The first test—motives—posits that "I will follow you If you are primarily committed to the success of the group or institution, rather than to your own self-aggrandizement" (Maister, 1997, p. 66). Does the leader have a track record of helping other people? Does he or she have a history of bringing others into internal or external relationships and passing on responsibility to them? Does he/she have a habit of helping other people succeed? Can he or she provide an example of choosing to put the interests of the group and/or organization ahead of his or her own interests? Does he or she take the time to teach and coach? Maister emphasizes that intention or future promises don't matter. The best test of someone's motives is the actual track record.

Maister then shifts to "core values." Is the leader committed to continuously getting better at serving internal and external stakeholders? Is he or she fascinated by the concerns and problems that internal and external clients or [citizens] are faced with? Does he or she go the extra mile to insure that excellence is achieved? Does the leader care deeply about achieving something meaningful? Does he or she care more about long-term success than short-term appearances? These values constitute a philosophy of practice for achieving extraordinary results over the long term.

Once professionals trust your motives and values, they will want to know about your "competence." Do you have constructive new ideas on how to help the group accomplish goals? Can staff turn to you for helpful suggestions? If you can be substantively helpful, they will likely listen to you.

His last criteria relates to "style." Does the leader provide you with challenging goals that build on your capabilities? Is your manager a "friendly skeptic, a loving critic, a challenging supporter, someone not afraid to give both positive and critical feedback?" Do staff members feel that their voices are heard and taken into consideration in decision making? Does the leader engage in extensive prior consultation on major issues? Only if these trust-building behaviors are done, will s/he fully engage your energies (Maister, 1997, pp. 65–75).

There are additional behaviors that also foster trust (Zauderer, 1994; Dubrin, 2003). Among these are:

- Honoring agreements by following through on commitments
- Accepting blame by acknowledging personal responsibility
- Communicating truthfully, especially on matters about which individuals have a right to know
- Respecting the dignity of individuals by giving earned recognition, inviting and giving genuine consideration to suggestions, and exhibiting courteous behavior
- Forgiving individuals for mistakes or wrongdoings
- Extending self for others by providing help in times that matter
- Exhibiting humility by keeping self-importance in perspective
- Avoiding unbridled ambition and the emphasis of rank and status differences
- Building rapport and partnerships
- Refraining from disclosing information provided in confidence
- Minimizing telling people "what they want to hear"
- Readily accepting feedback on behavior from others
- Maintaining eye contact with people

People are drawn to individuals they can trust. Stephen Covey (2006) states that: "When trust is high, the dividend you receive is like a performance multiplier, elevating and improving every dimension of your organization and your life" (p. 19). Leaders who are trustworthy have the potential to harness the collective energy of staff to achieve bold and challenging goals. Feelings of distrust, however, are often the consequence of incivility at the work place; this is the fourth dimension of integrity explored here.

Fostering Civility

Larry Greenberg was a very successful Senior Executive Service leader in a large federal agency. He was asked if he would like to compete for a promotion that would enhance his level of responsibility and pay. He agreed to apply for the position. The selection committee determined that Larry and one other internal candidate, Bill Thompson, were the finalists. On a specified afternoon, Larry and Bill would engage in separate interviews in the seventh floor conference room. Larry went first. After the interview—which he thought went well—he was shepherded to an unoccupied office. He sat there for an hour. Finally, he heard a commotion in the hallway. After about 10 more minutes, the door opened, and a member of the selection committee said, "Would you like to join us in the next room to celebrate Bill's promotion?"

Larry was devastated, not only because he wasn't selected, but also because the committee didn't provide him the courtesy of a private conversation describing the outcome, the reasons for the decision, and career implications going forward. Larry never felt the same about the organization and put in retirement papers within a month of this event.

In an article entitled "Workplace Incivility and the Management of Human Capital" (2002), I defined incivility as "disrespectful behavior that undermines the dignity and self-esteem of employees and creates unnecessary suffering" (p. 38). Common acts of incivility are: taking credit for work accomplished by someone else; malicious gossiping; consistently discounting others' comments during meetings; withholding information that is needed to conduct business; bullying; and attempts to imprison another person in a false identity.

Acts of incivility have consequences. In one study of 775 white-color workers by Christine Pearson and Christine Porath (2005), 20% of respondents indicated they experienced incivility at least once a week. Of those surveyed, 53% reported that they lost work time worrying about the incident; 37% believed that their commitment to the organization declined; and 22% reported that they decreased their effort at work. Forty-six percent contemplated changing jobs, and 12% actually changed jobs to avoid the instigator (p. 7).

People who are targets of incivility differ in the way they cope. These coping styles range from just living with the harsh reality since things may be worse elsewhere to withholding full commitment to the organization, confronting the perpetrator(s) hoping that the behavior will change, getting even by withholding information or whispering behind the scenes to undermine the reputation of the perpetrator, emulating the behavior toward others to conform to the organization culture, and leaving the division or the organization to distance themselves from the perpetrator(s). With the exception of confronting the perpetuator, the other coping styles drain energy from achieving organizational goals.

What, then, can a leader do to create a civil environment? The first thing is to recognize that he or she is responsible for the climate in the unit. Once this responsibility is accepted, the leader can engage staff in designing norms of conduct that foster a meaningful and productive organization. What, then, are the duties and responsibilities people have to each other as members of this interdependent community? Among the conduct values to consider are: listening, sharing your knowledge and wisdom with colleagues, sharing information, and helping each other—especially in times of need—and dealing with conflict directly before complaining or seeking the help of your supervisor.

Leaders should also find ways to reinforce the importance of these values. Civility discussion could be included in performance improvement conversations. A simple survey can be developed to monitor the quality of civility. The results of the survey should be distributed to staff with follow-up discussions as needed. The leader should model civility in daily interactions with people. In addition, the subject of civility should be included in the training offered to staff. Lastly, leaders should have private feedback sessions with staff who fail to adhere to the civility values.

Given the potential of defensive reactions among some staff members, it takes courage and caring to bring these issues to their attention. This may be the most important work-related career conversation they ever have. These conversations are worth having because they help individuals get ahead in the long run and because the leader's job is to build a strong and effective organization. This cannot happen when fear and distrust permeate the office environment (Zauderer, 2002). While the creation of a civil environment is important, a true leader will have to exhibit courage to protect staff, advocate for resources, speak truth to power, and confront ethical wrongdoing.

Exhibiting Courage

Lynn Jamison is a statistical analyst for a federal defense agency. A highly respected colleague, Jordon Smith, asks her for help in developing the analytical foundation for a study that he will present at a decision-making meeting of top officers of the organization. The decision to commit millions of dollars will be based, in part, by the information that is provided by Jordon. Jordan begins preparing the presentation and decides to invite Lynn to help him create the analytical foundation and to organize the statistical data. A month into the project, he invites Lynn to observe the decision-making meeting and sit in a chair in the back row of seating in the conference room.

As Jordon moves into his presentation, it becomes clear that he has skewed the data to support the emerging consensus that was developing to commit the resources. Lynn was a single mother and needed this job. If she stands up to speak, she might be severely criticized for her audacious behavior, which could place limits on any future career enhancing possibilities. Yet, she cannot help but think that the commitment of millions of dollars on this initiative may not be in the public interest. What should Lynn do?

Lynn's dilemma is just one example of the kinds of ethical challenges faced by professionals in the public service. People may observe that money is wasted; administrative staff is mistreated; people are not receiving credit for their accomplishments; some people are falsely blamed for programmatic breakdowns; critical information is being withheld from the public; or a political appointee is asking staff to do things that are either unethical or illegal.

Rushmore Kidder (2005) states that "courage is the willing endurance of significant danger for the sake of principle" (p. 9). Among these principles are honesty, respect, fairness, responsibility, and compassion. One may, for example, want to stand up for a colleague who is being falsely blamed for a programmatic breakdown. The principle of fairness and compassion may be prompting an individual to stand up to protect this colleague.

Confronting a wrong, whether minor or highly significant, brings with it risk. Kidder (2005) urges us to proceed with caution, and to examine the following three questions before committing to take action:

- Am I willing to face up to the ambiguity and confusion that surrounds this problem? Do I have confidence in my ability to figure things out?
- Do I acknowledge that by acting with moral courage I may be thrust into a highly visible leadership role, whether I want it or not?

- Do I grasp the peril to my income and position, as well as to personal relationships and public reputation? Have I underestimated or overestimated the risk? (p. 138)

Is the risk of ambiguity, public exposure, and personal loss low, moderate, or high? Am I willing to exercise formidable persistence and determination to see this through? And do I have a strategy for addressing the issue in a way that moderates my risk? How do you achieve this outcome?

Bernard H. Rosen (deceased), a former distinguished adjunct professor at American University and Executive Director of the U.S. Civil Service Commission, was called to the Nixon White House and told to take pictures of all federal employees who joined the protest demonstrations on the Vietnam War. Rosen said, "We can do this, but the *Washington Post* might do a series of articles that would be damaging to this Administration." The White House official said, "Do it anyway." Rosen replied, "We can do it but there may be a protracted legal challenge regarding First Amendment rights that may be damaging to this administration." The conversation continued in the same vein for some time. Finally, the official said, "I'll get back to you." He never followed up to press him on the matter. The teaching point here is that one way to stand up to power is to respectfully point out that the "consequences" may not be in their interest. Be prepared for a prolonged dialogue, but be armed with a long list of reasons that the proposed actions is not in their interest. Keep articulating the negative consequences, like a broken record stuck on one short segment of music (Chaleff, 2015).

Another senior government executive, Jack Young (deceased) who served as a professor at American University, once told me that he never wanted to be in a position where he could not be absolutely candid with his bosses. To provide him this freedom, Jack and Virginia, his wife, budgeted carefully so they had "quitting money" to pay bills in the event that he quit or was fired. At his funeral, his previous boss, the former Secretary of Defense, James R. Schlesinger, said that Jack's risk taking and candor was the thing he most admired about him. Jack's integrity was reflected by his willingness to speak the truth to power. Secretary Schlesinger's integrity was reflected by his ability to listen and reflect on diverse perspectives—even ones provided by strong-willed colleagues.

When people find that their values are at odds with the prevailing culture of an organization, how can they stick to their values without jeopardizing their career standing in the organization? How do they walk the tight rope between conformity and rebellion? Debra Meyerson (2001), in her book *Tempered Radicals,* provides a spectrum of five options from lower to higher risk (pp. 37–121). The following is an adaptation of her framework:

Make a Request and Set a Precedent

John Izsak worked for a company that placed no limits on the hours employees are expected to work. He, on the other hand, loved his job and worked long hours but did not want to compromise family time with his wife and children. He decided to tell his colleagues that he wanted to be a loving and responsible husband and would they please refrain from scheduling meetings after 5:00 p.m. with the exception of emergencies, and from calling him at home between 6:30 p.m. and 9:00 p.m. Before long, this became the general norm in the department, and people worked faster and smarter during the regular hours. Sometimes, a small incremental intervention can change the organizational culture.

Teaching and Learning in Everyday Conversation

Common interactions in organizations can provide an opportunity for learning. One of Bill Smith's colleagues complained about a gay manager who displayed a picture of his partner in the office. In his words, "I just don't understand why gay people have to announce their sexual orientation in the workplace." Bill replied by saying that the picture of your wife and children in your office also announces your sexuality. Bill saw this as a subtle opportunity to help a colleague understand the double standard implicit in his statement.

Using Dialogue to Find Common Ground

The risk level moves up a bit when there is a disagreement and you attempt to find common ground in a negotiation. In a senior care community a resident with modest but significant Alzheimer's condition wanted to remain in the independent setting—and promised the non-profit entity four million dollars if he could remain there. The clinical staff didn't believe that he was well enough to live independently, and that to do so would put himself and other residents at risk. The fund raising and corporate development staff were firmly in favor of letting him remain in his current setting. A senior member of the clinical staff, Loren Acheson, asked to meet with senior staff in the development office. After much discussion, looking at the issue from many perspectives, they decided to permit him to stay but only under the condition that 24 hour on-site care be employed. This negotiation brought about an integration of perspective that satisfied the interests of two sections of the organization (Zauderer, 2000).

Leverage Small Wins

Leveraging small wins is the fourth strategy. Wendy Ker worked in the educational branch of a state supported museum of modern art. The educational approach used at the museum was to have docents lecture to patrons with some question-and-answer opportunity. This was a deeply held value based upon 50 years of educational practice. Wendy, on the other hand, believed that lecturing denies the patron the opportunity to use his or her creative instincts to make sense of the painting. Wendy believed that when the patron is actively engaged, the learning is deeper and more meaningful.

Working with a docent, she decided to use experiential methods in one out of five presentations. Even though she endured some severe criticism at first, the reviews from patrons were extraordinary. Within a year, classes were offered on experiential methods, and many of the professional staff and voluntary docents began to experiment with these methods.

Build a Network to Push Change

Organizing collective action is the most visible and risky approach to change. Professor Carter was a young untenured chairman of an academic department. When he examined the curriculum, he discovered that almost every course was irrelevant to the needs of people entering that profession. He felt it was unethical to offer a curriculum that would not help young professionals succeed in their careers. Unfortunately, many of the respected faculty did not share this perspective. These changes would have required faculty to revise their syllabus, learn new material, or create new courses. A number of faculty members were just indifferent to curriculum matters, choosing to focus their energy on research and teaching.

Pushing ahead anyway, Carter put together a network of colleagues to serve as a design team. He also selected respected outside practitioners to gain their valuable insight on the relevance of different subjects and also to discourage faculty from simply protecting their interests in the curriculum discussions. A long series of meetings was held, some quite contentious. In the end, a new curriculum was formulated and successfully voted on at various levels in the university. Carter received criticism, accolades, and indifference for his work. Within the next two years, the enrollment tripled as prospective students and organizational sponsors saw the direct connection between the content of these courses and the professional success of these students. In the absence of this network, Carter would have been marginalized and pushed aside by more senior faculty. This story teaches that professionals can substantially moderate their risk as change agents by building a network of professionals committed to a common goal (Brandon & Seldman, 2004, p. 107).

The Thinker's Way to Ethical Decision Making

We all face tough choices as we carry out our professional responsibilities. If faced with a difficult decision, we could just accede to our emotions and impulses. But, when human beings simply follow an impulse, they can damage themselves as well as others. It is far better to pay attention to our emotions while also seeking guidance from facts and guiding principles. Through reason, we can analyze the ethical situation, evaluate alternatives, and make the decision based on reflection and choice (Chaffee, 1998, p. 320).

The rightness or wrongness of some decisions is fairly clear. It is wrong to cheat on taxes, pad expense accounts, bully people at work, disrespect administrative staff, hoard information, and punish risk takers. In right versus right situations, however, one "right" value is pitted against another "right" value. As a case in point, John Loriant, a senior manager in a local government, believes that his branch managers are good but don't function at a level of excellence. He is inclined to give them a "good" rating. According to policy, however, an "excellent" rating is necessary to be considered for promotion. He is also aware that other senior leaders are quite generous with their evaluations, and thus all of their branch managers are eligible for promotions. Should he evaluate on the basis of an absolute standard or a lesser standard used by others? This is a deeply troubling issue for him because he wants to be truthful but not to the extent of disadvantaging his branch managers. What should he do?

Rushmore Kidder (1995), in his book titled, *How Good People Make Tough Choices,* contends that most ethical dilemmas involve a clash of core values: truth vs. loyalty; individual vs. community; short term vs. long term; and justice vs. mercy (pp. 16–20). In this case, the value of truthfulness based on a standard of excellence clashes with the value of loyalty to his branch managers. One might even consider this a clash between justice and mercy. What decision-making framework can one apply in this situation?

A Clash of Core Values

1. Truth vs. Loyalty
2. Individual vs. Community
3. Short Term vs. Long Term
4. Justice (Common/Distributive) vs. Mercy

Definitions

- ***Truth*** The obligation to pass on information to others, especially when they have a right to know.
- ***Loyalty*** The obligation to be faithful in allegiance to another individual, group, institution, or state.
- ***Individual*** The obligation to address the specific needs of an individual, often due to unique circumstances.
- ***Community*** The obligation to address the needs of a larger aggregate of individuals, often seeking to achieve the greatest good for the greatest number.
- ***Short Term*** The obligation to address immediate problems or needs, often without regard to longer-term consequences.
- ***Long Term*** The obligation to make decisions that effectively address problems in the future. This may necessitate some form of immediate sacrifice.
- ***Justice*** The obligation to impartially administer policy or law to determine rewards or punishment. In its distributive form, justice refers to a fair share of rewards, sacrifice, or punishment.
- ***Mercy*** The obligation to exhibit compassion in a way that forbears punishment.

I use the following Kidder decision-making framework in my workshops on "Leading with Integrity":

1. Is this a right vs. right or right vs. wrong ethical dilemma?
2. What are the facts as distinguished from assumptions, desires, beliefs, and theories?
3. What ethical principles are considerations in this case?

4 What are some reasonable options to consider? What are the ethical values associated with each option? Can an alternative be crafted that integrates elements from two or more options?
5 What are the likely consequences of each option?
6 Commit yourself to a decision you are willing to defend and act upon, and for which you can present a clear rationale.
7 What ethical principles and standards have been honored by the recommendation?
8 How would you defend your decision to others?

John's dilemma is clearly a right vs. right ethical situation. We know that John's personal values would be compromised if he wasn't honest, that other managers are inflating the appraisals, and that organizational policy places limits on those who do not receive an "excellent" evaluation.

The ethical principles in this case are truth vs. loyalty and justice vs. mercy. In terms of options, John could: use an absolute standard; use the prevailing standard; use the prevailing standard but provide the branch managers with honest feedback about their strengths and shortcomings; and engage the entire division in a discussion of standards to heighten the level of uniformity. There may be other options as well.

In terms of consequences, if John uses an absolute standard, his staff might feel discouraged and feel it is being treated unfairly. If he adopts a prevailing standard, his managers might have a false impression of their true value and not strive for excellence. The absolute standard honors the value of truth and justice. The prevailing standard honors the value of loyalty and mercy. If he engages the entire division in creating uniform standards, his fellow managers may still find a way to manipulate the assessment to favor their branch managers. The intent would be to create a more just system, but his fellow managers might still be generous with their ratings. What set of values trumps the other set of values in this circumstance? Different individuals and groups will likely come up with different choices. There is no single right answer. The best one can do is to submit to a reasoned process in determining the right thing to do in a given circumstance.

Cultivating Your Integrity

The Greek philosopher, Socrates, stated: "The unexamined life is not worth living" (Plato, 399 BCa, 38a)—a statement he uttered at his trial for impiety. Some might quarrel with Socrates by arguing that those who fail to examine their lives may still gain pleasure and meaning in their existence. The thinker's way, however, provides an opportunity to appraise your level of integrity in light of universal ethical principles, strengths and shortcomings, and aspirations to contribute to the lives of others. Socrates in Plato's *Republic* (399 BC) said, "We are discussing no small matter but how we ought to live" (1, 352d). I invite you to answer the following questions about your own integrity. I hope it provides an opportunity to reflect and develop new personal development goals and an enhanced self-portrait. Please answer each question rating yourself on a scale of 1 to 5—1 being low and 5 being high:

1 To what extent are you able to constrain destructive self-interested impulses? ________
2 To what extent do you serve in deputyship to the service of others? ________
3 To what extent do you exhibit an intense commitment to agency mission? ________
4 To what extent do you search for new and innovative ways on how to better fulfill agency mission? ________
5 To what extent do you identify and reinforce core values that create a healthy and productive work environment? ________
6 To what extent do you strive to learn about the strengths and flat sides of your personality and identify a clear vision of where you need to improve? ________
7 To what extent do you exhibit personal humility? ________
8 To what extent do you do you exhibit fierce resolve in turning a vision into reality? ________
9 To what extent do you model and reinforce civility? ________
10 To what extent do you exhibit courage to do what is right, even if there is risk? ________
11 To what extent do you speak truth to power? ________
12 To what extent do you consider ethical principles when making decisions? ________
13 To what extent do you maintain a consistent commitment to do what is right, especially under conditions of adversity? ________

I encourage you to ask other trusted individuals about how they view you in regard to these questions of integrity. Consider making a conscious decision to reflect on your answers and comments by others in your journey of self-examination and self-transformation. In George Eliot's words, "It is never too late to be what you might have been." In a similar vein, John Chaffee (2009), a distinguished philosopher, declares, "You are an artist, creating your life portrait, and your paint and brush strokes are the choices you make each day of your life" (p. 4). Make your professional life a masterpiece.

References

Bonhoeffer, D. (1955). *Ethics.* New York, NY: Simon & Schuster.

Brandon, R., & Seldman, M. (2004). *Survival of the savvy: High-integrity political tactics for career and company success.* New York, NY: Free Press.

Brooks, D. (2015). *The road to character*. New York, NY: Random House.

Chaleff, I. (2015). *Intelligent disobedience: Doing right when what you're told to do is wrong.* Oakland, CA: Barrett-Kohler.
Chaffee, J. (1998). *The thinker's way.* New York, NY: Back Bay Books.
Chaffee, J. (2009). *Thinking critically.* Boston, MA: Heinle.
Collins, J. (2001). *Good to great.* New York, NY: HarperCollins.
Covey, S. M. (2006). *The speed of trust: The one thing that changes everything.* New York, NY: Free Press.
Dubrin, A. (2013). *Leadership: Research findings, practice, and skills.* Mason, OH: South-Western.
Eliot, G. (n.d.). BrainyQuote.Com. Retrieved July 3,2016, from BrainyQuote.com Website: http://brainyquote.com/quotes/quotes/g/georgeelio161679.
Gardner, J. (1990). *On leadership.* New York, NY: Free Press.
Goleman, D. (1998). *Working with emotional intelligence.* New York, NY: Bantam Books.
Kidder, R. (1995). *How good people make tough choices.* New York, NY: Fireside.
Kidder, R. (2005). *Moral courage.* New York, NY: HarperCollins.
Maister, D. (1997). *True professionalism.* New York, NY: Touchstone.
Meyerson, D. (2001). *Tempered radicals.* Boston, MA: HBS Press.
Ostrom, V. (2008). *The political theory of a compound republic.* Lanham, MD: Lexington Books.
Pearson, C., & Porath, C. (2005). On the nature, consequences and remedies of workplace incivility. *Academy of Management Executive, 19*(1), 7–18.
Plato. (399 BCa). *Apology.*
Plato. (399 BCb). *Republic.*
Sherman, N. (1989). *The fabric of character: Aristotle's theory of virtue.* New York, NY: Oxford University Press.
Telford, D., Gostick, A. (2005). Integrity works: Strategies for becoming a trusted, respected and admired leader. Salt Lake City, UT: Gibbs Smith, Publisher.
Trescott, J., & Grimaldi, G. (2007, March 27) Smithsonian's small quits in wake of inquiry. *The Washington Post.*
Trust [Def. 1b & 5a(2)]. (n.d.). In *Merriam Webster Online*, Retrieved February 23, 2016 from http://www.merriam-webster.com/dictionary/trust.
Wilson, J. (2003, July 6). What I didn't find in Africa. *The New York Times.*
Zauderer, D. (1994). Winning with integrity. *The Public Manager, 23*(2), 43–46.
Zauderer, D. (2000). The benefit of dialogue in public management. *The Public Manager, 29*(4), 27–30.
Zauderer, D. (2002). Workplace incivility and the management of human capital. *The Public Manager, 31*(1), 36–42.
Zauderer, D. (2005). Leading with character. *The Public Manager, 34*(1), 44–50.

8 Communicating to Drive Engagement and Trust

Angelo Ioffreda

> The greatest challenge to organizations is the balance between continuity and change. You need both. … [B]alance is basically the greatest task in leadership. Organizations have to have continuity, and yet if there is not enough new challenge, not enough change, they become empty bureaucracies, awfully fast.
>
> —Peter Drucker

Federal government agencies, like other organizations, must communicate with a variety of stakeholder communities, particularly during times of change and disruption. However, they face unique challenges that constrain but do not close off potential opportunities for improvement in the administration of the great public trust that has been given to the federal government's executive branch. At a time when trust in government is at an all-time low, both in the United States and in other developed democracies (Edelman, 2015), effective communications within and by government have never been more critical or more challenging.

There are signs of progress, new approaches are promising, and the way forward is clear. But it will require a faster, concerted, and sustained effort to refocus the leadership and culture of our public sector institutions to rebuild trust and deliver the 21st century government the public expects. Effective communication is foundational to that effort.

This chapter examines the challenges of and the unique constraints on communication in government and suggests five major opportunities for improvement:

- Leading with purpose.
- Shifting the mindset to be customer-centric.
- Focusing on organizational health (including the development of robust internal communication practices).
- Ensuring that leaders lead and managers manage.
- Adopting best practices.

The federal government provides a wide range of services. This chapter attempts to capture that breadth of services with respect to effective communication practices as a way to improve the overall functioning of the federal government.

The starting point of this analysis is that almost every government action, process, or service can be improved with strategic communication that is clear, intentional, and proactive. "[T]he way an organization communicates can be the difference between success and failure" (Marx, 2015).

We know that private sector firms with highly effective communications outperform those without by a large margin, according to communication studies by Towers Watson (2013). We also know that effective communication practices are needed to help lead an organization, support organizational alignment, and execute on its business strategy. "The most successful companies actively build a culture to support and drive behaviors aligned with their business strategy" (p. 3).

A host of factors make communication in and by government more challenging than in other sectors. Some of these are unique to the public sector, and some are shared across the private and non-profit sectors and may be more acute in government due to statute, culture, mindset, structure, organizational capacity, and politics. We know that even a small increase in communication effectiveness can have a big impact on employee and stakeholder engagement and overall agency performance. It is therefore worth the effort to invest in improving government communications.

Common Communication Challenges

First, it is important to acknowledge that the current context is different due to rapid technological change, globalization, the 24/7 news cycle, the rise of social media, and the speed at which organizations are being asked to communicate. Across all sectors, public and private, traditional approaches that may have worked well in the past are being upended by changing technology and rising public expectations.

Expectations for how government should communicate and interact with the public have changed radically. These expectations are set not by the government but by the Amazons, Googles, and Apples of the world. These companies, and others like them, make purchasing, searching, and customer service experiences simple and easy. The public would like its own experience with government to be just as simple and easy as "one-click" or "one swipe." The public doesn't understand why government can't seem to do this easily. Consequently, government service delivery pales in comparison with the industry leaders that are setting expectations (American Customer Satisfaction Index [ACSI], 2015; Partnership for Public Service & Accenture, 2016).

Government is not alone in facing this situation: private sector firms also suffer from the same comparison. Rising customer expectations enabled by technology create a disruptive force. In a 2015 IBM Study *Redefining Boundaries: Insights from the Global C-suite Study*, a chief marketing officer cited in the study underscores the challenge: "We know expectations are rising but what, exactly, will customers expect? We don't know that yet. And those expectations aren't set by us or by our competitors; they're set outside our industry by Apple or Amazon. That's who we're competing against, really" (IBM, 2015, p. 24).

A McKinsey Center for Government study (Baig, Dua, & Riefberg, 2014) entitled "Putting Citizens First" observed that citizens "care most about speed, simplicity, and efficiency—key elements of the interaction 'process' with government" and that overall customer satisfaction correlates with their online experience (p. 6). Furthermore, the top priority for citizens in interacting with government was the ability to complete processes online (Baig et al., 2014).

Simplicity Is Not Simple: Struggles with Technology

Delivering simplicity and ease-of-use is not simple. There may be an unrealistic perception by the public about the actual costs involved in delivering first-rate service. When one looks at companies that do an exceptional job of customer service, there is a substantial investment in infrastructure and training behind the delivery of those services.

Those companies are organized to deliver on their promise to customers. They pay great attention to the customer experience and invest in it. They map the customer journey and ensure they can deliver their branded experience across multiple customer touch points including the range of digital platforms (website, mobile, or mobile apps). Government can do this too (Dudley, Lin, Mancini, & Ng, 2015). Many organizations struggle to keep up with technology, but the government lags in implementing new technologies, and this has serious implications for effective communications, the ability to deliver streamlined services, and civic engagement.

The Office of E-Government and Information Technology (n.d.) states that:

> Information technology (IT) advancements have been at the center of a transformation in how the private sector operates—and revolutionized the efficiency, convenience, and effectiveness with which it serves its customers. The Federal Government largely has missed out on that transformation due to poor management of technology investments, with IT projects too often costing hundreds of millions of dollars more than they should, taking years longer than necessary to deploy, and delivering technologies that are obsolete by the time they are completed.

Technology is also a barrier to more effective communications within government agencies themselves. This problem was brought to light during the September 11 attacks and led to an investment in technology for first-responders that is still not complete, as documented by the Inspector General's Office at the Department of Homeland Security (Naylor, 2015). Multiple antiquated systems, with information and data in siloes, is too often the norm.

Overrelying on Email and Ignoring Everything Else

The government is not unique in an overreliance on email to communicate with employees. Email is our most loved and hated form of communication (Lafrance,

2015). Some agencies do a good job of determining the purpose of an email, e.g., providing information or a call to action, and developing a clear message in simple language.

However, there is a distinct bias toward top-down or "push" communications rather than multi-directional communications that invite feedback that would allow agencies to continuously improve. Government employees, like many workers, feel like they are drowning in email. In any organization, there is a need to provide some measure of traffic control so that employees are not inundated with email messages.

It is worth stating an obvious fact about communications—everything communicates. An employee or other stakeholder evaluating an organization's communications considers a broad spectrum of activities to be "communication." What a CEO or agency head says or does or doesn't say or do, processes, procedures, rules, how people are treated, reputation, customer service, onboarding, a website, a social media site or post, etc., are all viewed as communication. In short, "communication" is far broader than the spoken or written word.

Communication Challenges Inherent to Government

Government exists because it serves multiple purposes and does essential work that we as a citizenry have decided that it should do. The vast majority of today's public sector workforce consists of knowledge workers, and they work in organizational structures with processes better suited to another era.

The federal government, although often portrayed as a monolith, consists of 15 cabinet level departments and more than 1,500 operating units as defined by the Office of Management and Budget (OMB, 2015) and employs more than 2 million civilians (Office of Personnel Management [OPM], 2015b) with another 1.5 million in the military services (OPM, 2015f). It is better to think of government as an ecosystem consisting of chartered national, regional, state, and local entities with both overlapping and distinct areas of responsibility that deliver an array of public services and are bound by regulatory constraints.

Taxpayer Dollars Are Involved

Public expectations for government services are high (Pew Research Center, 2015; Sides, 2015). At the same time, there is an expectation of careful stewardship of taxpayer dollars in managing public sector institutions. Things cannot be too expensive or appear too expensive. It is an open question whether the public would be willing to pay to get the level of automation of key services available in the private sector. At the same time, there is skepticism that government can effectively manage major projects.

A Pew Research Center study (2015) showed a mismatch in major areas between what the public wants the government to do and confidence that the government can do it well. According to the Pew Research Center, only "19% say they can trust the government always or most of the time, among the lowest levels in the past half-century," and "[o]nly 20% of the survey's respondents would describe government programs as being well-run" (p. 4).

A Large Audience and Consequential Work: Checks and Balances

The number of people federal government agencies serve is large, and the work is consequential. Social Security, the Postal Service, the Centers for Disease Control, and the Food and Drug Administration (FDA), serve, either directly or indirectly, the nation as a whole—all of the 360 million of us. These are not niche organizations serving a small clientele; they serve the entire citizenry or very large segments of it.

The challenge is to deliver those services as efficiently and cost-effectively as possible on a large scale, and the consequences of not doing so are significant. Although Facebook has 1.5 billion active users monthly, the political and economic consequences of it going offline are less significant than Social Security checks not arriving to recipients on time or a food-borne illness spreading widely before it is detected.

Ours is a complex society with more than 360 million people and a federated system of government with built-in checks and balances. It is not designed to be the most efficient and effective or even fast. It is designed to restrain power. The complexity of the federal system is mirrored at the state and local levels. Even so, the public would like repeatable services to be made as routine, digital, and user-friendly as possible. Such services include obtaining or renewing a passport, making tax payments, finding information about programs or benefits, etc.

The Political Context in Government

The domestic consensus around the size and scope of government is under stress in the United States and in other developed democracies around the world. Nowhere has this been more apparent than with the Internal Revenue Service (IRS), the nation's collection agency. Opponents have sought to constrict agency funding to impair its ability to function.

In an unprecedented step, in the fall of 2015 six former IRS commissioners wrote to Republican and Democratic leaders in the House and Senate appropriations and tax committees to layout the consequences for the United States of continued budget cuts including a diminished ability to provide good customer service to the public.

> Over the last 50 years none of us has ever witnessed anything like what has happened to the IRS appropriations over the last five years and the impact these reductions are having on our tax system. It is clear to each of us that the [reductions] over the last five years materially and adversely affect the ability of the IRS to assist taxpayers … as well as the ability of the IRS to detect and deter taxpayers who have not complied with their tax obligations.
> (Rein, 2015, para. 3)

Continued cuts and political pressure make it difficult for an agency administrator to maintain morale and engagement, even when employees are fully committed to the mission of the organization. A similar situation is apparent with other agencies, such as the U.S. Secret Service, where sustained budget cuts are impacting the organization's ability to fulfill its mission. The political environment sets the environmental context in which public policy is made and carried out. In our system of government, elected political leaders set the agenda for public policy while the career federal employees—the permanent government—are charged with making recommendations, influencing policy choices, and carrying out policies to deliver goods and services to the public.

Administrations impose their vision on the federal government through the appointment of agency leaders and other political appointees in senior level positions throughout the agencies. Career federal workers need to understand the political context in which these leaders are operating. This can help senior civil servants identify and address concerns, educate and influence political leadership where appropriate, and prioritize decision making.

Because governmental organizations operate in a highly politicized environment, they want to avoid any "mistakes" or the appearance of mistakes that will open them up to criticism. A partisan political context fosters high levels of risk aversion and caution that constrain the potential for innovation and innovative service delivery. Of necessity, innovation, experimentation, and the ability to learn from mistakes are necessary to bring new products and services to market. This is an accepted part of life in the private sector where "failed" experiments take place regularly with little fanfare and are understood as part of doing business.

In the public arena, this is hard to do: failed government efforts make the news, and failed experiments can be seen as another strike against an administration, or government service more broadly (Markon, 2015). Considered in this context, government agencies want to make sure that the information is completely correct and error-free, not a formula for speed or responsiveness.

But we live in a world in which transparency is the new normal. We rate books, purchases, restaurants, movies, professors, doctors, rides, potential dates, etc., through a variety of online tools and apps. Transparency is ever more important to the public and a partisan political context makes it even more so. Americans want a public sector that communicates with them in a clear, transparent way that can be easily understood. They want to know how tax dollars are spent.

Because the federal government operates within a political environment, with multiple political agendas and factions, agencies must demonstrate independence of judgment by outlining the process to be used in making those evaluations (Wholey, Hatry, & Newcomer, 2010). Thus, transparency of both the process to be used to study a subject and the delivery of a study's findings are critically important to ensuring credibility in government. Also, under the Freedom of Information Act, citizens have the right to request information from government agencies. This is why government is so focused on process, a factor that is underappreciated by the public and even by government critics.

This has been evident in the debate over climate change. A letter to the editor of *The Washington Post* by the chair of the House Committee on Science, Space and Technology (Rep. Lamar Smith, R-Texas, 21st district) spells out the argument in transparency terms: "scientists who are federal employees and use taxpayer dollars for their research have an obligation to be transparent" (Smith, 2015, A18). This argument is being used to justify the GOP-led House's requests for unprecedented access to the e-mails of NOAA employees who worked on climate change research and has provoked a sharp rebuke from scientists.

The unfortunate reality of today's political environment is such that even if a leader or an agency is willing and able to do all the things necessary to develop state-of-the-art communications with internal and external stakeholders, there will be political and other impediments. Politicians will attack agencies whose missions or findings they do not agree with or starve those agencies for funds, and they will seek to politicize for their own political gains issues that arise or mistakes that are made. Leaders and agencies need to push on despite this political reality.

Adapting to Change Is Difficult

The work of government was once predictable. The partisanship of recent years has led to uncertainty over year-to-year budget allocations, which has spilled over into government operations and communications. A business, in contrast, develops a budget based on a forecast and can make faster changes to adapt to changing conditions. It can also decide it will no longer deliver a service or be in a certain line of business. Government agencies don't have this luxury.

Because change has been slower in government than in other sectors, structural change when it does occur is more wrenching. It is also more difficult especially when changes must be approved in advance by Congressional oversight committees and when one or more unions must also be involved. This necessarily complicates the process of making change and being able to communicate with employees about it in a timely manner. In contrast, private sector firms are continually restructuring to meet changing business needs, and this is seen as completely normal and necessary, even if it is often painful. Change management expert John Kotter (2012) observes, "Perhaps the greatest challenge business leaders face today is how to stay competitive amid constant turbulence and disruption" (p. 4). This is true of government as well.

Concerns over privacy have added to the government's difficulties in marketing services and creating behavioral change. While the public's views on privacy wax and wane, in general, the public is more comfortable with a private firm or a political campaign collecting information about us than with the government's collecting information about us. Private firms know a lot about us. Consider the sophistication of Target's analytical models that allow it to predict with great accuracy whether a woman is pregnant based on her purchasing patterns and thus deliver coupons in an effort to shift her buying habits to purchase more at Target (Duhigg, 2012). Our commercial and political campaign worlds are moving to one-to-one marketing, and sophisticated market segmentation strategies backed by reams of data to predict purchasing and voting behaviors, respectively.

Government relies on a broadcast model of communication with citizens even as commercial firms and political campaigns move in a more sophisticated direction that allows for micro-targeting. Achieving a comparable level of sophistication in government marketing would require citizens to accept higher levels of data collection and use so that government agencies could communicate and market to them more effectively. However, government agencies are not able to follow this trend due to political and legal constraints as well as the public's wariness about government access to personal information and concerns over government's ability to keep it secure.

There are alternatives. A smaller step forward would be for government agencies to use other marketing techniques such as developing "personas" of customers, i.e., descriptions of individuals with names who represent different customer segments, to help public sector employees understand the diverse perspectives of the people they are serving (GovLoop, 2015; Partnership for Public Service & Accenture, 2016). By putting themselves in their customers' shoes, government agencies could better understand their wants, needs, and interests and thus create tailored communications to more effectively address their concerns.

Suspicion of Government PR and Legal Constraints

Americans have been suspicious of government public relations and marketing, fearing propaganda and manipulation by the government. Concerns over propaganda and manipulation in the aftermath of WWI, coupled with the Gillett Amendment of 1913, led the government to back away from the use of the term "public relations" at a time when industry was moving in the opposite direction.

Instead, government communicators were given different labels and titles, such as public information officer or public affairs officer. The idea, which was reinforced over time through custom and practice, was that pubic information officers would disseminate information and not engage in a dialogue with customer stakeholders or attempt to shape public perceptions or market goods and services to them (Carvajal, 2015; Turney, 2015).

Legal considerations have a large impact on government communication. For instance, Section 508 of the 1973 Rehabilitation Act requires that the websites for all federal agencies and organizations that receive federal funding be 508 Compliant, i.e., they must be accessible via technology such as screen readers to people with disabilities. The ability of agencies to carry out certain activities must be authorized by law or statute. There has been a great deal of discussion post-9/11 over whether the Department of Defense (DOD) had the authority under its mission to conduct strategic communications abroad as part of its overseas missions in the war on terror or whether this treaded on the purview of the State Department. Ultimately, the DOD's effort to create a strategic communication infrastructure was disbanded for a variety of reasons, including the confusion it created over issues of legal authority.

In addition, government agencies' structures and cultures get in the way. They generally have inward-facing cultures that foster insularity and siloed behavior both within and across agencies. Insularity constrains the ability to perceive what is occurring in the marketplace and the public at large. Government agencies, like many organizations, also tend to favor traditional media relations over internal communications because they focus more on getting their message out rather than on listening to stakeholders and aligning internal activities—and they have been slow to "get" digital compared to their private-sector counterparts. When an agency does have both external and internal functions, the staff may not be integrated or collaborate, just as sometimes occurs in private sector and non-profit organizations.

There is also an overreliance on positional power to get things done rather than use "softer" influencing or persuasion skills. Governmental organizations are hierarchical and top down. Consequently, they lack many of the characteristics that are most conducive to open and honest communication (D'Aprix, 1999; O'Toole & Bennis, 2009). These include open and multi-directional flows of communication and information including feedback loops; honest, direct communication that allows for the safe delivery of "bad" news rather than a tendency to "shoot" the proverbial messenger; communications that provide the context for action; leaders who have a responsibility to communicate and are held accountable for doing so; and limited organizational politics in which arguments are over best approaches to issues rather than about personal or political power (D'Aprix, 1999).

Government Writing Is Dense

The Center for Plain Language's 2015 *Federal Plain Language Report Card,* which grades agencies on compliance and writing and information design (i.e., visual elements) observed that: "Agencies are making progress in using plain language, but much writing still uses a bureaucratic, overly technical style with an un-reader-friendly structure" (Crane, 2015, p. 3).

Government writing is improving but remains dense and bureaucratic (Clayton, 2015). On October 13, 2010, President Obama signed the Plain Writing Act with the purpose of improving "the effectiveness and accountability of Federal agencies to the public by promoting clear Government communication that the public can understand and use" (The Plain Writing Act, 2010, § 2).

Executive Order (EO) 13563 on Improving Regulation and Regulatory Review, issued under President Obama on January 18, 2011, was designed to require "public participation and an open exchange of ideas" in the regulatory review process and to "ensure that regulations are accessible, consistent, written in plain language, and easy to understand" (EO No. 13563, 2011, Section 1 (a)). This built on two previous executive orders that addressed the use of plain language in regulations. EO 12866 on Regulatory Planning and Review of September 30, 1993 said "Each agency shall draft its regulations to be simple and easy to understand, with the goal of minimizing the potential for uncertainty and litigation arising from such uncertainty" (EO No. 12866, 1993, Section 1. (b) (12)). EO 12988 on Civil Justice Reform of February 7, 1996, requires agencies formulating proposed legislation and regulation to use "clear language," a term that appears five times in this six-page document (Sunstein, 2011).

The guidance document listed some of the benefits of clear and simple communication, including: making it easier for members of the public to understand and apply for important benefits for which they are eligible and assisting the public in complying with applicable requirements simply because people better understand what they are supposed to do. "Plain writing is thus more than just a formal requirement; it can be essential to the successful achievement of legislative and administrative goals, and it also promotes the rule of law" (Sunstein, 2011, p. 1).

Despite efforts to improve the use of language, acronyms and jargon abound in government. Acronyms have become shorthand for laws, departments, interagency groups, etc. Politicians seem to love "clever" acronyms: in 2015, more than 350 acronym-named bills were introduced in Congress (Bump, 2015).

The result is a plethora of acronym clutter in the public sector. The Freedom of Information Act is FOIA, the Department of Defense is the DOD, the Federal Employee Viewpoint Survey is the FEVS, a Contracting Officer's Representative is a COR, Chief Human Capital Officers are CHCOs (pronounced Chico) … the list goes on and on. Even the official inter-agency group to provide plain writing guidance has its own acronym—PLAIN (The Plain Language Action and Information Network).

Acronyms and jargon become a separate language that obfuscates and acts a barrier to communication especially with individuals outside of that governmental entity. There is no harm in using a few acronyms in proportion or when it makes sense, such as a mnemonic that helps one remember. When you need a decoder or dictionary to explain them, however, it may be time to examine whether these make communication easier or more difficult for employees and stakeholders alike.

A Leadership Communications Gap

According to the Federal Employee Viewpoint Survey (FEVS), agency senior leaders are not providing sufficient leadership at the agencies they lead. While there have been "better internal communication from leaders to employees, greater input from employees in how their agencies operate, increased training opportunities, and more explicit recognition for a job well done," surveys indicate that leadership is a challenge at many agencies (OPM, 2015b, p. 1; Cordell, 2015).

Federal government employees have a more favorable view of their immediate supervisors than they do of agency leadership, a finding consistent with engagement surveys in other sectors (Cordell, 2015; OPM, 2015b). The component questions for the area of Leaders Lead underscore the importance of communication:

- In my organization, senior leaders generate high levels of motivation and commitment in the workforce.
- My organization's senior leaders maintain high standards of honesty and integrity.
- Managers communicate the goals and priorities of the organization.

- Overall, how good a job do you feel is being done by the manager directly above your immediate supervisor?
- I have a high level of respect for my organization's senior leaders (OPM, 2015b, p. 30).

These results point to a striking fact evident in many organizations across all sectors: "Communications is an undervalued, lightly regarded discipline in the theory and practice of corporate leadership. … Chief executives need to focus on communications as a management capability much more seriously than they typically do" (Montgomery, 2015).

Many barriers get in the way of good leadership communications ranging from not valuing communication to being reactive to an unwillingness to be visible or to make the time to do the necessary preparation to do it right. Communication is critical to helping employees understand the goals and priorities of the organizations they work for and how they contribute to achieving them—drawing that connection contributes to employee motivation and engagement.

The FEVS results may reflect the fact that there are new expectations for leaders. According to human capital expert Josh Bersin of Deloitte Bersin, "Leaders have traditionally been selected based on experience and company loyalty, but those leading today's biggest organizations aren't necessarily those who have spent the most time climbing the corporate ladder. The nature of management has changed, and this has resulted in new expectations for senior leadership" (Lindzon, 2015).

Lack of Resources and Professional Standards

Communications is labor-intensive and requires resources such as knowledgeable, well-trained staff and up-to-date technology. It is challenging to get the requisite resources when budgets are tight or when, as in the case of the IRS, the agency is targeted for sustained budget cuts. This situation is no different than that in other sectors, where organizations are reluctant to invest in what they may shortsightedly see as "overhead."

But without the needed investment, government risks falling further behind each year. When it comes to technology, if you are not moving forward then you are falling behind. When you are not investing in people, it is hard to attract the necessary talent. This leads to a self-fulfilling prophecy; service quality may erode or be perceived as eroding relative to the private sector, therefore, some may conclude that government shouldn't deliver a certain service or that it should be privatized.

Internal communication, in government and elsewhere, is often seen as a nice-to-do, an "overhead" expense that one pays for reluctantly, when you get into trouble or are undergoing a major change, rather than a capability critical to one's ability to lead an organization and make things happen more smoothly. One can argue that the failure of many government initiatives has been due to poor communication from poor project conceptualization to the design of a change management process and communications plan to support it.

Poor operational communication—whether due to insufficient internal capacity or budget—costs agencies in multiple ways. Change may take longer to implement or may fail altogether. As many have observed, there has been a hollowing out of government capabilities over the past few decades as more government work has been contracted out. This leaves government even more dependent on contractors to get work accomplished, elevates the importance of contract management for government, and leaves government agencies even more dependent on having sufficient budget to pay for needed communication services.

In contrast to other developed democracies like the United Kingdom, there are no established guidelines for what it means to be a professional communicator in government or for communication standards in government. There is no recognized career path as a government communicator or body of work about what exactly it means to be a government communicator. There is no internal community of practice. Fortunately, there are professional communication organizations to provide a network of support and set professional standards. These include the National Association of Government Communicators (NAGC), the International Association of Business Communicators (IABC), and the Public Relations Society of America (PRSA).

The Way Forward

Government must affect a sea change to meet rising public expectations with greater speed and focus. Attention to the communication approaches described below will help enable government to change, adapt, modernize, and rebuild public trust. The most promising areas for government to focus its communication efforts are described below.

There are five main ways to improve government communications:

- Lead with purpose
- Shift the mindset to be customer-centric
- Focus on organizational health
- Ensure leaders lead and managers manage
- Adopt best practices

Lead with Purpose

Despite the considerable challenges outlined above, government agencies have an advantage that is underutilized in their communications with the public, in their own branding, and in engaging with employees. That advantage is *purpose*, which is typically described in the federal government as an agency's mission. Public agencies from the U.S. Marine Corps to the Treasury to the Centers for Medicare and Medicaid (CMS) to NASA have a compelling mission that engages public sector employees' hearts and minds.

The opportunity is for senior leaders to internalize this sense of purpose and communicate it effectively. Being able to communicate purpose involves explaining the agency's rationale for being—and thus worthy of citizens' tax dollars and trust—to the public, and reminding employees of why they are there and the outcome of their efforts. In this sense, senior leaders need to become storytellers for their organization with a purpose narrative that presents a unifying story about the organization and includes sharing the stories of the impact the agency's work has had on citizens' everyday lives.

Purpose is a powerful motivator, as is a sense of service or public duty. The Office of Personnel Management (OPM) underscores this point in a September 2015 report that defines employee engagement as: "The employee's sense of purpose that is evident in their display of dedication, persistence, and effort in their work or overall attachment to their organization and its mission" (OPM, 2015a, p. 3). Organizations focused on leading with purpose have seen significant improvements in engagement and performance (Pfau, 2015). To further deepen engagement, OPM encourages agencies to focus employees on customer service at all levels and to communicate how the results of their work affect stakeholders or "consumers" of specific government services and programs (OPM, 2015a).

Shift the Mindset to be Customer-Centric

Shifting to a customer-centric perspective means designing customer experiences from the citizen end-user point of view. A customer-centric/end-user perspective means shifting the public sector mindset from thinking "inside out"—i.e., what an agency wants to tell, to "outside in"—i.e., what do citizens need from us and how can we deliver that good or service most effectively to them? That shift has to be led with "anytime, anywhere, any device" digital focus that is "mobile first," especially as smartphones are ever more ubiquitous, and adults are spending more time on mobile devices than computers (Meeker, 2015).

With an end-user perspective, a government website or app would be designed around what the customer needs to do or know rather than what the agency wants to tell. The creation of the U.S. Digital Service Corps under President Obama following the stumbled launch of healthcare.gov could be a large step forward if it can be sustained. When announcing the launch of the Digital Service Corps, President Obama said, "I want us to ask ourselves every day, how are we using technology to make a real difference in people's lives" (VanRoekel, 2012).

The United Kingdom's experience provides a striking example of the way forward. The United Kingdom was able to take 24 Ministerial departments and 331 other agencies and public bodies and create a front-end portal (www.gov.uk) for citizens built around their needs and interactions with government. The gov.uk site is universally recognized as a best practice in the public sector worldwide. Website statistics are available for all to see (Gov.UK, n.d.), and the U.K. government markets the site to citizens via e-zines and social media (Williams, 2015). The USA.gov site pales by comparison.

Not surprisingly, a "relentless" focus on the end-user drove the design of www.gov.uk, according to chief designer Ben Terrett (2014). The number one design principal for the design team was to "figure out what the end user is trying to do, and then design the service around that, not what the government process is." In his words, the relentless focus on the user-experience "is about changing government, changing the way government thinks—the digital transformation of government" (pp. 68–69). This is the mindset shift that is needed.

A good example of digital thinking from the end-user perspective is the new Federal Consumer Protection Board website (http://www.consumerfinance.gov/). Without the burden of legacy systems and having the ability to start fresh, the Federal Consumer Protection Board was able to design a site tailored to customer needs—one that is simple to use and easy to navigate.

Closely related to adopting an end-user perspective is to focus on simplicity, i.e., striving to make the government easy to deal with, using clear simple language, avoiding acronym and jargon clutter, and sharing the vast bank of data that government has in a way that is simple and easy to use. A good example is the increased use of infographics by the Government Accountability Office (GAO) to succinctly communicate the highlights of its extensive written reports, which used to be communicated primarily through the written word.

There is also an opportunity to improve government agencies' report writing processes to make them more efficient and cost-effective both in terms of time and the number of people needed to produce and clear them. Streamlined processes will strengthen writers' and editors' sense of ownership and will allow for a more consistent voice throughout a written report. It will also help with communications to employees. A leader's authentic "voice" can get lost in the editing process, and thus is lost the potential to make a connection with employees. Too often, employees, knowing that messages are overly edited, read between the lines to find out the "real" message, both a reflection of and a contributor to low trust.

Take a Holistic View

Internally, agencies should take a systems view of communicating with staff to foster multi-directional communications and make use of a mix of media, including intranets, apps, email, training, in-person meetings, instant messages, collaborative tools, new work spaces, etc. The goal should be to create workplace cultures of communication, candor, and collaboration with more inquiry, and less telling and informing, to provide for better outcomes and a more engaged workforce.

This change needs to start at the top with leaders being more prepared and equipped to manage in this new context. Training, coaching, and greater preparation to develop communication skills can help senior leaders be more effective in their roles, rather than look to on-the-job training to develop these skills once people have assumed a leadership position. Since everything communicates, agencies should take a holistic view of their internal and external communications.

While digital engagement is the most promising path to engaging citizen stakeholders, there is also a need to ensure a consistent positive customer experience across multiple touchpoints. A state-of-the-art website will not compensate for a poor customer service experience. There is a need to provide customer service training to government personnel who interact with the public, which OPM is encouraging (GovLoop, 2015; OPM, 2012a). Increasingly, agencies are looking to create customer experience officers, another positive development. More is needed. Fortunately, there are good resources to support a holistic move to a more customer-centric government, including the *Government for the People: The Road to Customer-centric Services* by the Partnership for Public Service and Accenture, GovLoop's *The Customer Service Playbook for Government*, the *U.S. Public Participation Playbook*, and the *U.S. Digital Services Playbook*.

We know that agencies can improve when they focus holistically on customer service. The Postal Service, one of the top ranked government agencies in terms of customer service, improved its services by gathering more actionable feedback from customers (Konkel, 2015). At the same time, public satisfaction with most interactions with federal services has declined, according to the American Customer Satisfaction Index (ACSI, 2015): "Customer ratings of service (specifically, courteousness and professionalism of agency staff) have declined the most" (p. 2). There is also a perception gap with agency leaders believing they understand their customers' needs better than they actually do: In fact, "only 45 percent think agency representatives understand their needs, compared with 66 percent of private-sector customers" (Partnership for Public Service & Accenture, 2016, p. 11; Konkel, 2016).

Put on a Marketing Hat

With few exceptions, government agencies and employees don't think in terms of marketing what they do. Exceptions include the military services that use advertising to recruit, the Postal Service, and agency "marketing" units that work with the film industry on movies.

A Center for Disease Control (CDC, 2015) campaign called "Zombie Preparedness" designed to raise public awareness has morphed into a major component of CDC's marketing to the public by tapping into popular culture interest in zombies. The CDC site says:

> Wonder why Zombies, Zombie Apocalypse, and Zombie Preparedness continue to live or walk dead on a CDC web site? … what first began as a tongue in cheek campaign to engage new audiences with preparedness messages has proven to be a very effective platform. (para. 1)

Focus on Organizational Health

Government agencies should boost support for operational and strategic internal communications, which offer the single-best opportunity for improving government communications and alignment. Improving communications with the workforce has been key to the Department of Housing and Urban Development's strategy to improving morale and employee engagement (Fox, 2016).

Every initiative within an agency requires communication support. This is something that agencies neglect to their own detriment. When communications are lacking, employees don't have a good understanding of what is happening, they don't see how they contribute to the mission (line of sight), they are less engaged, and initiatives take longer to implement or may not succeed at all. In the modernization of the U.K.'s Government Communication Service, internal communications was recognized as the area for greatest improvement (Russell Grossman, Profession Head for U.K. Government Internal Communications, Skype interview, December 2, 2015).

Consider the challenge of implementing new IT systems. A key to organizational transformation is the deployment of new IT systems that necessarily lead to changes in processes and procedures.

> Without effective communication, the IT leader of a government organization will not be able to achieve very much. To gain consensus, he must convince stakeholders that he is doing the right thing. ... However, the task of elevating the impact of IT in government requires the CIO to be a highly effective communicator. He must be the in-house guru who can speak eloquently about the transformational potential of IT in the organization.
>
> (Graudenz & Hirsch, 2008, p. 11)

Brand Themselves as Best Places to Work

The federal government and distinct agencies must do more to brand themselves as employers of choice. They should emphasize purpose as an attractor as well as the ability to do certain kinds of work that are unique to government, e.g., Peace Corps volunteer, Marine Corps officer, astronaut, forest ranger, etc. There is intense competition for talent, and agencies must recruit the skills, talents, and competencies they need amongst the Millennials and the so-called Generation Z.

Government agencies don't necessarily need to be seen as hip, but they will be challenged to find new talent if they are perceived as stodgy or old-fashioned. The Millennials are the first generation of digital natives entering the workforce, and their expectations for employers—including for the technology they will be working with and the way they will be working—will set the tone for all that comes afterwards. They will want the opportunity to learn, grow, and develop. Consequently, government workplaces must be more attractive and interesting places to work, and the process for applying for federal jobs must be simplified and speeded up. Realizing this, OPM is overhauling the USAJOBS website to make it more user-friendly following principles of "human centered design" (Katz, 2016).

Tying the work to purpose will be an especially powerful attraction for the next generation public sector workforce, just as it has been for previous generations (Calling Brands, 2012). All organizations are grappling with this challenge. According to Josh Bersin,

> Employers are trying to figure out how to make work easier and more meaningful to people, to attract both the very ambitious people that want to really move up and drive change and run things, and the people who want to work hard but not ruin their lives.
>
> (Lindzon, 2015)

All organizations are also struggling with the pace of change, but government agencies being traditional hierarchies created in and for another era, struggle even more acutely. Government needs to build the capacity to shift more rapidly by exploring novel ways of working. A first step is to find ways to break down internal organizational silos. Leadership programs that foster skill building and networking can be an important mechanism. Government agencies must build greater capacity for change management and more importantly, change leadership in which senior leaders have the competencies to spearhead change, manage culture, and set a positive tone at the top.

Ensure Leaders Lead and Managers Manage

Leaders need to do a better job of communicating. The Executive Core Qualifications (ECQs) for senior government executives provide a thorough list of competencies. In terms of communication skills, the ECQ list includes "vision" defined as "Tak[ing] a long-term view and builds a shared vision with others; act[ing] as a catalyst for organizational change. Influenc[ing] others to translate vision into action" (OPM, 2012b, p. 3). It also includes "political savvy," "influencing and negotiating," "interpersonal skills," "oral and written communication skills," and "commitment to serve the public" (p. 5).

Some in leadership roles may see communication as extra work. In fact, Nitin Nohria, the Dean of the Harvard Business School, has stated that "Communication is the real work of leadership" (Blagg and Young, 2001). It is through proactive, intentional communication that leaders make things happen within and across organizations.

Support Managers in their Communication Roles

A manager or supervisor has the greatest impact on an employee's work experience. The frontline manager is where the communication rubber meets the proverbial road in organizational communications. Managers must be equipped with the information and tools to communicate with their staffs in a timely way and be a conduit for upward feedback to leadership. Equipping managers is a recognized communication best practice across all organizations. "The best companies invest in effective training so that managers can support employees, demonstrating the courage to hear and share tough feedback during times of change" (Towers Watson, 2013, p. 7). This requires effort and resources to develop and manage a managerial communications program. In the absence of such communications, there may be a tendency for frontline managers to identify more with employees than with leadership, as in "us vs. them."

Cultivate Political Savvy but Stay Focused on the Mission

There is often a gap between the senior civil servants who see themselves as the permanent government and the political leadership that varies by administration. Senior civil servants should cultivate political savvy rather than seek to avoid politics altogether. Cultivating political savvy does not mean becoming involved in the political process; it does mean understanding the political pressures and motivations of key actors, including their agency's political leadership.

Political savvy can help senior civil servants understand the relative importance of initiatives and key stakeholders. It is also important to know the biases of political leadership, especially in the final two years of any administration when a given administration or agency administrator is looking to leave a legacy. The advice offered by a former government official remains sound: "Focus on the mission and don't get sidetracked by personalities" (Cunningham, 2015).

It can be argued that there is insufficient attention to mission and clearly communicating it through the ranks. In his analysis of government failures, Paul Light (2014) says there is a need to "sharpen" the focus on the mission and communicate it clearly and succinctly. In his view, "Far too many of the failures involved lack of clear direction on the policy mission. … [M]any failures began with the failure to compress the mission into an understandable set of expectations and commitments that can be measured, managed, and rewarded" (p. 24).

Adopt Best Practices and Find the Bright Spots

Government agencies should adopt best practices that are based on the development of meaningful metrics of performance to demonstrate the value of the work being done both externally and internally. This is not just counting what can be counted, to paraphrase Einstein, but identifying what the actual impact is on citizens' lives. For instance, while it is important to know how many seniors receive their social security checks on time, it would also be good to know about the importance of social security in seniors' lives to inform messaging (Center on Budget and Policy Priorities, 2015).

The Digital Government initiative is encouraging a move to common performance metrics across federal websites as well as open web analytics for all .gov websites; less than 10% of the 24 major agencies currently use the same performance metrics. The Digital Analytics Program is making progress in tracking government website utilization (analytics.usa.gov) through a government-wide deployment of Google analytics. It's a start.

Within any sector—or even within a single organization—there are people who are doing things well and are role models for others (Heath & Heath, 2010). Within the federal government, the new Consumer Financial Protection Board is a bright spot. As a new agency, the notion of good external and internal communication is built into their DNA. The agency's website is a model for user-centered design, and its outlook is oriented to the consumer marketplace. There are opportunities to learn from the Consumer Financial Protection Board the practices and approaches that can be adopted for use by other agencies.

Another good example is the Federal Emergency Management Agency's FEMA Mobile App. The app provides tips on disaster preparedness, allows the user to receive weather alerts, locate shelters and apply for disaster assistance, and to connect via social media including the ability to upload one's own disaster photos. It recognizes that we live in a mobile world, and it provides citizens with an easy-to-use tool to plan for and manage in a potential disaster situation.

Delivery of government services is a universal situation. This means that we can observe and learn from other governments who have been successful in communicating or implementing innovative solutions to public problems. For instance, the government can learn more effective approaches to reporting writing by examining major consultancies (Trendwatching, 2015). There are lessons from cities like San Diego and Rio and from countries like Denmark about addressing citizens' needs by working across traditional organizational boundaries (Williams, Gravesen, & Brownhill, 2015).

The United Kingdom developed the Government Communications Services (GCS) "to deliver world-class public sector communications. The service helps improve the lives of people and communities in the United Kingdom, assists with the effective operation of our public services and delivers responsive and informative communications 24 hours a day" (Brown, 2015, p. 2). The GCS has defined a recommended "Modern Communications Operating Model" (MCOM; see also *UK Internal Communications Standard Operating Model*, GCS, n.d.) with four key functions: strategic communications, media and campaigns, strategic engagement, and internal communications (including supporting organizational and cultural change) built into recommended communication structures for large and small agencies. The GCS follows international best practices (Brown, 2015).

Tell Stories

Just as other organizations have tapped into the power of storytelling, so too should government. Stories engage the listener and provide for greater engagement than telling or informing. But stories don't just happen by themselves. All organizations face the challenge of gathering, packaging, and disseminating relevant stories. This takes work and resources and people with an ear for a compelling organizational or leadership story.

A popular saying goes that: "If you don't tell your story, someone else will." There is a need for government agencies to improve their ability to tell compelling stories as part of citizen engagement and outreach strategies. Stories will help simplify the complexity of government for citizens. In the current era, heralded more than 15 years ago by *The Cluetrain Manifesto* (Levine, Locke, Searls, & Weinberger, 1999), there is a need for government to also speak in a human voice, to listen to the conversations in the markets, and to engage communities in solving problems. The advent of social media is enabling this shift as never before and further eroding the boundaries between the inside and outside of organizations. Within agencies social platforms can foster dialogue and collaboration. Externally, social media helps agencies reach citizens in new ways that reflect their own media consumption preferences. Social media requires agencies to strike a human tone.

Do the Basics Well

There are many routine communication practices that agencies do well and should continue to do well, even as these practices evolve. Government agencies, like other organizations, have the need to deal with traditional media for outreach, respond to media requests, and tell their story. There is a symbiotic relationship between communicators and the press. They need each other: communicators need the media to get their message out to stakeholders, and journalists need content to write about, access to subject matter experts or political leadership, and someone to answer questions as they arise in developing stories.

Approaches will vary by agency, issue, the background, and temperament of the lead agency communicator and agency leadership. Government communicators need to follow best practices of strategic communication and marketing—understanding audiences, developing messages that resonate, identifying ways to influence and reach them, determining effective spokespeople, approaches and channels, analyzing results, gathering feedback and adapting, as part of a continuous dialogue with citizen stakeholders.

Government agencies also need to continue to be well practiced in crisis communications. There is an expectation that the government will lead in an emergency. The range of potential crises that governments face is large, including plane crashes, food borne illnesses, natural disasters (hurricanes, fires, earthquakes), etc. Citizens naturally look to the government to take the lead in responding to crises.

Government has not always handled responses to crises well, and this has contributed to eroding confidence in government and political leadership. "Communication continues to be a major source of failure, in part because information has to flow up through multiple layers to reach the top of an agency, while guidance must flow down through the same over-layered chain" (Light, 2014, p. 23). Most after-the-fact reporting of government errors show that government officials were often aware of problems well before the news hit the press, raising questions of why agency leaders were not more proactive.

Agencies should continue to refine their understanding of stakeholder wants and needs in order to sustain a dialogue, be of service, and identify opportunities to make better use of their resources and influence. They could think of stakeholders more broadly as "stakeholder communities." These communities may consist of small, medium, and large suppliers, interested non-governmental organizations, influencers, and bloggers in addition to traditional stakeholders such as affected businesses, lobbyists, and potential employees, etc. "Customer-centered organizations are in constant communication with the people they serve" (Partnership for Public Service & Accenture, 2016, p. 24). This dialogue allows them to better understand their customers' evolving needs.

It is also worth recognizing that the government, unlike the private sector, has tremendous power, and often legal obligation (in the case of rulemaking), to convene, i.e., to bring diverse groups together on a range of issues of the day to create a dialogue or momentum or to frame a potential solution, e.g., social justice, gun violence, bullying, drug addiction, etc. Ongoing dialogue with stakeholders will help the government identify opportunities to be a convener.

Engage the Public through Social Media

Social media is radically altering the mechanisms by which government agencies engage stakeholders. It is an integral part of communication and media planning to launch, amplify, and expand the reach of a given message or campaign. In the current fragmented media landscape it is no longer sufficient to work through traditional media.

President Obama likely will be viewed as "the first social-media president" (Heinke, 2015). Social media was key to his success in reaching the Oval Office, and as president he has developed this capacity in his White House operations. His 20-person Digital Strategy team manages his Twitter feed (@POTUS), his Facebook page, and Instagram account. Their role is to look "for ways to establish a digital identity for Mr. Obama" and "to bring his voice directly to people" (Davis, 2015).

Even intelligence agencies like the CIA and NSA are tweeting. Marking this new era was when the CIA, tongue-in-cheek, launched its first tweet in June 2014, "We can neither confirm nor deny that this is our first tweet" (https://twitter.com/CIA; Griggs, 2014). Perhaps the greatest potential for social media in the public sector is to engage the public real time in an authentic way and humanize the government and the people who dedicate their lives to public service for the benefit of the rest of us.

Conclusion

In sum, government agencies are like other organizations with the same communication challenges and needs. While they do face some unique constraints, these are not necessarily limiting, and progress is possible. By focusing on dialogue, leadership, internal communications, and delivering positive digital experiences to simplify citizens' interactions with government, the government can go a long way to improve effectiveness and rebuild public trust. It will require a new mindset and leaders leading with purpose. Best of all, it is completely do-able.

References

American Customer Satisfaction Index (2015). *ACSI federal government report 2015.* Ann Arbor: University of Michigan. Retrieved from: http://www.theacsi.org/images/stories/images/reports/16jan_Gov-Report.pdf.

Baig, A., Dua, A., & Riefberg, V. (2014). *Putting citizens first: How to improve citizens' experience and satisfaction with government services.* Washington, DC: McKinsey Center for Government.

Blagg, D., & Young, S. (2001, April 2). What makes a good leader. *HBS Working Knowledge.* Retrieved from http://hbswk.hbs.edu/item/what-makes-a-good-leader.

Brown, S. (2015). *Modern communications operating model.* London, England: The Government Communication Service. Retrieved from https://gcs.civilservice.gov.uk/wp-content/uploads/2015/11/6.1288_CO_CP_Modern-Comms-Team-Document_for-print-FINAL-2-2.pdf.

Bump, P. (2015, August 3). 364 bills that have been introduced in Congress, ranked by acronym quality. *The Washington Post.* Retrieved from https://www.washingtonpost.com/news/the-fix/wp/2015/08/03/364-bills-that-have-been-introduced-in-congress-ranked-by-acronym-quality/.

Bush, M. (2014, January 19). *Trust in government plunges to historic low* [Press Release]. Retrieved from http://www.edelman.com/news/trust-in-government-plunges-to-historic-low/.

Calling Brands. (2012). *Crunch time: Why purpose is everything to the modern workforce. If you've got it you can change the world.* London, England: Author. Retrieved from http://cms.callingbrands.com/wp-content/uploads/2014/09/CB_CrunchTime_Report_A4_ST1_6.pdf.

Carvajal, J. (2015). *History of the National Association of Government Communicators (NAGC).* Retrieved from http://www.nagc.com/AboutNAGC/HistoryNAGC.asp.

Center for Disease Control. (2015). *Zombie preparedness.* Last updated April 10, 2015. Retrieved from http://www.cdc.gov/phpr/zombies.htm.

Center on Budget and Policy Priorities. (2015). *Policy basics: Top ten facts about social security.* Retrieved from http://www.cbpp.org/research/social-security/policy-basics-top-ten-facts-about-social-security.

Chinn, D., Dimson, J., Goodman, A., & Gleeson, I. (2015, March) *World-class government. Transforming the UK public sector in an era of austerity: Five lessons from around the world* [Discussion Paper]. McKinsey & Company. Retrieved from http://www.mckinsey.com/search.aspx?q=toward+a+more+efficient+public+sector.

Clark, C. (2015, November/December). Everyone wants transparency until their agency is on the line. *Government Executive.*

Clayton, V. (2015, October 26). The needless complexity of academic writing. *The Atlantic.* Retrieved from http://www.theatlantic.com/education/archive/2015/10/complex-academic-writing/412255/.

Cordell, C. (2015, October 6). FEVS: Satisfaction edges up; leadership stays low. *Federal Times.* Retrieved from http://www.federaltimes.com/story/government/management/agency/2015/10/06/fevs-satisfaction-edges-up-leadership-stays-low/73475388/.

Crane, C. (2015). *Plain language report card.* Center for Plain Language. Retrieved from http://centerforplainlanguage.org/wp-content/uploads/fedreportcards/2015_Brief_Report_Card_final.pdf.

Cunningham, L. (2015, November 5). Why the head of AARP thinks you shouldn't retire. *The Washington Post.* Retrieved from https://www.washingtonpost.com/news/on-leadership/wp/2015/11/05/why-the-head-of-aarp-thinks-you-shouldnt-retire/.

D'Aprix, R. (1999) Communication in effective organizations. In A. Wann (Ed.), *Inside organizational communication* (3rd ed., pp. 1–9). New York, NY: Forbes Custom Publishing.

Davidson, J. (2014, December 9). Obama praises federal senior leaders, announces new programs to support them. *The Washington Post.* Retrieved from: https://www.washingtonpost.com/politics/federal_government/obama-praises-federal-senior-leaders-announces-new-programs-to-support-them/2014/12/09/dfccaa36-7fdf-11e4-9f38-95a187e4c1f7_story.html.

Davis, J. (2015, November 8). A digital team is helping Obama find his voice online. *The New York Times*. Retrieved from http://www.nytimes.com/2015/11/09/us/politics/a-digital-team-is-helping-obama-find-his-voice-online.html?_r=0.

Dennis, B. (2015, November 13). Cantaloupes to cauliflower, pineapples to plantains: FDA finalizes first federal safety rules for produce. *The Washington Post*. Retrieved from https://www.washingtonpost.com/news/to-your-health/wp/2015/11/13/cantaloupes-to-cauliflower-pineapples-to-plantains-fda-finalizes-first-federal-safety-rules-for-produce.

Drucker, P. F. (1995). The world according to Peter Drucker: The corporation that plays together, stays together [Interview transcript]. Retrieved from http://myownstory-boochonuan.blogspot.com/2006/12/peter-drucker-world-according-to-peter.html.

Dudley, E., Lin, D., Mancini, M., & Ng, J. (2015, July). *Implementing a citizen-centric approach to delivering government services.* McKinsey Center for Government. Retrieved from http://www.mckinsey.com/insights/public_sector/implementing_a_citizen-centric_approach_to_delivering_government_services.

Duhigg, C. (2012, February 16). How companies learn your secrets. *The New York Times Magazine*. Retrieved from http://www.nytimes.com/2012/02/19/magazine/shopping-habits.html.

Edelman. (2015). *Trust barometer executive summary.* Chicago, IL: Edelman. Retrieved from http://www.edelman.com/insights/intellectual-property/2015-edelman-trust-barometer/trust-and-innovation-edelman-trust-barometer/executive-summary/.

Executive Order No. 12866, 3 C.F.R. 638 (1994), reprinted as amended in 5 U.S.C. § 601 (2000). Retrieved from https://www.whitehouse.gov/sites/default/files/omb/inforeg/eo12866/eo12866_10041993.pdf.

Executive Order No. 13563. 3 C.F.R. 215–217 (2012). Retrieved from https://www.whitehouse.gov/the-press-office/2011/01/18/executive-order-13563-improving-regulation-and-regulatory-review.

Federal Emergency Management Agency. FEMA [Mobile app software]. Retrieved from http://www.fema.gov/mobile-app.

Fox, T. (2016, January 11). Inside HUD's efforts to improve employee morale. *The Washington Post*. Retrieved from https://www.washingtonpost.com/news/on-leadership/wp/2016/01/11/inside-huds-efforts-to-improve-employee-morale/.

Gibbs T., Levy A., & Sneader, K. (2011). Toward a more efficient public sector, *McKinsey on Government,* (Spring), 18–23. Retrieved from http://www.mckinsey.com/~/media/mckinsey/dotcom/client_service/public%20sector/pdfs/mck%20on%20govt/change%20under%20pressure/tg_mog_6_toward_public_sector.ashx.

GOV.UK. (n.d.). *Activity on Gov.UK: web traffic*. Retrieved from https://www.gov.uk/performance/site-activity.

Government Communications Services. (n.d.). *Internal communications standard operating model*. Retrieved from https://communication.cabinetoffice.gov.uk/ic-space/wp-content/uploads/2015/05/standard-operating-model.pdf.

GovLoop. (2015). *The customer service playbook for government*. Retrieved from https://www.govloop.com/resources/the-customer-service-playbook-for-government/.

Graudenz, D., & Hirsch, T. (2008). *The case for government transformation*. Washington, DC: McKinsey Center for Government. Retrieved from http://www.mckinsey.com/~/media/mckinsey/dotcom/client_service/public%20sector/pdfs/mck%20on%20govt/it/tg_case_for_government_transformation.ashx.

Griggs, B. (2014, June 6). The CIA sends its first tweet, or not. *CNN.com*. Retrieved from http://www.cnn.com/2014/06/06/tech/social-media/cia-first-tweet/.

Heath, C., & Heath, D. (2010). *Switch: How to change things when change is hard.* New York, NY: Broadway Books.

Heinke, C. (2015, November 9). The president of the United States now has an official Facebook page: Obama continues to socialize the oval office. *Adweek.* Retrieved from http://www.adweek.com/news/technology/president-united-states-now-has-official-facebook-page-168035.

IBM. (2015). *Redefining boundaries: Insights from the global C-suite study* IBM Institute for Business Value. Retrieved from http://www-935.ibm.com/services/c-suite/study/.

Kamensky, J. M. (2015, November 10). Strengthening the links in government. *Government Executive*. Retrieved from http://www.govexec.com/excellence/promising-practices/2015/11/strengthening-links-government/123538/.

Katz, E. (2016, February 24). OPM unveils overhaul of federal hiring site USAJOBS. *Government Executive*. Retrieved from http://www.govexec.com/management/2016/02/opm-unveils-overhaul-federal-hiring-site-usajobs/126176/?oref=govexec_today_nl.

Konkel, F. (2015, December 3). Why the U.S. Postal Service has the Best Customer Service in Government. *Nextgov.com*. Retrieved from http://www.nextgov.com/cio-briefing/2015/12/why-us-postal-service-has-best-customer-service-government/124187/.

Konkel, F. (2016, February 22). Reports suggest divide between government and customers it serves. *Nextgov.com*. Retrieved from http://www.nextgov.com/cio-briefing/2016/02/reports-suggest-divide-between-government-and-customers-they-serve/126115/?oref=nextgov_today_nl.

Kotter, J. P. (2012, November). Accelerate! *Harvard Business Review*.

Lafrance, A. (2015, January 6). The triumph of email: Why does one of the world's most reviled technologies keep winning? *The Atlantic*. Retrieved from http://www.theatlantic.com/technology/archive/2016/01/what-comes-after-email/422625/.

Levine, R., Locke, C., Searls, D., & Weinberger, D. (2000). *The Cluetrain Manifesto: The end of business as usual.* Boston, MA: Perseus Books.

Light, P. (2014). *A cascade of failures: Why government fails and how to stop it.* Washington, DC: Brookings Institution. Retrieved from http://www.brookings.edu/research/papers/2014/07/14-cascade-failures-why-government-fails-light.

Lindzon, J. (2015, November 2). Six ways work will change in 2016. *Fast Company*. Retrieved from http://www.fastcompany.com/3052836/the-future-of-work/6-ways-work-will-change-in-2016.

Markon, J. (2015, November 8). A decade into a project to digitize U.S. immigration forms, just 1 is online. *The Washington Post*.

Marx, W. (2015, October 13). The new rules of corporate communications. *Fast Company*. Retrieved from http://www.fastcompany.com/3051881/know-it-all/the-new-rules-of-corporate-communications.

Meeker, M. (2015). *Internet trends 2015 – code conference.* San Francisco, CA: Kleiner, Perkins, Caufield, Byers (KPCB). Retrieved from: https://kpcb.com/InternetTrends.

Montgomery, W. (2015, August 17). How CEOs can adopt a 21st-century approach to communication. *knowledge@wharton*. Retrieved from http://knowledge.wharton.upenn.edu/article/how-ceos-can-adopt-a-21st-century-approach-to-organizational-communication/.

Naylor, B. (2015, June 8). After spending millions on communications, Homeland Security fails radio test. *National Public Radio*. Retrieved from http://www.npr.org/sections/thetwo-way/2015/06/08/412919097/after-spending-millions-on-communications-homeland-security-fails-radio-test.

O'Toole, J., & Bennis, W. (2009, June). Creating a culture of candor. *Harvard Business Review*.

Office of E-Government & Information Technology. (n.d.). Retrieved from https://www.whitehouse.gov/omb/e-gov/.

Office of Personnel Management. (2012a). *Customer service plan*. Retrieved from https://www.opm.gov/about-us/our-people-organization/support-functions/planning-and-policy-analysis/2012-customer-service-plan.pdf.

Office of Personnel Management. (2012b). *Guide to the senior executive service qualifications*. Retrieved from https://www.opm.gov/policy-data-oversight/senior-executive-service/reference-materials/guidetosesquals_2012.pdf .

Office of Personnel Management. (2015a). *Engaging the federal workforce: How to do it & prove it*. Retrieved from https://admin.govexec.com/media/gbc/docs/pdfs_edit/engaging_the_federal_workforce_white_paper.pdf.

Office of Personnel Management. (2015b). *Federal employee viewpoint survey results: Employees influencing change*. Retrieved from http://www.fedview.opm.gov/2015FILES/2015_FEVS_Gwide_Final_Report.PDF.

Partnership for Public Service & Accenture. (2016). *Government for the people: The road to customer-centered services*. Retrieved from http://ourpublicservice.org/publications/viewcontentdetails.php?id=934.

Pew Research Center. (2015). *Beyond distrust: How Americans view their government*. Retrieved from http://www.people-press.org/files/2015/11/11-23-2015-Governance-release.pdf.

Pfau, B. (2015, October). How an accounting firm convinced its employees they could change the world. *Harvard Business Review*. Retrieved from https://hbr.org/2015/10/how-an-accounting-firm-convinced-its-employees-they-could-change-the-world.

The Plain Writing Act of 2010, Pub. L. No. 111–274 § 2, 124 Stat. 2861 (2010). Retrieved from https://www.gpo.gov/fdsys/pkg/PLAW-111publ274/pdf/PLAW-111publ274.pdf.

Rein, L. (2015, November 13). Former commissioners tell Congress, "The IRS is stretched to the breaking point," so stop slashing its budget. *The Washington Post*. Retrieved from https://www.washingtonpost.com/news/federal-eye/wp/2015/11/13/former-commissioners-tell-congress-the-irs-is-stretched-to-the-breaking-point-so-stop-slashing-its-budget/.

Sides, J. (2015, November 23). Americans don't trust government. But they still want government to do a lot. *The Washington Post*. Retrieved from https://www.washingtonpost.com/news/monkey-cage/wp/2015/11/23/americans-dont-trust-government-but-they-still-want-government-to-do-a-lot/.

Smith, L. (2015, November 18). Eroding trust in scientific research [Letter to the editor]. *The Washington Post*, p. A18.

Sunstein, C. R. (2011, April 13). *Final guidance on implementing the plain writing act of 2010*. [Memorandum for the heads of executive departments and agencies]. Washington, DC: Office of Information and Regulatory Affairs. Retrieved from https://www.whitehouse.gov/sites/default/files/omb/memoranda/2011/m11-15.pdf.

Terrett, B. (2014, March 24–April 6). Overthrow the .Gov. *Business Week*.

Towers Watson. (2013). *How the fundamentals have evolved and the best adapt:2013–2014 Change and Communication ROI Study Report*. Arlington, VA: Author. Retrieved from https://www.towerswatson.com/en-US/Insights/IC-Types/Survey-Research-Results/2013/12/2013-2014-change-and-communication-roi-study.

Trendwatching. (2015, August). *Government & public sector industry update*. Retrieved from www.trendwatching.com.

Turney, M. (2015). *Government public relations.* On-line reading in public relations. Retrieved from http://www.nku.edu/~turney/prclass/readings/government.html.

U.S. Digital Service. (n.d.). *U.S. Digital Services playbook.* Retrieved from https://playbook.cio.gov/.

U.S. Public Participation Playbook. (n.d). Retrieved from http://participation.usa.gov/.

VanRoekel, S. (2012, May 23). Roadmap for a digital government. *The White House Blog.* Retrieved from https://www.whitehouse.gov/blog/2012/05/23/roadmap-digital-government.

Wholey, J., Hatry, H., & Newcomer, K. (2010). *Handbook of practice program evaluation.* San Francisco, CA: Jossey-Bass.

Williams, N. (2015, November 20). 2 billion and counting. *UK Government Digital Services Blog.* Retrieved from https://gds.blog.gov.uk/2015/11/20/2-billion-and-counting/.

Williams, P., Gravesen, J., & Brownhill, T. (2015, November 24). Achieving joined-up government. *Government Executive.* Retrieved from http://www.govexec.com/excellence/promising-practices/2015/11/achieving-joined-government/123952/.

9 A Review of Federal Government Reform Initiatives Since the Passage of the Government Performance and Results Act of 1993

Nancy Kingsbury

> The key concepts of this performance-based management are the need to define clear agency missions, set results-oriented goals, measure progress toward the achievement of those goals, and use performance information to help make decisions and strengthen accountability.
>
> —James F. Hinchman

Throughout the past two and a half decades, initiatives in both the legislative and executive branches have been proposed and implemented to improve government management and accountability. Most of these initiatives have focused on and expanded on the fundamental objectives of the Government Performance and Results Act (GPRA). Taken together, they have offered many opportunities to make government more efficient and effective, more transparent, and more accountable to the American people.

While each Congress and each presidential administration can be expected to continue to revisit many of these issues, key elements and lessons from recent past experience can provide useful strategies for addressing management challenges going forward. The purpose of this chapter is to review these experiences and identify strategies that senior government managers can adopt within their own organizations to continue to move ahead to achieve the goals of these reforms.

Legislative Reform

While the focus of government reform broadly was initiated with GPRA, the current era of management reforms as framed in legislation arguably began with the Chief Financial Officers Act of 1990 (CFO Act), as expanded by the Government Management Reform Act of 1994 (GMRA) and further amended by the Federal Financial Management Improvement Act of 1996 (FFMIA). These statutes constitute the basis for identifying and correcting financial management weaknesses that had cost the federal government billions of dollars and left it vulnerable to waste, fraud, and abuse.

The expanded CFO Act spelled out a long overdue and ambitious agenda to help the government remedy its lack of timely, reliable, useful, and consistent financial information. A key provision of the act required the 24 largest agencies (referred to consistently as the "CFO Act agencies") to prepare audited financial statements annually. Over time, the requirement for audited financial statements extended to most federal agencies.

GMRA also required the U.S. Department of the Treasury to prepare each year a government-wide consolidated financial statement that the U.S. Government Accountability Office (GAO) audits. FFMIA built on the CFO Act by requiring financial statement auditors to report whether agencies' financial management systems complied with federal financial management systems requirements and applicable federal accounting standards in order to provide uniform, reliable, and more useful financial information.

Since the CFO Act and related laws were enacted, most agencies have succeeded in issuing financial statements and having them successfully audited. Most individual agency audits are conducted by the relevant agency inspector general. GAO has issued reports each year on its audit of the government's consolidated financial statement and has reported significant improvements over time in the quality and availability of financial management information.

In its most recent report, however, GAO was still unable to render an opinion on the overall financial statements of the federal government because of serious financial management problems at the U.S. Department of Defense (DOD; GAO, 2015a). These prevented DOD's financial statements from being auditable, rendered the federal government unable to adequately account for and reconcile intra-governmental activity and balances among federal entities, and impeded the preparation of consolidated financial statements. In recent years, Congress has stepped in to encourage DOD to develop and implement specific plans to bring its financial systems and records to the point where accurate financial statements can be prepared and DOD's financial statement as a whole could be audited by September 30, 2017.

The CFO Act implementation has resulted in many significant improvements, notably more reliable financial reporting and auditing, and other congressional initiatives are contributing to better availability and transparency of financial data. The investment in improved financial systems has been more expensive than and not as successful as many would like, so further improvements are needed.

There is considerable variation in the role of CFOs in different agencies, and their role could be made more strategic. CFOs should move beyond basic accounting and financial reporting to provide services to program managers and the agency-level enterprise strategies. Financial management systems improvements continue to be implemented in some agencies, but it might be more effective to focus on improving financial business processes, more accurate data, and the use of business intelligence systems to streamline financial activities and better prevent improper payments. Finally, given the complexity and transparency of financial transactions and data, a new concern about cyber risk may need to be given higher priority (Corporate Partner Advisory Group, 2015; Maitner, 2010; Steinhoff & Cherbini, 2010).

Government Performance and Results Act

The cornerstone of legislative government reform in recent decades is the Government Performance and Results Act of 1993 (GPRA). Implemented over several years, GPRA required each federal agency to develop strategic plans that covered at least 5 years.

An agency's strategic plans were to include:

- a comprehensive mission statement for major functions and operations, general and outcome-related goals;
- a description of how the agency would achieve the goals and the operational processes and resources required;
- a description of how the goals would relate to annual performance plan goals;
- an identification of the key factors both external to and beyond the control of the agency that could significantly affect its achieving its goals; and
- a description of program evaluations the agency used in establishing and revising general goals.

When developing strategic plans, agencies were to consult with Congress and solicit and consider the views and suggestions of entities potentially affected by or interested in the plan (referred to as stakeholders). Under GPRA, agency strategic plans were to be the starting point for agencies to set annual program goals and measure performance in achieving them.

GPRA also required each agency to submit to the Office of Management and Budget (OMB) an annual performance plan that provided the direct link between the strategic goals outlined in the agency's strategic plan for each program in the agency's budget and what managers and employees do day to day. The agency plan was to:

- establish goals that define the level of performance to be approved by a program activity;
- express goals in an objective, quantifiable, and measurable form;
- describe the operational processes and resources required to achieve the goals;
- establish performance indicators for measuring the relevant outputs, service levels, and outcomes of each program activity;
- provide a basis for comparing actual program results with the established goals; and
- describe the means to be used to verify and validate measured values.

GPRA originally provided that OMB would use individual agency plans to develop an overall federal government performance plan that would be submitted annually to the Congress with the president's budget. In practice, successive administrations have interpreted this as a requirement that is satisfied by the president's budget itself, so no government-wide performance plan per se has ever been produced.

GPRA also required that each agency submit to the president and to the appropriate congressional authorization and appropriations committees an annual report on program performance for the previous fiscal year and several prior years. The agencies' reports were to review how successfully performance goals had been achieved and, where goals were not met, explain and describe why not. When a goal is not met, the agency's report is expected to explain why and present plans and schedules for meeting the goal in the future or to explain modifications to the goal and further recommended actions.

The CFO Act and GPRA followed a number of efforts in the previous decades intended to link spending decisions with expected performance. These initiatives included the Planning-Programming-Budgeting-System (PPBS), Management by Objectives (MBO), and Zero-Based Budgeting (ZBB). All these efforts failed to shift the focus of the federal budget process from its long-standing concentration on the items of government spending to the results of its programs. Through better information on the effectiveness of federal programs and spending, GPRA sought to help federal managers improve program performance. It also sought to make performance information available for congressional policy making, spending decisions, and program oversight with a stronger focus on the link between resources and results.

Other Government Management Reforms

In addition to the CFO Act and GPRA, Congress passed a number of important management reforms in the 1990s. Implemented together, these laws provide a powerful framework for developing and fully integrating information about agencies' missions and strategic priorities. They also show the relationship of information technology investments to the achievement of performance goals. These legislative management reforms are summarized in Table 9.1.

Government Performance and Results Act Modernization Act of 2010

The Government Performance and Results Act Modernization Act of 2010 (GPRAMA) significantly enhanced GPRA by addressing a number of federal performance management challenges that had become evident during the intervening 17 years. It focused attention on cross-cutting issues, enhanced the use and usefulness of performance information, increased transparency, and ensured leadership commitment and attention to improving performance. GPRAMA's initial implementation achieved the development of agency-level and government wide goals, designating officials to key leadership roles, and using the Performance Improvement Council to facilitate the exchange of information to strengthen agency performance management. GPRAMA has also led to OMB's and agencies' establishing agency priority goals and cross-agency priority goals and focusing attention on programs with similar goals across multiple agencies, identifying the highest priorities in each agency. In addition, GPRAMA provided a further statutory basis for key leadership positions, including chief operating officers, performance improvement officers, and goal leaders.

Table 9.1 Legislative Reforms Supporting the CFO Act and GPRA, 1990–1996

Clinger-Cohen Act of 1996, P.L 104–208	The purpose of the Clinger-Cohen Act is to improve the productivity, efficiency, and effectiveness of federal programs through the improved acquisition, use, and disposal of information technology resources. Among other provisions, the law requires agencies to base decisions about IT investments on the costs, benefits, and risks of the investments and to appoint Chief Information Officers.
Paperwork Reduction Act of 1995, P.L. 104–13	The purpose of the PRA is to minimize the public's paperwork burdens resulting from the collection of information by or for the federal government and to improve the dissemination of public information, and other matters.
Debt Collection Improvement Act of 1996, P.L. 204–134	The Debt Collection Improvement Act builds on the Debt Collection Act of 1982 (P.L. 97–365 as amended) to require the heads of agencies to collect debts owed the government, to authorize the compromise of some debts, and to authorize federal agencies to use certain collection tools available in the private sector.
Federal Credit Reform Act of 1990, P.L. 101–508, as amended	The purpose of the Federal Credit Reform Act is to accurately measure the costs of federal credit programs by placing the cost of credit programs on a budgetary basis equivalent to other federal spending and to improve the allocation of resources.

Source: *Managing for Results* (1997).

GPRAMA, expanding the spirit of GPRA, requires regular review of progress in achieving goals and objectives through performance reviews, including annual high-level strategic reviews and the scheduling regularly (at least quarterly) of data-driven performance reviews that organizational leaders and managers use to review and analyze data on progress toward key performance goals and other management improvement priorities. Transparency and public reporting were strengthened under GPRAMA through the requirement to develop a government-wide website to communicate government and agency performance information. The website—implemented by OMB as performance.gov—is required to make available information on agency and cross-cutting priority goals, updated quarterly. Performance.gov also includes agency strategic plans, annual performance plans, annual performance reports, and an inventory of all federal programs (GAO, 2015c).

The DATA Act of 2014

The Digital Accountability and Transparency Act (DATA Act) required OMB and Treasury to work together to establish government-wide data standards for reporting financial spending data to permit the measuring of the cost and magnitude of federal investments and share data across agencies to improve decision making and oversight. In addition to beginning to issue data standards, the act requires OMB to develop an inventory of government programs, creating a consistent framework for reporting spending information. This data framework will have to be supported by structures for project management and data governance as well as for obtaining stakeholder input and maintaining data integrity over time (Federal Data Transparency, 2014).

High Risk and Duplication, Overlap, and Fragmentation: The Role of the Government Accountability Office

One area of government reform that is legislatively directed, although not in statute, is GAO's focus biannually on alerting the Congress about major areas of government management that are at high risk due to their greater vulnerability to fraud, waste, abuse, and mismanagement. Since 1990, GAO's High Risk List has included more than 30 government programs that need management focus and reform.

The most recent list, issued in 2015 (GAO, 2015b), includes 32 major government challenges including: management of insurance and benefit programs, enforcement of tax laws, management of federal contracts, ensuring of public safety and security, transforming management at the Department of Defense, management of federal real property, and many others.

Since 1990, more than one-third of the areas previously designated as high risk have been removed from the High Risk List because sufficient progress was made in addressing the problems identified. Congressional oversight and legislative action have been critical to the progress that has been made. Congress passed numerous laws targeting both specific problems and the high-risk areas overall.

Additionally, in recent years, top administration officials have shown their commitment to ensuring that high-risk areas receive attention and oversight through regularly convening meetings attended by OMB officials, senior agency officials, and GAO. Lasting solutions to the high-risk areas offer the potential to further implement government reform, save billions of dollars, dramatically improve service to the American public, and strengthen public confidence in the government.

Experience with the High Risk List has demonstrated that several broad elements are essential to making progress. First, leadership commitment and support, in such areas as developing long-term priorities and providing continuing oversight and accountability, is a key challenge. Second, the agency must develop the people and resources necessary to address the high-risk program. Third, evaluating root causes for the problem and identifying corrective measures, including regular monitoring, is necessary to make further progress (GAO, 2015b).

In response to a statutory mandate, GAO also issues an annual report on federal programs, agencies, offices, and initiatives (both within departments and government wide) that are fragmented, overlapping, or duplicative as well as opportunities for cost savings or enhanced revenues. Over the past four years, the executive branch and Congress have made progress in addressing the approximately 440 actions across 180 areas that GAO has identified. Fully addressing the actions identified could lead to tens of billions of dollars in additional savings with significant opportunities for improved efficiencies, cost savings or revenue enhancements in areas such as defense, information technology, education and training, health care, energy, and tax enforcement (*Government Efficiency and Effectiveness*, 2015). This annual report also focuses on reducing improper payments, which have significantly increased in recent years to an estimated $124.7 billion in fiscal year 2014. Recent laws and guidance have focused on the issue of improper payments, including the Improper Payments Elimination and Recovery Improvement Act of 2012.

Executive Branch Reform

While the Congress focused on management reform in the 1990s and later, each executive administration since 1992 also adopted significant management reforms, while at the same time implementing many of the legislative reforms. In the early years of President Bill Clinton's administration, Vice President Al Gore led an initiative known as the National Performance Review (NPR). In the fall of 1993, NPR issued a report containing almost 400 recommendations intended to make the government "work better and cost less." In part, these recommendations built on initiatives that were already underway in various federal agencies. NPR subsequently identified a series of about 1,200 action items necessary to implement the recommendations. Many of the recommendations were in fact implemented.

Many agencies established NPR "reinvention labs" designed to test ways in which they could improve their performance and customer service by re-engineering work processes and eliminating unnecessary regulations. While these "labs" may have identified a number of promising approaches to improving existing agency work processes, their real value was to be realized only when the operational improvements they initiated, tested, and validated achieved wider adoption. All of these initiatives, however, were carried out within the legislative reform framework (National Partnership for Reinventing Government, 2001).

President George W. Bush's President's Management Agenda

The administration of President George W. Bush adopted a President's Management Agenda that in part was shaped by legislative management reforms and by GAO's High-Risk List. It focused on five major management areas, including improved financial management with a special initiative for reducing improper payments. Other areas were improving human capital reform; integrating management and performance issues with budgeting; starting e-government initiatives, including the development of a federal architecture; and managing real property assets.

With respect to financial management, agencies were expected to implement integrated financial and performance management systems that routinely produced information that was timely, useful, and reliable. Agencies and OMB were able to accelerate financial statement reporting by several months, and most agencies were able to obtain unqualified audit opinions on their financial statements. The federal agencies were also able to make progress in efforts to modernize their financial management systems and improve financial management performance.

However, improper payments (that is, inadvertent errors in payments including miscalculations or duplicate payments, payments of inadequately documented claims, payments for services not rendered, payments to ineligible beneficiaries, and payments resulting from fraud and abuse) continued to be a problem. Many improper payments occur in federal programs that are administered by entities other than the federal government, such as states, municipalities, and intermediaries such as insurance companies. Entities using successful strategies to help address their improper payments share a common focus of improving the internal control system. The recent implementation GAO's *Standards for Internal Control in the Federal Government* provides new criteria and ideas for such improved internal control systems (GAO, 2014).

Also under President Bush, OMB developed and implemented the Program Assessment Rating Tool (PART) to create a consistent approach to evaluating federal programs during budget formulation and consideration of the budget's program activities. This initiative illustrated the potential to build on GPRA's foundation to more actively promote the use of performance information in budget decisions.

While OMB went to great lengths to encourage consistent application of PART in the evaluation of government programs, including pilot testing of the instrument, issuing detailed guidance, and conducting consistency reviews, any tool is inherently limited in providing a single performance answer or judgment on complex federal programs with multiple goals. PART defined "program" as a line item in the president's budget, and it covered four broad topics for each programs reviewed: (a) program purpose and design, (b) strategic planning, (c) program management, and (d) program results (that is, whether a program is meeting its long-term and annual goals; *Performance Budgeting*, 2004).

While the tool was similar across government programs, certain questions were specific to major approaches to delivering federal programs, such as competitive grants, block and formula grants, capital assets and service acquisition programs, credit programs, regulatory-based programs, direct federal programs, and research and development programs. PART provided an opportunity to consider strategically targeting the assessment on groups of related programs contributing to common outcomes to more efficiently use scarce analytic resources and focus decision makers' attention on the most pressing performance issues cutting across individual programs and agencies. PART also had a positive impact in stressing the importance of performance information and the results of program evaluations in the assessment.

In the end, PART was assessed by researchers as not as useful as other approaches to performance measurement in part because, although it purported to be analytic in nature, it was largely a subjective OMB-driven assessment. PART also failed to provide for adequate stakeholder consultation (including congressional consultation) and public participation as GPRA advocated (Brass, 2004).

President Barack Obama's Evidence-Based Management Agenda

Following the formal management agendas of President Clinton (National Performance Review) and President Bush (Management Agenda and PART), President Obama did not announce a big formal government reform initiative. In a series of budget essays, President Obama presented (and continues to do so) a shift from individual agencies and programs to more broadly defined services and results.

Certainly, goal setting and performance reporting continued to be emphasized in an increasingly transparent way. To that end, President Obama's OMB maintained the results of the Bush administration's PART process on the OMB website ExpectMore.gov, where it can still be found. While that information is arguably dated, it provides some interesting insights into program operations (Kamensky, 2010).

In his first term, President Obama focused on problem-solving networks and enhancing the federal government's perspective on performance and management by naming a national Chief Performance Officer, Chief Technology Officer, and Chief Information Officer. The agenda also emphasized the importance of evidence-based policy making, and in the first couple of years the president's budget offered some additional funding to agencies that wanted to conduct program evaluations.

With the passage of the American Recovery and Reinvestment Act of 2009 to address the financial crisis that the administration was presented with in its early months, resources were provided for the inspector general community led Recovery Act Transparency Board to build an open data source to make information available at the zip code level to the public and researchers about the recipients and projects funded under that Act. (The Board went out of existence at the end of fiscal year 2015.)

In his second term, President Obama's agenda has focused on delivering better customer service experiences for citizens and businesses, smarter information technology investment and management, and increasing quality and value in core operations through such activities as strategic sourcing and shared services. The agenda also focused again on reducing improper payments, reducing federal real estate costs, and improving the federal workforce.

Contributions to Government Reform from Federal Managers

As this history suggests, Congress over time and each presidential administration have adopted management reform as a major focus. This trend is likely to continue. By understanding the challenges of such reforms and developing the tools to apply them in their own work, individual federal managers can make considerable improvements in the efficiency and impact of federal programs, whatever new or reinvented government reform initiatives are enacted or proposed.

A number of challenges arise for federal managers, especially during a presidential transition or implementation of new initiatives. One such challenge is the reality of turnover in political appointees. For federal managers, that challenge involves both the need to provide information to new appointees and at the same time integrate new ideas to ongoing (and often legislatively required) program management activities.

Another challenge is the multiple viewpoints that arise concerning a program, especially in a divided government where one branch or opinion holder is controlled by one party and the other branch by another party. Many of the past government reforms have encouraged improved communication between the program agencies and relevant congressional committees, although that communication has often not been timely or strategic. Nonetheless, understanding and to the extent possible reflecting congressional and other stakeholder viewpoints as programs are implemented is an important lesson from past reform initiatives.

Providing the training and staff capacity to effectively manage programs is also a challenge. And, for many federal programs, the responsibility to carry out federal programs rests with other government or non-governmental entities. Improved information from performance measures and spending data may provide some progress in bridging that gap.

The experience of management reform initiatives, however, provides a number of tools and capabilities to address many challenges. These include a focus on goal setting and performance measurement as tools for management as well as accountability. Program evaluation to assess the implementation or effectiveness of a program can also help to provide information for improved program management (GAO, 2013).

Improved financial information available through financial statements and financial audits brought about by the CFO Act of 1990 as amended, and current spending information that is to be available under the DATA Act, should help to have improved oversight over program management details. Several government reforms also provide focus on the importance of strategic human capital management and improved acquisition practices, especially (in management functions) for information technology system acquisitions, as key to improving government performance. Recent reforms under GPRAMA have led to the identification and monitoring cross-agency priorities and agency focus on periodic, data driven reviews of program activities. Participation in such activities also offers tools and techniques to better inform program management.

Conclusion

This chapter documents a constellation of congressional intent, presidential ambitions, and federal manager roles concerning government reform efforts. Managers are not only still free to follow the best practice of their mentors and leaders, the clear intent of Congress has always been to facilitate achievement and encourage good practice.

The experiments and programs that have grown out of these legislative and executive initiatives have added volumes of knowledge and experience to the realm in which federal leaders manage programs. These initiatives have provided experience from which to build improvements and lessons learned. The basic tools that the best managers have always used are still in the toolbox. In the end, it is up to each manager, whatever level he or she is at, to do what is fundamentally right, to treasure the first principles of our government and national traditions, and the collective goals of the organization within which he or she works. The manager and colleagues are there to foster work to achieve the purposes their particular organization is charged with and the broader goals of U.S. constitutional government.

At the executive level, these same principles apply, although the challenges may be greater. Through these years of government reform, organizational goals have been made clearer, performance data has been developed and refined, workforce diversity has increased, and managers have been given additional management tools and lost nothing important. At the same time, public trust in government has steadily declined, and public appreciation for government service has withered.

Government executives have an unusual opportunity as we approach a transition to a new presidency to demonstrate the long tradition of understanding governmental priorities and responsibilities and carrying out responsibilities to the best of their abilities, recognizing the balance of political, legal, and managerial prerogatives. In doing that, it is important for executives to foster organizational integrity and trust, respect the skills and abilities of those they lead, share information up and down their organization, and model government service for the following generation.

References

Brass, C. T. (2004). *The Bush administration's program assessment rating tool* (CRS Report No. RL32663). Washington, DC: Congressional Research Service.

Corporate Partner Advisory Group. (2015). *The CFO Act at 25: Perspectives from two decades of CFO surveys & prospects for the future survey series.* Washington, DC: Association of Government Accountants.

Federal data transparency: Effective implementation of the DATA Act would help address government-wide management challenges and improve oversight: Hearings before the House Committee on Oversight and Government Reform, 113th Cong. (2014) (Testimony of Gene L. Dodaro, Comptroller General of the United States, Government Accountability Office, GAO-15-241T).

Government Accountability Office. (2013). *Program evaluation: Strategies to facilitate agencies' use of evaluation in program management and policy making* (GAO-13-570). Washington, DC: Author.

Government Accountability Office. (2014). *Standards for internal control in the federal government* (GAO-14-704G). Washington, DC: Author.

Government Accountability Office. (2015a). *Financial audit: U.S. government's fiscal years 2014 and 2013 consolidated financial statements* (GAO-15-341R). Washington, DC: Author.

Government Accountability Office. (2015b). *High-risk series: An update* (GAO-15-290). Washington, DC: Author.

Government Accountability Office. (2015c). *Managing for results: Agencies report positive effects of data-driven reviews on performance but some should strengthen practices.* (GAO-15-579). Washington, DC: Author.

Government efficiency and effectiveness: Opportunities to reduce fragmentation, overlap, duplication, and improper payments and achieve other financial benefits: Hearings before the Senate Committee on the Budget, 114th Cong. (2015). (Testimony of Gene L. Dodaro, Comptroller General of the United States, Government Accountability Office, GAO-15-440T).

Kamensky, J. M. (2010, March/April). Obama's performance revolution: Changing how government works. *PATimes.*

Maitner, R., Jr. (2010). The CFO Act of 1990: Current systems considerations, modernization, and achieving compliance. *Journal of Government Financial Management, 59*(4), 38–44.

Managing for results: The statutory framework for improving federal management and effectiveness: Hearings before the Senate Committee on Appropriations and Committee on Governmental Affairs, 105th Cong. (1997) (Testimony of James Hinchman, Acting Comptroller General, Government Accountability Office, T-GGD/AIMD-97-144).

National Partnership for Reinventing Government (2001). Accomplishments, 1993–2000: A summary. Retrieved from Archives, NPR Version 3.0 http://govinfo.library.unt.edu/npr/whoweare/appendixf.html.

Performance budgeting: OMB's performance rating tool presents opportunities and challenges for evaluating program performance: Hearings before the House Subcommittee on Environment, Technology, and Standards, Committee on Science, 108th Cong. (2004) (Testimony of Paul L. Posner, Managing Director, Federal Budget Issues, Strategic Issues, Government Accountability Office, GAO-04-550T).

Steinhoff, J. C., & Cherbini, J. (2010). The CFO Act turns 20 years old: As we blow out the candles, where are we today and where do we go from here? *Journal of Government Financial Management, 59*(4), 10–26.

10 Change Management in Federal Government Organizations

Ruth S. Wagner

> As the recognition grows that part of every manager's job is to plan, initiate, and manage change, so will the concepts and methods in this area come to be seen as integral to the management process itself.
>
> —Edgar Schein

Organizational change is a constant in 21st-century organizations, and managing organizational change constitutes an essential skill for leaders in all organizations. Edgar Schein, Professor Emeritus at the MIT Sloan School of Management, made the statement in the epigraph almost 40 years ago, and it is even truer today. Schein has made significant contributions to our understanding of organizational change, change management, organizational culture, and leadership (Schein, 1988, 1992, 1996). Planning, initiating, and managing organizational change typically presents these difficulties: inability to anticipate all the major problems that arise, grossly underestimating the time needed to overcome the unforeseen problems and win acceptance by people involved, and the struggle to overcome resistance and turn resistance into acceptance of the change (Argyris, 1999).

For leaders in federal government organizations, change has become an integral part of organizational life (Sims, 2010). The thinking behind this chapter is that planning, initiating, and managing change are inherent competencies for every manager, because today's federal government organizations confront a maze-like landscape of multiple change initiatives. To be successful, managers need to develop nuanced approaches to organizational change tailored to their specific organizations and attend to the human element during organizational change.

The purpose of this chapter is to broaden leaders' understanding of organizational change, to provide insights into the complexity of change, and to present some practical ways to improve the management of change. This chapter begins with a summary of challenges facing leaders in federal government organizations; reviews relevant theories, models, and concepts associated with organizational change; and offers 10 recommendations for enhancing the management of change.

What Is Organizational Change?

Historically, organizational change theories result from melding concepts from the fields of social psychology, sociology, political science, management, and leadership; some have even incorporated concepts from epidemiology (Ford, 1999).

The interdisciplinary field of organizational change lacks any overarching unifying theory, which many leaders and practitioners find frustrating. Instead, there is a wide variety of change theories, models, and concepts; like organizational change itself, the study of organizational change is complex and multifaceted.

Tacit Assumptions about Organizational Change

As a leader seeking to make managing change integral to his/her management process, ask yourself: What is my philosophy of change? As a leader, you approach this chapter with your own assumptions and theories of organizational change. These assumptions and theories may be tacit, thus out of your conscious awareness. As you read this chapter, strive to identify your own thinking about organizational change; when you encounter a model or concept that you wish to reject, ask yourself: Why am I not willing to consider this? All of this influences how you interpret the world around you. In this chapter, you are encouraged to expand your thinking by adopting additional theories and concepts about organizational change.

Definitions of Organizational Change

A popular definition of change states: "Change means the new state of things is different from the old state of things" (French & Bell, 1995, p. 3). However, this definition does not do justice to the complex reality of organizational change. A well-known scholar of organizational change poses this question: "What does organizational change really 'mean'?" (Bartunek, 2003, p. x) and suggests why organizational change is so complex. First, there is rarely only one change initiative going on in an organization at a given time; rather there are multiple change initiatives existing simultaneously, some beginning, some in progress, and some having been around for a while but refusing to end. Second, measuring the effectiveness or success of a change initiative is difficult, because different stakeholder groups may have different criteria for assessing the effectiveness and success of the change initiative. Third, organizations are awash with competing popular approaches to implementing change.

Concept of Multiple Levels of Systems

An important concept is the existence of multiple levels of systems within an organization. There are numerous cuts at the concept of multiple levels. One is to look at the role hierarchy or "hierarchical differentiation" (Armenakis, Harris, & Mossholder, 1993), such as executives, middle managers, and staff; where someone sits in the organization influences one's perspective. Another concept of level is to look at the levels of analysis, such as environment, organization, and unit. The organization and its units form different levels. The environment is not one entity but consists of a general environment with multiple sectors, such as social, cultural, legal, political, economic, and technological (Hatch, 1997, pp. 68–70).

The essential point is to understand that what people see; their perspective may vary depending on their level in the system; their levels also influence how they make sense of a situation and how they define success. A slightly different concept of levels of systems is where people engage to make meaning of a situation; these levels are individual, group, and organization. Those planning, initiating, and managing change programs must understand and be able to work with this concept of multiple levels of systems.

Competing Perspectives on Planned Change Theory

Just to be clear, there is "no one, all-embracing, widely accepted theory of organizational change" (Dunphy, 1996, p. 541). There are numerous ways to group and contrast change theories; however, a helpful comparison contrasts two competing approaches to implementing planned change: socio-technical change theory, as espoused by Trist (1977), and strategic change theory, as represented by Kotter's (1996) eight-stage change model. In comparing these two theories of change, two differences arise: who leads the change effort and which stakeholders are involved and when.

Socio-technical Change Theory

In socio-technical change, the internal workforce is the figural stakeholder, and it is involved in the initial phases of the change effort; employee participation is considered an ethical imperative that provides a source of energy to sustain the change. Socio-technical change "directs analysis primarily toward internal factors" and "is strongly committed to placing the major initiative for the direction of change with key groups within the workforce itself" (Dunphy, 1996, p. 544).

Strategic Change Theory

In strategic change, leaders typically conduct an environmental scan, formulate a plan, and then communicate it to the workforce. Consequently, "the major challenge for senior management then is to align the workforce to the strategy and to involve them in translating the strategy into coordinated actions" (Dunphy, 1996, p. 544). In strategic change, the external stakeholders are figural and, typically, the internal stakeholders are not engaged until the implementation phase. Many scholar/practitioners contend the primary approach to change in federal government organizations is strategic change that is led by executives and driven by budgetary or political objectives and not driven by the needs of internal stakeholders as practiced under socio-technical change. Executive lead change is consistent with the strategic management literature and the military model, in which the top executives develop the strategy and then lead the organization through its implementation. The strategic change proponents view employee participation only as a means to obtain employee support or buy in for the change.

This chapter focuses on the strategic change using Kotter's eight-stage model as a framework, augmented with concepts first conceptualized under socio-technical change theory and more recent insights into how to implement successful organizational change.

Planned and Emergent Change

French and Bell (1995) distinguish planned change, which is deliberate, from unplanned change, which is accidental. The term *planned change*—the "conscious, deliberate, and collaborative effort to improve the operations of a human system" (Bennis, Benne, Chin, & Corey, 1976, p. 4)—entered the American rhetoric around 1900 when the salient question was: "Should or should not men seek, through deliberate and collaborative forethought in the present, to mold the shape of their collective future?" (Bennis & Chin, 1976, p. 14). A hundred years later, planned change has become ubiquitous in organizations (Beckhard & Pritchard, 1992; Kotter, 1996; Nadler, Shaw, Walton, & Associates, 1995). Scholars and practitioners sought multiple approaches, which Mills (2003) calls "popular theories of change" (p. 1); some examples are organizational learning (Argyris & Schon, 1974), Total Quality Management (TQM) (Deming, 1986), Business Process Reengineering (BPR) (Hammer & Champy, 1993), Organization Development (OD) (French & Bell, 1995), change management (Kotter, 1996), and organizational transformation (Adams, 1998).

Weick and Quinn (1999) distinguished between two types of change: planned change and emergent change, as described in Table 10.1. Note the multiple terms for each type of change. Readers are sometimes confused about the distinctions among these terms. In many federal organizations a new planned change initiative is layered over other planned change efforts and existing emergent change.

Planned Change

Other terms for planned change are second-order change, transformational change, and episodic change. Bartunek (1984) defined second-order change as

Table 10.1 Planned and Emergent Change: Features, Descriptions, and Synonyms

Features	*Planned change*	*Emergent change*
Level of analysis	Macro level	Micro level
Level of change	2nd order change	1st order change
Change pattern	Episodic, intermittent, discontinuous	Evolving, incremental, continuous
Degree of change	Transformational change, revolutionary change, deep change	Transitional change, ongoing adaptation and adjustments
Frequency of change	Change is infrequent, aperiodic	Change is a constant
Role of change agent	Prime mover who creates change	Sense maker who interprets change

Source: Adapted from Weick & Quinn (1999).

a "radical, discontinuous shift in interpretive schemes" in which "organizational perspectives are reframed and norms and worldviews are changed" (p. 356).

Emergent Change

Weick (2000) presented the concept of emergent change that "forms the infrastructure that determines whether planned, episodic change will succeed or fail" (p. 223). He added, "Emergent change consists of ongoing accommodations, adaptations, and alterations that produce fundamental change without ... intentions to do so. Emergent change occurs when people reaccomplish routines and when they deal with contingencies, breakdowns, and opportunities in everyday work" (p. 237). Emergent change is a relevant concept for this chapter, because planned organizational change, directed from the top of the organization, cannot address all the details throughout the organization; internal stakeholders are left to figure out these details, thus creating opportunities for emergent change.

Contrasting Planned and Emergent Change

Planned, episodic change is triggered by inertia, "failures to adapt," whereas, emergent, continuous change "never starts because it never stops" (Weick & Quinn, 1999, p. 381). Romanelli and Tushman (1994) referred to episodic change as transformational change and to continuous change as transitional change. The two types of change also differ in their level of analysis: planned change is typically seen from the macro or whole system level where the leader measures the effect of the change on the whole organization. In contrast, emergent change is typically viewed from the micro or local level; individuals put in place small changes to accommodate a larger change imposed from above. Another difference is the role of the change agent; in planned change, typically the leaders are the creators and drivers of change. With emergent change, anyone can be the change agent, who interprets, adjusts, and makes sense of the change.

Theory E and Theory O

Two scholars from Harvard Business School propose an archetype or two underlying theories of change: Theory E (economic value) and Theory O (organizational capability) (Beer & Nohria, 2000). A leader employing Theory E to maximize economic value would focus on changes to structures and systems and lead a programmatic effort. In contrast, a leader employing Theory O would focus on changes to culture and would lead through participation as an emergent effort. The authors contend that both theories have value and should be used jointly. Their research findings suggest that the effectiveness of a change management initiative would be improved by applying both of these theories.

Having presented an overview of organizational change theories, the next sections discuss federal government organizations and the challenges confronting them.

Challenges Facing Leaders of Federal Organizations

In recent decades, a growing amount of change has created turbulent environments that threaten the survival of many organizations (Laszlo & Laugel, 2000; Nadler et al., 1995; Vaill, 1989). The management literature highlights the large and growing amount of change facing organizations (Laszlo & Laugel, 2000; Nadler et al., 1995). For example, federal managers face a new president every four or eight years, along with changes in agencies' appointed leadership. Those in the career civil and military service lead most sub-organizations, and their challenge is to deal with the new leaderships' desire to make changes while maintaining ongoing commitments. They are influenced by law, tradition, values, relationships, mission, and the directives of superiors, while maintaining responsibility for ensuring the survival of their organizations—all without bringing unwanted attention from the media. Theirs is a difficult job! "The greatest challenge public sector organizations will face in the years to come is to achieve their mission and do so while swiftly adapting to change" (Sims, 2010, p. 23).

Organizations as Context for Change

Organizations—including federal government organizations—provide a complex context for our contemporary lives (Sims & Gioia, 1986), and this complexity amplifies the challenges faced by those who try to change them (Daft & Weick, 1984). A critical competency for leaders in the 21st century is leading planned change (Shaw & Walton, 1995), seeking to change everything from work processes to information systems and culture. In the public sector, these responses are referred to as planned change programs (Nutt, 1992). The bureaucratic and political aspects of federal government organizations exacerbate the challenges faced when undertaking change. Public managers exist in a dynamic, complex environment with multiple demands on their energies. For example, some of their activities are to identify a set of goals, monitor the environment for changes that will affect them, balance between following orders from their superiors and maintaining their independence, relate to other organizations that are in the same policy arena, and navigate the controversies among the various branches of government (Heymann, 1987). Public sector organizations have specific needs with respect to planned change: "Identifying the beliefs and needs of the authority networks, using bargaining tactics, balancing contractor and user concerns, learning public expectations, and determining stakeholder views" (Nutt & Backoff, 1993, p. 299). While coping with these tasks, they must also deal with the day-to-day stewardship of their organizations. Federal government leaders and managers are rewarded for maintaining stability and reliability rather than for being creative and innovative; it is challenging to do both (Sims, 2010). In addition, the American public sometimes does not respect these leaders and managers or what they do. Consequently, these leaders and managers frequently feel overwhelmed and unappreciated, as their organizations face downsizing, being asked to "do more with less," privatization, outsourcing, increasing media scrutiny (Nutt & Backoff, 1993), and an aging civil service workforce.

Complicating Factors of Public Sector Organizations

There are factors inherent in public sector organizations that complicate and impede the public managers ability to bring about change: fragmented decision making; balance of public good and public needs and wants; low appetite for risk; large stakeholder communities consisting of interest groups, lobbyists, demonstrators, and constituencies; and funding through legislation, all while being closely scrutinized (Sims, 2010).

In "The Deadly Sins in Public Administration," Drucker (1980) proposed six deadly sins associated with public sector organizations: lofty, unspecific, unmeasurable objectives; lack of focus; throwing resources at problems; lack of experiment in favor of dogmatism; failure to learn from experience; and the inability to abandon a project or program (pp. 36–40). Public sector organizations have specific needs with respect to planned change: "Identifying the beliefs and needs of the authority networks, using bargaining tactics, balancing contractor and user concerns, learning public expectations, and determining stakeholder views" (Nutt & Backoff, 1993, p. 299). Public sector organizations exist in a world of constraints that limit "flexibility and autonomy, goals are often vague … the leader's authority is limited, political interference and scrutiny by outsiders can be expected … and performance expectations continually shift" (Nutt & Backoff, 1993, p. 300). For example, public sector organizations have an indirect relationship with who pays for the services they provide.

In summary, several factors influence planned organizational change in public sector organizations: size of organizations, number of people impacted, complexity, and magnitude of the change. Change may create difficulties for leaders of sub-organizations, as it may require them to downsize or consolidate their organizations, which is in conflict with their responsibility to ensure the survival of their organizations (Rainey, 1997).

Drivers of Change Confronting Federal Government Organizations

Multiple situations drive change in federal government organizations; some are created internally and some externally. Examples of both are discussed.

Internally Driven Change

Executive, legislative, or judicial elements of government give directives, pass laws, and interpret the constitution. These actions from the internal environment of the federal government are enacted to change some aspect of the government operations and services. Relevant federal organizations then have to analyze, plan, design, and implement actions to bring about the desired changes. Some historical examples of this type of internally driven change are:

- *Civil Service Reform Act of 1978*
- *Government Performance and Results Act (GRPA, 1993)*
- *National Performance Review (NPR) (Gore, 1993a)*
- *Transformation of the Defense Department (Bush, 2001)*

Table 10.2 Examples of Internal Drivers of Change

Popular change theories	*Popular structural changes*
• Balanced scorecard (Kaplan & Norton, 2001)	• Downsizing
• Business process reengineering (Hammer & Champy, 1993)	• IT package implementation
• Change management	• Leadership change
• Culture change (Schein, 1992)	• Outsourcing
• Organization development (French & Bell, 1995)	• Restructuring
• Six sigma (Carnegie Mellon, 2005)	
• Total quality management (TQM) (Deming, 1986)	

Not all internally driven changes are initiated by actions taken in one of the three branches of government. Internally driven change can also result from applying popular theories of change and structural change within individual federal government organizations. See Table 10.2 for a list of popular change theories and structural changes that, when adopted within federal government organizations, drive change internally; most experienced public managers will have lived through many of these change efforts.

Externally Driven Change

Not all changes are driven from inside the federal government; some can also be in response to events from outside. Two examples are: the terrorist attacks of September 11, 2001 (Department of Defense, 2003) and the economic recession of 2008 (Baily & Elliott, 2009). Both of these external events then resulted in internally driven changes.

Confronted with the enormous amount of change facing leaders in federal government organizations, leaders need some theories for how to lead and manage change. The White House released a Behavioral Science Insights Policy Directive (Exec. Order No. 13707, 2015) that instructs executive departments and agencies to identify opportunities to apply behavioral science insights to programs. The following section presents three theories of change developed by applying behavioral science insights. The field of organizations development (OD) is defined as a planned and sustained effort to apply the behavioral science knowledge to bring about planned change (French, Bell, & Zawacki, 1994). The following section presents three theories of change that are based on behavioral science insights.

Overview of Three Theories of Change

"There is nothing so practical as a good theory" is attributed to the social psychologist Kurt Lewin (1951), who is considered the father of the field of organization development. At first his statement appears illogical, as a theory is a "a mental schema of a way of doing something" (Brown et al., 1993), whereas practical implies constructive, helpful, and worthwhile. For students of change, theories are practical in that theories are like lenses through which we can "see" a situation through the elements of the theory. Applying different theories to the same situation allows the viewer to see different aspects of the same situation. This chapter focuses on the theories of change developed by three scholar/practitioners: Kurt Lewin, John Kotter, and William Bridges. Each is presented in the next subsections.

Lewin's Change Theory

According to Hatch (1997), prior to the mid-20th century, there were few theories of change because stability was prized over change; the emphasis in organizations was on becoming routinized, efficient, and effective. The original organizational change theory is attributed to Lewin (1951), who borrowed concepts from Newtonian physics to depict the forces present in organizations. He contextualized the psychological field present and highlighted its multiple levels of human systems: individuals, groups, and organizations. Lewin introduced the concept of an organization as a balance between driving forces, which exert pressure to change, and restraining forces, which act like barriers against change in order to protect the status quo. He developed a four-part concept of organizational change that consisted of force fields, group dynamics, action research, and a three-step change model; together they constitute Lewin's change theory (Burnes, 2004).

Field Theory

Lewin conceived of human social systems as being acted on by driving and restraining forces. He stressed that an individual's behavior must be seen within the context of the larger system and reflected this concept in his equation $B=f(P, E)$ (Lewin, 1951, p. 239), which reads: individual behavior (B) is a function (*f*) of the person (P) and the environment (E). Applying this element of Lewin's change theory suggests that an individual's behavior cannot be assessed without considering the context in which he or she resides. For example, there are influences on behavior depending on the level in the organization, which can be characterized as top, middle, or bottom (Oshry, 1995); the functional area and role, such as being a logistician or a financial manager; and membership in a specific group, such as the group that plans and directs the change initiative or the group that is a recipient of the change initiative (Wagner, 2006).

Group Dynamics

Lewin was the first social psychologist to coin the term group dynamics and to describe the positive and negative forces existing within a group that influenced the behavior of its members (Burnes, 2004). The study of group dynamics spawned dozens of group dynamic theories such as Tuckman's (Tuckman & Jensen, 1977) forming, storming, norming, and performing; Bion's (1961) group-as-a-whole theory; and Hackman's (2002) research identifying the five conditions that foster team success. Group dynamics provides insight into how the elements of the group, such as structure, norms, roles, and processes impact the behavior of the group.

Action Research

Lewin also coined the term action research. Rather than start with a solution, action research poses three questions: "1. What is the present situation? 2. What are the dangers? 3. And most importantly of all, what shall we do?" (Lewin, 1946, p. 34). There are many variations on action research, but in its simplest form, it consists of an iterative process: planning the change, acting and observing the change and its consequences, and reflecting on the results. This is then followed by another cycle of plan, act, observe, reflect, and replan (Denzin & Lincoln, 2000). Action research has become an accepted method for use for implementing change in organizations and communities. "Action research is only possible with, for and by persons and communities, ideally involving all stakeholders both in the questioning and sensemaking that informs research and in the action which is its focus" (Reason & Bradbury, 2006, p. 2).

Three-step Change Model

Lewin's model of change consists of three steps or stages: unfreeze, change, and refreeze. His was the original stage theory. Figure 10.1 depicts how this change theory would apply. There is a present state, which begins as stable, but because of an imbalance between driving and restraining forces, becomes unstable and ultimately unfrozen. During this unfreezing stage, an emphasis is on creating readiness for change; leaders can begin by assessing two perceptions: the discrepancy between the current state and the proposed end state and the efficacy or perceived ability to change (Armenakis et al., 1993). As a result of this readiness assessment, the leaders can develop interventions using "influence strategies," such as "persuasive communication" and "active participation"(Armenakis et al., 1993, p. 574). A barrier to unfreezing the present state is the organization's culture, which seeks stability and organizational preservation. In the next state—the transition state—the driving forces for change must overcome the restraining forces that seek to maintain the status quo; Lewin suggests that to bring about change, reduce the restraining forces, rather than increase the driving forces. Activities in the transition state may include changing the organization's structure, shifting management behavior, or putting in place different reward systems. In the final state—the desired state—the changes are in place, the organization is back in a stable state, and the changed organization is symbolically refrozen in place. The concept of refreezing may be dated, as some contend that there is no longer time to refreeze before the next wave of change comes along. Lewin's theory presents a static view of organizational change (Hatch, 1997); however, it has proven to be the basis for subsequent change theories.

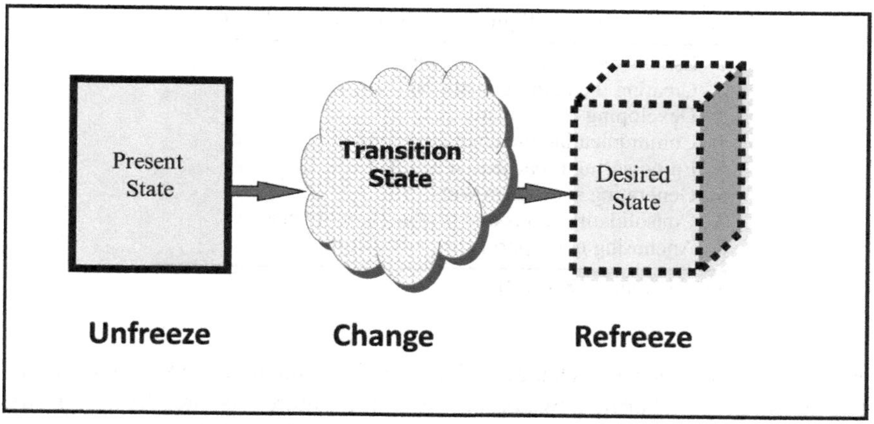

Figure 10.1 Lewin's Original Change Theory: Unfreeze-Change-Refreeze.

Schein (1964) applied Lewin's three-step theory while looking at change at the individual level and explored what would be required by an individual to go through these three steps. At the individual level this would require a change in an individual's attitudes and behavior. For example, in the unfreeze stage, the focus for an individual is on "creating motivation to change"; for the change stage, the focus is on "developing new responses based on new information"; and in the refreezing stage, the focus is on "stabilizing and integrating the changes" (Schein, 1964, p. 79).

In the 21st century, several factors complicate this simplistic picture. First, the rate of change has increased, so there is seldom only one change initiative occurring within a given organization. It is this layering of change initiatives that adds to the complexity of leading change. Second, the new, desired state is frequently a moving target and often unclear. Finally, there is change fatigue that exists amongst organizational stakeholders, who have experienced so many change initiatives that they are unable to generate the energy needed to undertake change.

Kotter's Eight-Step Model of Change

In the modern perspective, an organization is seen as an objective, rational entity that exists in an environment and is acted upon by environmental forces (Hatch, 1997). Multiple models of planned change developed in this modern perspective. With the emphasis on rationality, these models usually include a series of prescribed steps in the planning process. Kotter's (1996) eight-stage change process is a popular example of a model of planned change in the modern perspective; readers may be familiar with Kotter's model. Overlaying Kotter's model with Lewin's earlier model demonstrates Kotter's expansion of Lewin's concepts. Kotter's first four stages are intended to unfreeze the current state: establishing a sense of urgency, creating the guiding coalition, developing a vision and strategy, and communicating the change vision. During the next three stages—empowering broad-based action, generating short-term wins, and consolidating

Table 10.3 Kotter's Eight-Step Process for Leading Change

1	Establishing a sense of urgency
2	Creating the guiding coalition
3	Developing a vision and strategy
4	Communicating the change vision
5	Empowering broad-based action
6	Generating short-term wins
7	Consolidating gains and producing more change
8	Anchoring new approaches in the culture

Source: Kotter (1996, p. 21).

gains and producing more change—change is implemented in the organization. The last stage—anchoring new approaches in the culture—is intended to solidify the changes and refreeze the organization in the new, desired state.

Kotter's model reflects two basic assumptions of the modern perspective: a rational plan based on an assessment of the internal and external environments and the leaders having knowledge and power to design and direct the rational plan. Many current approaches to bring about change in organizations emerged from the modern perspective. Kotter's (1996) is a widely popular stage theory. Stage theories consist of distinct series of steps or stages; Lewin had the original stage theory, and there is a long tradition of stage theories in the change literature. Numerous authors have presented models tailored for public sector organizations, such as Bryson's (2004) 10-step strategic change cycle; his steps include forming initial agreements, responding to mandates, conducting environmental scans, formulating strategy, implementing based on the strategy, and reassessing the entire change process (p. 33). Another stage theory in the public sector is Joyce's (2000) model of four elements for strategic change: preparing, leading, changing, and partnering, which is built on Heyman's (1987) earlier public sector strategy model that focused on external support, desired goals, and organizational capacity (p. 15). Kotter followed in the tradition of stages theories; his eight stages or steps are presented in Table 10.3.

Kotter's eight-step process is an example of leader-driven change consisting of directive strategies. Some critics refer to Kotter's model as a framework, as if it were a skeleton, but to take shape, it needs to have meat added to the bones (Mackinnon, 2007). Later in this chapter, insights from other theories, models, and concepts will be applied to fill out and enhance Kotter's framework. In a subsequent book Kotter (Kotter & Cohen, 2002) addresses a persistent challenge: how to change people's behavior. He emphases the shift from "analysis-think-change" to "see-feel-change" (Kotter & Cohen, 2002, p. 2), thus emphasizing the importance of individual emotions during a change imitative and aligning with the next change model, which focuses on the individual emotions.

Bridge's Model of Change

The third model enables the reader to focus on what happens to the individual during a change initiative. Bridges (2004), an academic and organizational consultant, first published his change theory in 1980; his model focuses on the internal, psychological process that individuals go through when they encounter change. According to Bridges, there are three stages to any transition:

1 The Ending
2 The Neutral Zone
3 The New Beginning

These are not separate, clearly delineated stages. An individual may be in all of these stages at the same time; however, over time which stage is dominant for an individual may shift as depicted in Figure 10.2.

His model adds a great deal to the literature on change highlighting the individual level of analysis, emphasizing the role of human emotions, and distinguishing between change and transition:

> It isn't the changes that do you in, it's the transitions. Change is not the same as transition. Change is situational: the new site, the new boss, the new policy. Transition is the psychological process people go through to come to terms with the new situation. Change is external, transition is internal.
>
> (Bridges, 1991, p. 3)

This may seem like a subtle distinction, but leaders must recognize that there is always an emotional response to a change. A major insight from this model is that whatever the external change, the internal process is one of transition and that

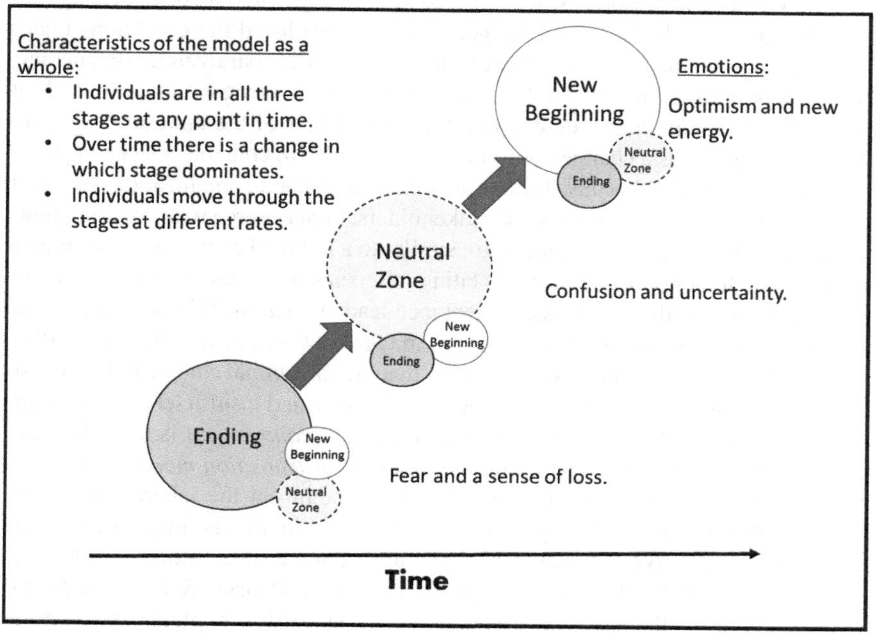

Figure 10.2 Bridges' Transtions Model Depicting the Dominance of the Three Phases over Time.

transition begins with an ending; that ending is associated with loss and letting go. If an individual does not deal with the ending, the loss, and the letting go, then he or she may be stuck in the first stage and be unable to move on. At the start of the change, the individual predominant experience is one of loss, however there are elements of the neutral zone and the new beginning, although the sense of ending dominates. These are not discreet stages, and the boundaries between them are not clearly defined. As Bridges (1991) says, "… you are in more than one of these phases at the same time and the movement through transition is marked by a change in the dominance of one phase as it gives way to the next" (p. 70). "It isn't changes themselves that people resist. It's the losses and endings that they experience and the transition that they are resisting" (p. 21).

Having reviewed three change theories, the next section explores the phenomenon of failure in organizational change.

Why Change Efforts Fail

There is no definitive study of what percentage of planned change efforts fail, but estimates range from 50% to 80% (Cameron, 1997; Kotter, 1996; Robertson & Seneviratne, 1995); even if it is only half that is a huge number considering the financial and human costs of change. Organizations often undertake planned organizational change without considering the potential for failure. Scholars and practitioners posit diverse explanations for the high failure rates; some examples are presented here. When Kotter (1995) researched why planned change efforts failed, he discovered eight reasons, which evolved into his eight-step theory of change. In his subsequent book, *Leading Change*, Kotter (1996) listed the conditions under which change would fail: "… inwardly focused cultures, paralyzing bureaucracy, parochial politics, a low level of trust, lack of teamwork, arrogant attitudes, lack of leadership in middle management, and the general fear of the unknown" (p. 20). Based on 30 years as a change consultant, Axelrod (2010) contends that change initiatives fail most often because leaders are unable to generate organizational support for the change across employees and stakeholders. Others agree with Axelrod, touting the need for a persuasion campaign, similar to a political campaign, to convince stakeholders to support the change, stating: "Persuasion promotes understanding; understanding breeds acceptance, acceptance leads to action. Without persuasion, even the best of turnaround plans will fail to take root" (Garvin & Roberto, 2005, p. 112). Bridges (1991), however, contends that organizational change fails because of an overemphasis on the future, the new beginnings, and insufficient emphasis on the endings; he writes, "… the first task of *change management* is to understand the destination and how to get there, the first task of *transition management* is to convince people to leave home" (p. 32). Others point out the inherent difficulty most people have with altering their own behavior. Finally, the high instances of failed change initiatives have created a weariness among stakeholders, resulting in disenchantment and distrust with any proposed changes (Garvin & Roberto, 2005).

Confronted by the high failure rates, the next section explores the various approaches in the field of change management.

Change Management in Federal Government Organization

If organizational change is ubiquitous and has such high failure rates, what are those who lead these changes to do? The field of change management attempts to address this challenge.

What Is Change Management?

Change management has many definitions. Here is the one used in this chapter: change management is "a systematic approach to helping the individuals impacted by 'the change' to be successful by building support, addressing resistance and developing the required knowledge and ability to implement the change" (Creasey, 2009, p. 6). In essence, change management focuses on the people or the "human element" aspect of the change. The field of change management was originally described as "highly prescriptive" (Cummings & Worley, 1997, p. 152) and initially focused on resistance and how to overcome it (Maurer, 1996). Kotter's model is an example of an expanded view of essential areas of focus from a change management perspective.

Old Change Management verses New Change Management

Over the course of a thirty year career as a change management consultant, Axelrod (2010) contrasts what he calls the old change management and the new change management. Under the old change management, which is still prevalent, a small group of leaders, consultants, and select employees is tasked with designing and implementing a change initiative. This small group works in isolation to develop the ideal solution, while the rest of the organization is left in the dark, resulting in what Axelrod calls the "engagement gap" (p. 14). Axelrod characterizes the old change management with four unique characteristics: (a) "the few decide for the many;" (b) emphasis is on "solutions first, people second;" (c) the creation of a burning platform resulting in fear; and (d) "inequality is the norm and life isn't fair" (p. 13).

There are structural flaws inherent in the old change management; for example, the leaders, consultants, and select employees immerse themselves in planning the change initiative and become defensive when others, with limited exposure or knowledge of the change initiative, do not support it. An "us versus them" atmosphere emerges; the planners begin to objectify the others and begin labeling them as resistors and change targets.

Axelrod (2010) proposes a different approach to change management based on the insight that people most support what they help create; the basic concept underlying the new change management is engagement. He proposed four principles for creating real engagement: "widen the circle of involvement, connect people to each other, create communities for action and promote fairness" (p. 22). Rather than seeking buy-in for change after most of the decisions are made, the new change management calls for engaging a critical mass of people in the change initiative from the beginning.

In Axelrod's (2010) consulting practice he does this by bringing together a cross section of stakeholders in conferences where participants work in small groups to analyze the situation, develop a vision for the future, and collaborate to design the change. By bringing together a diverse set of stakeholders in large group settings, he allows people to have an opportunity to get to know those beyond their normal working group. Creating communities for action brings a diverse group of people together around a specific topic; in these communities, members develop a compelling purpose, engage and relate to each other through dialogue, learn to value different perspectives, and commit to supporting what they create. At a micro level, communities for action become forums for emergent change. Under the new change management, Axelrod advocates three essential leadership practices: speak honestly, be transparent, and build trust; these should certainly resonate with leaders in federal government organizations.

Can Change Be Managed?

One burning question in the field of change management is: Can change be managed? Palmer and Dunford (2002), both academics, assert that judgments about successful management are conditional on two images: the image of what management means and the image of expected outcomes. They propose two images of management: "management as controlling and management as shaping" (p. 243); in the first, the change agent controls the activities in the change initiative and in the second, merely shapes the capabilities of the organization. The image of outcomes range from "intended, partially intended, and unintended" (p. 244). This combination results in "six change management images: directing, navigating, caretaking, coaching, interpreting, and nurturing" (p. 248). The authors argue that if the perspective on change is to control the change to achieve specific outcomes, then the answer may be that it cannot be managed. However, if the leaders are open to what unfolds or if the leadership is one of shaping rather than directing, then maybe change can be managed.

Assuming change can be managed, the next section provides recommendations for improving the management of change.

Recommendations for Enhancing Change Management

This chapter highlights the numerous theories, models and concepts available when designing and leading a change initiative. Many factors influence one's choice for a specific change initiative. For example, one could choose Kotter's change theory as a basic framework and then enhance it by applying additional theories, models, or concepts. Regardless of the nature of the change initiative, this section makes recommendations for specific activities to enhance the success of any change initiative. These are presented in Table 10.4.

Roughly inspired by the Theory E and Theory O framework (Beer & Nohria, 2000), these recommendations for enhancing change management fall in two categories: developing a nuanced approach to organizational change and attending

Table 10.4 Recommendations for Enhancing Change Management

Develop nuanced approaches to organizational change	
1	Apply multiple theories of change.
2	Identify layers of change.
3	Leverage emergent change within planned change.
4	Reframe resistance.
5	Recognize different philosophies of change.
Attend to the human element during organizational change	
6	Acknowledge emotional responses to change.
7	Nurture energy through data collection and feedback.
8	Identify and engage stakeholders.
9	Support sense making.
10	Adopt a learning stance.

to the human element during organizational change. Each recommendation is discussed in the following subsections.

Develop Nuanced Approaches to Organizational Change

As stated earlier, there is no one overarching approach to organizational change. All organizations are complex, and every organizational change initiative is unique; so each organizational change initiative should be approached by looking at what elements make it unique and complex. To determine the most appropriate approach for a given change initiative, consider three dimensions that impact the change: the context for the change, the content of the change, and the change process to be used (Pettigrew & Whipp, 1991). A starting place is to pose three questions: What is to be changed? Why and where is the change to occur? How is the change to be implemented? To assist in customizing an approach for change, consider using insights developed by scholars and practitioners in the behavioral sciences. Addressing the multifaceted challenges facing leaders in federal government organizations requires a multifaceted approach. The recommendation is to unite the insights gained from understanding the multiple approaches to change and to propose an enhanced, integrative approach. The following are some recommendations for enhancing an organization's change strategy.

Apply Multiple Theories of Change

Different theories, models, and concepts highlight different aspects of organizations and are based on different underlying assumptions of organizations and organizational change. In thinking about organizations using systems thinking, there is a fundamental principle to "take as many different perspectives as possible" (O'Connor & McDermott, 1997, p. 140). For example, Theory E and Theory O highlight two different perspectives on how to approach organizational change, and the authors' advice is to apply both in sequence (Beer & Nohria, 2000). Other models encourage looking at an organizations through multiple lenses; for example, leaders can view an organization through four distinct lenses or frames: structural frame, human resource frame, political frame, and a symbolic frame (Bolman & Deal, 2008). Earlier in this chapter, Bridges's model highlighted the difference between change, which is the external situation, and transition, which is the internal adjustment to the external situation.

Identify Layers of Change

Before launching a new change initiative, determine if there are existing change initiatives underway, as it is likely that other change initiatives exist. For example, if the new change initiative is focused on structural change, such as introducing new technology, ask: what other changes are currently underway that will be impacted by this new technology? If the new change initiative is coming from headquarters, what other change initiatives are underway locally? Try identifying and mapping out all the existing change initiatives to develop a broad picture of the summative changes that employees and stakeholders are being asked to absorb. Look for pre-existing change initiatives that are underfunded and struggling along on life support; some decisive action may be needed to close these down before beginning a new change initiative. Determine if the existing change initiatives are in support of or contrary to the new change initiative. How might the existing change initiatives be integrated into the new change initiative? The capacity for change is finite, and some new change initiatives are doomed from the start because they are layered over other, unrelated, or conflicting change initiatives.

Leverage Emergent Change within Planned Change

Planned and emergent change constitutes two distinct styles of change, as depicted in Table 10.1. There are advantages to planned change over emergent change (Weick, 2000), for example, when viewed within the context of large-scale organizational change, planned change has the advantage of sponsorship by the people in power, who have the resources to focus on an "explicit, compact mandate" (Weick, 2000, p. 228) and "conveys to key stakeholders the impression of being a rational program" (Weick, 2000, p. 227). If the planned change is being directed from headquarters, it is unlikely that the planners will understand the impact their directed changes will have on the lower-level organizations. A frequent complaint about planned change programs directed from headquarters is that they have a 10,000-foot perspective and are unaware of the impact on local organizations. As a leader, acknowledge that the planned change directive cannot address the small changes that will be required at the local level; engage the people at the local level to identify micro level, emergent changes that will support the overall planned change; and support and empower the local organizations to carry out emergent change. Weick (2000) linked sensemaking and change; he argued that emergent change is most conducive to sensemaking and contended emergent change creates a positive environment for undertaking planned change.

Table 10.5 The Change Equation

$D \times V \times F > R$
Where:
D = Dissatisfaction with the status quo
V = Vision of the future
F = First steps to bring about change
R = Resistance.

Source: Beckhard & Harris (1987).

Reframe Resistance

Anyone who has attempted to bring about organizational change surely has encountered resistance. Resistance takes many forms, ranging from quietly ignoring the change to overt opposition. Through the years, authors have focused on models to explore the nature of resistance and how to overcome it. Table 10.5 depicts a well-known change equation relating essential elements of a change initiative with the concept of resistance (Beckhard & Harris, 1987).

The equation highlights the critical roles that dissatisfaction, vision, and first steps play in creating a fertile environment for change to occur. Kotter addresses the need for dissatisfaction by emphasizing the critical need for a burning platform; his model also has two steps that highlight the need for a vision and a strategy for how to get there. This equation facilitates in communicating and persuading the stakeholder of the value of vision and first steps.

Historically, resistance is represented in the change literature metaphorically as a physical, restraining force focused on maintaining the status quo (Lewin, 1951). If change is to occur, the resistance is something to be overcome, as represented in Maurer's book *Beyond the Wall of Resistance* (1996). The practice has developed to label those who resist as resisters or even cynics, thus encouraging leaders to dismiss the concerns expressed through the metaphor of resistance rather than paying attention to what may be valid concerns. More recently authors are reframing resistance as a person's struggle to make sense of a change initiative (Wagner, 2006) and seeing questions not as a negative but as a search for answers to help make meaning of the change. To embrace this insight of resistance being in support of sensemaking would enable a leader to reframe resistance as people struggling to understand and make sense of the change rather than labeling those asking questions as resistors and dismissing potentially valid concerns. One indication of falling into the trap as seeing questioning as resistance is to notice if there is language that polarizes the supporters and the resistors as "us" verses "them."

Recognize Different Perspectives of Change

Weick and Quinn (1999) acknowledged two different perspectives taken by observers: a macro perspective and a micro perspective. If an observer takes a macro perspective, that is looking at the organization as a whole or from afar, then the organization "looks like repetitive action, routine, and inertia dotted with occasional episodes of revolutionary change" (p. 362). According to Weick and

Quinn, the macro perspective produces a theory of stability and occasional episodes of change. However, if an observer takes a micro perspective, scrutinizing the organization up close, then what he or she sees is suggestive of "ongoing adaptation and adjustment. Although … small, they also tend to be frequent and continuous across units, that means they are capable of altering structure and strategy" (p. 362). Again, be aware that one's level in the organization influences one's perception of the change.

Earlier in the chapter, a concept of levels was introduced to provide examples of a range of differences across a change initiative. Stakeholders at each different level will likely see the change from a different perspective. For example, executives may see the change from a macro perspective, while staff may see the change in a more micro or personal perspective. Stakeholders in headquarters may experience the change in fundamentally different ways than those in field offices. In the external environment, customers and the public may have unique perspectives on the change, and these perspectives may differ by stakeholder group. For those tasked with managing change, recognizing these different perspectives and trying to understanding them is critical to developing a successful change effort.

Attend to the Human Element During Organizational Change

John J. Garstka, an assistant director for Concepts and Operations in the Defense Department's Office of Force Transformation, highlights the importance of the "human element" of organizational transformation: "The human component of change is the most complicated factor in transformation, regardless of whether the setting is private, public or military. Consequently, leaders charged with guiding change must focus on the human element" (Garstka, 2005, p. 5). This insight is shared by Kotter; in his book *The Heart of Change* (Kotter & Cohen, 2002), the sequel to his book *Leading Change* (Kotter, 1996), he spotlights the importance of changing people's behavior by engaging their feelings not just their thinking. The rest of this section describes specific recommendations for supporting the human element—the people—to increase effectiveness during organizational change.

Acknowledge Emotional Responses to Change

Research has found that intense emotions are frequently part of individuals' experiences in organization (Weick, Sutcliffe, & Obstfeld, 2004), yet emotions are often ignored during a change initiative. Bridges' transitions model of change (see Figure 10.2) highlights the presence of emotions and advocates acknowledging those emotions. At the beginning of any change initiative when the change is announced, an individual will likely experience an ending or a sense of loss; this may be accompanied by emotions of fear, sadness, disorientation, and anger (Bridges & Mitchell, 2002). An individual in the neutral zone may experience uncertainty and impatience, which may manifest as insecurity about job, status or even personal identity; there is often frustration, skepticism, and a drop in morale and productivity during this middle stage. One only arrives at the last stage—the new beginning—after having successfully dealt with the first two stages. In the new beginning, an individual may start to find acceptance for the change and increased hope and energy.

Nurture Energy Through Data Collection and Feedback

Scholar/practitioners emphasize the role of organizational energy in bringing about change (Nadler, 1977); borrowing from the world of physics, nothing changes without energy being expended. In most change initiatives, the change agents collect data through surveys, focus groups, or interviews; this is not a benign act, as collecting data can generate energy. The amount and the direction of the energy depend on expectations around data collection and perceptions for how data are to be used. Energy is generated in support of a change initiative when data are used to shed light on a problem area or move a change initiative forward. The second essential action associated with data collection is to share the results of the data analysis. Nothing drains energy from a change initiative more than sending out a survey and never sharing the results. Consider asking people in the organization to participate in the data collection, analysis, and feedback cycle. Scholar/practitioners encourage us to find innovative ways to mobilize human energy during a change initiative (Axelrod, 2010).

Identify and Engage Stakeholders

Observing what authors are including in revisions to textbooks is one way to identify recent shifts in thinking about strategic change. In the third edition of the widely used textbook *Strategic Planning for Public and Nonprofit Organizations,* Bryson (2004) adds chapters on stakeholder analysis and the need for collaboration across stakeholder groups (Bryson, Crosby, & Ackerman, 2004). Stakeholder is defined as: "any group or individual who can affect or is affected by the achievement of the organization's objectives" (Freeman, 1984, p. 46). Stakeholder(s) can be any individual or group who has (have) a "stake," that is an interest, in the organization and its outcomes. In federal sector organizations, there is typically a complex network of both internal and external stakeholders; obvious internal stakeholders are agency leaders and employees, oversight organizations, and congressional budgetary committees. Depending on the organization and the planned change, external stakeholders might include customers, suppliers, and industry associations. Practitioners and leaders of change contend that stakeholders are critical to achieving successful outcomes of planned change (Farias & Johnson, 2000; Maddock, 2002).

Stakeholder theory posits that if an organization understands its stakeholders—their wants, needs, and perspectives on the organization—the organization will be in a better position to manage those stakeholders and, ultimately, to be successful (Freeman, 1984). From a change management perspective, leaders can identify the stakeholders affected by the change and pose these questions: Who are the stakeholders? What is their stake (i.e., what do they want or need)? How do they influence the organization? (Rowley, 1997). Who will be impacted by this change? Seeing the change from the perspective of the various stakeholder groups provides the leader with a nuanced awareness of how the various stakeholders perceive the change initiative and leads to insights about how to engage them.

Identifying stakeholders is a necessary first step but is insufficient to promote a successful change initiative. Next, determine stakeholder saliency in terms of power, legitimacy and urgency (Mitchell, Agle, & Wood, 1997, p. 853). Then reach out to a representative sample of these stakeholder groups and invite them to participate in the change process. Bring them in not just to hear about the change initiative in a one-way communication, but to listen to them in a two-way exchange in order to understand their unique perspectives. Any change initiative is likely to be perceived differently depending on where the stakeholder sits—top, middle, or bottom of the organization—or what is his or her role—funder, supplier, or customer. Include representatives of all stakeholder groups in an action research cycle to define the current situation, develop a vision for the future, and determine how to get there.

Support Sensemaking

The concept of sensemaking was introduced by organizational psychologist Karl Weick (1979), who defined sensemaking as the "making of sense" (Weick, 1995, p. 4) and explained that sensemaking deals with "how [people] construct what they construct, why, and with what effects" (Weick, 1995, p. 4). Weick (2001) viewed organizations as "collections of people trying to make sense of what is happening around them" (p. 5). Weick introduced seven properties, or characteristics, of sensemaking: social context, personal identity, retrospect, salient cues, ongoing projects, plausibility, and enactment. Within the context of an organization, Weick held that sensemaking highlighted "the important role that people play in creating the environments that impose on them" (Weick, 1979, p. 5).

In writing about change in organizations, Weick (2000) proposed four "bare-bones conditions" necessary for successful sensemaking—that people must "stay in motion, have a direction, look closely and update often, and converse candidly" (p. 232). People "stay in motion" when they continue productive work, rather than suspending work because of the pending change. To "have a direction" implies that people understand how the change influences their work and what change is expected of them. In order to stay informed with the progress made, "look closely and update often" implies staying tuned in to what is happening to the change effort and using this current information to feed the sensemaking process. To "converse candidly" advocates the need to speak openly about the change; this last condition is important, as sometimes speaking candidly is perceived as resistance and results in the person's being labeled as a resistor. However, another way to perceive these candid conversations is as individuals asking question as they struggle to make sense of the situation (Barrett, Thomas, & Hocevar, 1995, p. 370). Even these bare bones conditions are difficult to promote during times of organizational change.

One study of a planned change in the Defense Department investigated the differences in experience between two stakeholder groups: planners/implementers and contributors/recipients (Wagner, 2006). The findings revealed that individuals in the planner/implementer stakeholder group perceived more support for their sensemaking compared to those in the contributor/recipients stakeholder group. Being involved during the planning and having a significant role during implementation provides opportunities for dialogue with others and thus provides support for sensemaking.

Adopt a Learning Stance

Change scholars contend that "an integral part of a fundamental change strategy must be a conscious decision to move to a learning mode, where both learning and doing are equally valued" (Beckhard & Pritchard, 1992, p. 4). What this looks like during a change initiative is people being open to examining how they make sense of the change and being curious how others make sense of it. Senge's (1990) concept of a learning organization can be applied to enhance effectiveness during organizational change (Albert, 2005). One helpful technique is to observe your response when someone has a different perspective on the change initiative you are leading. A common reaction is to judge the person who has a different perspective; instead strive to suspend judgment and shift to a stance of curiosity. Ask: what is this person seeing that makes her not support the change? What can I learn by being curious rather than judgmental? Taking a stance of curiosity and being open to learning from others can provide invaluable insight as to why someone is opposed to the planned change.

In many federal government organizations, the culture values and rewards leaders for being experts, whereas when dealing with organizational change, what is needed is expertise. There is a difference between being an expert and having expertise. From a cultural perspective, an expert always has the right answer and can tell people what to do. In contrast, a person who had expertise understands enough about what is going on to bring the right people together, to ask the questions, but does not claim to have all the answers. Leading a change initiative from a position of having expertise demonstrates a willingness to be open to learning and not possessing all the answers.

This concludes the discussion on the recommendations for enhancing change management.

Conclusion

This chapter opened with a quotation from the eminent scholar/practitioner Edward Schein (1977): "As the recognition grows that part of every manager's job is to plan, initiate, and manage change, so will the concepts and methods in this area come to be seen as integral to the management process itself" (p. ix). In today's federal sector organizations, most managers will likely agree with the assertion that planning, initiating, and managing change are inherent competencies for every manager. However, there is likely less agreement on which concepts and methods of change should be studied, understood, and applied. The intent of this chapter has been to provide leaders of federal sector organizations with a cross section of theories, models and concepts from the behavioral sciences concerning organizational change. The selection of theories and concepts and the 10 recommendations are derived from the author's years as an executive leading planned change, as an organizational consultant assisting clients develop and implement strategic change, and as a professor teaching courses on organizational change. This chapter reflects the insight that to be successful, mangers need to develop nuanced approaches to organizational change tailored to their specific organization and to attend to the human element during organizational change. It is hoped that this chapter will provide an introduction to the field of organizational change and an entree into the vast selection of literature on organizational change.

References

Adams, J. D. (Ed.). (1998). *Transforming work* (2nd ed.). Alexandria, VA: Miles River Press.

Albert, M. (2005). Managing change: Creating a learning organization focused on quality. *Problems and Perspectives in Management, 1*, 47–54.

Argyris, C. (1999). *On organizational learning* (2nd ed.). Malden, MA: Blackwell Publishers.

Argyris, C., & Schon, D. A. (1974). *Theory in practice: Increasing professional effectiveness*. San Francisco, CA: Jossey-Bass.

Armenakis, A. A., Harris, S. G., & Mossholder, K. W. (1993). Creating readiness for organizational change. In W. W. Burke, D. G. Lake, & J. W. Paine (Eds.), *Organization change: A comprehensive reader* (pp. 569–589). San Francisco, CA: Jossey-Bass.

Axelrod, R. H. (2010). *Terms of engagement: New ways of leading and changing organizations* (2nd ed.). San Francisco, CA: Berrett-Koehler.

Baily, M. N., & Elliott, D. J. (2009). *The US financial and economic crisis: Where does it stand and where do we go from here?* Business and Public Policy at Brookings. Washington, DC: Brookings Institution.

Barrett, F. J., Thomas, G. F., & Hocevar, S. P. (1995). The central role of discourse in large-scale change: A social construction perspective. *Journal of Applied Behavioral Science, 31*(3), 352–372.

Bartunek, J. M. (1984). Changing interpretive schemes and organizational restructuring: The example of a religious order. *Administrative Science Quarterly, 29*, 355–372.

Bartunek, J. M. (2003). Foreword. In J. H. Mills (Ed.), *Making sense of organizational change* (pp. ix–xi). London, England: Routledge.

Beckhard, R., & Harris, R. T. (1987). *Organizational transitions: Managing complex change* (2nd ed.). Reading, MA: Addison-Wesley.

Beckhard, R., & Pritchard, W. (1992). *Changing the essence: The art of creating and leading fundamental change in organizations*. San Francisco, CA: Jossey-Bass.

Beer, M., & Nohria, N. (2000). Resolving the tension between theory E and theory O of change. In M. Beer & N. Nohria (Eds.), *Breaking the code of change* (pp. 1–33). Boston, MA: Harvard Business School Press.

Bennis, W., & Chin, R. (1976). Planned change in America. In W. Bennis, K. D. Benne, R. Chin, & K. E. Corey (Eds.), *The planning of change* (3rd ed., pp. 13–22). New York, NY: Holt, Rinehart and Winston.

Bennis, W., Benne, K. D., Chin, R., & Corey, K. E. (1976). *The planning of change* (3rd ed.). New York, NY: Holt, Rinehart and Winston.

Bion, W. (1961). *Experiences in groups*. New York, NY: Routledge.

Bolman, L. G., & Deal, T. (2008). *Reframing organizations: Artistry, choice, and leadership* (4th ed.). San Francisco, CA: Jossey-Bass.

Bridges, W. (1991). *Managing transitions: Making the most of change*. Reading, MA: Addison-Wesley.

Bridges, W. (2004). *Transitions: Making sense of life's changes, revised 25th anniversary edition*. Cambridge, MA: Da Capo Press.

Bridges, W., & Mitchell, S. (2002). Leading transition: A new model for change. In F. Hesselbein & R. Johnston (Eds.), *On leading change*. San Francisco, CA: Jossey-Bass.

Brown, L., Hughes, A. M., Sykes, J., Trumble, W. R., Hole, G., Knowles, E. M., ... Stevenson, A. (Eds.). (1993). *The new shorter Oxford English dictionary*. New York, NY: Oxford University Press.

Bryson, J. M. (2004). *Strategic planning for public and nonprofit organizations: A guide to strengthening and sustaining organizational achievement* (3rd ed.). San Francisco, CA: Jossey-Bass.

Bryson, J. M., Crosby, B. C., & Ackerman, F. (2004). Resource C: Strategic planning in collaborative settings. In J. M. Bryson (Ed.), *Strategic planning for public and nonprofit organizations: A guide to strengthening and sustaining organizational achievement* (3rd ed.). San Francisco, CA: Jossey-Bass.

Burnes, B. (2004). Kurt Lwein and the planned approach to change: A reappraisal. In W. W. Burke, D. G. Lake, & J. W. Paine (Eds.), *Organization change: A comprehensive reader* (pp. 226–253). San Francisco, CA: Jossey-Bass.

Bush, G. W. (2001). *National security strategy of the United States of America*. Retrieved February 18, 2005, from http://www.comw.org/qdr/fulltext/nss2002.pdf.

Cameron, K. S. (1997). Techniques for making organizations effective: Some popular approaches. In D. Druckman, J. E. Singer, & H. Van Cott (Eds.), *Enhancing organizational performance*. Washington, DC: National Academy Press.

Civil Service Reform Act of 1978, Pub. L. No. 95–454, Stat 2640 (1978). Retrieved from http://www.eeoc.gov/eeoc/history/35th/thelaw/civil_service_reform-1978.html.

Creasey, T. (2009). Defining change management: Helping others understand change management in relation to project management and organizational change. *Change management tutorial series.* Retrieved from http://www.change-management.com/Prosci-Defining-Change-Management-2009.pdf.

Cummings, T. G., & Worley, C. G. (1997). *Organization development & change* (6th ed.). Cincinnati, OH: South-Western College Publishing.

Daft, R. L., & Weick, K. E. (1984). Towards a model of organizations as interpretive systems. *Academy of Management Review*, *9*(2), 284–295.

Deming, W. E. (1986). *Out of the crisis*. Cambridge, MA: MIT Press.

Denzin, N. K., & Lincoln, Y. S. (Eds.). (2000). *The handbook of qualitative research* (2nd ed.). Thousand Oaks, CA: Sage.

Department of Defense. (2003). *Transformation planning guidance.* Retrieved May 23, 2005, from http://www.oft.osd.mil/library/library_files/document_129_Transformation_Planning_Guidance_April_2003_1.pdf.

Drucker, P. F. (1980). The deadly sins in public administration. In R. C. Kearney & E. M. Berman (Eds.), *Public sector performance: Management, motivation, and measurement* (pp. 36–44). Boulder, CO: Westview Press.

Dunphy, D. (1996). Organizational change in corporate settings. *Human Relations*, *49*(5), 541–553.

Executive Order No. 13707. 80 F.R. 56365 (2015). *Using behavioural insights to better serve the American people.*

Farias, G., & Johnson, H. (2000). Organization development and change management: Setting the record straight. *Journal of Applied Behavioral Science, 36*(3), 376–379.

Ford, J. D. (1999). Conversations and the epidemiology of change. In W. A. Pasmore & R. W. Woodman (Eds.), *Research in organizational change and development* (Vol. 12, pp. 1–39). Stanford, CT: JAI Press.

Freeman, R. E. (1984). *Strategic management: A stakeholder approach.* Boston, MA: Pitman.

French, W. L., & Bell, C. H. (1995). *Organization development: Behavioral science interventions for organization improvement* (5th ed.). Englewood Cliffs, NJ: Prentice Hall.

French, W. L., Bell, C. H. J., & Zawacki, R. A. (Eds.). (1994). *Organization development and transformation: Managing effective change* (4th ed.). Chicago, IL: Irwin.

Garstka, J. J. (2005). *The transformation challenge.* Retrieved May 18, 2005, from http://www.oft.osd.mil/library/library_files/article_447_041805_nato_reviewl.doc.

Garvin, D. A., & Roberto, M. A. (2005). Change through persuasion. *Harvard Business Review, 83*(2), 104–112.

Gore, A. (1993). *NPR 93-a report of the national performance review: From red tape to results: Creating a government that works better & costs less.* Washington, DC: U.S. Office of the Federal Register.

Government Performance and Results Act of 1993, Pub. L. No. 103–62, 107 Stat. 285. (1993). Retrieved from https://www.whitehouse.gov/omb/mgmt-gpra/gplaw2m.

Hackman, J. R. (2002). *Leading teams: Setting the stage for great performances.* Boston, MA: Harvard Business School Press.

Hammer, M., & Champy, J. (1993). *Reengineering the corporation.* New York, NY: Harper Business.

Hatch, M. J. (1997). *Organization theory: Modern, symbolic, and postmodern perspectives.* Oxford, England: Oxford University Press.

Heymann, P. B. (1987). *The politics of public management.* Binghamton, NY: Vail-Ballou Press.

Joyce, P. (2000). *Strategy in the public sector: A guide to effective change management.* Chichester, England: John Wiley & Sons.

Kotter, J. P. (1995). Leading change: Why transformation efforts fail. *Harvard Business Review, 73*(2), 59–67.

Kotter, J. P. (1996). *Leading change.* Boston, MA: Harvard Business School Press.

Kotter, J. P., & Cohen, D. S. (2002). *The heart of change: Real-life stories of how people change their organizations.* Boston, MA: Harvard Business School Press.

Laszlo, C., & Laugel, J. F. (2000). *Large-scale organizational change: An executive's guide.* Woburn, MA: Butterworth-Heinemann.

Lewin, K. (1946). Action research and minority problems. *Journal of Social Issues, 2*(4), 34–46.

Lewin, K. (1951). *Field theory in social science.* New York, NY: Harper & Row.

Mackinnon, L. (2007, June 30). Book review: John Kotter on change management [Review of Leading change and the heart of change]. *Think differently.* Retrieved from http://www.think-differently.org/2007/06/book-review-john-kotter-on-change/.

Maddock, S. (2002). Making Modernisation Work. *Journal of Public Sector Management, 15*(1), 13–43.

Maurer, R. (1996). *Beyond the wall of resistance: Unconventional strategies that build support for change.* Austin, TX: Bard Books.

Mills, J. H. (2003). *Making sense of organizational change.* London, England: Routledge.

Mitchell, R. K., Agle, B. R., & Wood, D. J. (1997). Toward a theory of stakeholder identification and salience: Defining the principle of who and what really counts. *Academy of Management Review, 22*(4), 853–886.

Nadler, D. A. (1977). *Feedback and organization development: A data-based method.* Reading, MA: Addison-Wesley.

Nadler, D. A., Shaw, R. B., Walton, A. E., & Associates. (1995). *Discontinuous change: Leading organizational transformation.* San Francisco, CA: Jossey-Bass.

Nutt, P. C. (1992). *Managing planned change.* New York, NY: Macmillan.

Nutt, P. C., & Backoff, R. W. (1993). Transforming public organizations with strategic management and strategic leadership (Special Issue: Yearly Review of Management). *Journal of Management, 19*(2), 229–348.

O'Connor, J., & McDermott, I. (1997). *The art of systems thinking: Essential skills for creativity and problem solving.* Hammersmith, London, England: Thorsons.

Oshry, B. (1995). *Seeing systems: Unlocking the mysteries of organizational life.* San Francisco, CA: Berrett-Koehler.

Palmer, I., & Dunford, R. (1996). Understanding organization through metaphor. In C. Oswick & D. Grant (Eds.), *Organization development: Metaphorical explorations* (pp. 7–20). London, England: Pitman.

Palmer, I., & Dunford, R. (2002). Who says change can be managed? Positions, perspectives and problematics. *Strategic Change, 11*, 243–251.

Pettigrew, A. M., & Whipp, R. (1991). *Managing change for competitive success.* Oxford, England: Blackwell Publishing.

Rainey, H. G. (1997). *Understanding & managing public organizations.* San Francisco, CA: Jossey-Bass.

Reason, P., & Bradbury, H. (Eds.). (2006). *Handbook of action research: The concise paperback edition.* London, England: Sage Publications.

Robertson, P. J., & Seneviratne, S. J. (1995, November/December). Outcomes of planned organizational change in the public sector: A meta-analytic comparison to the private sector. *Public Administration Review, 55*, 547–558.

Romanelli, E., & Tushman, M. L. (1994). Organizational transformation as punctuated equilibrium: An empirical test. *Academy of Management Journal, 37*, 1141–1167.

Rowley, T. (1997). Moving beyond dyadic ties: A network theory of stakeholder influences. *Academy of Management Review, 22*(4), 887–910.

Schein, E. H. (1964). The mechanisms of change. In W. W. Burke, D. G. Lake, & J. W. Paine (Eds.), *Organization change: A comprehensive reader.* San Francisco, CA: Jossey-Bass.

Schein, E. H. (1977). Foreword. In D. A. Nadler (Ed.), *Feedback and organization development: Using data-based methods* (pp. vii-ix). Upper Saddle River, NJ: FT Press.

Schein, E. H. (1988). *Process consultation: Its role in organization development* (Vol. I). Reading, MA: Addison-Wesley.

Schein, E. H. (1992). *Organizational culture and leadership* (2nd ed.). San Francisco, CA: Jossey-Bass.

Schein, E. H. (1996). Kurt Lewin's change theory in the field and in the classroom: Notes toward a model of managed learning. *System Practices, 9*, 27–47.

Senge, P. (1990). *The fifth discipline: The art and practice of the learning organization.* New York, NY: Doubleday.

Shaw, R. B., & Walton, A. E. (1995). Conclusion: The lessons of discontinuous change. In D. A. Nadler, R. B. Shaw, & A. E. Walton (Eds.), *Discontinuous change: Leading organizational transformation* (pp. 272–276). San Francisco, CA: Jossey-Bass.

Sims, H. P. J., & Gioia, D. A. (1986). *The thinking organization.* San Francisco, CA: Jossey-Bass.

Sims, R. R. (Ed.). (2010). *Change (transformation) in government organizations*. Charlotte, NC: Information Age Publishing, Inc.

Trist, E. (1977). A concept of organizational ecology. In J. M. Shafritz & J. S. Ott (Eds.), *Classics of organization theory* (3rd ed., pp. 316–328). Belmont, CA: Wadsworth Publishing.

Tuckman, B. W., & Jensen, M. A. (1977). Stages in small group development. In W. E. Natemeyer & J. T. McMahon (Eds.), *Classics of organizational behavior.* (3rd ed., pp. 241–251). Prospect Heights, IL: Waveland Press, Inc.

Vaill, P. B. (1989). *Managing as a performing art*. San Francisco, CA: Jossey-Bass.

Wagner, R. (2006). *The human element of organizational transformation: A phenomenographic study of how internal stakeholders in federal defense organizations experience and make sense of planned organizational change.* (PhD), Fielding Graduate University, Santa Barbara, CA.

Weick, K. E. (1979). *The social psychology of organizing* (2nd ed.). New York, NY: McGraw Hill.

Weick, K. E. (1995). *Sensemaking in organizations*. Thousand Oaks, CA: Sage.

Weick, K. E. (2000). Emergent change as a universal in organizations. In M. Beer & N. Nohria (Eds.), *Breaking the code of change* (pp. 223–241). Boston, MA: Harvard Business School Press.

Weick, K. E. (2001). *Making sense of the organization*. Malden, MA: Blackwell.

Weick, K. E., & Quinn, R. E. (1999). Organizational change and development. *Annual Review Psychology*, *50*, 361–386.

Weick, K. E., Sutcliffe, K. M., & Obstfeld, D. (2004). *Organizing and the process of sensemaking*. Retrieved February 18, 2005 from http://web.gsm.uci.edu.

11 Leading in the Context of Constitutional Government

Joseph V. Kaplan

There may be times when we are powerless to prevent injustice, but there must never be a time when we fail to protest.

—Elie Wiesel

Imagine this scenario, unfortunately not rare anymore in the United States. You are nearby when a mass shooting takes place. Think of Columbine, Virginia Tech, Aurora, or San Bernardino. In the aftermath, TV news crews swoop down on the scene hoping to get reactions of local citizens. You are simply passing by, on your way to work at a nearby large retailer, when the TV reporter asks if you would mind giving a brief interview. You agree. During this brief interview, you are asked about your reaction to the horrific events. You respond by saying that you think access to guns in the United States is far too easy. The interviewer asks if you think that gun sellers should be held legally liable when their products are used in mass killings. You respond by saying that you do not know enough to offer a legal opinion, but you are just concerned with the easy availability of guns. You conclude your comments to the interviewer by stressing that you are merely espousing your personal opinion of course. When the interviewer asks you what brought you to the vicinity of the shooting, you replied that you work at the large retailer nearby, naming the retailer, and that are on your way to work. The interviewer thanks you for your time saying she would not want you to be late for work. This brief interview concludes and you continue on to work.

It is now the following day. When you arrive to work, your supervisor calls you in for a meeting. He tells you that the store manager saw your interview on TV last night and, because of that, your employment is being terminated. The supervisor admonishes you for mentioning your opposition to guns, because the store sells a lot of guns. In disbelief, you remind the supervisor that you merely expressed your personal opinion and specifically told that to the reporter. You remind your supervisor that you have been an outstanding employee with an unblemished record for the past seven years. Your supervisor tells you there's nothing he can do about the situation and that you need to pack up your personal belongings and be escorted out the door. That's it! You are fired for having expressed your personal opinion on a matter of public importance.

By now you might be thinking, "This isn't right! We have freedom of speech in this country. You cannot fire an employee for expressing an opinion like that." If that's what you're thinking, you would be wrong. In this imagined scenario, the employee worked in the private sector. The First Amendment to the Constitution protecting freedom of speech concerns the relationship between the United States government and the states and the relationship between the U.S. or state governments and the people. With the one exception of the 13th Amendment outlawing slavery, the Constitution does not concern the relationship between people, including the relationship between employers and their employees. Therefore, our public-minded employee in our scenario may legally be fired by his employer for merely expressing his opinion on a matter of public concern, even though that expression had absolutely no adverse effect on the employer. In our scenario, the employee is an "employee-at-will," who can be terminated at any time, without notice, for a good reason, a bad reason, or no reason at all, as long as the reason does not contravene some other state or federal statute. In the United States of America, most workers are employees-at-will.

Stop and think for a moment of the impact on this employee suddenly losing his job. Imagine for a moment the employee is you. How would you pay your mortgage or rent? How would you continue making your car payment? What will you do when your child's college tuition bill comes due? Not to mention the daily expenses that you and your family incur.

The scenario above would be quite different if our employee had been employed by the United States or a state government. In that event, the First Amendment would apply. It is doubtful therefore whether, under the facts given above, the employee could have been legally terminated for expressing his opinion on a matter of public concern, absent some demonstrated harm to the government agency for which he worked.

This brings us to another scenario. Imagine that you and your husband are both lawyers for the U.S. Environmental Protection Agency (EPA). Because of decades of work at the EPA, you and your husband have formed an opinion that the president's initiative for "cap and trade" to reduce carbon emissions is fundamentally flawed. Obviously, this is an issue in which your agency has quite a stake. As a parent and citizen, you feel so strongly about this issue that you take to the media. You and your husband publish "letters to the editor" in prominent newspapers and even post a YouTube video explaining why the proposed cap and trade program being debated in Congress not only fails to solve the problem of carbon emissions, but exacerbates it. Then imagine being called into your supervisor's office where your supervisor tells you that he read your newspaper letters and saw your YouTube video and demands that you immediately take down your video because you have engaged in acts contrary to the position taken by the administration. You are threatened with discipline, which could include termination, if you fail to take down the video.

But now, let's change up the scenario just a bit. Rather than imagining that it is you and your husband who are the lawyers disagreeing with the cap and trade proposal, you are those lawyers' supervisor. It is *you* who read the letter to the editor in the newspaper and *you* who watched the YouTube video. It is *you* who is made uncomfortable from your employees' public disagreement with administration views. What do you do? (This scenario is based on real events, see Plitz, 2009.)

Employment with the federal government is a mixed blessing. As a federal employee, which all supervisors and managers are, you are protected by a plethora of rights. The Constitution, laws enacted by Congress, government-wide regulations, agency-specific regulations, agency-specific policies and rules, all combine to set out a framework of rights and responsibilities. As a federal employee, you would not have to worry about the arbitrary termination suffered by our employee in the first scenario, fired after expressing a public opinion regarding gun violence.

But as managers and supervisors, it is *you* who has the responsibility to apply that plethora of rights in a manner that lets you take action against employees when there are legitimate adverse consequences to the efficient accomplishment of the agency's mission. First, you would have to have an understanding of what rules (statutes, regulations, agency policies) the employee violated, which will allow you to consider taking action against the employee. Then, as you desire to take action against the employee, there are separate statutes and regulations that govern the very manner in which you may discipline the employee. Hence the mixed blessing: federal employees—which include leaders, managers, and supervisors—are protected from arbitrary action. You as a supervisor must comprehend the rules that apply when taking action.

Tension between the Law and Administrative Convenience

As a federal employee, you were required to take this oath:

> I do solemnly swear (or affirm) that I will support and defend the Constitution of the United States against all enemies, foreign and domestic; that I will bear true faith and allegiance to the same; that I take this obligation freely, without any mental reservation or purpose of evasion; and that I will well and faithfully discharge the duties of the office on which I am about to enter. So help me God.
>
> (Oath of office, 5 U.S. Code § 3331)

First and foremost then, as a federal employee and federal manager, your obligation is to the law. There are many laws and regulations that tell you what you *can't* do. Of course, well known are our anti-discrimination laws, which prohibit employment decisions motivated by animus due to race, color, religion, sex (the EEOC has held that discrimination on the basis of sexual orientation is within the prohibition of Title VII's discrimination based on sex, *Complainant v. Anthony Foxx, Secretary, Department of Transportation*, 2015), national origin, disability, age, pregnancy, and genetic information. Added to these are prohibited personnel practices (5 U.S.C. § 2302(b)) which prohibit, among other things, reprisal for whistleblowing, discrimination on the basis of marital status or political affiliation, violation of veterans' preference, coercion of political activities, retaliation due to the filing of any grievance or appeal rights, and the hiring of family members.

There are still other prohibitions such as those found in the Standards of Ethical Conduct for Employees of the Executive Branch (5 C.F.R. Part 2635), which regulate, among other things, gifts between supervisors and their employees and outside employment. And still on top of these restrictions are those imposed by individual departments and agencies. Additionally, (that's right, I'm not done!) almost every aspect of federal employment rights are regulated by other statutes and regulations. Pay, leave, and retirement benefits are established by Congress. Procedures for awarding promotions and within-grade increases, granting leave, and issuing performance awards, to name but a small few, are established through the Office of Personnel Management's regulatory authority (most regulations involving federal personnel matters are found on Title 5 of the Code of Federal Regulations).

All of these legal obligations, in a real sense, restrict managers from making decisions they might want to otherwise make. Have a stellar employee you want to promote two grade levels? Sorry, you cannot do that. Have a poor performer you'd like to immediately terminate? Sorry, you cannot do that either. Your ability to manage—to lead—is constrained and confined by these restrictions. The natural reaction of managers, faced with a "can't do" situation, is to become frustrated. You look at your mission objectives, which may be expressed in a declaration from your department head or captured in your own job elements and performance standards, and conclude, naturally, that they are your prime objectives. Those are the tasks you have been chosen to perform. Those are the goals you have been chosen to meet. And, of course, in a real sense you are correct.

But, what those mission objectives and performance standards do not expressly convey is that whatever discretion has been entrusted to your judgment in how those objectives and standards are achieved, they must be achieved within the legal framework that proscribes federal employee conduct. And it is that realization—that I cannot meet my goals and standards as *I* want to—that leads to the frustration. But it is frustration borne of the lack of a perspective that should be taught to every federal supervisor and manager to enable him or her to be an excellent leader, but sadly is not.

What is that perspective? I suggest it is this: *Your first and foremost loyalty is to the law*. Our Founders in our Constitution, our Congress through statutes, and our president, as leader of the executive branch, through those delegated with the president's authority, have established your overriding objectives and performance standards: to perform your daily duties consistent with legal obligations and requirements. Not that your mission-oriented goals and performance standards should be viewed as *hampered* by the law, but that in a government such as ours it is specifically understood and mandated that those goals and standards be accomplished with a high and conscious regard for the law.

The two do not compete; they are symbiotic. Meeting the requirements and obligations of the law should be viewed as being a part of meeting agency mission and performance standards as much as how many audits will be conducted each year, how many program reviews will be undertaken, or how many tax returns will be examined. Unfortunately, for most federal managers and supervisors, until they run afoul of their legal obligations, or find those obligations seemingly "getting in the way" of mission accomplishment, once they take that oath of office promising to "support and defend the Constitution of the United States" and to "well and faithfully discharge the duties of the office," there is no later time or emphasis devoted to an understanding that meeting the objectives and performance standards within the legal requirements *is* the mission.

Treating Law as Policy and Values

Training—if and when supervisors get it—often will contain a brief legal unit on the basics of equal employment law and maybe the Hatch Act's prohibitions on political activity. This may keep federal leaders from running afoul of certain laws but does nothing to frame the essential *attitude*. What should be impressed from day one is that all federal managers have been chosen to lead in the context of the law. Perhaps a better way to inculcate federal managers and supervisors is to refer to law by what it really is: *policy*.

We know it is against the law to discriminate in employment on the basis of such factors as race, religion, sex, and disability. But what does that really mean? That means that our country, through our Congress, has adopted a *policy* that, in our nation, we want employees treated a certain way. When Congress supplements minimal Constitutional due process protections before federal employees can be terminated, Congress has adopted a *policy* that employees are to be afforded certain protections against arbitrary actions according to the will of any one superior. When Congress passed the Whistle Blower Protection Enhancement Act in 2012, enlarging free speech protections for federal employees, Congress adopted a *policy* encouraging that speech by prohibiting retaliation for that speech.

The same can be said of all civil service laws or regulations. They constitute *policy* decisions about how federal service is to be managed. These policies are statements of our collective *values* about how the federal civil service is to be managed and led. Chances are, unless you have taken a course such as "Leading in Context of Constitutional Government" at American University's Key Executive Leadership Development Program, you have not thought of the plethora of laws and regulations governing the federal civil service as statements of values.

Rather than presented or thought of as "obligations" or "prohibitions," if the civil service rules were taught, from the beginning, as a system of values to be embraced and incorporated into the way federal managers manage and lead, then there would be no frustration when one such rule "prevented" action. Rather, adherence to these requirements, both proscriptive and prescriptive, would be integrated into the manner and methods of accomplishing the mission requirements and meeting performance expectations. Civil Service *policies* would not be obstacles to overcome or avoid, but rather part of the very methodology of managing and leading.

The Role of Leaders

What better example of excellent leadership is there than demonstrating that *values* guide the accomplishment of the agency's mission in all decisions affecting day-to-day assigned tasks?

As your managerial training doubtless did not teach you to embrace all of the civil service rules as an expression of values, it is quite likely that you have considered them as obstacles or impediments to efficiency. Hence, the frustration.

But now you see how the attitude toward these rules can be reframed. While you have been selected as a manager and leader to exercise your best judgment and skills to solve the problems faced by your agency, embrace the fact that part of your job is to also implement and apply the values expressed through the amalgamation of Constitutional provisions, statutes, regulations, and Executive Orders that construct and constrain our civil service system. To the extent that as leader you are also teacher, use your leadership to imbue others with this "attitude adjustment."

Formalizing the need for an attitude adjustment in the development of performance objectives for subordinates is one way to accomplish this goal as a leader. Performance standards, which often do incorporate equal employment policies, should go further and incorporate a wider range of ethical and legal values. Being a leader in the federal government is a calling to public service. Tasks that are solely "results oriented," like the cliché "the ends justifies the means," have no place in leading a workforce that has a higher calling than just how many widgets are produced and is responsible to the law.

Changing attitudes to embrace the law as part of our performance goals and objectives will not happen overnight. But to happen at all, it takes leaders to enlighten those above them in the chain-of-command that in the context of a constitutional government, a career in federal service means a career where the "how" we perform and serve goes hand-in-hand with "what" we perform. You, the federal service leaders, must not shrink from the obligation (yes, it is your obligation) to instill in all in your chain-of-command, above or below, that "how" the agency's mission is accomplished is not just about measurements of quantity, quality, and timeliness, but also whether the performance was in accordance with those "policies"—those "values" that have been established through our civil service rubric. If you do not shrink from this obligation, you will help to bring all of the employees in your agency closer to really fulfilling that oath of office to "*faithfully discharge the duties of the office*."

Practical—The Need for "Constitutional Competence"

Hopefully, you have been won over on the reasons to embrace compliance with civil service laws and regulations as part of the very heart of accomplishing your agency's mission. But there are other practical reasons as well. In their preface to *Constitutional Competence for Public Managers,* Rosenbloom, Carroll and Carroll (2000) wisely admonish that "public managers should have constitutional competence because they pledge to uphold the Constitution. However, there is a second, very practical reason for such competence—avoiding *personal* liability for violating individuals' constitutional rights."

In 1982, in the aftermath of abuses of power by the Nixon administration, the U.S. Supreme Court, in the case of *Harlow v. Fitzgerald* (1982), held "that government officials performing discretionary functions, generally are shielded from liability for civil damages *insofar as their conduct does not violate clearly established statutory or constitutional rights of which a reasonable person would have known*" (457 U.S. 818). Said another way, as a public administrator, you may be held *personally* liable for violating a citizen's constitutional rights if those rights were clearly established and a reasonable person in your position should have known of those rights. Liability may also attach for the violation of statutory rights (Civil action for deprivation of rights, 42 U.S.C. § 1983).

So, from personal interest and necessity, embracing constitutional values in meeting agency missions is more than just a way to avoid being frustrated at having to follow various rules in managing and leading your agencies. It is a necessity to avoid possible personal financial loss and professional ruin. This may sound dramatic, but it is grounded in law and experience. (While you can be held personally liable for constitutional violations, Congress has acted to insulate federal employees for acts of ordinary negligence that injure an individual's person or property. In such situations, if the harm occurred while you were acting in the scope of your employment, e.g., think of a traffic accident while you are driving from one agency office to another to attend a briefing, the federal government is substituted as the defendant, and you would not be personally liable, even if you were responsible for the harm. See 28 U.S.C. § 2679, commonly referred to as "The Westfall Act").

But even if you are not concerned about being held personally responsible for violating the constitutional rights of individuals, there is yet more reason to be "constitutionally competent." Even though you are not personally liable, violating the rights of others may lead to *your agency* being held liable for *your actions*. While the financial loss would not be yours, the consequences may certainly be. It is certainly not unreasonable to think that your agency may take action against you for causing an event that resulted in financial or other liability to the agency.

So, there are practical reasons for the need to embrace the civil service rules as you manage and lead your agency. While this practical need may be a motivator, hopefully the prime motivator will always be the desire to adhere to rules because, in a society where the rule of law is paramount, adhering to the rules is part of our social contract with one another.

I Want to Make a Difference: Can I Lobby for Change?

As a leader, you obviously want to affect and implement positive change in your own agency. You may also want to be more active, believing that the ability for change rests with congressional action. However, as a federal employee, there are some restrictions on your right to lobby Congress. In 1919, Congress enacted the Anti-Lobbying Act (18 USC § 1913) designed to prohibit agencies from using appropriated funds to lobby Congress. The Act has been amended as well as interpreted more recently by the U.S. Department of Justice because of concerns about First Amendment Free Speech.

In its essence, the Act (18 USC § 1913) prohibits the use of agency appropriated funds for lobbying "intended or designed to influence in any manner a member of Congress, a jurisdiction, or an official of any government, to favor, adopt, or oppose, by vote or otherwise, any legislation, law, ratification, policy or appropriation, whether before or after the introduction of any bill. …" The Act specifically allows federal employees to respond to congressional requests, and for agencies "through the proper official channels, requests for any legislation, law, ratification, policy or appropriations which they deem necessary for the efficient conduct of the public business. …"

Department of Justice interpretations allow government entities to make direct communications to other federal officials, including Congress, in support of administration or agency positions. But bear in mind that agencies will generally designate certain personnel as congressional liaisons for this purpose. Additionally, each agency may have its own rules concerning the ability of its employees to lobby Congress. You should not ever represent that you are speaking on behalf of your agency without express approval to do so. The Anti-Lobbying Act (18 USC § 1913) says that you cannot be paid by your agency to lobby Congress. But, that does not mean that you are denied your First Amendment rights to "petition the Government for a redress of grievances."

On your own, as a citizen, you can lobby Congress on your own time as a First Amendment constitutional right. Congress made this clear in adopting a provision protecting Employees' Right to Petition Congress (5 U.S.C. § 7211):

> The right of employees, individually or collectively, to petition Congress or a Member of Congress, or to furnish information to either House of Congress, or to a committee or Member thereof, may not be interfered with or denied.

Of course, again, such lobbying must be done on your own time. If being done electronically (including telephone calls and emails) use your personally owned equipment and be off government-owned, leased, or occupied property.

How Can I Affect Agency Change Through the Budget Process?

As a leader and innovator, you might think that your agency needs to adopt or change certain priorities. Sometimes, the change you want or need has to be effectuated through the appropriations process. But, what if for whatever reasons, you cannot convince policy makers to whom you report that they should seek the appropriations in accordance with what, in your judgment, is best in keeping with the agency's mission or the ability to serve the public? Or, what if those policy makers agree with you but are not successful in the budgeting process of getting the administration's support to realign its budgeting priorities or to seek the funding you believe is necessary? You might be thinking that since you have constitutional free speech rights, as reaffirmed by Congress, you can go directly to Congress to lobby for a change in your agency's budget. Not so fast!

Lobbying for changes to your agency's budget may not be an appropriate role for you. The Office of Management and Budget's (OMB) Circular No. A-11 (2015a) states, in pertinent part, the following:

> The nature and amounts of the President's decisions and the underlying materials are confidential. Do not release the President's decisions outside of your agency until the budget is transmitted to Congress. Do not release any materials underlying those decisions, at any time, except in accordance with this section … Do not release any agency justifications provided to OMB and any agency future plans or long range estimates to anyone outside the executive branch, except in accordance with this section. (Sec. 22.1)

Therefore, if you are involved in your agency's budgeting process, or are privy to budget information *before* the president's budget transmission to Congress, you should not be releasing that information or discussing it outside your agency without approval. This obviously will lead to its own frustration. The challenge is how to reconcile your judgment with the realities of your agency's budgeting.

This brings us full circle (well, kind of) to what we discussed at the beginning of this chapter. While not necessarily "embracing" the realities of your agency's budget in the same way, you should embrace the legal framework of the civil service, being able to *accept* financial (and perhaps policy-determinative) limitations, rather than lament them, should enable you to work within those limitations and to accept them as challenges to overcome in meeting agency objectives rather than as obstacles to those objectives. What theologian Reinhold Niebuhr taught in his "serenity prayer" seems very apt here:

> God grant me the serenity to accept the things I cannot change, the courage to change the things I can, and the wisdom to know the difference.
>
> (Wygal, 1940, p. 25)

This is when exceptional leaders must rise to their very best. This is when inclusive decision making, tapping the best skills and talents of those on the team, lead to best solutions. Seize the opportunity.

In a 1995 interview (Glaze, 2014), Apple co-founder Steve Jobs told what is now referred to as his "Parable of the Rocks" to demonstrate the characteristics of teamwork. In its essence, Jobs recalled an elderly neighbor who showed Jobs a homemade rock tumbler, made out of an old coffee can. He then led the young Jobs into the garden where they gathered some ugly rocks. They placed the ordinary rocks into the tumbler with some liquid and grit powder, and turned on the tumbler to a loud rattle. "Come back tomorrow," the neighbor bade. When Jobs returned the next day and they opened the can, out came beautifully polished stones. Many years later, after successfully founding Apple, Jobs said the stone polishing experience was a metaphor for teamwork:

> It's that through the team, through that group of incredibly talented people bumping up against each other, having arguments, having fights sometimes, making some noise, and working together they polish each other and they polish the ideas, and what comes out are these really beautiful stones.
> (Glaze, 2014, para. 7)

If you feel hampered by the inevitable lack of resources, especially when you feel that your own expertise or judgment has not been heeded by the policy makers above you, accept that in the federal civil service, the best and brightest career leaders still answer to some superior (unless, of course, you happen to be elected president of the United States!). For a variety of reasons, some political, some genuine differences in opinion, you will not always be able to convince your superiors that your, and/or your team's, priorities are desired or appropriate at this time. The excellent leader, who also is a subordinate to someone, accepts the budgetary limitations and leads the team within those limitations and without lamenting the "what-might-have-beens" if your advice had only been followed. Collaborate with your team and make the best lemonade that you can out of the lemons.

Sometimes the Leader Feels the Need to Speak Out

Imagine this scenario. You are the head of a major division within your agency, which is concerned with protecting public health and safety. Your position can be described as a "high profile" one. Due to budget allocation decisions made by your own superiors, with which you disagreed during internal deliberations, your division's budget does not allow you to assign enough personnel to vital safety inspections. In your sincerest opinion, these budgetary allocations place the public's health and safety in real jeopardy.

Because of your visibility, and the public's concern about the safety issues involved, you are interviewed by the local newspaper. In the interview, you admit that safety hazards have increased because you do not have adequate staffing. You state that you no longer have adequate staffing to do the inspections necessary. You continue that rather than having safety inspectors perform the inspections, you will have to contract out for lower-level inspection "technicians" to take up the slack for the lack of actual inspectors. In our scenario, all of these statements are truthful. It is also very true that these statements show your own superiors, who made these budgetary decisions, in a very bad public light. Were these comments appropriate to make? Were these comments *legal* to make? (This scenario is loosely based on the case involving former U.S. Park Police Chief Teresa C. Chambers.)

This is the type of dilemma that leaders face often: doing what is perceived as "right" from the vantage point of the general public welfare and what is "right" from the standpoint of maintaining solidarity and an *esprit de corps* within the agency hierarchy. The question of whether such comments are "appropriate" is largely a question of conscience and one's perspective of duty. What are the consequences to the public your agency serves if you remain quiet? What are the consequences to your colleagues if you remain silent? These are difficult questions of ethics and morality. The question as to whether such public remarks are legally protected is easier to answer but only somewhat. We will come back to our scenario and answer these questions in a bit.

We start from a basic legal premise that public sector employees do not relinquish their First Amendment rights to free speech simply because they accept employment with the government (*Pickering v. Board of Education*, 1968). However, because the government as employer also has interests in ensuring workplace decorum and meeting the agency missions, there is a balancing that must take place. The more a public employee is speaking out as a citizen on a matter of public concern, the more likely the employee's speech will be protected under the First Amendment. The more the employee is speaking about a personnel matter personal to the employee, or is being critical of others in the agency with whom the employee must have a close personal relationship, the more the interests of the agency-employer outweigh the free speech rights of the employee (this balancing of interests is referred to as the Pickering Balancing Test).

Under this balancing test, a teacher's letter-to-the-editor critical of the school board's planned usage of funds raised by publicly approved bonds was protected speech under the First Amendment (*Pickering v. Board of Education*, 1968). A low-level employee in a sheriff's office, who was not a policy maker and had no contact with the public, could not be fired for commenting that she wished the attempted assassination of a president had been successful, as a way of expressing her opposition to President Reagan's social welfare programs (*Rankin v. McPherson*, 1987). But, an assistant district attorney who circulated an employee questionnaire soliciting her colleagues' opinions about office procedures and the truthfulness of the agency's supervisors did not engage in protected speech because she was speaking out mostly on internal office issues, which sounded like an employee grievance personal to her, and her comments were disruptive to the office (*Connick v. Meyers*, 1983).

In 2006, the Supreme Court put a major roadblock in the way of public employees' free speech rights in holding that if the speech occurred in the normal course of an employee's duties, the speech was not protected under the First Amendment because the employee was speaking out as an employee, not as a citizen. Hence, an assistant district attorney was not protected under the First Amendment from reprisal when he complained about false statements by police officers in affidavits to procure search warrants, because speaking out on such issues was a normal part of his job duties. The Supreme Court, however, has held that if you are subpoenaed to give testimony about information you obtained during the course of your normal duties, such testimony *is* protected under the First Amendment (see *Lane v. Franks*, 2014).

As you can surmise, navigating the boundaries of what is and what is not permissible speech can be difficult. Luckily, for federal employees, this navigation has been made easier because Congress passed the Whistleblower Protection Act and the Whistleblower Protection Enhancements Act (referred to collectively as the WPA) to give federal employees much greater protection when they speak out.

The lynchpin of First Amendment free speech is that an employee speaks "as a citizen on a matter of public concern." But, under the WPA, Congress defined the speech that is protected, and it need not be about a matter of "public concern." Moreover, the employee need not be speaking as a citizen out of some altruistic motive. If the protected speech—disclosure as it is referred to under the WPA—is within the covered definition, then the employee is protected from retaliation, unless the agency can convincingly prove that it would have taken the action anyway, based on grounds unrelated to the whistleblowing. The categories of protected disclosures under the WPA are as follows:

- A violation of law, rule, or regulation,
- Gross mismanagement,
- Gross waste of funds,
- An abuse of authority, or
- A substantial and specific danger to public health or safety (5 U.S.C. § 2302(b)(8)).

Now, let us return to our scenario where you are the head of a major division within your agency, concerned with protecting public health and safety. The disclosure about the lack of adequate safety inspectors *might* not be protected under the First Amendment if the information was obtained and given as part of normal job duties. Also, if you, a high-level agency official, were being openly critical of superiors with whom you work closely, that speech could be deemed to be too disruptive to the workplace. But that is the First Amendment analysis. We can think of the First Amendment as "minimal" rights, or a "floor" that protects public sector employees. But Congress has augmented these minimal rights and expanded the definition of protected speech.

Under the WPA, the disclosure about inadequate safety inspectors would be a disclosure about "a substantial and specific danger to public health or safety" and therefore protected. The Whistleblower Protection Enhancement Act of 2012 made it clear that the fact that the disclosure was made in the normal course of duties does not take the speech outside the protected categories (5 U.S.C. § 2302(f)(2)).

Now that you have a *basic* understanding of your Free Speech rights, you have an appreciation as to whether your disclosure would be legally protected. Now, you must wrestle with the question, *should you make the disclosure*? If an aspect of leadership is about acting ethically and if public service is about doing public good, the question answers itself. As 1986 Nobel Peace Prize winner Elie Wiesel (1986) said, "There may be times when we are powerless to prevent injustice, but there must never be a time when we fail to protest" (para. 29).

Questions of conscience are always difficult to answer. They are more difficult to answer when there is personal risk that your job or position within your agency, one you worked so hard to attain, could be in jeopardy for speaking out. But leadership in the federal civil service is not about your grade level or nature of your appointment. Leadership is not shirking from hard choices; it is about confronting such choices responsibly and ethically and, of course, within the law. Hopefully, with the firm grounding you find from resources like this handbook, you will confront those hard choices with confidence.

Conclusion

There are many resources out there to help you understand your legal rights and responsibilities as federal employees, managers, and leaders. Some resources are right within your own agency. Your agency undoubtedly has an ethics office that will answer your queries about whether your actions, or those of others, fall within government-wide or agency ethics guidelines. Your agency's office of legal counsel (in some agencies referred to as Office of General Counsel, in others the Solicitor's office) should be another place you can turn for legal advice and guidance with respect to action you may be contemplating or about actions of others that you may question.

There is a caveat, however. Always remember that the ethics officers and the general counsel do not work for you personally. They work for, and represent, the agency as an entity. Their interpretations of legal rights and responsibilities may be geared to those that most favor the agency-desired outcome and minimize the rights of individual employees, such as you. This caveat is in no way intended to disparage anyone who works in the ethics or legal offices. Rather, it reflects that those opinions may be reflective of the agency's "agenda" or viewpoint.

Remember the scenario discussed above about the EPA attorneys who were threatened with discipline if they did not take down their YouTube video because it was at odds with the agency's viewpoint? That ended with the EPA having to withdraw the threats because the two EPA lawyers did nothing wrong in posting their own personal opinions on a matter of public concern. That's an example of an agency legal counsel or ethics office offering an opinion that fit the agency's "agenda" but was actually overly restrictive in its interpretation. If the issue is important enough to you, you can always seek advice from experienced legal counsel outside your agency.

There are various publications concerning administrative law issues and the legal rights of federal employees. Internet searches may also provide you with resource material. Of course, as a layperson, be careful about legal opinions offered on line or interpreting the law on your own. Here are some resources that may be helpful:

- *The Federal Employees Legal Survival Guide* (Kaplan & Passman 2014).
- *Constitutional Competence for Public Managers* (Rosenbloom, Carroll, & Carroll, 2004).

- *Employee Relations, Employee Rights and Appeals* (Office of Personnel Management, https://www.opm.gov/policy-data-oversight/employee-relations/employee-rights-appeals/).
- *Your Rights as a Federal Employee* (Enforced by the U.S. Office of Special Counsel, https://osc.gov/Resources/Your%20Rights%20as%20a%20Federal%20Employee.pdf).
- *Overview of the Privacy Act of 1974* (Department of Justice, 2015 Edition, http://www.justice.gov/opcl/overview-privacy-act-1974-2015-edition).
- *Merit System Principles (5 USC § 2301)* (U.S. Merit Systems Protection Board, http://www.mspb.gov/meritsystemsprinciples.htm).
- *A Guide to the Hatch Act for Federal Employees* (U.S. Office of Special Counsel, https://osc.gov/Resources/HA%20Pamphlet%20Sept%202014.pdf).
- U.S. Office of Government Ethics (http://www.oge.gov/).
- U.S. Office of Special Counsel (https://osc.gov/).
- *Federal Sector EEO Overview* (U.S. Equal Employment Opportunity Commission, http://www.eeoc.gov/federal/index.cfm).
- *Restrictions on Government Entities Lobbying the Federal Government* (Public Citizen, https://www.citizen.org/documents/Govt-Lobbying-Govt.pdf).

Summary

Seeking a leadership position in the federal civil service is a choice. Heaven knows you did not make that decision because the pay is fantastic or because you will receive high public esteem. Rather, you had a call to public service that you answered. With all your responsibilities, you are facing that "mixed blessing": a plethora of protections not enjoyed in the private sector, combined with a plethora of legal constraints. If you ever get to the point of feeling overwhelmed, take time to take stock. You have these legal constraints because you live in a society where "We The People," through elected representatives, make the law. You are leading in the context of a constitutional government. The experiment that began in Philadelphia, resulting in the 1787 adoption of our Constitution, is still going strong. Our Constitution is a marvel and the envy of the world. Every day that *you* lead your agency in fulfillment of the oath you swore to *support and defend the Constitution of the United States* is another day that that experiment continues because of *you*.

References

Complainant v. Anthony Foxx, Secretary, Department of Transportation (Federal Aviation Administration). (2015). WL 4397641 (EEOC, July 17, 2015).

Connick v. Meyers. (1983). 461 US 138.

Garcetti v. Cebellos. (2006). 547 US 410.

Glaze, S. (2014, November 25). The impact of teamwork and Steve Jobs' parable of rocks. *Great Results Teambuilding.* Retrieved from http://greatresultsteambuilding.net/impact-teamwork-steve-jobs-parable-rocks/.

Harlow v. Fitzgerald. (1982). 457 U.S. 800.

Kaplan, J. V., & Passman, E. H. (2014). *Federal Employees Legal Survival Guide* (3rd ed.). Washington, DC: Passman & Kaplan.

Lane v. Franks. (2014). 573 U.S. __, 134 S. Ct. 2369.

Office of Management and Budget. (2015). Communications with the Congress and the Public and Clearance Requirements. *Office of Management and Budget circular No. A-11* (Section 22). Retrieved from https://www.whitehouse.gov/sites/default/files/omb/assets/a11_current_year/s22.pdf.

Pickering v. Board of Education. (1968). 391 US 563.

Plitz, R. (2009, November 25). EPA attempt to limit free speech by agency lawyers Laurie Williams and Allan Zabel violates the law. *Climate Science & Policy Watch.* Retrieved from http://www.climatesciencewatch.org/2009/11/25/epa-attempt-to-limit-free-speech-by-agency-lawyers-laurie-williams-and-allan-zabel-violates-the-law/.

Public Law 112–199, November 27, 2012.

Rankin v. McPherson. (1987). 483 US 378.

Rosenbloom, D., Carroll, J., & Carroll J. (2000). *Constitutional Competence for Public Managers*. Belmont, CA: Wadsworth Publishing.

Whistle Blower Protection Enhancement Act of 2012. (2012). Pub. L. No. 112–199, 126 Stat. 1465.

Wiesel, E. (1986, December 11). Nobel lecture: Hope, despair and memory. Retrieved from http://www.nobelprize.org/nobel_prizes/peace/laureates/1986/wiesel-lecture.html.

Wygal, W. C. (1940). We plan our own worship services: Business girls practice the act and the art of group worship. New York, NY: The Woman's Press.

12 Understanding the Federal Budget

Where Policy Meets Money

Neile L. Miller

You can't always get what you want
But if you try sometime you might find
You get what you need.

—The Rolling Stones

Whether you are a government executive or a government executive-in-training, chances are you are recognized as an expert in whatever program or project you've been asked to lead. You may have spent years building your reputation, either by working your way "through and up" the government—in related programs at ever higher levels—or by your academic or private sector efforts that eventually led to an offer to come into the government. This is true whether your subject is energy or defense or affordable housing or finance or anything else related to something the government spends money doing.

But one of the interesting facts about life in government is that subject matter expertise is absolutely no guarantee that you will be able to do what attracts people to government positions in the first place: get something important to happen, move the needle, change the game, and make a lasting difference. While it's true that politics can triumph over even the most well-considered and well-intentioned policy or program, much of the frustration that leaders experience can be traced to a different truth: nothing that people need or want the federal government to do occurs without money.

This is as true for implementing a treaty as it is for prosecuting a war, conducting research, constructing a regulatory regime, carrying out drug trials or managing the money supply. In every case, the government has to buy people, goods, infrastructure, and/or services. For this reason, *arguably the most interesting place in the government—the place to focus on if you really want to have an impact—is at the nexus of policy and money*. That's where the "what" of government programs meets the "how": commitments and promises coupled with the means to translate them into action.

Yet it is the rare government manager who sees it as her or his job to have more than a cursory involvement with the budget side of the program. Typically, leaders view themselves as the programmatic experts and either believe that it's the job of the "bean counters," the "green eye-shades folks," or the "number crunchers" to worry about getting sufficient resources or are under the impression that since what they are managing is a "presidential priority," sufficient resources are a given, *because the president wants it.*

Very few high profile initiatives and programs launched in a given presidential administration, however, actually take root and become part of the baseline work of the agency. If they do manage to hang on, they are often crippled by diminishing appropriations and burdensome oversight; worst of all, few of their objectives are ever accomplished.

Succeeding in government—ensuring the progression of ideas to implementation, and sustaining the effort—requires understanding that the getting and keeping of resources is as integral to what you are trying to do as the policy objective that got it all going in the first place. Just as you are the acknowledged expert on the substance of the program, you need to master the funding part.

The central lesson that all aspiring federal government executive branch leaders eventually learn is that the ability to make progress, create change, and successfully lead is directly connected to actively engaging in in the process of getting money, managing money, and keeping money—in other words, formulating the budget request, overseeing the execution of the appropriated dollars, and effectively working with those who will determine funding for subsequent fiscal years. This is particularly true of career federal executives because the political leadership, which changes often, will want to influence the annual budget process to implement the president's agenda, but it is the responsibility of career leaders to take the long view when it comes to budget.

It's not hard to master the basics, despite the fair number of moving parts. Doing so will not only give you more control over ensuring your program will succeed in the long run; it will also put you at an advantage vis-à-vis your colleagues. Most of them—and this is especially true the higher up the food chain one looks—fail to see the connection between policy and money until it's too late. When it comes to the federal budget, as in many things, knowledge is power. If you understand the process and players and you're prepared to step up and engage with both, you will enjoy a major advantage in the intense competition for federal funding.

This chapter will provide an overview of *federal budget concepts and rules*, as well as *the process for creating and defending the president's budget (PB)*, and *spending the money appropriated by Congress in accordance with the law.* All of this requires an understanding of the political component—who's who, why they do what they do, and what you should do about it. Knowing that there is always only a limited amount of resources to go around, you should come away with the knowledge of how to get what you need—if not always what you want—out of the annual tournament that produces (in most years) the budget of United States government.

One note: this chapter is not intended to provide a definitive compendium of budget-related regulations and statutes. This chapter is written from the perspective of a former agency budget officer, Office of Management and Budget (OMB) budget official, and senior program manager. The regulations and statutes are easily accessible from other sources, and current practitioners should consult both the latest OMB circulars providing guidance on budget formulation and execution, as well as the relevant appropriation and authorization statutes. Similarly, an agency's budget office, as well as its political leadership, provides specific formulation direction in a given fiscal year.

Finally, owing to political dysfunction, in recent years the federal budget process and the role of the Congress to ensure that the new fiscal year starts on schedule (October 1st) have been turned on their heads. This chapter will make reference to this development, but for the most part it should be assumed that what is described here is how it all works, when it works according to the rules.

Budget Concepts and Some Rules of the Budget Road

The federal government is associated with a lot of jargon, and the budget is no exception. Unless you are working at OMB or in an agency budget shop, there's no need to know every acronym or abbreviation. However, some fluency in the language will help you make your way further in the land of federal money. Here are some of the key terms and concepts.

- **Budget year, a.k.a. fiscal year** The federal fiscal year (FY) begins on October 1 and ends on September 30 of the next calendar year.
- **The color of money** As you will see, there are many different ways to characterize the money that pays for government programs. Whether you are putting together a budget proposal for your established program or a new initiative that the president has proposed and Congress has authorized you to lead, it's vital that you know the color of the money involved—the source of the funds and the authority to use them, the type of appropriation, its lifespan and how it can be spent, and its budget function or classification. These features are key to understanding what is possible and what is not, both as you build your budget and when you go to spend the money.
- **Where does the money come from? *Federal funds and trust funds*** The federal budget has two main components: *federal funds* and *trust funds*. Federal funds include all taxes not designated in law as trust fund receipts, all expenditures except those from trust funds, and cash receipts from borrowing against the federal debt. About 91% of the receipts are from individual and corporation income taxes; the remainder includes excise taxes on alcohol and tobacco, customs fees, and estate and gift taxes (Gessaman, 2010).
- **Deficit spending** Although it may seem that deficit spending is a relatively recent development for the federal government, since 1960 the federal funds have run deficits every year, except for FY 2000. Federal funds deficits are covered by borrowing from the public and from the trust funds. Trust finds are designated in law and receive receipts for which expenditures are made for specific purposes. The largest trust fund is Social Security, which accounts for two-thirds of trust fund receipts. Federal civilian and military retirement, Medicare, and unemployment compensation are the other major trust fund components. Excess funds in the trust funds are invested in federal securities—debt issues to cover the deficit in the federal funds. As of 2010,

except for five years, the trust funds have run annual surpluses since 1934 (Gessaman, 2010). When expenditures from the Social Security and Medicare trust funds begin to exceed annual receipts, monies borrowed by the federal funds will have to be repaid.

- **Budget authority, obligations, and outlays** Federal funding for the activities of government agencies has three components to its spending cycle: the agency must first receive *budget authority* from Congress; it can then *obligate* or commit the money for a purpose; once it has received the goods or services for which money has been promised, the agency can *outlay*—or pay out—the funds. Here is an explanation of these components.
  - ***Budget authority (BA)*** is the authority for government agencies to enter into obligations to pay for the delivery of goods, services, employee salaries and benefits, grants, and subsidies. For example, every time the government signs a contract to buy a product or hire an employee, it incurs an obligation to pay. Before making an obligation to pay, the agency or department must have the budget authority to make the obligation. Entering into an obligation without the corresponding budget authority is a criminal offense (Gessaman, 2010). BA is provided through legislation in four forms:
    - *Appropriations* permit the government to incur obligations and make payment from Government funds. There are two types: *Permanent appropriations* and *annual appropriations*. Programs that have permanent appropriations—that is, they never need additional appropriations once they have been created, are called direct or *mandatory programs*. Annual spending levels are set in law. This spending will occur forever, unless there is no money at all in the Treasury. Social Security, Medicare, federal government retirement programs, and interest on the federal debt are all funded through these permanent appropriations. Programs that require annual appropriations are known as *discretionary spending programs*. Funds are provided annually in one of 12 appropriations acts and in supplemental appropriations acts. Discretionary programs include national defense, housing assistance, energy R&D, and the space program.

      Most discretionary appropriations have a lifespan of *one year*. This means that the agency must commit all of the money during a specific fiscal year. *Multiple year* appropriations are available for a definite period in excess of one fiscal year. *No-year* appropriations are available for obligation indefinitely until expended.
    - *Borrowing authority* permits obligations to be incurred from borrowed funds, usually from funds borrowed from the general fund of the Treasury. It's often done for business-type activities that are expected to produce income and repay the borrowed funds with interest.
    - *Contract authority* allows obligations in advance of an appropriation or in anticipation of a receipt that can be used for payment.

- *Spending authority* permits the obligation of funds received from user fees, e.g., Medicare Supplementary Insurance.

  Obligations are binding agreements that result in outlays of money, immediately or in the future. Sufficient budgetary resources—BA—must be available before obligations can be incurred legally. For most agencies and programs, BA provided in a particular fiscal year must be *obligated*—though not *outlayed*—in that year. Exceptions include when an appropriations act states that the funds are for investment programs covering a period of years. If the authority to obligate has expired, it may be possible for the payments to be made to settle obligations. Appropriated money is not actually spent until it is outlayed. *Outlays* are generally cash payments, but they include accrued but unpaid interest on public issues of Treasury debt and cash-equivalent transactions such as the subsidy cost of direct loans and loan guarantees. One general rule: the federal government does not pay for the delivery of goods and services before such delivery has happened. It may incur an obligation to do so, but it doesn't cut the check until it's happened.

  Thus, it is rare that the BA provided for a program is fully spent in the year that it is made available. Usually the outlays in a given fiscal year are the result of BA that's provided both in the current year and in prior years. It's not hard to understand why: for a major construction project, such as building a ship or a new research facility, the cost of the project may be provided in a single appropriation, but the work and the outlays will happen over several years.

  For these reasons, what an agency spends—or writes checks for—in a given fiscal year, is usually for considerably more than the BA it has received for that fiscal year. But it cannot incur obligations for more than it has actually received in budget authority, and it does not write those checks—outlay the funds—until it has received that for which it has obligated the money in the first place.

- **Budget functions** The federal budget is organized into functions and sub-functions according to the major purpose the spending serves—such as agriculture or national defense. There are 20 functions, most of which are divided into sub-functions. For example, the Agriculture function comprises the sub-functions Farm Income Stabilization and Agricultural Research and Services. There are then program accounts under each of these sub-functions. The sub-function Farm Income Stabilization has several program accounts, including Agricultural Credit Loan Program and Commodity Credit Corporation Fund (The White House, n.d.). The functions include all spending for a given topic, regardless of the federal agency that oversees the individual federal program. An example is the budget of the Department of Energy (DOE), which has funding from Function 270 (Energy), Function 250 (General Science), and Function 050 (National Defense). Both the president's proposed budget submitted to

Congress and the Congress's budget resolution are organized this way. The functional classification system provides a way to capture spending and resources according to "national needs."

The reason the classification of the money is significant is that each function has a target for spending, reflecting the spending goals and objectives of the president in his/her budget and those of the Congress in its budget. These targets allow for more or less spending, not merely as a way to control the overall sum of the budget, but as a means of making policy through fiscal policy. Once again, budget planning can be seen as a zero-sum activity: if the target in a given function, say, for basic R&D, is meant to increase as a reflection of the president's or Congress's commitment to science, and yet deficit reduction is in play, then spending in (an) other function(s), say, education, will be constrained, and new or additional spending in education will require an offsetting reduction in current education spending.

A Few Words About the Deficit and the Federal Debt

The deficit and the federal debt are not the same thing. For purposes of determining funding for federal programs, the deficit, not the debt, matters. A *deficit* occurs when government expenditures exceed the receipts in any fiscal year (FY). For example, if the government spends $3.5 trillion but only collects $3 trillion from taxes and other sources, the deficit for that FY would be $500 billion.

The *debt* is the cumulative effect of annual deficits and annual surpluses. Every time the government ends a year with a deficit remaining, the shortfall goes on the government's "tab." If the government runs a surplus in a given year, the deficit is reduced. The government pays interest on its debt, just like businesses and people do, and there are valid arguments for maintaining debt, as there are in private business. For decades, it has been government policy to maintain debt and leverage funds, and as a result, the tab is equivalent to three or four years of total expenditures (Gessaman, 2010).

Deficits can increase through any number of factors, including:

- emergency funding for unforeseen circumstances, such as the economic stimulus in 2009, war, or a natural disaster like Hurricane Sandy;
- a downturn in the economy, leading to a decrease in receipts and additional expenditures for unemployment compensation and food stamps;
- a stock market downturn, leading to lower receipts from capital gains taxes;
- an increase in inflation, which can lead to higher costs for programs where expenditures are related to inflation, such as Social Security;
- an increase in interest rates that would increase the cost of borrowing funds from the private sector to finance the federal debt.

As you will see in the discussion on the annual budget process, if deficit reduction is a key focus of the administration and/or Congress, as it has been in recent years, proposals for spending on discretionary programs will be heavily scrutinized for their effect on the deficit, i.e., does a given proposal add to the deficit or help offset the deficit, or is it deficit "neutral"?

Very few agency budget proposals will result in revenue generation or other means to directly reduce the deficit, so except in the rare years where there is a budget surplus, building a budget is mostly a zero-sum game—with a net zero effect on the deficit the objective. The primary way to achieve this is to look for an *offset*: the spending that could be ended or reduced to allow for an increase somewhere else. Even though discretionary spending in total is only about 30% of the annual budget, many see it as the answer to deficit reduction, mainly because the non-discretionary components—mandatory programs and servicing of the federal debt—are "must-pay" items. A new space shuttle and basic R&D are not "must pay."

Who's Who in the Federal Budget World

In addition to the senior leaders of the departments and agencies, the key stakeholders in the federal budget process within the government are the following:

- Principal people in the department or agency who are responsible for budget development
- Key staff people in the:
    - Office of Management and Budget (OMB)
    - Congressional Budget Office (CBO)
    - Government Accountability Office (GAO)
    - Appropriations subcommittees that handle budget and appropriations issues concerning that department or agency
- Outside stakeholders, such as associations and lobbyists

Of these, the most prominent players outside of the agency are the staff of the House and Senate Appropriations Committees and Subcommittees and the staff of OMB. The products of both the GAO, which investigates for Congress how the government uses appropriated money and CBO, which provides Congress with analyses of economic and budgetary issues, are arguably much more significant factors in the budget process than are these units' individual staff members.

Appropriations Committees

Each of the House and Senate Appropriations Committees and Subcommittees has a majority and minority staff that examines the administration's budget proposals from the perspectives of the majority and minority parties (Gessaman, 2010). Staff handles all aspects of the budget work, from preparing the questions and managing the witnesses for the budget hearings to writing the draft legislation that becomes the appropriations bill to negotiating with counterparts in the other chamber to reconcile differences in the two bills.

Typically consisting of fewer than 10 people combined, the majority and minority staff usually work closely with each other to ensure the appropriations process accomplishes the objectives and priorities of the committee members in a timely manner.

Office of Management and Budget

OMB staff maintains an ongoing presence throughout the budget formulation process in two ways: by overseeing the preparation of the president's budget and by overseeing the 2010 Government Performance and Results Modernization Act. The budget formulation process is overseen by an OMB Resource Management Office, within which program analysts or "examiners" focus on specific program areas. Examiners are responsible for the evaluation, formulation, and coordination of the budget, management procedures, and program objectives affecting federal agencies.

Other players within OMB include the Budget Review Division, responsible for developing the estimates and projections used in preparing the guidance for formulating the PB; the Legislative Reference Division, responsible for coordinating all agency and department interaction with Congress on the budget and other legislative matters; the Office of Federal Financial Management; and the Office of Information and Regulatory Affairs.

Under the Government Performance and Results Act of 1993 (GPRA) and the follow-on GPRA Modernization Act of 2010, OMB is also tasked with producing a report on agency performance. This is delivered to Congress annually along with the president's budget. Other White House offices, including the National Security Council staff, the Office of the Science and Technology Policy, and the National Economic Council, can play in the budget process, depending on the interests of the staff. OMB, as it considers the agencies' requests, will often reach out to these staffs for input on a given agency's proposal, especially regarding new initiatives that may require additional funding.

Outside Stakeholders

There are many stakeholders in the budget process outside of the executive and legislative branches. From trade associations to non-governmental organizations, corporations, foreign governments, and labor unions to lawyer-lobbyists representing all manner of special interests, every year a vast number of groups and individuals attempt to influence the budget process.

Of course since we know that budgetary resources usually determine whether or not the government will act on something, it is not surprising that all of these entities focus their own resources on trying to achieve the most favorable outcomes for their particular interest. Many outside stakeholders are extremely knowledgeable about how the process works, who the real federal players are, and the specific inflection points when they are most likely to be successful in influencing the outcomes.

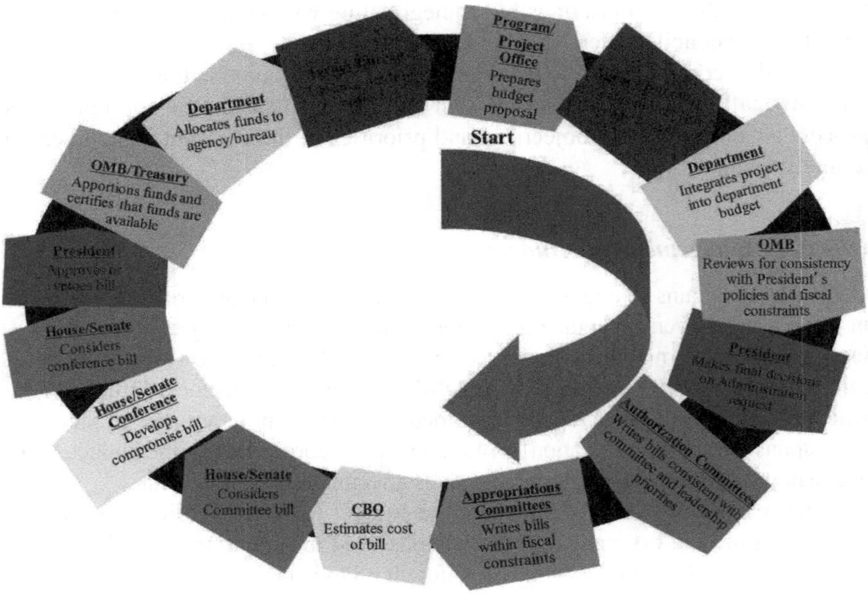

Figure 12.1 "The Vicious Cycle": Organizational Involvement in Budget Process
Examples of insertion points: March-ish: Lab is working at the 'Start' box; Summer: Agency decisions; Fall: Present to OMB.

Formulation, Execution, and Defense: The Three-Ring Circus of Federal Budgeting

At any given time, the federal government is working on three budgets:

- Formulation of the PB that will be sent to Congress next February;
- Congressional action on the budget for the coming fiscal year that begins next October 1; and
- Execution of the budget for the current fiscal year that began last October 1.

If you are working in the executive branch, you will be involved in some way with all three budgets at some point during a calendar year and sometimes all three simultaneously. In addition, you will be involved in the performance management and strategic planning processes associated with the budget formulation process that has been institutionalized by the 2010 GPRA Modernization Act. Those performance management and strategic management processes are described elsewhere in this handbook, but their primary influence has been to encourage agencies to consider their work from the perspective of outcomes and outputs, not just ongoing, level-of-effort activities. The idea is that agencies at all levels should tie their resource planning to specific goals and performance and should have their follow-on proposals evaluated against the progress—or lack thereof—toward their stated strategic plan.

Ring 1: Formulation of the President's Budget

Annually, by law, the president must submit a budget to Congress sometime between the first Monday in January and the first Monday in February (Center on Budget and Policy Priorities, 2015). Sometimes the submission is delayed—particularly when a new administration takes office or congressional action on the prior year's budget has been delayed. The PB is developed through an interactive process between federal agencies and OMB and lays out the president's relative priorities for federal programs.

The PB is very specific and includes details on each of more than 1,300 appropriation accounts. Fiscal policy and budget priorities are sketched out not only for the coming year but also for the next 10 years. In addition to the official budget volumes issued by OMB, agencies typically produce their own explanations, with even more detailed descriptions of the programs and the proposed funding levels and justifications for any proposed programmatic or funding level change. Some agencies produce volumes that slice and dice the budget by state or facility, making it easier for an individual member of Congress to see his or her state's or district's "winners and losers"—i.e., entities affected positively or negatively by programmatic funding proposals.

Inside the Agency

Work on the PB starts about 12 months in advance of its delivery to Congress and 18 months before the start of the fiscal year. That's when the agencies, at their most fundamental programmatic levels, begin to figure out what level of effort will be required of ongoing programs and how much that will cost and what new or additional initiatives could or should be proposed. If we consider this on a calendar basis, the aforementioned activities typically take place in late January into early spring. In early spring, the agency's budget office will usually issue some preliminary guidance as the program offices begin shaping the "building block" budget requirements into proposals for consideration by the agency's senior leaders.

At the same time, OMB begins establishing the budget targets for the outyears (years beyond the budget year that was submitted to the Congress in February). The targets include considerations of:

- decisions reflected in previously enacted budgets, including the one for the fiscal year in progress,
- reactions to the last proposed budget (which Congress is considering at the same time the process of preparing the forthcoming budget begins), and
- evaluations of program performance all influence decisions concerning the forthcoming budget, as do projections of the economic outlook, prepared jointly by the Council of Economic Advisers, OMB, and the Treasury Department (OMB, 2012, p. 125).

Additionally, any legislation that has a direct effect on spending targets is considered in the development of the guidance. An example of this is the Budget Control

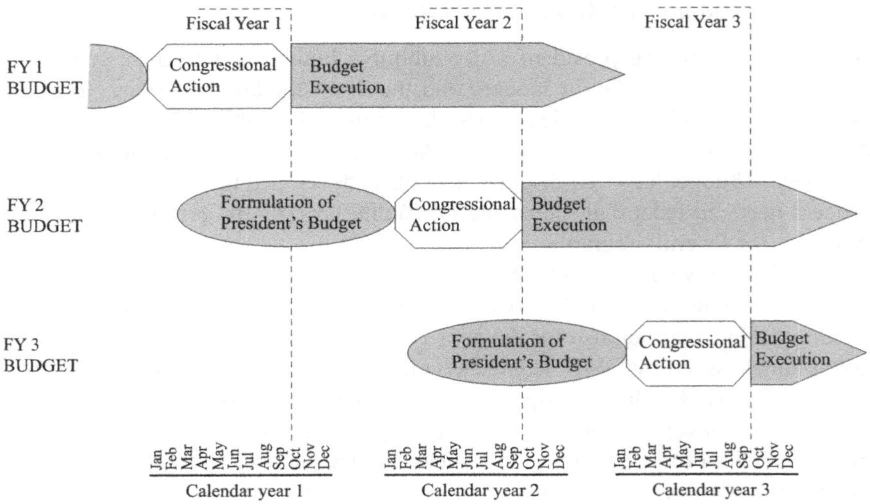

Figure 12.2 Federal Budget Process Overview.

Act of 2011, which introduced 10-year mandatory spending caps for discretionary programs as a mechanism for reducing the deficit. In May, OMB issues formal planning guidance to the agencies, which includes specific policy directions and funding levels for the budget year and for at least four of the following years. Under law, the departments and agencies prepare budget requests in accordance with presidential guidance (Preparation and submission of appropriations requests to the president, 2010).

At that point, the process inside the agencies kicks into high gear, and it is the beginning of a critical period for anyone leading federal programs. Over the next couple of months, usually culminating in July or August, the agency must come up with a consolidated proposal that will be submitted to OMB at the beginning of September. Understanding that there will always be more activities deserving of funding than the OMB guidance levels will accommodate, ultimately the head of the agency must decide what's in and what's out. Most agencies engage in some form of intra-agency collegial decision making along the way to presenting the head with a discreet set of choices to be made at the executive level.

Up to this point (roughly May), depending on your overall set of responsibilities, you may not have paid much attention to the budget building going on within your program area. But now the agency's budget office takes over. Their goal is to develop an agency-wide budget that allows senior management to see how it can assure the essential work of the agency is funded while reserving enough money to pay for the administration's—and their own—priorities. The budget office often starts by asking the programs to provide their funding proposals under several scenarios, such as budgets built at the OMB guidance level and at perhaps a two and a five percent cut to that level. Program managers may be asked to order their spending priorities and then to accommodate the cuts by spreading the pain equally across activities or absorbing the full cut in the lowest priority items and describing the relative merits or catastrophes associated with each approach.

You can probably see why it becomes critical for you to stay engaged from this point on. Among other reasons, this means being physically present and avoiding travel during this period for the intra-agency meetings where you may be asked to defend your proposal and help develop options for meeting the budget guidance. Otherwise, you are very likely to find yourself with a budget that say, either kills a new initiative you have poured your heart, soul, and professional expertise into crafting or undercuts everything else your office does in a way that makes real progress impossible—even if it keeps it all "alive."

As described at the outset of this chapter, this is the nexus of policy and money. Accordingly, you need to know a few things cold:

- Your real programmatic priorities—what are you really ready to live without and what are you defending at all costs?
- The rationale for your prioritized spending list.
- The numbers associated with that list and the supporting documentation for the recommended spending levels, including past program and budget performance.
- A strong understanding of the administration's priorities and those of your agency's chief executive—which may or may not be in complete agreement.

As the summer plays out, you are likely to be called to defend your budget proposal in front of various groups at your agency, up to and possibly including the head of the agency. As in all negotiations, you must know your bottom line and also that you are unlikely to get every dollar you seek. But the better informed you are about the story and data behind your proposal, the easier you are likely to find its defense.

Over to OMB

Once the agency's budget proposal is finalized and delivered to OMB in September (in October for DoD), OMB staff spends the next two months reviewing the proposals, hearing supporting presentations from the agencies, and preparing issue papers that discuss the requests, program performance, political considerations, and congressional and public reaction. During this "budget season," OMB staff is expected by management to scrub all proposals both for their comportment with the president's policy priorities and for the soundness of the resource request. As noted earlier, policy officials and staff in OMB, the National Economic Council, and other parts of the Executive Office of the President provide their views on program priorities and trade-offs among departments and budget functions (Gessaman, 2010).

In late November, the OMB director "passes back" decisions to the departments on what has been accepted for the PB, in a process known as *passback*. These decisions include the overall budget level (BA and outlays) and usually budget and policy guidance for specific programs. Not surprisingly, the departments generally appeal OMB passback decisions, both the specific programmatic guidance and the overall budget level. Appeals are usually resolved by early to mid-December, with OMB and the agency trying to reach agreement at the staff level as quickly as possible, but with the ability for an agency chief executive to appeal unresolvable issues (usually no more than 1 to 3) to the president or a board established by the president for resolution.

The Budget Review Board (BRB) usually consists of some combination of senior White House officials, such as the vice president, chief of staff, and director of OMB, together with the secretary of the Treasury. Appeal to the president remains an option for issues that can't be resolved by this board, but it should be emphasized that as it is only a very few issues that even go to the BRB, it is rare for issues to go beyond the BRB (Gessaman, 2010).

When everything has been resolved, the remaining work focuses on preparing the budget documents for submission to Congress. OMB leads the preparation of the written justification for the president's proposal, and as stated earlier, the agencies also prepare more detailed justification data and "sales pitches" for their specific portions of the budget. The budget goes to print in late January, in time for its presentation to Congress in February, as previously described.

Ring 2: Congressional Action on the Budget

Following the submittal of the PB to Congress, the focus of the budget process shifts away from the executive. Throughout the spring, the role of officials in the executive branch is to testify to Congress about the rationale for the president's proposed policies and program and the budgetary resources required to support them.

The congressional budget process can be divided into four stages, each governed by its own procedures outlined in the congressional budget, the rules of the House and Senate, and other relevant statutes. The last three stages shown below often occur simultaneously (U.S. House of Representatives, n.d.).

Adoption of the Congressional Budget Resolution (CBR)

House and Senate Committees hold hearings on the president's budget throughout the spring, those testifying range from the head of the agency to the managers of individual programs, depending on the committee and its level of interest in the details. When the hearings are completed, each congressional committee provides funding and revenue recommendations for the programs under its jurisdiction, including the programmatic assumptions used in developing the amounts for each budget function, to the Budget Committee of the relevant house.

After each chamber passes a resolution, the Committees on Budget work together to report a concurrent resolution on the budget that sets each committee's allocation of spending authority for the next fiscal year and aggregate spending and revenue levels for at least five years. The CBR also establishes aggregate totals with respect to revenues and spending for the entire federal budget. Although the CBR is not law—since the president does not sign it—Congress often attempts to obtain presidential agreement because the allocations included in it set the overall funding levels that become the basis of the appropriations bills sent to the president for approval.

Congress, by law, must adopt a budget resolution by April 15th (Reconciliation, 2010), however it has happened several times that the Congress has been unable to adopt a budget resolution. This is usually because the politics in one chamber are significantly different from those in the other—for example, when one house is focused on achieving deficit reduction by slashing discretionary spending below levels that the other house finds acceptable.

Passage of Appropriation Bills

In May, the House begins consideration of the 12 annual appropriation bills for the next fiscal year based on the discretionary spending allocation in the budget resolution. As these bills move through hearings, markups, floor consideration, and conference they are constrained by the levels and allocations in the budget resolution and the enforcement of the Budget Act and through House and Senate rules (U.S. House of Representatives, n.d.).

The Appropriations Committee in each chamber allocates the discretionary amount approved in the CBR among its subcommittees (Gessaman, 2010). Although the CBR includes "appropriate" levels of discretionary spending by budget function—i.e., so much for defense, so much for general science, etc.—the appropriations subcommittees are not required to follow the guidance. The only thing that matters is the total funding allotted to the subcommittee. It can spread it around any way it chooses.

For a federal manager, this can provide an opportunity to revisit the budget levels laid out in the president's budget. Members of an appropriation subcommittee often act on a bipartisan basis, sharing concerns about the performance of federal programs and not necessarily committed to the same initiatives that made it into the PB. Members and their staffs often use the budget hearings and attendant background briefings to pursue information on ways they can affect the items of interest to them—from a policy perspective or because of their location—that may not have been funded as the members would have wanted.

It is not beyond imagination that a federal manager may find him-/herself more in line with appropriators who are eager to support, say, a new supercomputer at a national laboratory than with those who favor further investment in clean coal technology and may use the questioning of the subcommittee as a way to provide supporting information that does not appear in the PB. While it is the expectation of the administration that its officials will support and defend the PB to Congress, it is also the case that when a member or subcommittee requests information on a matter of interest, the agency is expected to provide it.

In this way, proposals that were declared dead on arrival at OMB, or long-established programs that a new administration decides are no longer priorities and has therefore outright killed in the PB, sometimes have new life breathed into them in the latest appropriation bill.

Reconciliation

When spending targets in the CBR do not match anticipated revenue, a reconciliation resolution would contain instructions to committees to report legislation containing statutory changes that would enable the CBR spending levels to be "reconciled" with revenue. For example, to increase revenue there could be a change in tax levels, a requirement that a government charge fees, or a change in the eligibility for benefits received through an entitlement program like Social Security. Like many other aspects of the budget process, the deadline for completing reconciliation, June 15th, is seldom met by the Congress.

Program Authorization

Authorization acts come from the practice of distinguishing between laws that set federal policies and laws that fund them. Authorization laws establish, continue, and modify federal programs. With respect to funding authorizations, there are a few important points:

- Some authorizations are annual, some for a specified number of years, and others are for an indefinite period. The military programs of DOD, for example, require annual authorizations, which address every line in the appropriations bill. Other agencies, such as DOE, can and do go for years without an authorization bill because their activities are considered authorized by their establishing legislation.
- Although the authorization of an appropriation usually precedes the appropriation, it is not always the case. Sometimes the authorization bill never passes and Congress can enact an appropriation that is its own "authorization."
- Authorizations of mandatory spending programs set policy and make funds available without further appropriations. As previously discussed, more than half of all federal spending is for programs for which appropriations are provided in the authorization legislation, without the requirement for separate appropriations.

A Word about Continuing Resolutions

As noted earlier, for most of the past 10 years, Congress has had difficulty maintaining the schedule for all of the actions that comprise the congressional budget process. In particular, appropriations bills are often not completed in time for the start of the fiscal year. As October 1 gets closer, the Congress will usually pass a joint "continuing resolution" (CR), which provides appropriations for any affected agency (and often all of them are still waiting when October 1 rolls around) to continue operations at some specified level (usually close to the level of the expiring fiscal year) until a specific date or until their regular appropriations bill has been enacted.

As with regular appropriations, CRs must be presented to the president for approval or veto. For the affected agency, although CRs have become an almost inevitable fact of life, their ability to wreak utter havoc with programmatic objectives and the effective use of federal resources cannot be overstated. Whether they last a few days, weeks, or months (and some have gone on for the whole fiscal year), CRs pose one of the biggest challenges federal leaders face.

All of the planning that went into the front end of developing funding requirements; the ability to maintain construction project schedules and to hire staff as planned is thrown out the window since agencies do not have the resources they expected on the scheduled for which they were told to plan. Operating with such uncertainty requires leaders to remain flexible and to think creatively, especially in managing the effect on staff morale.

Ring 3: Budget Execution, or Spending the Money

At some point, you will have money to spend on your program. As a federal leader, you may find yourself with responsibility for overseeing expenditures in the tens or even hundreds of millions of dollars. It is not an exaggeration to say that as far removed as you might feel from the reality of those resources, your ability to sustain the funding that you and your team fought long and hard to obtain rests squarely on how well the budget is executed—which is to say, how the dollars are spent.

This doesn't mean necessarily that you are on the line to ensure, say, the success of an experimental space program—after all, you can't be expected to guarantee the success of an experiment. But when considering your budget request OMB and Congress will ask a lot of questions trying to understand how well you planned and whether you maintained good control over your money. Questions such as:

- How closely matched are the activities that received resources over the fiscal year to the detailed plans for expenditures that you presented when you were seeking the funds?
- How much money was left over at the end of the fiscal year and why?
- If the answer is more than 20%, were you unrealistic in your expectation for what could get accomplished during the fiscal year? Perhaps your current "ask" is similarly overstated?

It is a common mistake to think that the whole point of the federal budgeting process is to get the appropriation you requested. This is only part of the story. If the execution of those resources is not well managed, not only are you in danger of losing out in the internal agency competition for budget resources, and of getting next year's request cut, but the mechanisms exist to take previously appropriated money away from one program and give it to another.

Program planning, monitoring, and evaluation—which are called for in GPRA 2010 and other "government reform" initiatives—put the burden on federal leaders to effectively and efficiently manage public resources. Continuous oversight of your resources will help guard against this and is becoming a prime responsibility of federal senior leaders.

Execution Mechanisms

Budget execution mechanisms are where the rubber meets the road. Understanding the basic terminology will enable federal leaders to manage their programs much more effectively and efficiently.

- ***Apportionment*** Before any appropriated funds can be used, they must be released by OMB to the organizational unit that will carry out or execute the program. The process for preleasing the funds is called *apportionment.* Agencies submit apportionment requests on a standard form to OMB for each budget account within 10 days of the approval of the appropriation. OMB approves or modifies the apportionment specifying the amount of funds agencies can use by time period, program, project, or activity. Generally, apportionments are done every quarter of the fiscal year to reduce the chances of a funding shortage in an account before the end of the year. In addition to the apportionment by OMB, the Department of the Treasury issues a warrant certifying the amount of funds that can be withdrawn from the Treasury. This is based on the language of the bill and the OMB apportionment. The president may delay the use of funds—which is to say, OMB may withhold the apportionment—for a number of reasons, such as:
    - After reviewing the execution data, it may be determined that the full amount of available funding is not needed.
    - The president may not want to spend the money for a specified program.
    - It may not be feasible to use the funds immediately.

Depending on the situation, the president can also ask Congress to rescind the budget authority; however, this rarely occurs (Gessaman, 2010).

- ***Reprogramming*** In order to respond to new requirements that arise during the year, most departments have the authority to reprogram BA among programs within an account and to transfer BA from one account to another after informing their congressional appropriations subcommittees. Although not required by statute, in practice agencies will not reprogram funds until receiving a positive response from Congress.

The Political Component

David Stockman (1986), President Reagan's first OMB director, titled his memoir of his time in that job *The Triumph of Politics*. His point was: many budget decisions ultimately did not reflect what President Reagan claimed were his policy priorities nor did they support his economic program. Sometimes they were in direct contravention of these things (Stockman, 1986).

So why is the budget so politicized?

To answer this question it's helpful to once again consider that nexus of politics and money. We've noted that most everything the government does, from research to building to regulating, requires money. It follows that if you want to stop the government from doing something, the most direct way is to assure that there is no money for it is to cut off the flow of funds, which are oxygen in the federal system. And since the effort to determine one year's worth of funding takes a full year and a crowd of participants, it is easy to understand that there are plenty of opportunities for politics to be injected into what, on paper, looks like a very mechanical process.

The political facets of the budget are clear from the time the PB begins to be formulated within an agency, for example, when a cabinet secretary may shave funding from some programs to free up resources to fund one of his or her priorities to establish new research collaborations or a new affordable housing program. Within the White House, an agency's proposal may be rethought, meaning funding is shifted away from some things toward others because members of the National Security Council staff believe the president's commitment to fighting terrorism requires more resources dedicated to increasing the U.S. presence somewhere overseas.

Once the president submits the budget to Congress, the political maneuvering is in full swing. "Typically, and regardless of which party proposes the Budget, opposing party leaders label presidential priorities and program policy objectives as unacceptable for America's future and pronounce the Budget '**dead on arrival**'" (Gessaman, 2010, p. 167).

In fact, most of the president's budget will be passed almost exactly as it has been submitted, if for no other reason than the fact that the relatively small congressional staff working on appropriations does not have the capacity for making wholesale changes on every program in every agency—even if it were so inclined. But the stakes are high for those charged with managing the process for a budget the sheer size of which is hard to fully grasp. There are many interests involved in getting it "right"—and that key word has as many different definitions as there are players in the process.

Getting What You Need

We live in a time of constrained federal resources. Apart from the stimulus funds provided by the 2009 American Recovery and Reinvestment Act, budgets have been tightening and even declining over the past decade, particularly following the passage of the Budget Control Act of 2011. As you try to navigate the budget process, here are some points worth considering:

1 Leading in a time of tight money is challenging, without doubt, all the more reason to pay as close attention to your federal resources as you do to your

program activities. Don't assume the "budget shop" can function well without your advice and guidance.

2 Hold your staff accountable for the proper execution of the resources you have and for developing defensible proposals for the resources you are requesting. It is better that you beat up the proposal first because you want it to have been tested before the experts in saying "no" to requests for money get their chance.

3 Know that in our separation of powers system, "But it's a presidential priority!" is not likely to get you the additional dollars you are seeking. Every president has many priorities and understands that there is not enough money to fund all of them. Congress and its members will also have priorities, as will your agency's stakeholders. That's why OMB staff, as the president's budget arm, is expected to push back on your request. You need to be able to articulate the reasons this deserves scarce resources.

4 Never propose to fund your most important activity—presidential priority or not—with additional funds that you are requesting above your base budget. The standard assumption at OMB is that if it's so important, it should be the first thing you fund, not the last.

5 The more your OMB examiner and congressional staff know about your program, the better placed they will be to support your proposals come the budget season. But do not wait until the budget season to begin this open education. These people like to be involved throughout the year, and it is in your interest to grab their attention early and often.

What is true for any negotiation is true for you and your budget: you are not necessarily going to get everything you want. But put in the effort to understand and become fluent in both your program and your budget and you just might get what you need.

References

Center on Budget and Policy Priorities. (2016). *Policy basics: Introduction to the federal budget process*. Retrieved January 10, 2016 from http://www.cbpp.org/sites/default/files/atoms/files/PolicyBasics_SocSec-TopTen.pdf.

Gessaman, D. E. (2010). *Understanding the budget policies and processes of the United States government*. Washington, DC: The EOP Foundation.

Lewis, D. E. (2008). *The politics of presidential appointments: Political control and bureaucratic performance*. Princeton, NJ: Princeton University Press.

Office of Management and Budget. (2012). *Analytical perspectives, budget of the U.S. Government, FY2013* Washington, DC: U.S. Government Printing Office.

Preparation and submission of appropriations requests to the president. 31 U.S. Code § 1108. (2010).

Reconciliation. 2 U.S.C. § 641. (2010).

Stockman, D. A. (1986). *The triumph of politics: Why the Reagan revolution failed*. New York, NY: Harper & Row.

The White House. (n.d.). *Functional classification*. Retrieved from https://www.whitehouse.gov/tax-receipt/functions.

U.S. House of Representatives, Committee on the Budget. (n.d.). *Budget Functions*. Retrieved January 10, 2016 from http://budget.house.gov/budgetprocess/.

13 Emerging Challenges for Federal Government Leaders

> If the rate of change on the outside exceeds the rate of change on the inside, the end is near.
>
> —Jack Welch

Developing federal government leaders who are prepared for complex and dynamic operating environments has been a recurring theme of this handbook. This chapter explores several areas of change that leaders in the 20th century did not have to confront but that are now creating enormous challenges, and opportunities, for the 21st-century leader. These challenges include managing change in an extraordinarily dynamic environment to ensure that organizations are resilient and can adapt to that changing environment, developing new ways to understand workforce and demographic changes through workforce analytics, using social media effectively and responsibly, and utilizing big data to manage programs and achieve the vital missions that federal agencies have been entrusted with by Congress and the president.

Data as an Asset—Big Data: Lost in Space

Joyce Hunter

> Ten years from now, when we look back at how this era of big data evolved … we will be stunned at how uninformed we used to be when we made decisions.
>
> —Billy Bosworth

Data now streams from daily life: phones, credit cards, televisions, and computers, from the infrastructure of cities to sensor-equipped buildings, trains, buses, planes, bridges, and factories. The data flows so fast that the total accumulation of the past two years—a zettabyte (Zettabyte, n.d.) dwarfs the prior record of human civilization. The amount of data in the private and public domains is experiencing exponential growth. Mobile devices, sensors, audio and video feeds, social media, and what has become known as "The Internet of Things" are all contributing to this increase in information variety, volume, and velocity.

This significant increase in data in recent years, coupled with the development of new techniques and technologies to analyze it ("Big Data"), enables disruptive business models to flourish and is now spreading into the more traditional corporate/government models and activities. When there is a significant amount of data, mathematical patterns can be created to come up with any answer. This has to do with a combination of sample size, pseudo randomness, and the sheer volume of possible patterns. By providing feedback that is incorrect, we guarantee future results that are also incorrect. *It's as if you keep telling spell checker to learn the words of the words you misspelled.*

This is what I would call a "Lost in Space" phenomena.

The Consequences of Being Lost in Space

For those of you old enough to remember the popular TV show (an American science fiction series that aired September 1965-March 1968), "Lost in Space" featured the astronaut family and robot of Dr. John Robinson, an Air Force pilot, who set out in the spaceship Jupiter 2 from an overpopulated Earth to visit a planet circling the star Alpha Centauri with hopes of colonizing it. The Robinsons, along with stowaway Dr. Zachary Smith, initially a doctor of Intergalactic Environmental Psychology who eventually became a bungling, self-serving, greedy, and manipulative coward after veering off course, attempted each week to return to Earth.

Unfortunately, with a series of bad data and interference from Dr. Smith, the lost crew ended up in challenging situations where they spent the rest of the season surviving a host of adventures. The "Lost in Space" problem occurs frequently in Big Data as it is an *adversarial environment.* There is an opponent (like Dr. Smith) who is purposely changing the environment in order to prevent your ability to understand the situation or predict it. There is also the fact that applications and users are constantly evolving how they use devices and the network. This changing environment means that models are always based in the past. As time proceeds without feedback, the model becomes more and more inaccurate until it's useless. *"Insufficient facts always invite danger"* (Spock in Coon, Wilber, Roddenberry, & Daniels, 1967).

Or, as the robot would say to young Will Robinson, "Danger! Danger!"

To better understand the challenges faced by organizations trying to leverage Big Data, Knowledgent (2015) recently conducted a survey designed to gauge the levels of difficultly experienced in key areas that in Knowledgent's perspective are potential pain points. In this survey, they asked questions relative to the status of Big Data initiatives and projects and the value being received by these efforts.

The survey found that:

- Big Data continues to grow in importance despite significant obstacles.
- The combination of traditional and more unstructured data sources, combined with advanced analytics, are contributing to the development of new business insights.
- Big Data initiatives are transitioning from Proofs-of-Concept to production.

More than 60% of respondents indicated that Big Data initiatives were either very or extremely important to their organizations. However, even with Big Data's growth and benefits, there are significant challenges to organizational adoption:

- Resources, both human and other, continue to be a major constraint.
- Putting together an overall "production grade" program, particularly those aspects related to standardizing process, is a notable challenge.
- The "Data Lake" architecture needs to evolve and mature to better support end users (Knowledgent, 2015, p. 2).

The Big Data concept is a huge challenge for those trying to assist organizations to manage change in these disruptive times—like trying to drink from a fire hydrant. There is just so much data that either isn't being collected or is being collected incorrectly, and there is no magic algorithm or sensor out there yet to make this easy. Encouraging contributors to be more diligent with the data collection process is critical, because correct data makes the difference in solution results.

The challenge is two-fold. First, we do not currently collect and scrub good enough data to support this recent fascination with numbers. Second, our brains are not wired to understand or comprehend the magnitude of all that data. And if you have a lot riding on bad data (aka "dirty data") that is poorly understood, then people will distort the data or find other ways to game the system to their advantage.

I do not recall whether the Robinsons ever made it back to Earth, but I do know that Big Data is creating big headaches for CIOs and IT managers—from management to infrastructure, storage, resourcing, and security. Based on its sheer volume, extracting value from big data is as daunting a task as the Robinsons' weekly challenges.

Current technologies and architectures are not equipped to handle massive volumes of data. Security and privacy are important issues associated with big data. To benefit from big data, agencies will need to rethink their data management strategies, invest in solutions, and acquire the skills needed to maximize the value of their information.

Data as a Utility—Going Where Data Has Not Gone Before

The enduring popularity of Star Trek is due to the underlying mythology and shared love of stories involving exploration, discovery, adventure, and friendship that promote an egalitarian and peace-loving society where technology and diversity are valued rather than feared and citizens work together for the greater good. Thus, Star Trek offers a hopeful vision of the future and a template we can aspire to for our lives and our society.

The same can be said for the promotion of Big Data, Open Data, and Open Government, which has the ability to accelerate the effective use of data by connecting vertical and horizontal levels of government with a focus on delivering services according to citizen need and promoting social good.

Big Data essentially describes very large datasets, but that's a somewhat subjective judgment that depends on technology. Today's Big Data may not seem so big in a few years when data analysis and computing technology improve. Open Government is a combination of ideas. It includes collaborative strategies to engage citizens in government; government releasing data about its own operations, such as federal spending data; and government releasing data that it collects on issues of public interest, such as health, environment, and different industries. Open Data is accessible public data that people, companies, and organizations can use to launch new ventures, analyze patterns and trends, make data-driven decisions, and solve complex problems. All definitions of Open Data include two basic features: the data must be publicly available for anyone to use, and it must be licensed in a way that allows for its reuse.

Starting with those basic descriptions, the intersection of these three concepts defines the six subtypes of data shown in the diagram. (There's no separate category for the intersection of Big Data and Open Government—anything in that category is also Open Data.) Figure 13.1 shows characteristic examples of each, referring to the numbers below:

1 ***Big Data That's not Open Data*** A lot of Big Data falls in this category, including some Big Data that has great commercial value. All of the data that large retailers hold on customers' buying habits, that hospitals hold about their patients, or that banks hold about their credit-card holders, falls here. It's

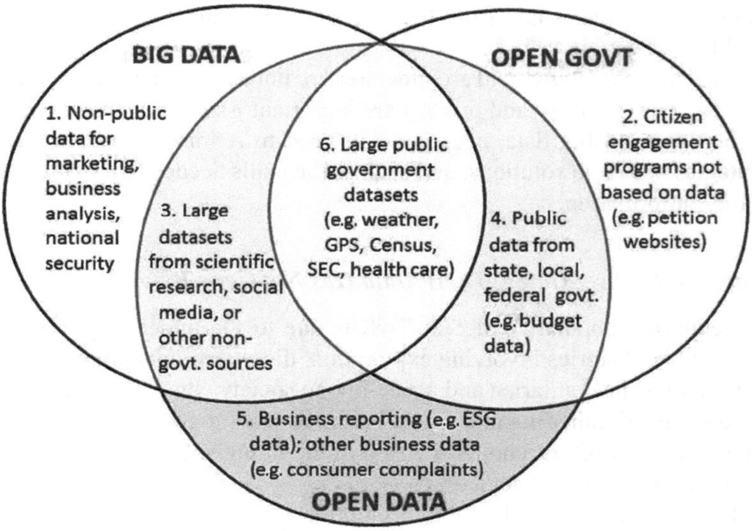

Figure 13.1 The Relationship between Big Data and Open Data

Source: Adapted from Gurin (2014).

information that the data-holders own and can use for commercial advantage. National security data, like the data collected by the NSA, is also in this category.

2 ***Open Government Work That's not Open Data*** This is the part of Open Government that focuses purely on citizen engagement. For instance, the White House has started a petition website, called "We the People" to open itself to citizen input. While the site makes its data available, publishing Open Data—beyond numbers of signatures—is not its main purpose.

3 ***Big, Open, Non-Governmental Data*** Here we find scientific data-sharing and citizen science projects like Zooniverse. Big data from astronomical observations, from large biomedical projects like the Human Genome Project or from other sources, realizes its greatest value through an open, shared approach. While some of this research may be government-funded, it's not "government data" because it's not generally held, maintained, or analyzed by government agencies. This category also includes a very different kind of Open Data: the data that can be analyzed from Twitter and other forms of social media.

4 ***Open Government Data That's not Big Data*** Government data doesn't have to be Big Data to be valuable. Modest amounts of data from states, cities, and the federal government can have a major impact when it's released. This kind of data fuels the participatory budgeting movement, where cities around the world invite their residents to look at the city budget and help decide how to spend it. It's also the fuel for apps that help people use city services like public buses or health clinics.

5 ***Open Data—not Big, not from Government*** This includes the private-sector data that companies choose to share for their own purposes—for example, to satisfy their potential investors or to enhance their reputations. Environmental, social, and governance (ESG) metrics fall here. In addition, reputational data, such as data from consumer complaints, is highly relevant to business and government and falls in this category.

6 ***Big, Open, Government Data (the trifecta)*** These datasets may have the most impact of any category. Government agencies have the capacity and funds to gather very large amounts of data, and making those datasets open can have major economic benefits. National weather data and GPS data are the most often-cited examples. U.S. Census data and data collected by the Securities and Exchange Commission and the Department of Health and Human Services are others.

The Age of Data-as-a-Utility

I know it sounds strange, but public and private customers are starting to think of data as a *utility*. Yes, *that* kind of utility: gas, water, electricity. Something they turn on with the press of a button or the flick of a switch. In this case, the ability to ask an ad hoc question and get an immediate answer. They don't particularly care where it comes from, as long as it's on when they want it and delivered without glitches.

The age of data-as-a-utility has arrived in the public sector, and it's the long-awaited platform fusion of a wide variety of government data programs, including open data, big data projects, and internal data sharing, which will dramatically accelerate the shift to high-performance, high-efficiency, and high-return government on nearly every continent. It's a transformative moment for data.

In the past, governments have turned water, electricity, and transportation into utilities, and now its data's turn. So, going forward, you can expect to see governments of all sizes using an abundance of data to create economic prosperity for the people they serve, to create new opportunities academically for children, to create safer, more livable cities—and to create a better standard of living for everybody.

Living Long and Prospering with Data

> The biggest barrier to innovation in digital engagement is not technology, but culture and lack of imagination.
>
> (Turnbull, 2013)

So what is it going to take going forward? Government agencies have been working according to predictable command-and-control structures and processes for years at the sacrifice of initiative and performance. The younger generations are more comfortable with the new ways of engaging and the adaptability required to respond to changing markets and citizens. Transformation in government should be an ongoing process.

Transformational leaders must be flexible and organizations agile enough to accept this truism. Information is a government, not a departmental asset designed to be used as a utility. Everyone involved in back office functions (including the CIO) needs to start thinking and acting more like enterprise leaders, providing value within the context of the bigger picture rather than focusing on the day-to-day technical challenges that they have typically been concerned with.

A number of obstacles need to be overcome for transformation to occur. The central agencies of government need to loosen their detailed reporting requirements while maintaining a balance between central oversight and initiative. Department and agency heads are typically appointed based on their background in government, policy work, and connections. Once they are appointed, leaders often do not serve long enough to see real change implemented. Tenures are short and depend often on parties in power; leaders tend to focus on policy reform rather than process reform.

And finally many operations are under scrutiny by organizations with conflicting agendas—including opposition parties, auditors and regulators, the public, watchdog groups, and the news media. The transformational leader will have to overcome outmoded government structures and old management styles to empower public servants to self-direct, make decisions, experiment, generate ideas, and take risks. Individuals and teams should be rewarded for outstanding performance. This fosters a sense of pride and ownership and focuses more on leadership than on management.

Throughout federal government departments and agencies, there are examples of significant performance improvements. The vision of transformation is continually being defined and recognized as one that will be in a perpetual state of flux, and forays down the path to making strategic vision a reality will be many and varied. Effective use of big data, open data, and open government will align objectives with the capacity for better outcomes. The good news is that the technology is available, and movement has begun toward implementing a comprehensive and effective strategy.

Workforce Analytics: Data-Driven Human Capital Management

Anita Blair

> The time to make up your mind about people is never.
>
> —Philip Barry

Of all resources, the hardest to manage is human resources. People are an organization's most valuable and precious asset: the source of invention, improvement, judgment, and wisdom. People are also costly and difficult to control. They think and do what they want. They come and go wherever and whenever they please. They require maintenance and don't last forever.

What if we could minimize the risks and costs and maximize the benefits of working with people by changing the way we manage human resources? About 30 years ago, the invention of inventory management systems revolutionized stock keeping. This not only freed human clerks from the drudgery of sticking prices on cans but also enabled businesses to track and use inventory data to improve products and profits. Later, the development of supply-chain management revolutionized logistics, which saved time, freed space, opened markets, and provided the foundation for today's worldwide online economy.

Suppose we could apply similar techniques to analyze large amounts of data about people and use that knowledge to enable people to do their jobs better, drive innovation, and use their talents to the fullest? That is the promise of workforce analytics (using data to make decisions about managing people), which is not a new practice. What is new in the 21st-century is the emergence of sophisticated tools to acquire and manipulate immense amounts of data.

A simple definition of workforce analytics (sometimes called Human Resources or "HR" analytics) is "an evidence-based approach for improving individual and organizational performance by making better decisions on the people side of the business" (Bassi, 2011, p. 16). Workforce analytics is also defined as "an advanced set of data analysis tools and metrics for comprehensive workforce performance measurement and improvement" (Gartner, n.d.).

Traditional HR data fields typically included basic personal, pay, and benefits information along with job history—sufficient to attract and track employees but not adequate to manage talent development or enhance performance. Modern technology enables us to gather and analyze almost unlimited amounts of information about people, including their skills, talents, personality traits, preferences, perceptions, opinions, and personal networks. Analyzing such data can help us optimize the ways we recruit, develop, assign, evaluate, and reward individual employees, as well as the ways we build, manage, and motivate workforces.

Strategic human capital management is important to all employers, including, perhaps especially, public sector organizations. Government agencies predominantly provide services, which means that people are among agencies' most valuable—and costly—assets. An agency's mission and budget performance directly depends on how well the agency manages people.

Managing the federal workforce more efficiently could save, or at least avoid wasting, a lot of money. The federal government in 2017 employs an estimated 4.1 million people, including about 2.1 million civilians in the executive branch, about 1.4 million in the uniformed military, and roughly 630,000 in the Postal Service and the Legislative and Judicial branches. Personnel compensation and benefits in 2017 are estimated at $337 billion for civilians and $146 billion for military personnel, with an additional $100 billion for civilian and $69 billion for military retirement pay and benefits—totaling about two-thirds of a trillion dollars in a four trillion dollar budget (Office of Management and Budget, 2016).

These are large numbers, but no one can truly say whether they are too large, or too small, or just right. With the right data and tools, workforce analytics could help determine whether the federal workforce is at the right size and cost for the federal government's mission. Applying workforce analytics could help identify ways to optimize the productivity of the federal workforce, perhaps by investing in training and development or by better matching investment levels to work priorities. With advances in social science research techniques, workforce analytics can help leaders and managers discern how to motivate workers to become more agile, adaptable, and flexible, as 21st-century challenges require.

Background: From 1990 to Now

Starting in the 1960s, inventory and supply chain management systems took decades to evolve, tracking improvements in computer power, memory, and data management. It is reasonable to expect workforce analytics to develop more quickly than earlier resource management systems did. Maintaining accurate, secure, reliable, current information about people, however, is a much greater challenge than doing the same for inventory. Today, we are closer to the beginning than the end of the evolution of workforce analytics.

Around 1990, the PeopleSoft system was introduced as the first major integrated web-based HR management system, part of a package of financial management and supply chain management systems (Oracle, n.d.). As recounted by analyst Josh Bersin, early HR analytics systems were intended to serve as single systems of record for multiple sets of HR data. In the 1990s, vendors such as PeopleSoft offered products to address this need, but these "didn't sell very well because companies had such complex HR systems they didn't have the budget or IT support to build the HR data warehouse" (Bersin, 2015).

At about the same time, in the federal sector, Congress enacted the Government Performance and Results Act (GPRA) (1993). GPRA represented the first time that Congress imposed statutory requirements on most agencies to set goals and measure performance and report to Congress on their plans and results. GPRA established a foundation for results-oriented planning, measurement, and reporting, but agencies encountered challenges in implementation. The Government Accountability Office (GAO) found that, among other things, "in certain areas, federal managers continue[d] to have difficulty setting outcome-oriented goals, collecting useful data on results, and linking institutional, program, unit, and individual performance measurement and reward systems" (2004, p. 1).

Both private and public sectors exhibited a strong appetite for workforce analytics—data-based decision-making for HR management and employee performance—for some time before the necessary technology and tools became available. Bersin describes "a shift in the market" around 2011, when "Big Data" and "predictive people analytics" began to take hold (2015).

Also in 2011, the GPRA Modernization Act (GPRAMA) took effect (GPRAMA of 2010). It mandated data-driven reviews by agencies on progress toward key performance goals and required agencies to ensure the accuracy and reliability of performance data (GAO, 2015, pp. 9-10). More recently, the Digital Accountability and Transparency Act of 2014 (DATA Act), promises to expand "the quality and availability of federal spending data [which] will better enable federal program managers to make data-driven decisions about how they use government resources to meet agency goals" (GAO, 2014, p. 10).

Since 2001, strategic human capital management has been designated by GAO as a government-wide, high-risk area. According to GAO (*Human Capital*, 2015), "strategic human capital management plays a critical role in maximizing the government's performance and assuring its accountability to Congress and to the nation as a whole. However, the federal government is facing workforce-related challenges that could affect the ability of agencies to cost-effectively carry out their missions" (p. 1). With continuing developments in technology and data management supporting the mandates of GPRAMA (2010) and the DATA Act (2014), federal agencies at last can begin to diagnose root causes and design effective solutions for long-standing human capital management problems through the use of use workforce analytics.

How Workforce Analytics Can Improve Public Sector Management

Workforce analytics operates at two levels to improve agency human capital management. First, workforce analytics can help assess the performance of the human capital management function itself. For example, time-to-hire and manager/applicant satisfaction data reveal whether the HR office is operating efficiently and effectively in filling positions. To comply with laws governing merit system principles (*e.g.*, 5 U.S.C. §§ 2301-2302), public sector HR functions must master and apply more complex employment rules than the private sector, making HR performance a significant factor in contributing to, or hindering, agency performance.

Second, workforce analytics can inform and support program decisions about how to improve management and performance of the workforce generally. For example, surveys of employee perceptions and attitudes, such as the Federal

Employee Viewpoint Survey (FEVS) (OPM, 2015), produce data that help managers address disincentives and improve employee engagement for better performance. The Office of Management and Budget (OMB) now requires federal agencies to review and analyze FEVS results and other human capital data as a basis for planning and action to promote employee engagement (Donovan, Corbert, Archuleta & McLaughlin, 2014).

In addition to general and HR-specific management perspectives, workforce analytics can provide both current and predictive management information and decision support. A key step in workforce planning is to analyze data about the workforce to assess the degree to which the current workforce meets, exceeds, or falls short of providing the capabilities required for the mission. Analytical tools such as data tabulations and visualizations describe current employee and workforce characteristics, performance, costs, and other conditions of interest to management. In addition, modern analytical tools can produce predictive models or logarithms to help understand and influence future human and system performance, behavior, and trends.

The types of data that feed workforce analytics tend to be wide-ranging, complex, dynamic, and challenging to secure and manage. Rear Admiral Grace Hopper, a 20th-century pioneer in computer programming and data processing, wrote:

> The application of systems techniques … meets difficulty when it is applied in social and political situations largely because people are not "well-behaved" mathematical functions, but can only be represented by statistical approximations, and all of the extremes can and do occur.
>
> (Hopper, 1976/2015)

HR has lagged behind finance and IT in its ability to make practical use of analytics tools. The HR community itself has not systematically developed computer and analytical capabilities among HR specialists. As a result, some question whether "HR" should be involved in workforce analytics. A recent essay concluded:

> HR analytics needs to evolve and transcend HR (as other functions' analytics will need to transcend their own functional boundaries), and will only become relevant when it takes an "outside in" approach, and is taken out of HR and integrated in existing end-to-end business analytics.
>
> (Rasmussen & Ulrich, 2015, p. 236)

Federal personnel regulations are substantially different from private sector rules, and they pervasively affect the management of federal employees and related resources. For workforce analytics to be useful and productive for the federal government, the federal HR function must participate in or lead the development, design, and use of HR analytics. Supporting this view, the GPRA Modernization Act of 2010 specifies roles and responsibilities for the Office of Personnel Management and agency Chief Human Capital Officers in adopting data-driven planning and performance evaluation relating to human capital management in the federal government (31 U.S.C. § 1115).

Next Steps

Successful adoption of workforce analytics will require coordination among all elements of federal resource management, including IT, Finance, Acquisition, and HR/Human Capital. In simple terms, each of these management officers has both an individual and a joint role in providing workforce analytics capability for the organization. As the subject-matter expert and customer, the HR/Human Capital Officer (CHCO) establishes the functional system requirements. The Chief Information Officer (CIO) translates the functional requirements into technical requirements. The Acquisition or Procurement officer (CAO) identifies the best sources and methods to purchase system(s) that will meet functional and technical requirements. The Chief Financial Officer (CFO) must assess how much the organization can afford to invest and continue to support during the lifecycle of the system(s). All of these officers must coordinate with one another regularly throughout the decision and implementation process so they can make informed trade-offs that support the best overall interests of the organization.

Emerging requirements for stronger IT management and governance will drive federal agencies to adopt a joint management approach. At the same time, federal agencies will recognize the need for workforce analytics to develop their workforces, which must maintain specialized competencies to operate under federal sector rules.

The Federal Information Technology Acquisition Reform Act (FITARA) was enacted as part of the National Defense Authorization Act for Fiscal Year 2015. FITARA assigned a significant role to federal agency CIOs in IT management, governance, and oversight processes. FITARA also directed the OMB to assist agencies in developing strategies, methods, and measures to improve IT investment performance.

OMB's memorandum, *Management and Oversight of Federal Information Technology,* defines the roles and relationships for the CIO, CFO, CAO, and CHCO, as well as the Assistant Secretary for Management and the Chief Operating Officer, in managing IT resources and programs. The OMB memorandum also requires agencies to address competency gaps and workforce planning in their IT and IT acquisition workforces, an exercise that will increase demand for workforce analytics capabilities (Donovan, 2015).

HR-related IT systems tend to be large because most organizations want to consolidate smaller HR systems to achieve economies of scale and better access to data. HR IT systems also tend to be complex and difficult to design and implement because of the need to protect privacy and prevent disclosure or misuse of personally identifiable information. Successful deployment of workforce analytics systems, which are fundamentally HR IT systems, will require agency management leads—CIO, CFO, CHCO, and CAO—to collaborate with personnel security, privacy, and records management officers. Some agencies have added specialized data management officers or "Data Stewards" to coordinate technical, privacy, and security issues relating to data across organizations.

Many trends are converging to drive agencies to adopt workforce analytics. Some of the trends include the successful development of other resource management information systems, rising personnel costs, changing missions, and changing technology. Perhaps the most compelling trend is the empowerment of individuals. Only people can transform data into knowledge and knowledge into innovation. Ultimately, the greatest value of workforce analytics is helping organizations create an environment in which people can excel.

Cultivating Resilience: A Modern Day Organizational Imperative

David A. Bray and Charles R. Rath

> In the twenty-first century, building resilience is one of our most urgent social and economic issues because we live in a world that is defined by disruption. Not a month goes by that we don't see some kind of disturbance to the normal flow of life.
>
> —Judith Rodin

This section seeks to demonstrate that:

1 modern public service confronts a rapidly changing external environment that requires organizations to embrace organizational resilience as a strategic imperative.
2 layers of legacy processes and technologies make embracing organizational agility—let alone resiliency to unexpected events—difficult to achieve, yet achieve it we must.
3 achieving resiliency requires public service to rethink how it organizes its human processes, technologies, and other human elements regarding who does what work and how.
4 more specifically: rapidly changing environments, which are to be expected for our foreseeable future, will require new ways of organizing who does what work and how to include bottom-up, more "entrepreneurial-on-the-inside" activities now typically associated with how public service has functioned in the past. This section concludes with a case study from one of the author's own experiences in a public service organization.

Organizational Resilience

Perhaps no buzzword has been bandied about more in the dawn of the 21st century than "resilience." Its presence is found in the strategic plan of nearly every cabinet agency. The mere mention of the word is celebrated, often without the celebrator fully understanding what the term means, much less how it can be applied in the modern bureaucracy.

So—what is resilience, why do we want it, and how do you get it for your organization? Many have tried to provide an authoritative definition of resilience for a variety of different purposes. However, for the sake of this discussion, let's go with Merriam-Webster's (n.d.): *resilience—"an ability to recover from or adjust easily to misfortune or change."*

This concept has gained remarkable traction as a top priority for nations, cities, and governments around the world: we are in the midst of unprecedented global, social, and technological change. These changes are occurring across a number of discrete areas—globalization, climate change, pandemics, increasing cybercrime, artificial intelligence, use of social media, rapidly emerging economies, aging populations, terrorism, and urbanism—just to name a few.

One idea of resiliency that we the authors think is worth highlighting is that of Judith Rodin (2014), head of the Rockefeller Foundation and author of *The Resilience Dividend: Being Strong in a World Where Things Go Wrong*. She states:

> In the twenty-first century, building resilience is one of our most urgent social and economic issues because we live in a world that is defined by disruption. Not a month goes by that we don't see some kind of disturbance to the normal flow of life. (p. 4)

Think of resilience as the mechanism by which an individual or organization can deal with a rapidly evolving environment. Thus, a resilient organization is one that can quickly adapt, or even thrive, when disrupted. Resilient organizations have the capacity to deal with a multitude of different threats or changes. Doing so requires a modern organization to rethink how it organizes its human processes, technologies, and other human elements regarding who does what work and how—they cannot be burdened by legacy processes, technologies, and other elements more appropriate for the less demanding 19th or 20th centuries. Resilient organizations can quickly embrace change and reconfigure themselves through physical, process, or institutional adaptations. They are proactive, not reactive. When disrupted, they often reemerge stronger than they were before.

Leaders at all levels—which we define as those individuals willing to "step beyond the status quo" of an organization, regardless of whether they have formal authority or not—of resilient organizations have a detailed understanding of how their systems function. Leaders at all levels understand the complex interconnectedness of their human capital, technologies, processes, and external stakeholder environment. They view their organizations' processes, technologies, and related elements akin to a human body—a harmonious balance of cardiovascular, skeletal, respiratory, and cognitive functions. They understand that each subsystem within the organization is dependent on the next and is easily stressed when unbalanced or shocked after trauma. Like good doctors, leaders at all levels can accurately diagnose the root cause of emerging issues and quickly design effective organizational remedies.

Characterizing our Rapidly Changing External Environment

With the definition and value of organizational resilience established, it is worthwhile to characterize the rapidly changing external environment. In 2013, there were the same number of humans as there were network devices globally on the planet: approximately seven billion. By 2015, the number of network devices globally had doubled (fortunately the number of humans had not) to 14 billion.

By 2022, industry estimates predict anywhere between 75 and 300 billion network devices globally (Bray, 2013). That's not linear change, that's exponential change.

Similarly, the amount of global data on the face of the planet is also doubling every two years. In 2013, there were four Zettabytes (4 billion Terabytes—or approximately 400 million Libraries of Congress) of data on the face of the planet. Less than 10 years later, by 2022, estimates are that there will be 96 Zettabytes (9.6 billion Libraries of Congress). This will be more data than all human eyes on the planet see in the course of a year. This is also more data than all spoken conversations the human species ever had with each other in the entirety of human history times two (Bray, 2013).

Over the next decade our world isn't experiencing linear change, it is experiencing exponential disruptive change: change that will challenge traditional notions of what it means to be an organization in either the public or private sector. The very definition of what it means to be a nation and national sovereignty may also be challenged—already we have seen the rise of non-state entities such as anonymous and networked terrorist cells. Even startup companies will be challenged. While startups currently have the advantage of no legacy infrastructure or processes, a successful startup in 2015 will find the world of 2022—just seven years later—dramatically different (March & Simon, 1993).

Such an exponentially changing environment explains in part the current fascination with startups because such organizations don't come with legacy processes and technologies. They can start with a blank slate and design the processes and obtain the technologies they perceive as most needed to be "fit" and thrive in the changing world. At the same time there are some elements of social life that we may not want to begin again with a *tabula rosa*—a blank slate. For example: the court systems, our national defense, even the behind-the-scenes provision of energy, resources, and trade. To stop any of these until a new system could be implemented would be incredibly detrimental to modern society. The public institutions that have developed over the last hundred years are important while at the same time in need of being both updated and being made more resilient to rapid world change.

Such a challenge for those institutions that cannot be treated as startups, to include those that underpin living in a republic with elected leaders, can be equated to attempting to redesign an MD-80 into a modern Boeing 777 while in mid-flight. Everything needs to keep on working while, at the same time, the way things have been working needs to incorporate new processes and technologies (as well as the elimination of outdated legacy processes and technologies) to scale with the external exponential change of our world.

How to Become More Resilient

How can public service organizations overcome such challenges and become more resilient? The answer begins with recognizing that organizations must reject the notion that leaders will have all the answers. The *Harvard Business Review* published an article in 2007 entitled "In Praise of the Incomplete Leader," noting

"It's time to end the myth of the complete leader: the flawless person at the top who's got it all figured out. In fact, the sooner leaders stop trying to be all things to all people, the better off their organizations will be," with the addition that, "the executive's job is no longer to command and control but to cultivate and coordinate the actions of others at all levels of the organization" (Ancona, Malone, Orlikowski, & Senge, 2007, p. 92).

The first step to increasing organizational resiliency begins with recognizing that leaders at all levels, regardless of whether they have formal authority or not in their roles, will be incomplete and will have "blind spots" in what they know or perceive.

The second step is to understand that leaders need to cultivate a culture that embraces change. Processes need to be created with the sole purpose of identifying future conditions, to include disruptive scenarios, technological advancements, and changing demographics. Leaders need to elicit this information from throughout the organization—recognizing that many times ideas from the "bottom-up" are best and a healthy "creative friction" is an attribute worth commending. Further, mechanisms need to be established to communicate these insights to the public—namely, external oversight organizations responsible for creating the administrative flexibility necessary to be adaptive.

The third step requires leaders to create cognitively diverse networks, within their organizations as well as outside their organizations, to compensate for the fact that they will have blind spots. Work by Thomas Malone and others at the MIT Center for Collective Intelligence have produced experiences that show a diverse set of participants will produce better decision outcomes (Bray, 2007). Expertise, while helpful in cultivating in-depth knowledge of a subject, also includes certain heuristics and lenses for making sense of the world. These heuristics and lenses can help reach insights yet also become blind spots themselves. This is why crowdsource can produce innovations better than one set of experts because of the diversity of heuristics and lenses for making sense of the world brought to bear on a topic.

The fourth step is to provide autonomy within a public service organization to "change agents" at all levels to help improve the organization. Note this is not a prescription for anarchy or chaos, but rather a recognition that each worker in the organization will have topics and issues that they will know and understand better than anyone else. If their topic changes or has a disruption, they will be the best equipped to spot these changes and raise an alert to respond to a positive or negative event.

Command and control are ineffective in managing knowledge in rapidly changing environments because they decrease a hierarchical organization's ability to maintain accuracy with its outside environment. This pivots the role of managers in a hierarchy into that of cultivators scanning for worthwhile insights to champion further up in the hierarchy should they arise. One might even think of employees as "change agents" operating akin to individual startups within the organization, making pitches to their manager or boss similar to a "venture capital" pitch, should the employee see a way to do something better, more cost effectively, or with results improved over existing outcomes.

These four steps together improve not only a public service organization's resiliency but also organizational agility. In 1991, prominent organizational scientist James G. March published a paper entitled "Exploration and Exploitation in Organizational Learning." He noted the tension between an organization's continuing to exploit what it had learned was beneficial and successful vs. an organization's exploring what might be a new beneficial way of being even more successful relative to a changing external reality. When faced with a changing environment, organizations that exploited doing what they had learned was previously beneficial quickly lost relevance with external reality. This is a real risk for public service in our exponentially changing world (March, 1991).

In contrast, those organizations that explored a new and beneficial way of being even more successful relative to a changing external reality obtained, through probabilistic searching, new ways of being even more relevant to more closely "match" external reality. Subsequent research by Bray and Prietula in 2007 showed that as an organization added more tiers to its organizational hierarchy, the loss of relevancy with a changing external reality was amplified if it focused on "top down" exploitation vs. exploration of new ideas. Focusing on "bottom up" exploration vs. exploitation improved its ability to more closely "match" external reality (Bray & Prietula, 2007).

The combined results of this research clearly show that public service going forward cannot be top down and still maintain relevancy with our changing world. While it cannot be flat, given the sheer scope and scale of everything public service includes, it can encourage "bottom up" exploration of new ways of working, collaborating, and delivering results to the public in an exponentially changing world.

Putting These Principles into Actual Practice

Lest this sound theoretical—these ideas to improve organizational resiliency have been successful put into motion with transformative results. Imagine, for a moment, being faced with these challenges and tasks while taking over the CIO role for a large government agency:

- You've inherited several legacy systems and many more business processes.
- You want to inspire your IT team to overhaul the aging systems, and you want to inspire the different programmatic bureaus and offices to simplify processes.
- You know a lot of history has preceded your arrival and that it will be important to listen and learn while also working to encourage a "think different" mindset about the agency's technology.
- You want all of your co-workers to know you're open to thinking outside the box while encouraging them to do the same.

Faced with these challenges, what would you say? How would you get your message across? One of the authors of this section found himself in this position 18 months ago, he when took over the chief information officer role for a national public service organization. In the eight years prior, there had been nine CIOs, either in a permanent or acting capacity. There had been sporadic efforts at change in the past that had not lasted. Staff morale was not at its highest. In order to be successful as a senior executive, the author was going to need to be more than a champion of change. The author was going to have to cultivate a network of change agents.

When he showed up at this organization, one of the first talks he gave to both the IT team and the broader organization as a whole was about the need for experimentation. He explained that "expertise" and "experiment" have the same root, meaning "out of danger." This is critical, because in order to gain expertise and keep up with the changes in our world, we're going to have to conduct experiments. Experiments by their nature are dangerousthey're risky, not every experiment will work, yet in a rapidly changing world, that's the only way for us to adapt and learn. Thus, it's important to create a space in which it's okay to experiment and learn how to adapt.

To get employees comfortable with doing more experiments, he told employees he was creating a safe space where they could feel comfortable bringing their ideas forward. The initial reaction was mixed. At first, maybe about 10 to 15% got it. Another 40% were on the fence, with a neutral mindset of: "That sounds nice, but we don't know if we see ourselves as being that proactive about change." Another 40% raised contrarian concerns akin to: "Well, wait. If we take risks and fail, will that hurt our careers? Why should we do anything more than the status quo? We don't want to jeopardize our jobs." That said, he expected that initially his proposal would be met with skepticism—it's healthy to a degree. There are times when some executives say they want change, yet really don't want to support risk takers. He needed to show the team he meant what he said.

So he worked with 10 or 15% of early adopters initially through lunches or at after-work happy hours, and the coalition of the willing grew to more like 35 to 40%. Even now, the network of positive "change agents" isn't the majority, and it might not ever become the majority, but that's okay. It's now grown as large as, if not larger than, the skeptics. And that's a good sign that the transformation movement has reached a tipping point and the "change agents" are sufficient in number to improve the organizational resiliency of the public service organization.

A Diversity of Views Including Skeptics Welcomed

Today's reality is that modern organizations have to do two things: One, they have to keep the lights on and hire people who are attracted to that consistent, repeatable work. Two, modern organizations must do the complete opposite, namely dramatically adapt to the exponential changes in our globalized world. To do that, organizations often need to attract a totally different personality than those who like to keep the trains running. A goal of any executive should be to recognize and reward both types of people—as a real-time evolving organization needs both.

Your organizational partners may have a diversity of views and differ on where things need to go, and that's actually okay. Diversity, to include skeptics, leads to better outcomes and avoids the risks of group think. Our rapidly changing world requires a diversity of perspectives on the changing organizational and global technology landscapes to then improve organizational resiliency.

Improving Organizational Resiliency by Encouraging Internal Risk Taking

It's interesting that we reward Silicon Valley for taking risks that might not always work out—including some that will fail to become a successful public offering. We have to do this to adapt to our rapidly changing world, particularly where technology capabilities in terms of speed and volume are growing exponentially. Risk taking is central to what entrepreneurs do, and they do so with resiliency. Yet within established businesses and within public service organizations, if we try that same model of experiments—then sometimes there can be a stigma for being an "intrapreneur," or entrepreneur on the inside, because you have to be a good steward of either your company's profits or a good steward of your taxpayers' dollars. We're not advocating for folks to go forth without a plan or do things without intentionality. Instead, we're saying our exponential era of change does not come with an existing textbook that shows us the way to go: in established businesses and within public service organizations, we're going to have to experiment to improve organizational resiliency to our rapidly changing world.

In addition, we need to recognize the important distinction between leadership and management. When you lead you intentionally step outside of the expectations of others—be it your boss, peers, reports, the Congress, the presidential administration, or the public. The root of the word leadership means "to send unto death," meaning that leaders confront friction and will need to manage it to avoid dying. Leaders in organizations will need to take the kind of bold action that risks the alienation of some of their workforce (Bray, 2013).

As aforementioned, to improve organizational resiliency, leaders at all levels must recognize they will be incomplete and will have "blind spots" in what they know or perceive. Second, leaders at all levels need to cultivate cognitively diverse networks, both within and outside of their organizations. Finally, organizational leaders must provide autonomy within a public service organization to "change agents" at all levels to help improve the organization. Such actions will improve organizational resiliency for our exponential era ahead.

Do's and Don'ts of Social Media in the Federal Government

Kim Mosser Knapp

> In the old days men had the rack. Now they have the Press.
>
> —Oscar Wilde

Back in the days before electrons took the place of ink as the primary way to communicate, Oscar Wilde knew that the press (or media) could ruin someone. Wilde would have found this to be even more relevant in today's world of social media, which has greatly expanded the options for public communication and the potential for use/misuse of that media.

This essay will briefly explore the current state of social media use in the federal government and will include three main messages:

- "Social media" is a set of tools in a communications expert's toolbox. This set of tools is not a replacement for traditional media management.
- Different platforms have different audiences and different rules of the road. Learn them.
- Real life lessons, learned the hard way, provide practical tips for social media managers.

Current State of Social Media

In 1995, 35 million people used the Internet, and 80 million people had mobile phones. By 2014, Internet usage had exploded to 2.8 billion people, almost 40% of the world's population, and 5.2 billion mobile phone users, 73% of the world's population (Meeker, 2015).

These twin communication platforms have led to an enormous increase in content controllers—the modern-day equivalent of ink barrels and printing presses—such as Yahoo (1995), Google (1998), Facebook (2003), Twitter (2006), YouTube (2007), Instagram (2011), Snapchat (2011), and Chromecast (2014).

The largest impact of this social media revolution has been on consumers, but it has been embraced by businesses, education, healthcare, and the security/safety worlds. By all accounts, however, the major sector that has been lagging behind is government (Meeker, 2015).

The National Academy of Public Administration's (NAPA) (2015) *Federal Leaders Digital Insight Study* provides some clues about why social media has not yet taken a strong foothold in the federal government. "The findings reveal a number of challenges, including concerns that the government cannot keep pace with the rate of technological advances and the perception … that the private sector procures and adopts technologies more effectively" (p. 12).

In addition, federal workers balked at being on call 24/7 by being tethered to their "crackberries," which is perhaps a reflection of the generational differences among Millennials, Gen-Xers, and Baby Boomers. Overall, the study contained no surprises for anyone who has worked in a federal agency's media shop, which is typically dominated by federal employees who are more comfortable with print, radio, and television media than emerging social media.

But there is evidence that social media is being used in surprising ways in the federal government. Terrorists have been given credit for being social media experts who can lure new recruits through social media outlets, but the U.S. intelligence community has been quietly combatting these efforts, with some success. Javier Lesaca (2015) notes that the State Department has published more than 300 YouTube videos "that counter the violent and extremist messages of radical jihadist groups," including a video of the daring 2015 U.S. Delta Force rescue of 70 Kurdish prisoners, receiving 120,000 views (para. 5).

What's in Your Toolbox?

Communications experts have long used press releases, reporter interviews, press conferences, and newsletters to share ideas and messages. Social media—primarily Facebook and Twitter, but there are some newcomers to the field that may or may not stick around—made it easier to go directly to constituents rather than filter through traditional media. Social media offers a way to amplify messages, get around traditional media, build a brand, connect with constituents, and conduct 'rapid response' (getting a message out quickly during a crisis). Constituents couldn't sign up to receive press releases—but now they can subscribe to an agency's social media feeds for a direct connection to that office.

Overall, this is a good thing. However, because taxpayers have direct access, they expect direct answers. You should try to answer respectful questions on Facebook and Twitter when you can. Don't get into debates with folks online, though. What you write is there forever, and it's not worth getting hot and bothered via the Internet.

While the government values the access social media gives us to the public, it is not a replacement for traditional media management. It's critical to have that skill even in today's tech-obsessed world. Some offices have a group of staff to work with the media and other staff to do social media. For example, in a large-scale media shop at a federal agency, there will be at least one dedicated "press secretary" to answer reporter inquiries quickly and accurately, pitch stories to editors and writers, book television interviews, and speak "on background" to the media. This is a craft that takes years of experience, relationship building, and discipline to "do well." A good press secretary will know what different reporters are likely to cover, how to protect his or her boss from leading questions during an interview, and understand the difference between "not for attribution" and "off the record."

The press secretary's role is critical to ensuring the media has a good impression of the agency. However, that person may not even know how to sign in to Twitter or what a hashtag is. That's where a "social media manager" comes in. This is usually a youngish, in-the-know person who understands the subtle differences among social platforms and the best way to tell if the message is getting through. However, the social media manager may not have the reporter contacts a senior press secretary might.

A particularly large operation—for example the department-wide press shop at one of the cabinet agencies or the Speaker's Office in the House of Representatives—might have someone dedicated to creating videos or just writing opinion pieces and speeches. But there are countless other press operations across the government that do not have staff dedicated to each communications function—so it pays to be good at the old fashioned press relations and the new media.

Picking Platforms

While there are dozens of social media tools available today—and some agencies try valiantly to adopt a new platform once in a while but inevitably give up—the government uses two primary "social networking" platforms to share content:

Facebook and Twitter. YouTube and Flickr are used heavily as repositories for video and photo content, but few constituents actually go directly to the site for information. They find YouTube videos and Flickr pics through Facebook and Twitter feeds.

This boils down to the fact that the public is not looking for content from the government on some of the smaller, niche platforms, but Facebook and Twitter have staying power, and nearly all government offices use them. Facebook is a conversation tool. Think of it as a real-life focus group or family conversation. Your goal is to get people to comment, share, react, converse. Families like to share pictures and stories. Make sure your pictures are appropriate, your boss looks good, and include a diverse group of people when possible, and you won't get anyone in trouble.

Supporters (and detractors) love to engage on Facebook. But they want to hear back from you. Set aside time each week to answer Facebook comments (and delete the profane ones).

Few reporters use Facebook for their jobs. They tweet. And they follow what agencies are tweeting. Twitter is a tool to reach people quickly and give them topline information. Example: "Senator Sanchez to host job fair Oct 10." Or "Breaking: Secretary Brown appoints war hero as chief of staff." Always link to more information in your tweet. Tweeting is also a great way to get information out in an emergency or crisis.

Getting from Good to Great with Social Media

The name of the game is numbers. How many Facebook likes do you have? How many Twitter followers? The more you have, the broader your message is shared. How can you get more, more, MORE!? You can do it organically or with your budget. Building an organic audience is hard. You have to be edgy (which is the exact opposite of what most federal agencies want to be), have the right mix of content, encourage debate, and generally be interesting 24/7. This is hard unless you're: (a) involved in a scandal or (b) likely to end up in a scandal. Advice: Don't end up in a scandal. Every federal agency media shop lives by the maxim: "Don't show up on the front page of the *Washington Post*."

A commonly used practice is to experiment with content and hashtags to see what gets the best engagement. How many shares and likes and comments are posts getting? Whatever is getting the most—do more of that (this is an art, not a science). SHORT videos are good. Music is good. Humor is good when appropriate. "Behind the scenes" is good. Kids, pets, food, smiling, laughing, veterans—all good.

What's bad: heavy text, run on sentences, and broken links. Post at least twice (preferably three times) a day. Strive for a good mix of playful, informative, and engaging. Keep your pictures fresh—change profile pictures weekly.

Agencies can also run ads on Facebook or Google to drive web traffic to a site or to announce an initiative. These ads are incredibly effective, but since taxpayer dollars are used they should be used judiciously. For example, in the House of Representatives, there are very strict rules about what messages you can spend money on. (Consult the Franking Commission with the House Committee on Administration for more info http://cha.house.gov/franking-commission.) But agencies do use ads, for example for recruitment by the armed forces or by the Veterans Administration to reach veterans and inform them about new benefits (Next Gov, 2013).

Tracking progress is critical. Measure "likes" and "follows" every month, and set goals by quarter and year. However, social engagement is more important than pure likes and follows. Reach out to the Facebook and Twitter government offices in Washington to help build your engagement numbers. They can also help set realistic goals for you.

Trending

The NAPA (2015) study points to the problem of information overload when it comes to new social media. The federal government is inherently conservative and adverse to change, so the rapidly evolving social media landscape can be daunting. What follows is a short description of some new tools that are trending and could be used by federal agencies.

- ***Instagram*** Purely promotional tool to share pictures of the softer side of agencies or document important moments. Not good for detailed information sharing. No room for discussion beyond comment feature, but great to build a brand or an image.
- ***Snapchat*** Fun way to share snippets of information or tease bigger news coming. Not for disseminating real information. Snapchat is booming in the campaign business right now.
- ***Google+*** We had high hopes for this, but it turned out to be a poor man's Facebook/Twitter hybrid that no one really checks or updates with regularity.
- ***LinkedIn*** Professional networking site that can help government professionals find each other to collaborate, but the business-to-consumer application hasn't really translated. Not being used with frequency to communicate with the public.

Other Tips

The unthinkable happens with great frequency: hitting "reply all" when the message was intended for only one person; disclosing classified or sensitive information in a press release; or some other public relations disaster. The following are some tips that can help avoid disaster at a time when response times are shortening and the scrutiny of agencies is increasing.

Proof Thrice, Post Once

Always have at *least* another set of eyes look at your post for grammar, content, and context. If possible, have someone with a political background review pictures to avoid embarrassing situations. Being tone deaf to public perceptions is what led Government Services Agency employees to stage an extravaganza in Las Vegas and for one senior executive to post a picture on his Facebook page sipping wine in a Jacuzzi.

Many times, however, trouble comes after purely innocent circumstances that could have been avoided with a bit more proofing and vetting. For example, your boss is at an event and you have great pictures of her at a ribbon cutting for a new public housing project, but behind is a toddler pulling his pants down. Or you have a great action shot to post of your boss from his career before government, but unfortunately his ex-wife is to his left. Ouch!

Always have policy experts review and fact check any official information you provide. Social media is typically executed by a communications person—not the legislative or policy expert. Sometimes a mistake is made and can be fixed quickly, but more frequently in our digital age, it's captured and recorded forever. Sites like Politwoops, for example, record every tweet you delete. This is a communications professional's worst nightmare, but the chances of disaster striking are increasing just as exponentially as the many social media apps and outlets.

When at all Possible, Keep Accounts Very Separate

Don't log in to personal accounts from official equipment. Aside from being frowned upon by the government, you run a high risk of posting something personal to an official account. I once published an invitation to a summer BBQ to my boss's official Facebook. #awkward. To keep it idiot proof, just don't toggle back between any of your official and personal accounts. It's a recipe for disaster.

Speaking of Disasters

If your boss is known for impulse tweets, don't give him/her access to the accounts. It's for his/her own good!

About Passwords

Keep them private. Don't share with more than three trusted staffers, and change them every three months. Never give to interns, who are just loaded guns waiting to go off.

Avoid the Crazies

There are some crazy people out there. Turn off geotagging when you're posting so the public doesn't know where you or your boss is. Or wait to post until you've left a location.

And, finally, don't forget to regularly update your Wikipedia page!

The Entrepreneurial Species within the Federal Government Innovation Ecosystem

Avery Sen

> Innovation is not an individual activity; it is a collective achievement.
>
> —Andrew H. Van de Ven

The key to innovation is organizing well. Our most wicked problems—from climate change to cancer—require people from different disciplines to work better together, and to navigate through diverse institutional norms. Simple problems require experts, but complex ones require teams and therefore team leaders. The entrepreneur is that leader: the captain of the ship, conductor of the orchestra. He or she is the person who drives innovation, and the organization is what is being driven.

An entrepreneur often draws power from being an outsider: one who has not been inculcated by conventional wisdom (Baumol, 2004) and can align multiple forces and bring them to bear on a single strategic focus. Hwang and Horowitt (2012) liken the entrepreneur to a keystone species within an ecosystem: he or she keeps things connected, actively bridging social distances and reducing the transaction costs within a system of innovation.

The innovation ecosystem in the U.S. federal government is uniquely complex, and the entrepreneurial species faces unique difficulties. There could be more entrepreneurs (or "intrapreneurs") within government than there are. Per the Partnership for Public Service's analysis of Federal Employee Viewpoint Survey (2015), "employees do not feel empowered in their work and are not being recognized for their efforts" (p. 2). The government's innovation score is 58.9 out of 100 in 2014, down 4.4 points since 2010. More specifically:

- 89.8% reported they are constantly looking for ways to do their jobs better; however,
- 54.1% reported they feel encouraged to come up with new ways to do their work,
- 42.5% reported they are recognized for providing high quality products and services, and
- 32.7% reported they believe creativity and innovation are rewarded in their organization.

These numbers trail comparable data from surveys of workers in the private sector by between 8 and 14 points, depending on the question.

Government institutions must be stable to fulfil their purpose in society, but, as in any system, a lack of flexibility can mean the difference between resilience and fragility. This section will explore two questions: why is it relatively difficult to be a change agent within government, and are there ways to make the institutions of government more accepting of innovation?

Organizational Challenges

It is difficult to innovate in any large organization (Mote, Jordan, Hage, Hadden, & Clark, 2015). As the diversity of expertise grows, so do the barriers to coordinating innovative work (Hollingsworth & Hollingsworth, 2011; Page, 2007). Bureaucracies function to standardize and stabilize organizational activity. And the federal government's executive branch is one of the largest bureaucracies of all. In the postwar period, the federal government grew dramatically in terms of budget, number of units, and number of missions. The number of federal employees has stayed relatively stable, but there are ever more contractors—though even the U.S. Congressional Budget Office (2015) cannot say how many.

In addition to sheer size and complexity, the context for innovation in government differs from the private sector in terms of the multiple professional and epistemological commitments of executive leadership. It is not uncommon for a non-government entrepreneur to have an MBA and experience in a number of different companies. This person would find that most others in his or her network—funders, partners, competitors, etc.—would share similar values and vocabulary as managers of private enterprise. However, this is not the case in government.

Within government, the entrepreneur may have a history in business administration or public policy or political science or law, while his or her colleagues have histories in one of the others or something else entirely. The professional perspectives and experiences that underlie leadership and that legitimate decisions are broader than those rooted in the management disciplines, and so the task of mobilizing diverse interests is harder.

Indeed, the proportion of executives operating from a political versus an administrative perspective is increasing. The number of senior positions in the U.S. government's executive branch filled by political appointees—rather than career civil servants—is more than any other industrial democracy (Vedantam, 2008) and has grown twice as fast as the government itself since the 1960s (Lewis, 2008). Performance, strategy, and finance matter, but so do power, personality, and ideology.

Rosenbloom (1983) distilled the different perspectives operating in government to three: the managerial (concerned with effectiveness, efficiency, and economy); the political (concerned with representativeness, responsiveness, and accountability), and the legal (concerned with procedures, rights, and fairness). These three perspectives are rooted in the shared authority of the three branches of government (executive, legislative, and judicial) and reflect the organizational structures and cognitive patterns unique to each (Rosenbloom, 2013).

Moreover, there are often highly stable constellations of power and influence that combine these perspectives on particular issues. Lowi (1979) described "iron triangles" made of interest groups, congressional committees, and agency bureaucracies. No one party is controlling the whole system, yet all parties want more money and the status quo to continue. As a result, government programs never go away; all of the pieces are allowed to grow.

The American public bureaucracy is, according to Moe (1990) "an organizational mess." Even within single agencies, diverse, technocratic expertise results in, as Kingdon (1984) describes it, "organizational anarchy," wherein "members have only fragmentary and rudimentary understandings of why they are doing what they are doing and how their jobs fit into a more general picture of the organization" (p. 84).

The interaction among diverse professional perspectives within the government system is in a perpetual state of transition, so the entrepreneur must remain conceptually flexible. This is, of course, true for every change maker, but especially so for those in the complex social, organizational environment of government. Compared to his or her private sector counterparts, the government entrepreneur must spend less time operating from a rationalist worldview. As Zalmanovitch (2014) puts it, public administration is not "confined to a strict, positivist rigor," but instead "should be treated as an art" (p. 813), that is, in the words of Wildavsky (1980), "the solving of problems that cannot be expressed until they are solved" (p. 15).

To institutionalize innovation in this complex ecosystem we must create habitats for the entrepreneurial species to be productive. Different institutional factors can produce different types and degrees of innovation (OECD, 2005). In the pages to follow, I describe two organizational patterns that have evolved to deal with the need for innovation within the executive branch of the US federal government. The first I call "island+bridge," which emerged over the course of the 20th century and is exemplified by the Defense Advanced Research Projects Agency (DARPA). The second I call "bridge+island," which has emerged in the 21st century and is exemplified by U.S. Digital Services (USDS) and 18F (Shueh, 2015).

These two types of organizations look different on the surface, but underlying both is a transdisciplinary, systems approach to structuring innovation. The first approach gives greater weight to the potential of metaphorical islands, the second to bridges.

Island+Bridge

A common organizational structure for innovation is isolation. Innovators are segregated from normal business operations in a distinct organizational unit that has greater freedom from the bureaucracy. Lockheed Martin's 'Skunkworks' and Xerox's Palo Alto Research Center (PARC) are notable examples. This is the general philosophy underlying any organization's choice to have an R&D division that is distinct from its other business units.

Another common innovation structure is an open network. Rather than conducting all R&D in-house, in one place, an organization may rely on the R&D conducted elsewhere (e.g., at universities or start-up companies). This occurs through licensing agreements or buy outs or, in the public sector, through grants and cooperative agreements. An open model assumes that one does not have to originate ideas in order to benefit from them and that many of the most knowledgeable people work somewhere else (Chesbrough, 2003).

Some structures are isolated and open at the same time. The best example of this is DARPA, which "was formed to address the problem of transformative innovation" during the Cold War because the centralized R&D units of the U.S. Army and Navy had become too focused on fundamental principles and produced innovation that was too incremental (Bonvillian & Van Atta, 2011, p. 470). DARPA is best known for developing the precursor of the Internet and stealth aircraft. Even the interactive graphical user interface, often held up as an example of private-sector innovation, began with DARPA funding (Fong, 2001).

The hybrid open/isolated model works in many contexts. It has been the basis for a number of innovative organizations in the federal sector that were modeled on DARPA, including the Advanced Research Program Agency for Energy (ARPA-E), the Intelligence Advanced Research Projects Activity (IARPA), the Advanced Technology Program (ATP), and In-Q-Tel, a non-federal partner of the Central Intelligence Agency. To better understand the management practices and beliefs underlying such organizations, one of the authors interviewed managers and analyzed strategic and operational guidance at three: DARPA, ARPA-E, and ATP (Sen, 2014).

A summary description of this organizational pattern borrows a metaphor from Bennis and Biederman (1997): an island with a bridge to the mainland (abbreviated here as island+bridge). The island is a refuge for experimentation and failure; the bridge is a conduit for the transfer of knowledge. Island-style work is *deliberately but delicately disruptive*: transforming systems while still working within a system of controls. Managers drive change by orchestrating creative, extramural researchers. Bridge-style work emphasizes *frank and frequent face time*: regular, detailed conversations between managing and performing teams about project progress, resulting in the co-creation of knowledge about technology as it evolves.

These agencies are organizationally separate from the service and the science and divisions of their departments. They are smaller, flatter, and less complex than most other federal institutions. There is little patience with the usual machinery of government. Program environments are brutal and fast-paced, but managers are empowered, not micromanaged. They have "fire in their belly" and are driven to change the world, not to pursue long, stable careers in government. ARPA and ARPA-E benefit from a flexible hiring mechanism, intergovernmental personnel assignments (IPAs), to bring managers on more quickly and off more regularly.

Managers are talented as specialists but more talented as generalists. They create social networks that span government, academia, and industry. Their skills in science are superseded by their skills in coordinating the work of scientists. Managers often play the role of problem solver and facilitator. Where processes cannot be simplified, managers work to navigate the bureaucracy. This was notably the case at ATP, where the bureaucracy was not very flexible, but managers at all three agencies carefully push certain limits while simultaneously working within others. Thus, if a separate chain of command is not feasible for the aspiring transformative agency, there may be other ways to exert freedom.

Unifying island and bridge—at the heart of every project—is an explicit, unambiguous vision statement, accompanied by concrete measures and milestones. Routine, in-person conversations about strategy, execution, and evaluation allow diverse specialists to share semantics and situational awareness. Manager and investigators carefully negotiate and renegotiate visions and metrics. In discussions that cross organizational boundaries, teams articulate problems, consider alternative solutions, agree upon the meaning of success, and share the understanding of whether or not success was reached.

Bridge+Island

Over the course of the Obama administration, a different model to increase innovation has gained popularity across the federal government. Bridge+island is, as the name would suggest, the inverse of island+bridge. Rather than advancing high-risk, high-reward technologies in the interest of specific social and political outcomes, it lays the foundational infrastructure to help a wide range of entrepreneurial clients advance smaller scale innovations. The units that embody bridge+island are not agencies and programs on an organizational chart, but rather places, practices, and people.

The places are what we might generically call "innovation labs"—physical spaces in which the interpersonal work of innovation can take place. These include The Lab at the Office of Personnel Management (GAO, 2014), the Innovation Lab at the U.S. Department of Housing and Urban Development (2015), and the Center for Applied Technology at the U.S. Census Bureau (Ravindranath, 2014). These labs are often venues for collaborative activities, such as hackathons and design workshops, as well as training on project management.

Other efforts go beyond the physical space and operate institutions for shepherding the maturation of new ideas into innovations. The U.S. National Science Foundation's (NSF, 2015) iCorps program provides grant recipients (whose expertise is in science) training and support in Lean Start-Up methodology (Blank, 2013) to facilitate the commercialization of their research results. The U.S. Department of Health and Human Services' (HHS) IDEA Lab is the federal front runner in this domain. It offers entrepreneurs within HHS a comprehensive system of practices such as crowd-based idea generation (often called "ideation"), incubator projects to grow viable business plans around new technologies, competitions for small venture funds, and innovation awards to recognize successes and failures (HHS, 2015).

Bridge+island is also embodied in people, specifically, uniquely talented people brought in from outside of government (often from renowned Silicon Valley technology firms). This was the solution to the healthcare.gov fiasco, and formed the basis for the U.S. Digital Services and 18F (Shueh, 2015), as well as the Presidential Innovation Fellows program (Balutis & Robbins, 2015). Indeed, a defining purpose of bridge+island—whether realized as places, practices, or people—is to bypass the program or manager that is the traditional home for activities in a particular mission domain and, instead, promote the alternative work of "outsiders," such as lower-level employees or rising stars from the private sector.

The assumption is that government institutions, no matter how well intended, ultimately grow inflexible and politically entangled over time, so countermeasures must be built into the organization. This assumption is shared with the island+bridge model, where program managers all serve under IPAs and agency directors short-circuit the chain of command by reporting directly to the Department Secretary. Also like island+bridge, bridge+island focuses on connecting means with ends, that is, inventions to outcomes. It places importance on linking nodes of expertise, on integrating technologies in addition to creating them.

However, there are differences. Island+bridge emphasizes the nodes of an ecosystem. Programs are defined by the particular mission needs of their parent departments, and projects are centered on developing and applying particular technologies. Bridge+island emphasizes the linkages of an ecosystem. Places, practices, and people support innovation projects by focusing on medium, rather than mission.

The bridge+island model specializes in mastering tools for transdisciplinary integration—the means for connecting across professional domains—and then applying these tools to assist change makers in endeavors aimed at various sorts of outcomes.

Such tools are not new (consider written language, mathematics, and the scientific method), but over the last few decades, innovations in information technology and social science have given us new, more powerful tools to improve the organization of innovation itself. These innovation media can be products and processes, the code underlying a new app, and the hackathon at which it was written.

Innovation labs may house coders and designers as well as facilitators of structured methods for ideation and mentors in project management forms. Practices such as Agile (Highsmith & Cockburn, 2001) and Human Centered Design (Brown, 2009) are systematic ways of empathizing with stakeholders, prototyping in multi-disciplinary teams, collecting feedback early and often, and iterating products incrementally and quickly. They combine the workstyle of designers and engineers ("makers" in contemporary vernacular) with social science methods (e.g., ethnography, grounded theory) for collecting and analyzing qualitative data.

The challenge that bridge+island operations face is being able to demonstrate success. Indeed, those from a traditional government bureaucracy perspective are skeptical of this sort of work, given its unorthodox, often playful nature. Recent assessments of innovation labs have focused on the need to develop better metrics (GAO, 2014; Piechowski, 2015). Island+bridge efforts are relentlessly focused on output- and outcome-oriented measures. They do not always succeed, but it is easy to see when they do, and it is easy to see which efforts are or aren't working. This is slightly more difficult for bridge+island efforts, which are further upstream in the value chain, benefiting outputs and outcomes only indirectly.

Conclusion

Those who aim to drive change in the federal government must acknowledge the complexity of the ecosystem in which that change would occur. They should expect to have to navigate and translate among the diversity of professional perspectives particular to administration in the public sector. The change maker would do well to seek out a supportive habitat—one that embodies an island+bridge or bridge+island approach. Alternatively, he or she may seek to establish one where there is an unmet demand, as a springboard for other change makers.

Fair warning to would-be government entrepreneurs: finding and creating these sorts of habitats is not easy. For one thing, institutional infrastructure for innovation is "mission extrinsic" to most agencies (Rosenbloom, 2014). That is, like workforce and capital management, it does not relate directly to a single mission, but indirectly to all missions and is often a second-tier priority. Island+bridge agencies are rare and managerial positions within them exclusive. Bridge+island operations are also still rare, but are multiplying. Those just starting out try to create demand, and so the opportunities to work with them are greater; those more mature will have built demand for their services, and it may be more difficult to work with them.

Furthermore, it is worth noting that any innovation endeavor will inevitably bring political risks for advocates, economic costs for incumbents. As Sapolsky and Taylor (2011) write, "innovation may benefit society, but it has its victims, and these victims fight back" (p. 33). As such, Bonvillian's (2011) advice is that organizations created for innovation must "ensure in program design that there will be a noteworthy political interest constituency" (p. 312).

Finally, the entrepreneur will have to decide upon the nature of his or her work within the federal system. There are many roles to play: civil servant, political appointee, private-sector contractor, not-for-profit advocate, etc. Federal positions can be difficult to obtain, but, once on board, the job security that federal employees enjoy can enable exploration and risk-taking that is not possible in other positions. Those who are not federal employees are, as outsiders, in a unique position to push for change; federal colleagues often rely upon them for an external perspective. Of course, appointees have the advantage of being at the top of a hierarchical bureaucracy and so can issue directives, define expectations, and provide "top-cover" for other change makers.

Whatever his or her role, the entrepreneur should carefully, constantly survey the organizational and political landscape and proceed in the way that best suits his or her situation. To be sure, innovation is not always serendipitous; more often, it is the result of method, not magic. However, following prescribed recipes can only get you so far. Change makers must be able to adjust to changing circumstances and make the rules up as they go along.

References

Ancona, D., Malone, T. W., Orlikowski, W. J., & Senge, P. M. (2007). In praise of the incomplete leader. *Harvard Business Review, 85*(2), 92–100.

Balutis, A. P., & Robbins, S. (2015, November 15). Wish they all could be. *FCW.* Retrieved from https://fcw.com/articles/2015/11/11/balutis-it-talent.aspx.

Barry, P. (1939). *The Philadelphia Story* [Play]. New York, NY: Samuel French.

Bassi, L. (2011). Raging debates in HR analytics. *People & Strategy, 34*(2), 14–18. Retrieved from http://mcbassi.com/wp/resources/pdfs/RagingDebatesInHRAnalytics.pdf.

Baumol, W. J. (2004). Education for innovation: Entrepreneurial breakthroughs vs. corporate incremental improvements. In *NBER Working Paper Series: Vol. 10578*. Cambridge, MA: National Bureau of Economic Research.

Bennis, W. G., & Biederman, P. W. (1997). *Organizing genius: The secrets of creative collaboration.* New York, NY: Basic Books.

Bersin, J. (2015, February 5). The geeks arrive in HR: People analytics is here. *Forbes*. Retrieved from http://www.forbes.com/sites/joshbersin/2015/02/01/geeks-arrive-in-hr-people-analytics-is-here/.

Blank, S. (2013). Why the lean start-up changes everything. *Harvard Business Review, 91*(5). Retrieved from https://hbr.org/2013/05/why-the-lean-start-up-changes-everything.

Bonvillian, W. B. (2011). The problem of political design in federal innovation organization. In J. Lane, K. Fealing, J. Marburger III, & S. Shipp (Eds.), *The science of science policy: A handbook* (pp. 302–326). Palo Alto, CA: Stanford University Press.

Bonvillian, W. B., & Van Atta, R. (2011). ARPA-E and DARPA: Applying the DARPA model to energy innovation. *The Journal of Technology Transfer*, *36*(5), 469–513.

Bray, D. (2007). Knowledge ecosystems: A theoretical lens for organizations confronting hyperturbulent environments. In T. McMaster, D. Wastell, E. Ferneley, & J. DeGross (Eds.), *Organizational dynamics of technology-based innovation: Diversifying the research agenda* [IFIP International Federation for Information Processing, Vol. 235] (pp. 457–462). Boston, MA: Springer.

Bray, D. A. (2013, September 8) *Leadership is passion to improve our world* [PowerPoint slides]. Retrieved from: http://ssrn.com/abstract=2685963.

Bray, D. A. & Prietula, M. (2007, December). Extending March's exploration and exploitation: Managing knowledge in turbulent environments, presented at *28th International Conference on Information Systems (ICIS)*, Montreal.

Brown, T. (2009). *Change by design: How design thinking transforms organizations and inspires innovation.* New York, NY: Harper Business.

Chesbrough, H. W. (2003). The era of open innovation. *MIT Sloan Management Review*, (Spring), 35–41.

Collins, J. (2005). *Good to great and the social sectors: A monograph to accompany Good to Great.* Boulder, CO: HarperCollins.

Congressional Budget Office. (2015). *Federal contracts and the contracted workforce.* Washington, DC: Author. Retrieved from https://www.cbo.gov/publication/49931.

Coon, G. L. (Writer), Wilber, C. (Writer), Roddenberry, G. (Creator), & Daniels, M. (Director). (1967). Space Seed [Television series episode]. In Coon, G. L. (Producer), Justman, R. H. (Associate Producer), Roddenberry, G. (Executive Producer), *Star Trek.* Los Angeles, CA: Desilu Production & Norway Corporation.

Department of Health and Human Services (2015). *Programs & initiatives*. HHS IDEA Lab. Retrieved from http://www.hhs.gov/idealab/what-we-do.

Department of Housing and Urban Development (2015). *Innovation lab*. HUD portal. Retrieved from http://portal.hud.gov/hudportal/HUD?src=/open/innovation_lab.

Digital Accountability and Transparency Act of 2014, Pub. L. No. 113–101, 128 Stat. 1146, (2014).

Donovan, S. (2015). *Management and oversight of federal information technology* [Memorandum for heads of executive departments and agencies, M-15-14]. Washington, DC: Office of Management and Budget. Retrieved from https://www.whitehouse.gov/sites/default/files/omb/memoranda/2015/m-15-14.pdf.

Donovan, S., Corbert, B., Archuleta, C., & McLaughlin, M. (2014). *Strengthening employee engagement and organizational performance*. [Memorandum for heads of executive departments and agencies, M-15-04]. Washington, DC: Office of Personnel Management. Retrieved from https://www.whitehouse.gov/sites/default/files/omb/memoranda/2015/m-15-04.pdf.

Federal Information Technology Acquisition Reform, Pub. L. 113–291, Subtitle D, 128 Stat. 3292, 3438–3450 (2014).

Fong, G. R. (2001). ARPA does windows: The defense underpinning of the PC revolution. *Business and Politics*, *3*(3), 213–237.

GAO. (2014). *Federal data transparency: Effective implementation of the DATA Act would help address government-wide management challenges and improve oversight* (GAO-15-241T). Washington, DC: United States Government Accountability Office.

Gartner. (2015). *IT Glossary*. Retrieved from http://www.gartner.com/it-glossary/workforce-analytics.

Government Accountability Office. (2004). *Results-oriented government: GPRA has established a solid foundation for achieving greater results* (GAO-04-38). Washington, DC: Author.

Government Accountability Office. (2014). *Office of Personnel Management: Agency needs to improve outcome measures to demonstrate the value of its innovation lab* (GAO-14-306). Washington, DC: Author. Retrieved from http://www.gao.gov/products/GAO-14-306.

Government Accountability Office. (2015). *Managing for results: Implementation of GPRA modernization act has yielded mixed progress in addressing pressing governance challenges* (GAO-15-819). Washington, DC: Author.

Government Performance and Results Act of 1993, Pub. L. No. 103–62, 107 Stat. 285. (1993). Retrieved from https://www.whitehouse.gov/omb/mgmt-gpra/gplaw2m.

GPRA Modernization Act of 2010, Pub. L. No. 111–352, 124 Stat. 3866. (2011).

Gurin, J. (2014). *Open data now.* New York, NY: McGraw Hill.

Highsmith, J., & Cockburn, A. (2001). Agile software development: The business of innovation. *Computer*, *34*(9), 120–127.

Hill, L., Brandeau, G. (2014). *Collective genius: The art and practice of leading innovation.* Boston, MA: Harvard Business Review Press.

Hollingsworth, J. R., & Hollingsworth, E. J. (2011) *Complexity design society: Major discoveries, creativity, and the dynamics of science* (Vol. 15). Vienna, Austria: Remaprint.

Hopper, G. (2015) *David and Goliath.* Naval History and Heritage Command. (Original work published 1976). Retrieved from http://www.history.navy.mil/research/library/bibliographies/hopper-grace-admiral-select-bibliography/david-goliath-hopper.html.

Human capital: Update on strategic management challenges for the 21st century: Hearings before the Senate Subcommittee on Regulatory Affairs and Federal Management, Committee on Homeland Security and Governmental Affairs, 114th Cong. (2015). (Statement of Yvonne D. Jones, Director, Strategic Issues, Government Accountability Office. GAO-15-619T).

Hwang, V. W., & Horowitt, G. (2012). *The rainforest: The secret to building the next Silicon Valley*. Los Altos, CA: Regenwald.

Kingdon, J. W. (1984). *Agendas, alternatives, and public policies* (Second edn.). New York, NY: Longman.

Knowledgent. (2015). *Big Data survey: Current implementation challenges.* New York, NY. Retrieved from http://knowledgent.com/wp-content/uploads/2015/06/Knowledgent-Big-Data-Challenges-Survey-Report-2015-Final.pdf.

Lesaca, J. (2015). Fight against ISIS reveals power of social media. *Brookings TechTank.* Retrieved from http://www.brookings.edu/blogs/techtank/posts/2015/11/19-isis-social-media-power-lesaca.

Lewis, D. E. (2008). *The politics of presidential appointments: Political control and bureaucratic performance*. Princeton, NJ: Princeton University Press.

Lowi, T. J. (1979). *The end of liberalism: The second republic of the United States* (2nd ed.). New York, NY: WW Norton & Company.

March, J. G. (1991). Exploration and exploitation in organizational learning. *Organization Science, 2*(1), 71–87.

March, J., & Simon, H. (1993). *Organizations* (2nd Edn.) Cambridge, MA: Blackwell.

Marks, J. (2013, July 12). VA spent $2 million on Facebook ads. *Nextgov*. Retrieved from http://www.nextgov.com/emerging-tech/2013/07/va-spent-2-million-facebook-ads/66458/.

Meeker, M. (2015). *Internet trends 2015 – code conference*. San Francisco, CA: Kleiner, Perkins, Caufield, Byers (KPCB). Retrieved from: https://kpcb.com/InternetTrends.

Moe, T. M. (1990). Political institutions: The neglected side of the story. *Journal of Law, Economics, & Organization, 6*, 213–253.

Mote, J., Jordan, G., Hage, J., Hadden, W., & Clark, A. (2015). Too big to innovate? Exploring organizational size and innovation processes in scientific research. *Science and Public Policy.* Published online July 31, 2015. Retrieved from http://spp.oxfordjournals.org/content/early/2015/07/31/scipol.scv045.abstract.

National Academy of Public Administration. (2015). *Federal leaders digital insight study*. Washington, DC: Author. Retrieved from http://www.napawash.org/reports-publications/1703-federal-leaders-digital-insight-study.html.

National Science Foundation. (2015). *About i-corps*. NSF News. Retrieved from www.nsf.gov: http://www.nsf.gov/news/special_reports/i-corps/about.jsp.

Office of Management and Budget. (2016). *Analytical perspectives, budget of the U.S. Government, FY2017*. Washington, DC: US Government Printing Office. Retrieved from https://www.whitehouse.gov/sites/default/files/omb/budget/fy2017/assets/ap_8_strengthening.pdf.

Office of Personnel Management. (2015). *Federal employee viewpoint survey results: Employees influencing change*. Retrieved from http://www.fedview.opm.gov/2015FILES/2015_FEVS_Gwide_Final_Report.PDF.

Oracle. (n.d.). *Oracle PeopleSoft applications*. Retrieved from http://www.oracle.com/us/products/applications/peoplesoft-enterprise/overview/index.html.

Organisation for Economic Co-operation and Development. (2005). *Oslo manual: Guidelines for collecting and interpreting innovation data.* Paris, France: European Commission. Retrieved from www.oecd.org/sti/inno/2367580.pdf.

Page, S. (2007). *The difference: How the power of diversity creates better groups, firms, schools, and societies.* Princeton, NJ: Princeton University Press.

Partnership for Public Service. (2015). *2014 best places to work in the federal government analysis.* Retrieved from http://bestplacestowork.org/BPTW/rankings/demographics/large/innovation.

Piechowski, D. (2015). Making innovation labs work. *IBM Center for the Business of Government.* Retrieved from http://www.businessofgovernment.org/blog/business-government/making-innovation-labs-work.

Rasmussen, T. & Ulrich, D. (2015). Learning from practice: How HR analytics avoids being a management fad. *Organizational Dynamics*, *44*(3), 236–242.

Ravindranath, M. (2014, April 6). Census bureau creates its own slice of Silicon Valley. *The Washington Post.* Retrieved from https://www.washingtonpost.com/business/on-it/census-bureau-creates-its-own-slice-of-silicon-valley/2014/04/06/5517d746-b5cb-11e3-8cb6-284052554d74_story.html.

Reinhold, M. D. (2015). *Federal supervisory and managerial frameworks and guidance* [Memorandum for human resources directors].Washington, DC: Office of Personnel

Management. Retrieved from https://www.chcoc.gov/content/federal-supervisory-and-managerial-frameworks-and-guidance.

Resilience. (n.d.). In *Merriam-Webster online*. Retrieved from http://www.merriam-webster.com/dictionary/resilience.

Rodin, J. (2014). *The resilience dividend: Being strong in a world where things go wrong*. New York, NY: PublicAffairs.

Rosenbloom, D. H. (1983). Public administrative theory and the separation of powers. *Public Administration Review*, *43*(3), 219–227.

Rosenbloom, D. H. (2013). Reflections on "public administrative theory and the separation of powers." *The American Review of Public Administration*, *43*(4), 381–396. doi:10.1177/0275074013483167.

Rosenbloom, D. H. (2014). Attending to mission-extrinsic public values in performance-oriented administrative management: A view from the United States. In J. P. Lehrke, E. Bohne, J. D. Graham, & J. C. Raadschelders (Eds.), *Public administration and the modern state: Assessing trends and impact.* Hampshire, England: Palgrave Macmillan.

Sapolsky, H. M., & Taylor, M. Z. (2011). Politics and the science of science policy. In J. Lane, K. Fealing, J. Marburger III, & S. Shipp (Eds.), *The science of science policy: A handbook* (pp. 31–55). Palo Alto, CA: Stanford University Press.

Sen, A. (2014). *Transformative innovation: What "totally radical" and "island+bridge" mean for NOAA research.* (Unpublished doctoral dissertation). The George Washington University, Washington, DC.

Shueh, J. (2015, October 6). White House plans to grow U.S. Digital Services, 18F in 2016. *Government Technology*. Retrieved from http://www.govtech.com/White-House-Plans-to-Grow-US-Digital-Services-18F-in-2016.html.

Simon, H. (1991). Bounded rationality and organizational learning. *Organization Science*, *2*(1), 125–134.

Turnbull, M. (2013, December 4). Australian minister calls for innovation in digital government. FutureGov Summit, Australia.

Van de Ven, A. H. (1986). Central problems in the management of innovation. *Management Science*, *32*(5), 590–607.

Vedantam, S. (2008, November 24). Who are the better managers—political appointees or career bureaucrats? *The Washington Post.* Retrieved from http://www.washingtonpost.com/wp-dyn/content/article/2008/11/23/AR2008112302485.html.

Wildavsky, A. (1980). *Speaking truth to power: The art and craft of policy analysis.* London: Macmillan.

Wilde, O. (1895). *An ideal husband.*

Zalmanovitch, Y. (2014). Don't reinvent the wheel: The search for an identity for public administration. *International Review of Administrative Sciences*, *80*(4), 808–826.

Zettabyte (n.d.). *Wikipedia*. Retrieved November 2015 from https://en.wikipedia.org/wiki/Zettabyte.

About the Editors

Patrick S. Malone, PhD is a professor and the Director of Key Executive Leadership Programs in the School of Public Affairs at American University. He teaches courses in leadership, executive problem solving, organizational analysis, and public administration. He is a frequent guest lecturer on leadership and organizational dynamics in state and federal agencies, professional associations, and universities across the country.

David H. Rosenbloom, PhD is a Distinguished Professor of Public Administration in the School of Public Affairs at American University (Washington, DC). His research and publications focus primarily on public administration and democratic constitutionalism. In 2017 and 2018, he will spend the spring and summer semesters at Renmin University of China in Beijing under the sponsorship of the Chinese Thousand Talents Program.

Bill Valdez retired from federal service as a career senior executive in 2014 and is now a senior vice president at an international consulting firm that specializes in energy, environment, and science/technology policy. In addition, he is an Adjunct Professor at American University's School of Public Affairs, where he specializes in federal government evaluation and strategic planning.

About the Contributors

Anita Blair is a Fellow of the National Academy of Public Administration and has served over 15 years as a federal executive, including as the chief Human Capital Officer of the Department of the Treasury and as deputy assistant secretary of the Navy in manpower and reserve affairs. The views expressed in this article are her own and not to be attributed to the federal government or any agency.

David A. Bray, PhD has led S&T responses to crises, including 9/11, anthrax, and SARS; later voluntarily deploying to Afghanistan to think differently. He serves as a senior executive and CIO for a national critical infrastructure organization. He also serves on the Council on Foreign Relations and as a Visiting Executive at Harvard. He was named an Eisenhower Fellow to Taiwan and Australia in 2015 and a Young Global Leader by the World Economic Forum in 2016.

Robert F. Durant, PhD is an Emeritus Professor of public administration and policy, School of Public Affairs, American University. His latest book is *Why Public Service Matters: Public Managers, Public Policy, and Democracy*. He is a Fellow in the National Academy of Public Administration.

Joyce Hunter is the deputy chief information officer for policy and planning for the Department of Agriculture. Ms. Hunter has over 30 years' experience in the information technology industry and previously served as the CEO of Vulcan Enterprises. Ms. Hunter earned an MBA in Marketing from the University of Pennsylvania, Wharton School of Business, has a certificate in Emotional Intelligence, and is a Wharton Fellow.

Angelo Ioffreda is the founder and chief engagement officer of io spark communications llc (www.iospark.biz), a strategic communications and management consultancy that helps leaders engage employees and lead, manage, and navigate change. He is an Adjunct Professor in the Key Executive Leadership Program in the School of Public Affairs at American University and began his career as a Presidential Management Fellow at the U.S. Department of State.

Joseph V. Kaplan, Esq. is a founding principal of the law firm Passman & Kaplan, P.C., where he primarily represents federal employees in the areas of employment, labor, and discrimination law. Mr. Kaplan was twice elected as national president of the Society of Federal Labor and Employee Relations Professionals (SFLERP) and currently serves on the adjunct faculty of American University's Washington College of Law and School of Public Affairs.

Nancy Kingsbury, PhD is an Adjunct Public Affairs Professor at American University. She is also managing director for applied research and methods at the Government Accountability Office where she is responsible for managing GAO's technical staff. She holds a PhD from The Johns Hopkins University and is a fellow of the National Academy of Public Administration.

Kim Mosser Knapp is a communications consultant with more than a decade of government and political experience. She has served as a staff member in the U.S. Congress, the White House, within the Directorate of National Intelligence, and at the Department of Homeland Security. She tries not to take herself too seriously. And neither should you.

Neile L. Miller is the former acting undersecretary of Energy for Nuclear Security and principal deputy administrator of the National Nuclear Security Administration. She also served as the U.S. Department of Energy's budget director and as a senior analyst at the White House Office of Management and Budget. She is currently a management consultant.

Andrew Rahaman, EdD has over 25 years working in diverse leadership positions, building teams in a variety of private and government settings. Andrew is a faculty member at American University's School of Public Administration and a leadership facilitator and coach in their Key Executive Leadership Program. He also works as an adjunct for the Center for Creative Leadership and has written on action learning, organizational culture, and performance.

Charles R. Rath is the President and CEO of Resilient Solutions 21 (RS21), a global consultancy created to help communities, cities, systems, and businesses flourish in today's changing world. He speaks globally on issues related to resilience, with a particular focus on systems thinking and next-generation urban analytics. He was identified as a 40 under 40 Vanguard by Next City in 2015.

Avery Sen, PhD's job is to help people anticipate and influence socio-technical change. He specializes in the strategy, organization, and evaluation of R&D programs. Avery has supported government executives on management issues for over a decade through his work at the Space Policy Institute, the National Oceanic and Atmospheric Administration, and (currently) Toffler Associates.

Robert M. Tobias is a distinguished practitioner-in-residence in the American University's Department of Public Administration and Policy. He teaches in the Key Executive Leadership MPA and Key Executive Leadership Certificate Program, which he founded. He is also a Senate-confirmed member of the IRS Oversight Board.

Ruth S. Wagner, PhD is an executive-in-residence in the School of Public Affairs at American University where she is also the director of the Master of Science in Organization Development program. She has over 30 years of management experience in various technology and consulting firms. For the past decade Ruth worked as independent consultant predominately in the public sector and focused on federal defense organizations undertaking change.

Ruth Zaplin, DPA is an executive-in-residence in the School of Public Affairs, Department of Public Administration & Policy at American University (AU). In AU's Key Executive Leadership Program, she serves as the director of executive coaching and designs the curricula for national and international programs/courses. She is a Professional Certified Coach (PCC) certified by the International Coach Federation.

Donald G. Zauderer, PhD is Professor Emeritus of public administration at American University, where he directed the Key Executive Leadership Program. Dr. Zauderer served as senior advisor at The Brookings Institution, and is currently Principal of Zauderer & Associates, providing leadership courses, executive coaching, and organization consulting. Dr. Zauderer serves as feature editor for the Public Manager and is a former member of the D.C. Bar Ethics Committee.

Index